"Issues surrounding race, war, and women have bedeviled the Pentecostal Movement from the beginning. Its pragmatism led to its alignment with Evangelicalism. Using the example of the Assemblies of God, Kenyon outlines the development of the Fellowship's historical decisions in all three areas. He challenges his readers to return to the sources that guided early Pentecostals in making their ethical decisions—Scripture and the contemporary working of the Spirit—in order to become more fully Pentecostal."

> —CECIL M. ROBECK, JR., Senior Professor of Church History and Ecumenics, Fuller Seminary

Ethics in the Age of the Spirit

Ethics in the Age of the Spirit

Race, Women, War, and the Assemblies of God

Howard N. Kenyon

FOREWORD BY
Martin W. Mittelstadt

PICKWICK *Publications* · Eugene, Oregon

ETHICS IN THE AGE OF THE SPIRIT
Race, Women, War, and the Assemblies of God

Pentecostals, Peacemaking, and Social Justice

Pickwick Publications
An Imprint of Wipf and Stock Publishers
199 W. 8th Ave., Suite 3
Eugene, OR 97401

www.wipfandstock.com

PAPERBACK ISBN: 978-1-4982-0174-2
HARDCOVER ISBN: 978-1-4982-0175-9
EBOOK ISBN: 978-1-4982-8522-3

Cataloguing-in-Publication data:

Names: Kenyon, Howard N., author. | Mittelstadt, Martin W., foreword.

Title: Ethics in the age of the Spirit : race, women, war, and the Assemblies of God / Howard N. Kenyon ; foreword by Martin W. Mittelstadt.

Description: Eugene, OR: Pickwick Publications, 2019. | Pentecostals, Peacemaking, and Social Justice. | Includes bibliographical references and index.

Identifiers: ISBN: 978-1-4982-0174-2 (PAPERBACK). | ISBN: 978-1-4982-0175-9 (HARDCOVER). | ISBN: 978-1-4982-8522-3 (EBOOK).

Subjects: LCSH: Christian ethics. | Ethics. | Assemblies of God. | Pentecostalism.

Classification: BJ1251 K36 2019 (print). | BJ1251 (epub).

Manufactured in the U.S.A.   OCTOBER 23, 2019

To my mother,
Anita Ruth Osgood Kenyon
1932–2017
A great preacher of the Word with the heart of a pastor and the love
of a mother
Ordained an Assemblies of God minister (1981)

"For we cannot but speak the things which we have seen and heard."

Acts 4:20 (KJV)

Contents

Foreword

I LOVED THE 1980s. During this decade, I finished high school, college, and seminary. On the one hand, a glance back to the 1980s may not appear distant, but on the other, it seems worlds away. For those not present during the eighties or for those of us in search of a blast from the past, I recommend the recent documentary miniseries produced by Tom Hanks and Gary Goetzman. *The Eighties* provides an entertaining and stark reminder of monumental generational shifts during these formative years. One episode focuses on the rise of a generation raised by visual and audio media, from 24/7 news by upstart cable companies such as CNN to the advent of MTV, or a new approach to music via the portables from the in your face boombox to handy CDs on a walkman. In another episode, the narrator chronicles the tumultuous political scene. The end of World War II failed to diminish tension among peoples around the globe. On the American front, Korea, Vietnam, and the Cold War produced a generation of young people unable to imagine America not at war (a depiction that remains to this day). Even the fulfillment of Ronald Reagan's now famous words, "tear down this wall," brought little relief. Hostage crises, corruption on Wall Street, bailouts, and you get the idea.

During this decade, Howard Kenyon begins PhD studies at Baylor University. A dreamer and optimist, Kenyon longs for better days. As a young man born and reared in the Assemblies of God, he becomes particularly interested in the moral issues of his day. But unlike many of his peers, he begins to wrestle with questions not typically on the radar of classical Pentecostals. While the church of his youth remains embattled in debate on abortion, divorce and remarriage, and secular humanism, Kenyon embodies—and envisions—a new generation. His dissertation stands as one of the early attempts by a Pentecostal to visit hot button issues—and three of them in one work!

Kenyon charges to issues concerning race, women in ministry, and war. Though Pentecostals were aware of these concerns, they did not take center stage. Focus on these issues would be found among the "liberal" mainline Protestants, particularly their civil rights activists, many of them products of the Jesus movement. Kenyon calls for Pentecostals to make these concerns primary. And for this reason, Kenyon remains an important voice for our current generation of Pentecostals.

In my opinion, Kenyon captures the essence of Pentecost. Pentecost—rightly understood—marks the beginning of the last days. Though Pentecostalism begins as an end-times revival, critics often chastise a movement bent only on escape from the world via Jesus' soon coming return. Instead, a full orbed eschatology must bring the future into the present. The Spirit poured out in the last days should elicit monumental change. Pentecostals should surely capture a glimpse of Jesus' prayer, "thy kingdom come," a realized eschatology. And to some degree, they did.

Consider for a moment the rise of American Pentecostalism in Los Angeles. The Azusa Street Revival embodies—at least through a glass darkly—holistic and egalitarian impulses. Who could have imagined a multiethnic revival with African-Americans, Hispanics, Asians, and Caucasians all under one roof? These Pentecostals caught a vision of "Spirit poured out upon all flesh." Within weeks and months of the revival and for subsequent decades, proponents of the raw and upstart movement would send female evangelists, missionaries, and educators "to the ends of the earth," thereby offering prophetic fulfilment of the Spirit given to "your sons and your daughters." And finally, if not already too radical, these embryonic Pentecostal denominations would declare themselves unable to participate in World War I. Race, women, and war! Indeed, is it possible that such a common, but very thin thread might capture the barrier-breaking and egalitarian essence of Pentecost(als)?

By the time we fast-forward to the 1980s, our early proclivities toward racial inclusivity, affirmation of women, and commitment to nonviolence fall prey to the currents of the twentieth century. Our prophetic imagination wanes. During these days, God raises up a prophet from among his own people to revisit our history and look to the future. And for this reason, Kenyon remains an important voice for our current generation of Pentecostals.

In 2018, a generation removed from the youthful Kenyon and a century beyond our humble beginnings akin to Los Angeles, Pentecostals march forward. We've walked more than a few miles, preached not a few sermons, and witnessed Pentecost(al) power. Yet these three questions remain. What are we to say of race, women, and war? On the one hand, hope is at a low ebb. The future looks bleak. Have we not learned anything? The evening news is exhausting. On Kenyon's three issues, I pause to think of #MeToo, Ferguson, Charlottesville, genocides, and ethnic cleansing. Whether questions concerning immigrants and refugees, poverty, hate crimes, sex scandals and abuse, or world leaders taunting each other with war-like speech, our response converges yet again, on race, women, and war. But on the other hand, hope reigns supreme. For in the worst of times, we witness the best of human behavior. When we feel like giving up, we witness stories of remarkable compassion.

For inspiration we look to the prophets. We remember the likes of Joel, Amos, and Micah! We remember the prophetic Jesus, who lived and ministered to the margins. We remember "Pentecost" and the new people of God raised up to embody the prophetic tradition! We remember the prophetic impulses of our Pentecostal foremothers and forefathers! We take to heart the poignant call of Roger Stronstad not only for a "priesthood of all believers," but "the prophethood of all believers." And to this choir of prophetic witnesses, we add the comparatively recent, but ever relevant voice of our friend Howard Kenyon.

In the spirit of the prophets, Kenyon invites Pentecostals to remember their (hi)stories. As he writes of racism, women's issues, or nonviolence, Kenyon traces the early impulses of the Assemblies of God and calls for contemporary action. He writes not only as an ethicist, but also a cultural historian. Both disciplines have a prophetic domain, for they seek to awaken a people from their sleep; Kenyon seeks to rescue Pentecostals from historical amnesia. As an insider, he understands the lay of the land and the DNA of an adolescent movement.

Finally, why does this work remain relevant? In his preface, penned thirty years ago and now revised into his first chapter, Kenyon offers a not-so-final conclusion. He calls for broader and sustained efforts, academically and pastorally, among Pentecostals. Following publication of his dissertation, Kenyon did not enter the academy. If ever the adage "our loss, your gain" rings true, I think it's appropriate here. Instead, Kenyon embodies his message and lives as the consummate practitioner. He and his wife Kim moved first to Asia for many years and then returned to live a quiet and productive (egalitarian) life in Portland, Oregon. While those closest to him reaped the dividends of his prophetic embodiment, his voice remained relatively silent in the academy. Amazingly, the work now before us found its way into the hands of upstart ethicists, historians, and theologians, particularly among Pentecostals. Though many students and ministers may not have seen or recall Kenyon's name, others with scholarly investment in Pentecostals will have surely stumbled on a foot-note and pressed onward to ProQuest dissertation publications. Kenyon's passion for greater engagement of these issues has found growing suc-cess among Pentecostal academicians. Today the Society for Pentecostal Studies includes a thriving interest group devoted to ethics. A number of Assemblies of God universities have ethicists in their theology and/ or philosophy departments. Scholarly efforts on the pacifistic impulses among Pentecostals are on the rise. Indeed, many contributors to this se-ries, *Pentecostals, Peacemaking, and Social Justice*, stand on the shoulders of Howard Kenyon. So I say yet again that it is for this reason that his work be more readily available.

With great affection and admiration.

Martin W. Mittelstadt

Summer 2018

Acknowledgments

I AM GRATEFUL FOR the many people who aided in the development of this work. Three faculty committee members at Baylor University—Daniel McGee, William Pitts, and Robert Miller—served admirably on the initial dissertation completed in 1988. A true mentor was found in Edith Blumhofer who contributed long hours of assistance in research and analysis. Without Wayne Warner, then director of the Assemblies of God Archives (now Flower Pentecostal Heritage Center), and his able staff, Joyce Lee and Glenn Gohr, the documentation would have been inconsequential. William Menzies and Gary McGee provided advice in the early stages. Not all denominational leaders shared my curiosity for these controversial subjects, but Joseph R. Flower showed much appreciated interest and his staff proved always willing to help. The libraries and staffs of Baylor University, Central Bible College, Southwest Missouri State University, and especially the Assemblies of God Theological Seminary were great resources.

Thanks to all these people—and to all the family, friends, and folks in my ministry who through the decade of 1978–88 provided encouragement and much needed "space." At the center of this "great cloud of witnesses" stood my parents and my wife. They kept the dream alive. For his great motivational strength, I dedicated my original dissertation to my father.

Thirty years passed. The dissertation remained on the shelf.

Then I was approached by Darrin Rodgers, Marty Mittelstadt, and Jay Beaman, who encouraged me to take the tome off the shelf, dust it off, rework it a bit, and submit it for publication. With the help of Mittelstadt, Beaman, and the editors and staff at Wipf & Stock, the dissertation has been turned into something accessible to a larger audience. For this second phase, I also thank Jon Stewart and Wesley Wilson for technical assistance, as well as my wife, Kim, for her ever-enduring patience and support.

1

Then . . .

I was born the year C. Vann Woodward published *The Strange Career of Jim Crow*. The book and I did not meet until we both turned twenty-five. By then its subject had already had a profound influence on my life even as Jim Crow himself was fading into the annals of history.

As a graduate student in Waco, Texas, I had come to a spiritual impasse. I could not fathom how people claiming to be led by the Spirit could be taken in by something as diabolical as segregation, to the point that they even allowed it to dictate a racist form of evangelistic triage. The questions then stirring in my mind grew into a lifelong pursuit of ever-elusive answers concerning the gap between belief and behavior.

Long before I was introduced to Woodward by Daniel B. McGee, Baylor University's distinguished professor of ethics, I had come to the bedrock conclusion that people of faith, particularly my own Pentecostal people, were called to a prophetic life, one that invariably set them apart, made them counter-cultural. Yet, we seemed also a people eternally in search of legitimacy and acceptability, so much so that this pursuit occasionally altered the way we interpreted Scripture and how we lived out what we knew to be true.

A fourth-generation Pentecostal, I was well aware of how much we were rejected by Fundamentalists, ignored by Mainline Protestants, and not even noticed, so we assumed, by Catholic and Orthodox believers. We felt like the step-children of the church world. To the earliest Pentecostals, this was a badge of honor. To succeeding generations, the badge grew unbearably weighty.

In the 1960s and 1970s, that church world experienced dramatic shifts. Roman Catholics embraced Vatican II and much of Christendom was immersed in ecumenism. Meanwhile, although some theologically conservative Protestants remained Fighting Fundies, the majority morphed into a more open evangelicalism, prodded on by their own Billy Graham and Carl F.H. Henry. Mainline Lutherans and Methodists, as well as Catholics, started raising their hands spontaneously and speaking in tongues, throwing church labels into disarray and dealing a severe blow to the comfortable habit of age-old denominationalism. For our part, we Pentecostals were shedding our persecution complex and fleeing our isolation wards as we embraced some of these changes and allowed them in turn to change us forever.

Some things, though, never do seem to change. People of faith, dually called to a prophetic, counter-cultural stance and to embedding incarnationally in the world, never quite know how to follow a leader who whips money handlers in the temple and parties with outcasts. All too often we opt for the safe route that prefers a skin of salvation to a core-shaking transformation.

Yet core-shaking transformation was what we Pentecostals were all about. Our movement was birthed in a sea change of prophetic utterance, a birthmark we chose to shed in a few short years for the safety of pseudo-acceptance. Gradually welcomed among emerging evangelicals mid-century, we continued to mute that prophetic voice for the sake of human approval, abandoning our original pacifist stance and hiding our women preachers. Goaded on at once by the likes of Billy Graham and a liberalizing society, we white Pentecostals slowly acknowledged our multi-racial roots. We also remembered our gender-free giftings. But instead of driving society toward racial reconciliation and acceptance of women in leadership, we rode sheepishly in the back of the bus.

Following the lead of the white evangelical world, my white Pentecostal subset hid in a cultural ghetto while the racial integration of the fifties and sixties passed us by. First as a teenager, then as a twentysomething, I struggled with our freakish race record. Why were we so white when we had started off so multicolored? Where else had we written off a single ethnic group as beyond the scope of the Great Commission the Spirit had empowered us to fulfill?

I grew up in New Jersey, a kaleidoscope of ethnic diversity. The state was more stew than melting pot, large ethnic chunks floating in and out, not always mixing together very well, no one dominating, except maybe as the butt of jokes. People were not white—they were German or Polish or Italian. People were not black—they were African American or Jamaican or East African. People were not Hispanic—they were Cuban or Puerto Rican. Though, as with elsewhere, there was a pecking order to these chunks, with newer or darker meaning lower.

Our very white statewide church network reflected a bit of this Jersey diversity long before our national organization, the General Council of the Assemblies of God,[1] began to. Quietly, the New Jersey District ordained black ministers in the 1950s—at the very time when the nationwide "fellowship," as the American Assemblies of God preferred to be known, was denying ordination for black people and debating at the highest levels what to do about the "colored problem," letting southern churches and districts dictate a national policy of segregation. In its own confused, awkward and quiet manner, that New Jersey body of churches would continue to pave the way for racial change in the denomination, electing the first black leader in the national church body.[2]

Imagine then the culture shock I experienced when I enrolled in Baylor University's graduate program in 1976. Deep in the heart of Texas, Waco was only a nanosecond from its segregationist days, and the church world—my church world—was no different than the culture in which it was enmeshed.

Engaged in my studies on theology and ethics, I began to wrestle practically with the perplexing question of why there were only a handful of black people in my denomination. While I was not naïve to the prevalence of racism in our American culture, I had never seen it so thoroughly personified in my church until, in the late 1970s, I met the presbyter who granted me my first ministerial credentials.

A presbyter is an overseer of pastors and churches. Mine was short, round, bombastic, and domineering, a man who staccatoed his sermons in a pattern of forceful "hunnns." Kindly, he took me under his wing and shepherded me through my initial ministerial processing. But his outsized

1. The term General Council denotes the entirety of the Assemblies of God within the United States and may also refer to the biennial denominational business conference of ministers and church delegates. Note the church's official title, "The General Council of the Assemblies of God."

2. Reverend Zollie Smith held statewide church leadership positions in the New Jersey District of the Assemblies of God before being elected to national executive office in the General Council of the Assemblies of God in 2007 until 2017, the first African American to hold executive office at both district and national levels in the denomination.

bigotry hit a raw nerve in me. His racist proclivities were epic. During the days of the civil rights movement, he went so far as to stand outside his church and defiantly shout that no N___ would ever be allowed inside. Not that any person of color would ever want in. The presence of him and his all-too-prevalent spiritual siblings in my church caused an acute crisis of faith in me. Not all were as blatant in their racism as he was, but the pervasiveness of and tolerance for bigotry in the church was more than I could stomach.

Out of my wrestling, a master's thesis was born: "An Analysis of Racial Separation within the Early Pentecostal Movement."[3] The thesis did not satisfy. Its answers were more like questions and I, meanwhile, was becoming increasingly aware that ethics, my chosen major, was an underappreciated field of study in the Assemblies of God. Ethics teachers and writers appeared to be a low priority for the denomination's publications and schools of higher learning. Frequently I was told that the Council had little interest in ethics. On hearing I was working on a doctorate in the field, a Bible college president asked hopefully if I could teach anything else.

However, no individual or group is void of a moral framework, even if such has never been adequately articulated. The problem I faced was how to go about the task of defining the ethical posture of such a large and dynamic organization.

Then a brief encounter with Murray Dempster in 1982 helped me turn the questions into theories. Dempster, at the time a professor at Southern California College (now Vanguard University) was recommended to me as the first person in the Assemblies of God to earn a doctorate in ethics. As no other, he got my pursuit.

A trilogy of issues—black-white relationships, women in ministry, and attitudes toward war—were what Dempster suggested, a means of getting at the whys, looking beyond a specific issue—race relations—to see larger patterns of ethical behavior and thinking in the fellowship. Much as a surveyor might propose three points to gain perspective, the three topics could point to something bigger: an ethical posture of an entire denomination.

These issues were not chosen because they had necessarily been self-evident concerns within the movement. Race relations was little more than a footnote embedded in Assemblies of God mythology,

---

3. Baylor University, 1978.

while pacifism, which dominated the attention of the denomination in its earliest years, disappeared from memory within a generation. In the twentieth century, few social-oriented topics ever achieved significance among either the leadership or the constituency. Occasional intrusions into political discussion were made by editors and leaders, as when the nation was "threatened" with a Roman Catholic for president. Only the topic of divorce and remarriage with its implications for church and family were of perennial concern. Otherwise, ethical discussion was limited to personal behavioral standards and to encroaching secular humanism.

As I began my research, I was warned I would find little useful material. On the contrary, each of the three issues proved to be a study in itself. But nothing, not even the idea of considering the very ethical foundations of the movement, was as controversial as the sole topic of racism.

In the national headquarters of the General Council, I walked carefully down the long and forbidding corridor of the third floor. This subdued and softly lit hallway sheltered the denomination's executive suites and harbored profound secrets. A short, skinny youth, I tried to step as confidently as I could in my blazer, tie, khakis, and top-siders, but I felt no match for that sacred hall and prayed I would be accepted by my host. I had nothing to fear.

When I reached the office of the general secretary, his receptionist ushered me in without delay. Short, thin, his balding head fringed with white hair, Joseph R. Flower invited me to sit and we briefly chatted up mutual connections. We had several, our family histories intersecting at various junctures, such connections perhaps my passport into this inner sanctum.

Abruptly and yet calmly he invited me over behind his desk, opening a right-hand drawer filled with file folders. "Much of this," he said, "has never before been seen. I am entrusting it all to you."

Brother Flower was a son of J. Roswell Flower, the first general secretary and a founding father of the Assemblies of God. A man of few words, all softly spoken, the son was intimidating only in title.[4] As with everyone else on that floor, he served in the shadow of larger-than-life Thomas F. Zimmerman, general superintendent of the fellowship.

I was on a quest, my holy grail the moral core of my wing of American evangelicalism, the Pentecostal movement, particularly the Assemblies of God. The beginning of the fellowship is well documented: how a

---

4. Joseph R. Flower served as general secretary 1975–1993. His father, J. Roswell Flower held the same post from 1914 to 1916 and again from 1935 to 1959.

small gathering in Hot Springs, Arkansas, in 1914, founded what would become a worldwide movement of fifty million adherents by the end of the century.

My quest had little to do with that gathering and even less with the phenomenal growth that was to follow. I wanted to understand how the Assemblies came to shift its moral ground—more than once—over the intervening years.

For some reason, Flower trusted me to walk out of that room with a box full of heretofore top-secret files, files that gave witness to a strange history of ecclesiastical shadow dancing and strict racial segregation. I could barely contain myself to get those files home and pour through them. Flower had told me he wanted them turned over, once I was finished, to the denomination's archives (now known as the Flower Pentecostal Heritage Center in honor of his family). The archives were under Flower's oversight, but I was to have first review of these records and for as long as I needed. And he expected me, a mere youth, to live up to his trust. What was in these files?

"You stop this research right now." My breath caught in my throat as I struggled to understand what my ears were hearing. "You stop this research," he repeated emphatically. Bartlett Peterson, tall and thin like Zimmerman, and almost as commanding as long as Zimmerman was not in the room, was reacting to my line of questioning.[5]

We had met at a local restaurant, I the twenty-something in search of a doctoral degree, he the retired-something responding to my request for an interview about his years as the denomination's assistant general superintendent. He was game enough to share his wealth of experience, but blanched when he realized where my line of questioning was leading. Right into that file drawer.

I was asking how and why the fellowship had reacted to the civil rights movement the way it had under his and Zimmerman's leadership. My questions had barely begun before I realized this interview was not going to end well. In fact, it ended immediately. Growing red-faced, he left abruptly, leaving me to wonder what on earth bothered him so much.

I do not remember my specific questions that day. I was in the early stages of my research and had been busy following every possible lead

5. Peterson served as general secretary for the Assemblies of God 1959–75; as an executive presbyter for most of the years from 1943 until 1975; as the Minnesota district superintendent in the 1940s; and as president of Central Bible Institute (later College, consolidated with Evangel University in 2013) 1948–58.

on this one of many visits to Springfield, Missouri, "international" head-quarters of the American Assemblies.

Boasting wide, tree-lined streets, loads of churches, and a family-oriented culture, Springfield was the kind of town where you wanted to raise your kids. With 130,000 souls, mostly either Baptist or religiously rebellious, the "Queen of the Ozarks" was also home to several Assemblies of God schools of higher education—and Maranatha Village, a sizeable denominational retirement center, filled with venerable preachers, missionaries, and leaders of the fellowship.

I had already visited Maranatha to see Ernest S. Williams and Alice Reynolds Flower, both in their nineties. Brother Williams, as everyone knew him, had been general superintendent longer than anyone except Zimmerman. When we met, details evaded him as did energy and strength, though he still had a firm grasp on his faith. Mother Flower, wife of J. Roswell and mother of Joseph R., was still full of vitality, wit and conviction. She had been a pioneer of the denomination as much as her husband had been. But it was obvious that though both Brother Williams and Mother Flower had been there back then, all of life's experiences had sifted into the murky memory pond advancing years tend to provide for data collection. However, I was struck by how these and other lingering pioneers were less uptight about my questions than they were concerned they could no longer recall the details I was pestering them about. They certainly did not blanch.

I grew up a multigenerational preacher's kid in a family that over the past century has produced some thirty Assemblies of God ministers, half of them women. My grandparents and parents even have the A/G logo on their tombstones. That is why, I've long assumed, Brother Flower trusted me, especially with our families sharing connections back several decades. In any case, those files bore account to some astounding proceedings.

The response I have often received when I have shared the topic of my research is that white Pentecostals in general and the Assemblies of God in particular were certainly no worse in their behavior, particularly on racism, than anyone else. But such a response is even more troubling than if we denied any wrongdoing. Amongst us has been a commonly held belief that we were and remain a cut above everyone else, that we as people of the Spirit are extraordinary, breaking all barriers, casting down all strongholds. Moreover, when were we as Pentecostal youth ever allowed to get away with the excuse that "everyone is doing it"? As a denomination, our history just might not have been that exceptional after all. There is the rub.

Ironically, as I was putting the finishing touches on my paper in the late 1980s, the General Council found itself in the midst of one of its greatest crises, one in which ethics had become the central concern. The issue—pertaining to the moral failure of some of its leading preachers—was much broader than the sexual immorality of television personalities. This crucial state of affairs raised many questions regarding the proper use of money and power, the need for personal and corporate integrity and accountability at every level, and the scope of the church's mission.

Through that crisis, it became evident that the Assemblies of God could no longer consider ethics an option secondary in importance to the Great Commission. A lack of moral consideration could, at the very least, impede fulfillment of the evangelistic mandate of the church; at most, it could bring down the whole house.

The actions of the fellowship then and now reveal the heart of the corporate body. What is at issue in the decision-making processes of the presbyteries and councils is the ethical development of the fellowship itself.

My professor, Dan McGee, taught me well that right belief and right experience alone provide incomplete orientation for the Christian life. An equal stress must be placed on right practice, both personal and corporate. The Assemblies of God had long defined Pentecostal experience and doctrine, but it had continuously sidestepped the task of delineating a suitable ethic of right action for its constituency. The Council prided itself on being a world leader for the Pentecostal movement; perhaps it was time for it to take a lead in developing a Pentecostal ethic.

In 1988, a good dozen years after my first musings and six years after proposing the topic, the work was at last complete—or, I should say, the work produced a whole new set of questions in need of answers. A great need presented itself—that more study be done on each of these topics and that the dialog over what the Pentecostal tradition could contribute to the study of ethics should continue. Three decades later, the core questions remain: Is Pentecostalism—with its distinctive theology and experience—also able to inform ethical thinking and right action? Are we any closer to understanding what it means to live in the Age of the Spirit? Have we yet become thoroughgoing Pentecostals?

2

In Search of the Fellowship's Ethical Pulse

FROM AN ORGANIZATIONAL GATHERING of approximately three hundred ministers and lay persons in 1914, the Assemblies of God emerged over the following century to become an acknowledged leader of the world Pentecostal movement and modern evangelicalism. With its international affiliates, it is now the world's fourth largest Christian denomination.

Over time, the American fellowship cultivated a collective consciousness. It perceived itself in the world of Christianity as a fellowship of ministers and churches at once distinctively Pentecostal and mainstream evangelical,[1] an attitude that has greatly affected the denomination's approach to theological, cultural, and social issues.

Protestantism was at a pivotal point when the denomination was born. Nineteenth-century American evangelicalism was then in the midst of the modernist–fundamentalist split, and another fifty years would pass before white evangelicalism could begin to regain a leading role in American society. Out of step with prevailing theological winds of the time, Pentecostalism leaned toward the fundamentalist wing, though the latter continued to reject Pentecostals.

---

1. The term "evangelical" is narrowly defined here and generally throughout this paper, referring to the contemporary post-Fundamentalist movement within orthodox Protestantism, which has emphasized the teachings and authority of the Scriptures and has stressed the importance of personal experience of repentance and reconciliation to God through Christ.

Acceptance, Unity, and Mainstreaming

Unlike other Pentecostal groups existing in 1914, the Assemblies of God was born rootless. Organizations in the holiness wing of Pentecostalism could trace their origins directly to the nineteenth-century holiness movement. For Council members, everything prior to their own Pentecost had been made new. There was little to connect them with anything before. Two primary social impulses at work in the fellowship at that time were acceptance and unity.

The drive for acceptance was born out of both necessity and alienation. Of necessity, these white Pentecostals sought ecclesiastical connection for railroad passes and conscientious objector status. Of alienation, the badge of intense persecution and ostracism Pentecostals had faced became burdensome. In addition to the antagonism of the Fundamentalists, the pioneers faced opposition from many segments of society, including legal authorities. Pentecostals were arrested for preaching, for converting Catholics to another faith, for healing, for emotionalism, and for speaking in tongues. They had their revival tents burned to the ground; they were mobbed, pelted, shot at, and imprisoned.[2] Though such persecution waned as the years wore on, it left its mark on succeeding generations.

The drive for unity was at the heart of the organizational impulse that led to the establishment of the Assemblies of God. With a desire to begin a unifying, Spirit-led movement, the founders were not seeking to establish a new denomination; they intended only to form a cooperative fellowship for the effective propagation of the gospel.[3] Doctrinal focus was minimal; diversity was evident even on the subject of the nature of the Trinity, the most basic of orthodox tenets.

Out of these two desires for unity and acceptance, the fellowship adapted a collective consciousness of mainstreaming. Mainstreaming refers to the significant attempt on the part of the denomination to accommodate itself in all "non-essentials" to prevailing Fundamentalist/evangelical thought.

From the first, the Assemblies of God concentrated on the primary task of evangelism at home and abroad and on organizing the cooperative fellowship into a more effective movement. It did not concern itself

---

2. Flower, "The Mark of the Beast," 1–2; Cox, "Hot Times in Maryland," 1–2.

3. "Twelfth General Council Meeting," 5–9.

with fostering distinctive features. Theological formulations, polity, and hymnology were adopted in part or borrowed wholesale.

From the very first council in 1914, dogma was not a primary concern. This attitude began to change within two years, a direct result of the New Issue[4] controversy. As the denomination matured, emphasis on the authority of Scripture made doctrinal integrity more and more a qualifier for affiliation. Even so, there remains hardly any issue apart from the "initial physical evidence" doctrine which can serve as a firm divider between the Assemblies of God and other evangelical churches.

Likewise, positions on social issues have been borrowed; the denomination has chosen over time to "mainstream." In other words, it has gravitated toward the middle of the stream of conservative white evangelical thought, and this, in turn, on occasion has produced a contradiction in the denomination's self-understanding. When the collective attitude of the Assemblies of God caused it to adopt whatever position was held by the larger evangelical community, it usually did so without considering possible contributions from its own heritage.

This struggle can be illustrated by noting a doctrinal alteration which occurred in 1961. In that year the Assemblies of God attached the word "verbally" to its statement of belief in inspired Scripture. There had been no controversy within the denomination itself to give rise to the change; however, other evangelicals were altering their documents to include the phrase, and the Assemblies of God simply conformed.[5]

A milestone in this mainstreaming process came in 1942 when, with much debate, the National Association of Evangelicals (NAE) invited the Assemblies of God to join its ranks. This was a crucial step for the sect in its drive for acceptance and recognition, one that eventually affected much of the denomination's social perspective through its alliance with a

---

4. The New Issue was a doctrinal controversy regarding the Trinity and water baptism formula which rocked the General Council within the first two years of its existence and caused a significant schism.

5. Dayton, "The Holiness and Pentecostal Churches," 789. Compare "General Council Chronicle," 9, 10. Only on four other occasions since it was first adopted in 1916 had the Statement of Fundamental Truths been altered or adjusted. Clarifying changes were made to the statement on speaking in tongues in the two subsequent General Councils. In 1927 the Statement of Fundamental Truths was incorporated as Article V in a new constitution. In 1933 the section titled "The Adorable Godhead" was added to the section "The One True God." Other revisions were made in 1961, none of which were substantial changes. Then in 1969, the articles governing the mission of the church were altered to conform to the statement on purpose written by the Study Committee on Advance.

movement that was on the verge of awakening to a new and developing social consciousness.

Beginning with Carl F. H. Henry's *The Uneasy Conscience of Modern Fundamentalism* in 1947, reborn evangelicalism found itself opening more and more to issues of social concern and social action. By the 1980s, the movement was divided between the radical evangelicals on one side and the New Right on the other. As white American evangelicalism became politicized, the New Right came to dominate. The Assemblies of God continued to follow an official attitude of political neutrality espoused by the NAE and repeatedly chose a middle road of nonalignment, even into the twenty-first century. Meanwhile, the rank and file followed the larger white evangelical trend of voting conservative and Republican.[6]

Evolving Social Positions

To understand how the Assemblies of God has determined its social positions, it is helpful to take a deep dive on three significant issues: race relations, women in ministry, and attitudes toward war. On none of these subjects has the fellowship remained static or predeterminant.

In the beginning Pentecostalism as a whole was interracial, and although the Assemblies of God formed as a white denomination, it struggled with the issue of race in unique fashion. Most of the African Americans who might have been in the Assemblies of God at its inception left in the New Issue exodus of 1916. Subsequently, the Assemblies of God came to perceive its "whiteness" in the context of the "Sisterhood Myth"[7] and understood its black counterpart to be the holiness-Pentecostal Church of God in Christ. While on the one hand the denomination has never overtly banned black members or relegated them to a segregated branch, on the other hand it severely restricted the ordination of black ministers. For much of its history, it made only token contributions to the civil rights movement and to ministering to black people in general. Beginning in the sixties, the denomination began to show official concern

6. See Hersch and Malina, "Partisan Pastor."

7. The Sisterhood Myth is a term designating the popular idea that the Church of God in Christ is the black counterpart of the Assemblies of God. See chapter 11 for a more complete discussion of the subject.

for America's inner cities and evangelism of the black community, yet by 1990, less than 1 percent of Assemblies of God ministers were black.[8]

From the start the sect demonstrated an openness to women clergy and the role of women in the church. Although the issue of ordaining women to pastoral ministry was not settled until the 1930s, women played a key role in the founding and development of the Assemblies of God as well as in the larger Pentecostal movement. But with the shift toward mainstreaming, this liberal attitude changed, particularly regarding women clergy. From the 1970s, ordination status became more open to women, but only recently have women been accepted into denominational eldership.

As was true of other Pentecostal groups at the time, the Assemblies of God in its earliest days had a strong non-combatant, even pacifist orientation, though there was no uniformity of opinion. Even so, it was not until World War II that involvement in war became acceptable. By the sixties the denomination had moved to a more obviously militaristic posture.

Finding the Pulse

As this research began in the late 1970s, some limited examination had been made of the issues of women in ministry and pacifism. But the attitude of the denomination toward American blacks remained entirely undocumented. Moreover, no known comprehensive study had been made of the Assemblies of God and its approach to social ethics.

The problem was how to get at the data of such a geographically diverse group spanning seventy-five years. Among available primary sources, the most important were the minutes of all General Councils[9] of the Assemblies of God and *The Pentecostal Evangel*. In addition, various notes, papers, sermons, and tracts were available, as well as some ordination records and reports.

8. Other ethnic groups could have been included in the study, but three considerations contributed to limiting the issue of race relations to blacks and whites only. One is the practical limitation of space. A second is that the black-white problem is of special historic significance in both secular and church relationships. Third, although the Hispanic element has become a very significant population in American life, the issues involved in black-white and Hispanic-white concerns are somewhat disparate.

9. General Council, in such instances, refers to the biennial denominational business conference of ministers and church delegates.

The membership of the Assemblies of God had been essentially non-literary at least through its first seven decades. Thus, for the researcher, there was much to be gleaned from the church's oral history and journalistic efforts; official references were few. Yet *The Pentecostal Evangel* simultaneously served as a mouthpiece for the organization's official attitudes as well as a reflection of the tenor of the grassroots. Nothing else within the Assemblies of God could be deemed so representative: the weekly's predecessors—the *Christian Evangel*, the *Weekly Evangel*, and the *Word and Witness*—were catalysts in the formation of the Assemblies of God, and the *Evangel* continued to serve as the official organ of the denomination through the remainder of the twentieth century.[10] The editors of the original publications were, from the beginning, among the most influential leaders in the new Council. Two of the three original editors—Eudorus N. Bell, of the *Word and Witness*, and J. R. Flower, of the *Christian Evangel*—held high office, Bell being the first chair of the General Council and Flower serving as general secretary for many years. The third, Alice Reynolds Flower, while never holding office, was well known and greatly respected. Subsequent editors John W. Welch and Stanley H. Frodsham[11] served respectively as chair and general secretary.

The official minutes of the General Council and the General Presbytery also contain more information than might at first be assumed. Though there are few documented actions involving the three issues, the contributions of these records are not insignificant.

In this study, examination of the three issues is concentrated on the General Council as a whole. The Assemblies of God is a denomination which was built on strong local self-determination, helping it to become increasingly diverse and to lose much of the homogeneity of its earliest days. At the same time, the church organization centralized, fostering a

10. The *Christian Evangel*, founded in June 1913 by J. Roswell and Alice Flower, was a weekly paper which went through several name changes; it was intermittently called the *Weekly Evangel* (13 March 1915–1 June 1918), until finally known as *The Pentecostal Evangel* (18 October 1919). *Word and Witness* (published as early as 1912) was a monthly which eventually merged with the *Evangel* (October 1915). In December 2014, *The Pentecostal Evangel* ceased printed publication and shifted exclusively to digital format as *PE News*. For more information, see "Pentecostal Evangel Moves," 5 January 2018.

11. Frodsham, an English Pentecostal, came into the movement in 1908. He helped formulate the Assemblies of God doctrinal statement in 1916 and was closely associated with the *Evangel* from 1916 to 1948, serving as editor after 1920. See Menzies, *Anointed to Serve*, 118, 133.

commonality of attitude despite the diversity. Thus, there is a case to be made for viewing the Assemblies of God as a movement with a unified sense of self-understanding, which in turn is reflected quite conclusively in the pages of *The Pentecostal Evangel* and in the actions of the General Council, as well as in the General and Executive Presbytery.[12]

12. These are smaller representative bodies which serve as official boards for the Assemblies of God when the General Council is not in session. The General Presbytery includes three representatives from each district council, of which there are sixty-one in the United States and Puerto Rico. The Executive Presbytery is composed of twenty-one members.

3

The Fellowship's Roots

THE ASSEMBLIES OF GOD was founded by a diversity of Pentecostal believers from all regions of the nation. No one person served as a "founding father" and no single tradition shaped the fledgling organization. The most identifiable unifying element was the Pentecostal experience of, and teaching on, the baptism in the Holy Spirit.

At least two traditions had their influence on Pentecostalism. The theological roots of the distinguishing Pentecostal doctrine, the baptism in the Holy Spirit, may be found in the teachings of John Wesley and the holiness movement. The reformed tradition helped define the understanding of sanctification in at least two branches of Pentecostalism.[1]

The Higher Christian Life

Wesley's doctrine of Christian perfection served as a theological foundation for the doctrine of Spirit baptism which developed a century later. Although holiness was a major theme among the earliest Methodists, it was already becoming a neglected motif in American Methodism as early as the 1830s; attention in the church had been centered on organization and expansion since the American Revolution. Then, as a younger generation took time to reflect on its roots, new interest in this basic tenet was aroused and aided by a diverse assortment of ministers and laity coming from a variety of backgrounds, particularly Methodist and Presbyterian.

---

1. For further discussion of the historical roots of the Pentecostal movement, see Synan, ed., *Aspects of Pentecostal-Charismatic Origins*.

Yearning for a Wesleyan concept of "the higher Christian life," they called the nation to a renewal of holiness.

At this time the American scene was charged with feelings of great optimism and destiny, and it was in this atmosphere that Charles G. Finney, a Presbyterian, and others called the new nation to explore the rich world of Christian living. During the 1830s, Finney's preaching engendered a great mood of revival that swept the country.[2] Another significant development, closely linked with Finney's revivalism, was the establishment of a regular weekly prayer meeting widely known as the "Tuesday Meeting," organized by two sisters, Sarah Lankford and Phoebe Palmer, members of New York City Methodist churches. This prayer movement, lasting until the 1900s, quickly became a catalyst for the revival of the original Wesleyan teaching of sanctification.[3]

The religious fervor of 1858–59 was greatly aided by the efforts of the Palmer sisters and other leaders in evangelicalism. Sometimes called the "Great Prayer Meeting Revival," it was characterized by lay people who prayed fervently for a deluge from heaven. Lay leaders helped spread the movement to the British Isles.[4] At the height of the revival, Presbyterian William E. Boardman's book, *The Higher Christian Life*, sold 200,000 copies here and abroad.[5] Finney himself was still conducting great union services in Boston, Buffalo, and New York, calling people to a life of holiness.

The Holiness and Keswick Movements

Only temporarily slowed in development by the Civil War, the holiness movement under Methodist leadership soon operated on an interdenominational basis. Within a decade of the awakening, the movement was officially organized as the National Camp Meeting Association for the Promotion of Holiness. Beginning at Vineland, New Jersey, in 1867,

2. Smith, *Revivalism and Social Reform*, 113. Finney himself referred to the term "baptism of the Holy Spirit" in his preaching and in his *Autobiography*, but it is used in a very general sense, referring both to his conversion of 1821 and a subsequent spiritual unction for the ministry. See Finney's sermons such as "Be Filled with the Spirit," in *Revivals of Religion*. See also, Bruner, *A Theology of the Holy Spirit*, 40–42, 332–35.

3. Dayton, *The American Holiness Movement*, 9.

4. Orr, *The Light of the Nations*, 101–109.

5. (Boston, 1858; Britain, 1860). Smith, *Called unto Holiness*, 11.

twenty-four "national" camp meetings were held within four years, with as many as twenty thousand in attendance.[6]

Through the efforts of Boardman and others, the Wesleyan emphasis was reintroduced into England. The predominant thrust on both sides of the Atlantic was that "the Christian can attain full holiness (sanctification) only when he abandons all efforts and allows the Holy Spirit to live within him the life of Christ."[7] Sanctification was understood as an experience subsequent to salvation, a "second blessing."

On the British side of the Atlantic, the spiritual tide became identified as the Keswick movement, after the Keswick Convention for the Deepening of the Spiritual Life.[8] The Keswick movement borrowed its evangelical ecumenism with its slogan "All One in Christ Jesus" as well as much of its leadership from the Revival of 1858–1859.[9]

In the two countries the religious momentum grew along separate lines and when the Keswick teachings were brought back to the United States by Dwight L. Moody, tension resulted in the holiness ranks. Significantly, the holiness movement in America remained for the most part within Methodism, whereas the Keswick movement with its leadership from non-Methodist churches was able to achieve a broader impact. Moreover, the Keswick adherents continued to be an evangelical and ecumenical force whereas the American group, lacking a spirit of revival unity, underwent division after division as splinter denominations were formed.

The Keswick and holiness schools both embraced the teaching on the baptism in the Holy Spirit, though they understood it quite differently. While the holiness supporters continued to see sanctification or the "second blessing" as "eradication from sin" or "cleansing," Keswick's teaching replaced that concept with the "enduement of power." Perfection was a process begun at salvation; the "second blessing" was power granted for service.

Both traditions were to find their way into Pentecostalism. For those of Keswick persuasion the process was but a simple step since the theological framework needed no adjustment. The holiness movement, however, was to undergo tremendous readjustment and further division.

---

6. Smith, *Called unto Holiness*, 16–21.

7. Smith, et al., *American Christianity*, 313.

8. Canon Dundas Hartford-Battersby, Vicar of St. John's, Keswick, aided in establishing the conventions during the 1870s. See Pollock, *The Keswick Story*, 11, 21–29.

9. Orr, *The Fervent Prayer*, 143.

Having received the "second blessing" of sanctification, many adherents looked for yet a third experience in grace which would bring the desired "baptism of power." Doctrinal thought moved toward a separation of the cleansing and empowering work of the Holy Ghost in the believer's life.

Adding to this agitation inside the holiness movement, the Keswick teaching was reintroduced into the United States with its emphasis on "enduement of power."

> These teachings—the denial of the eradication of inward sin and the emphasis on premillennialism, faith healing, and the "gifts of the Spirit"—opened a wide breach in the holiness ranks. The conflict spread to America when Dwight L. Moody, R. A. Torrey, first president of Moody Bible Institute, Chicago, Adoniram J. Gordon, father of Gordon College, Boston, A. B. Simpson, founder of the Christian and Missionary Alliance, and the evangelist J. Wilbur Chapman began to propagate in this country the Keswick version of the second blessing.[10]

A number of holiness denominations—or more properly, sects—were spawned from the holiness revival. Initially, an effort was made to maintain the holiness movement within the ranks of Methodism. By 1893 reaction had hardened against the holiness message in the existing denominations and during the next fourteen years twenty-five separate holiness groups came into existence. The largest of these were what were then called the Pentecostal Church of the Nazarene and the Pilgrim Holiness Church.[11]

The "third blessing" segment, the left wing of the holiness revival, was the actual parent of Pentecostalism. Such doctrine was condemned by mainline holiness people who taught that those seeking such phenomenal third experiences were those whose experiences were unsatisfactory.[12] Apparently there were many people dissatisfied with their spiritual life, for a significant segment of the holiness movement was swept into Pentecostalism around the turn of the century.

This splintering phenomenon greatly affected the structure of Pentecostalism, which began at the height of the holiness organizational activity. Several holiness churches came into the new movement already separated and structured. Other holiness people who were not

---

10. Smith, *Called unto Holiness*, 25.

11. Atter, *The Third Force*, 19.

12. Bresee, "The Gift of Tongues," 6.

yet organized brought into Pentecostalism their aversion to organization. Charles Parham, Pentecostal pioneer and holiness preacher, was a major voice against organization. "Brethren, let us cease wasting time at this juncture in systemetizing [sic] or organizing the work of God. Let each minister go forward doing his work, and leaving local Assemblies under local elders."[13] Aside from previous unhappy experiences with ecclesiastical authority, there was a genuine concern that as much freedom as possible be granted to the Spirit to do His work.

Eschatological Hopes

The year 1901 was not just the dawn of a new century; it was the beginning of the twentieth century since the first advent of Christ. Eschatological expectations were running high, including a partially realized eschatology that the Last Days would see the fulfillment of various Old Testament prophecies concerning the promise of the "latter rain."[14] Thoroughly restorationist, such fulfillment was expected to include an outpouring of God's Spirit as described in the book of the Acts of the Apostles.

Proponents of the Latter Rain teaching compared the history of the church with the pattern of rainfall in the Holy Land. Symbolizing the outpouring of the Holy Spirit, the early rains of a "copious" nature had fallen in the time of the Apostles. Spasmodic lighter rains, interspersed with hot, dry spells, followed. Now, according to prophecy, the final outpouring or latter rain, of a bountiful nature, was to be expected in the Last Days. The early Pentecostals believed they were in those last days and that their movement was the fulfillment of the promised latter rain.[15]

Numerous developments reinforced these expectations. The first was a nationwide revival in Wales in 1904–5. Under the leadership of Evan Roberts, the whole country was soon engulfed in a major awakening. Word of these events quickly reached expectant hearts in the United States, particularly in Los Angeles, fully a year prior to the introduction of Pentecostalism into that city in the great Azusa Street meetings. Frank

---

13. Parham, *The Life of Charles E. Parham*, 177.

14. Hos 6:3; Joel 2:23; Zech 10:1. See also Jas 5:7.

15. That such a belief did not end with Pentecostalism's first generation is evident in an exegetical article by Douglas, "The Former and Latter Rain," 8–9.

Bartleman, one of those "expectant hearts" later wrote, "The present world-wide revival was rocked in the cradle of little Wales."[16]

John Alexander Dowie

A second phenomenon which increased expectations in an end-time revival and which had direct impact on Pentecostalism was John Alexander Dowie's city of Zion. A Scotsman by birth, Dowie had been converted to Christianity in Australia and had become pastor of a Congregational church in 1872. He began conducting great healing meetings, which drew thousands. In 1888, he migrated to the United States where he founded the "Christian Catholic Church" and in 1900 established his headquarters and a new community near Chicago, which he called Zion, and which became home eventually for ten thousand people.

Dowie's ministry flourished briefly amid excesses and controversy, dissolving about the time the Pentecostal movement began. He is best known for his work in promoting the doctrine of "divine healing,"[17] a major tenet in Pentecostalism. But his social and ethical teachings were also noteworthy, particularly his commitment to pacifism, his advocation of racial intermarriage, and his attacks on capitalism and monopolies. A biblical literalist, Dowie favored the Gospels. According to Charles Kessler, former associate editor of *Leaves of Healing*, Dowie's spiritual and ethical attitudes were deeply linked. "I am convinced that Dr. Dowie's zeal for justice, his hatred for racial discrimination, his plea for pacifism, his interest in equal universal education, his belief in universal redemption *together with* his passion for Divine Healing, and his hatred of these things that destroy the individual *all stem from his intense inner, spiritual commitment to the compassion and love of God.*"[18]

Zion City was to be the place where Dowie's ideas of social reform could be implemented and the teachings of Jesus directly applied. It was one of numerous models of American attempts at building utopian communities and the thousands who flocked to the city came filled with great eschatological hope. Dowie espoused dispensationalist and premillennial views similar to those of J. Wilbur Chapman and Reuben A. Torrey,

16. Bartleman, *How Pentecost Came*, 21.

17. Atter, *The Third Force*, 20.

18. *Leaves of Healing*, 11–19, quoted in Hollenweger, *The Pentecostals*, 118. Emphasis in the original.

though he saw the foundation of the Christian Catholic Church and Zion City as the beginning of the millennial drama. Dowie pledged to buy up Jerusalem in preparation for the Second Coming. During the millennium, he asserted, Christ would reside in Jerusalem, but Zion City would be the real governing center of the world.[19]

In the waning days of Dowie's reign, Pentecostal pioneer Charles Parham invaded Zion City with a band of workers and formed a Pentecostal church. Though Dowie strongly opposed the Pentecostal intrusion, he could not stop a large defection of his followers to the new movement, especially after his own tragic downfall in 1905.[20] In time over two thousand Zion citizens would become Pentecostals, many of them serving as leaders in the Assemblies of God.[21]

The Birth of the Pentecostal Movement

The birth of the modern Pentecostal movement is commonly designated as occurring during the period 1901–1906, though, as will be discussed more fully in the next chapter, the date has occasioned much debate. Briefly, the doctrine of the initial physical evidence, which crystalized the teaching on the baptism of the Holy Spirit for Pentecostalism, was first developed at a Bible school run by Parham in 1900–1901. An ongoing series of meetings in Los Angeles, commonly known as the Azusa Street Revival, in 1906 served as a catalyst for launching the Pentecostal movement worldwide.

---

19. *Leaves of Healing*, 22 April 1905, 10–12; 13 May 1905, 114.

20. Before he was half-paralyzed by a stroke in 1905, Dowie had had delusions of grandeur. Then, with his health gone, the economic base of the city collapsed, and the onslaught of a famine, Dowie was deposed, later dying abandoned, broken, and sick. See Hollenweger, *The Pentecostals*, 118.

21. See Hollenweger, *The Pentecostals*, 459–60. Among Dowie's followers who later joined the Assemblies of God were Edith Baugh, an early associate of Marie Brown in New York City and who later went as a missionary to India; F. F. and B. B. Bosworth; Marie Brown, pastor of Glad Tidings Tabernacle, New York; Cyrus Fockler, pastor in Milwaukee, Wisconsin; F. A. Graves, pastor and hymn writer (whose daughter was the wife of Myer Pearlman); John G. Lake, missionary to South Africa and evangelist; "Dad" Richey and his five sons, all evangelists; Raymond T. Richey; Charles S. Robinson, author and for many years assistant editor of *The Pentecostal Evangel*; Dr. Lillian B. Yeomans, evangelist; and Dr. Phinehas Yoakum, who conducted a very successful healing home in California for many years.

In these first stages, Pentecostal teaching reflected the holiness concept of sanctification. At that time the dominant teaching in Pentecostalism was sanctification as a "second work" of grace since prior to 1910 the non-holiness doctrine of sanctification had not been clearly articulated. Then William H. Durham, pastor of the North Avenue Mission in Chicago, Illinois, preached that this second work was superfluous and posited instead his "Finished Work" doctrine: no second stage is necessary because salvation is adequate to change a man's heart and his nature, which, though formerly sinful and depraved, is now "dead in Christ."

The holiness-turned-Pentecostals had argued that one received the Holy Spirit baptism only after a period of cleansing, which occurred when a person was sanctified. Durham pointed to all the non-holiness people who had also received the baptism. His argument was that if they had not experienced this specific sanctification crisis experience and yet had received the Holy Spirit baptism, then sanctification must somehow be related to their conversion experience.

Influential here was the reformed view of sanctification, as held by Durham, a Baptist, which stressed process instead of crisis. So pronounced is this emphasis found in the Pentecostal movement that historian Klaude Kendrick termed the nonWesleyan Pentecostals "Baptistic."[22]

Controversy over Durham's teachings on sanctification led to bitter conflict within Pentecostal ranks. Many were his opponents, including Parham and William Seymour, the apostle of Azusa Street.[23] Durham died shortly after he began propagating his teaching on the "Finished Work of Calvary," but his influence continued to sweep the movement. The Finished Work doctrine became the accepted teaching on sanctification for the leading Pentecostal groups organized after 1912, including the Assemblies of God.

22. Kendrick, *The Promise Fulfilled.* See especially chapters 5 and 8.

23. Bartleman, *How Pentecost Came,* 145–53.

4

Development of the General Council

HISTORICAL DEVELOPMENTS, BOTH INSIDE and outside the Assemblies of God, did much to shape the denomination and its collective thinking with World War II generally serving as the dividing line for its two-stage development. Before the war, the movement was more homogenous. Uniformity was not stressed from the national headquarters, as the consistency was occurring organically. First-generation Pentecostals predominated. Somewhat set apart from the rest of society, the movement was young, and so were its leaders. It was a sect of lower class, white, heavily Southern Pentecostals.[1]

A rapid upward mobility marked the Council's membership following World War II. Among other causes, the change was assisted by a migration to the West Coast[2] and by the expansion of church members

---

1. Even as late as 1955, over 47 percent of adult members within the Assemblies of God resided in the states which formerly composed the Confederacy and the Border states. The percentage of members in the Assemblies of God in 1936 was 37.3 percent rural and 62.7 urban. This is fairly representative of all Pentecostals (37.6 percent rural), but somewhat more urban when compared to other predominantly white Pentecostal denominations (43.6 percent rural). See Anderson, *Vision of the Disinherited*, 168–69.

2. Although the Assemblies of God constituency was strongly represented in California early on, the movement long had its primary strength in the south-central part of the United States. J. R. Flower, interview by Menzies, 26 June 1967. Even so, the shift in influence was away from the Texas-Oklahoma-Arkansas stronghold for many years. Southerners totally dominated the top position in the General Council prior to 1929: E. N. Bell, of Florida and Texas, 1914, 1920–23; Arch P. Collins, of Texas, 1914–15; John W. Welch, of Oklahoma (though originally from New York), 1915–19, 1923–25; and W. T. Gaston, of Arkansas, 1925–29. Since 1929, only one Southerner, Ralph M.

into the middle-income levels in society. Also, there was an increasingly wide latitude of people within the denomination. In no small measure, this trend escalated in the sixties and seventies with an influx into the fellowship of members from the more middle-class and mainline charismatic movement.

Organization and Division

The organizational impulse which brought the Assemblies of God into existence came from leaders within the Finished Work segment of Pentecostalism. Although they were hesitant about starting a new denomination, these leaders saw a need for cooperative effort among the many nonaligned Pentecostals. There were already numerous Pentecostal organizations, but they were without exception of the older holiness persuasion.

During the first generation of Pentecostalism, the growth of the movement was served by numerous publications. Two of these publications, the *Word and Witness* and the *Christian Evangel*, provided the communications network which brought about the organizational General Council in April 1914.

The council, convened in the face of much opposition, was decidedly of the Finished Work persuasion. The keynote address by M. M. Pinson was entitled "The Finished Work of Calvary." Although no formal doctrinal position was developed in that first council, the "Preamble and Resolution on Constitution" which was adopted carried with it the implications of the Durham view of sanctification, for only two experiences are identified—salvation and the baptism in the Holy Spirit.[3] Sanctification is not even mentioned. The first two chairpersons, Bell and Arch P. Collins, were originally Baptists.

Though a new organization was established at Hot Springs, such was not the intention of the founders, who saw their initiative more as the creation of an annual council to be held together between sessions by a small advisory body carrying very limited authority.[4] The primary concerns which necessitated the cooperative effort were missions and

---

Riggs, of Mississippi, 1953–59, has served as general superintendent, though he spent all of his adult years outside the Deep South.

3. General Council minutes, 1914, 3.

4. Flower, "History of the Assemblies of God," 21.

ministerial education. Publishing interests quickly became a third concern when the *Evangel* and the *Word and Witness* were brought under the umbrella of the General Council. Doctrinal unity was simple in scope, the Pentecostal distinctive being the determinant of fellowship.

A major theological dispute already stirring was soon to alter the non-creedal disposition of the Council. Extensive shifts in doctrine were common during the first twenty years of the Pentecostal movement. The Assemblies of God was formed in an attempt to bring greater stability to this chaos, but it would be severely tested before doctrinal stability was achieved.

The New Issue, as it was termed, was a controversy regarding the doctrine of the Trinity. It was a unique form of unitarianism, centering on the name of Jesus. Originating in California a year before the Hot Springs Council, the new teaching began to have a nationwide effect among Finished Work Pentecostals in 1915. Soon the issue reached the point of hysteria, when Bell and other Assemblies of God leaders adopted the concept. Bell was not serving as chair at the time, but he was the editor of the two Assemblies of God publications, a position that he subsequently resigned. A special council was convened in 1915, but it was not until the 1916 General Council that the issue was settled. That conference, held in St. Louis, resolved the conflict by adopting a formal creed known as the Statement of Fundamental Truths. Bell, who had by this time "repented" of his errant beliefs, was one of the preparers of the statement that dealt extensively with the question of the nature of the Godhead.

An immediate result of the council was a significant defection of "Oneness" people, a term referring to their unitarianism. Under the leadership of G. T. Haywood, a black minister loosely associated with the Assemblies of God, a racially-mixed Pentecostal unitarian fellowship known as "The Pentecostal Assemblies of the World" was organized in 1916.[5]

Another result of the controversy was the restructuring of the executive leadership of the fellowship. A General Presbytery was instituted to serve more representatively the judicial and legislative needs of the Assemblies of God when the General Council was not in session.

---

5. It continued as an integrated body until 1924 when the white ministers withdrew to form a separate organization. Two white Oneness groups merged in 1945 to form "The United Pentecostal Church," largest of the Oneness bodies. See Kelsey, *Tongue-Speaking*, 242–43.

Youthful Flexibility and Consolidation

Even with this solidification, the Assemblies of God remained a loosely-organized fellowship. The doctrinal formulation had placed greater stress on scriptural authority, but the emphasis was still on being a Spirit-led movement.

Last Days preoccupation continued to be a dominant feature in the fellowship throughout the first decade. Four of the sixteen sections in the Statement of Fundamental Truths are eschatological in nature. These statements are premillennial, though not necessarily dispensational. Such teachings in the early years did carry a strong dispensational flavor, despite the fact that dispensational beliefs among Fundamentalists denied the possibility of a modern Pentecostal experience.[6] To this day, teaching on the subject in the Assemblies of God continues to be premillennial without adhering to dispensational categories.[7]

The prophetic concept of the Latter Rain served as a foundational perspective in the worldview of the entire Pentecostal movement during the first generation. These earliest Pentecostals thought that they were living in the "last days" as prophesied by Joel and evidenced by myriad workings of the Spirit such as healing and tongues. As people who believed they were living on the edge of time, they were not deeply concerned with tradition or status quo, and such lack of attachment to the present world order had its impact on how they responded to society's priorities.

With the passing of World War I, concern over the "end times" abated, only to be renewed with the onslaught of the second world war.[8] Eschatological emphasis has continued to cycle through the years. However, other factors common to aging movements have mitigated the radical tendencies of the earlier, youthful end times worldview.

The 1927 General Council served as a watershed occasion for the Assemblies of God. Until this time, denominational affiliation had been rather fluid. At that meeting a new constitution was adopted which

6. A classic example of Pentecostal adaptation of dispensationalism is Frank M. Boyd's *Ages and Dispensations*, published in 1949 by GPH.

7. Illustrative of this is a book published in 1967 by a significant Assemblies of God scholar in which the term "dispensation" does not even occur. See Horton, *The Promise of His Coming*.

8. More than one-third of the major articles printed in *The Pentecostal Evangel* during the first three months of 1941 were directly related to the war in Europe and biblical prophecy.

served to structure the fellowship more formally. Procedures for granting credentials were directly affected which caused some significant
adjustments in the ordination of women in the 1930s. During the next
two decades, particularly under the long-term leadership of general superintendent E. S. Williams, the Council experienced a period of great
stabilization and growth.

Aligning with Evangelicals

A second watershed in the history of the Assemblies of God came in the
midst of World War II. Internally, stability had been achieved. Externally,
acceptability was coming with the growth of the church.[9] One result of
the war itself was a greater world consciousness apart from missions,
which occurred with participation in the war both by laity serving in the
military and by ministers serving in the chaplaincy.[10]

Another very significant development quite separate from the war
was the founding of the NAE in 1941–43 and its openness toward the
Assemblies of God. Earlier there had been a strong sectarian spirit within
the fellowship. The Pentecostals had a message which was looked down
upon and despised by others "so we didn't care."[11]

The first forty years of the Pentecostal movement found these believers unaccepted by the larger church world. In 1928, *The Pentecostal
Evangel* reported a resolution passed at a convention of the World's
Christian Fundamentals Association (WCFA) held in Chicago, identifying the Pentecostal movement as "a menace in many churches and a
real injury to the sane testimony of Fundamental Christians." The WCFA
went on record as "unreservedly opposed to Modern Pentecostalism."[12]

The Pentecostal Evangel repeatedly defended Pentecostalism against
such attacks by Fundamentalists with whom they otherwise found much
in common,[13] not the least of which were "all the fundamentals of the

---

9. Between 1926 and 1936, traditional Protestant churches in the United States
lost two million members, or 8 percent of their total, whereas the Assemblies of God
had a 208.7 percent increase, for a new high of 170,000 members. See Sherrill, *They
Speak with Other Tongues*, 50.

10. J. R. Flower, interview by Menzies, 26 June 1967.

11. J. R. Flower, interview by Menzies, 26 June 1967.

12. Frodsham, "Disfellowshiped!" 7.

13. Williams, "Movement under Fire," 2–3.

faith." Frodsham and Williams called upon the Pentecostals to continue to love and accept those who had chosen to put them "without the camp."[14]

Attempting to find some basis for connection, Assemblies of God founders spoke of Pentecostalism in terms of "Fundamentalism Plus." David H. McDowell, who later served as an assistant superintendent, is credited with first coining that phrase at a meeting of the General Presbytery in 1924. He likened the modernists to the Sadducees of Jesus's day and stated, "We stand one hundred per cent [sic] with all who believe in the verbal inspiration and absolute authority of the Scriptures of Truth." But more than mere fundamentalism was needed. "We need the Scriptures plus the power of God."[15] The idea was picked up by J. Roswell Flower when thirty years later he reiterated, "We are fundamentalists, but we are more than that." Again, Flower pointed out the similarity of the modernists to Sadducees but added that the Fundamentalists were modern-day Pharisees who believed in the supernatural, "provided it is in the past."[16]

Though they were strongly rejected by the Fundamentalists, Assemblies of God leaders often supported the efforts of those who stood by the Bible as the Word of God.[17] Books by Fundamentalists were promoted in *The Pentecostal Evangel* and articles by such men as William Jennings Bryan appeared on occasion.[18] Though its sympathies lay with these other conservatives, the Assemblies of God was far removed from the fundamentalist-modernist debate itself.

However, in the 1940s, where previously there had been an indifference to cooperation and alignment, the desire grew to reach out for understanding and fellowship. On the part of evangelicals, there was reticence at first as to how cooperation with Pentecostals would work out.[19]

At a 1941 meeting in Chicago, some twenty leaders gathered to consider how they might develop a cooperative organization of evangelicals. Carl McIntire, who that same year had founded another body of Fundamentalists called the American Council of Christian Churches (ACCC), was invited to address the Chicago group about the objectives

14. Frodsham, "Disfellowshiped!" 7.

15. Cited in an editorial, *The Pentecostal Evangel*, 24 July 1924, 4.

16. Flower, "The Present Situation," 12–13; 23–24.

17. "The Editor's Notebook," 27 September 1930, 4–5.

18. Bryan, "A Defense of the Faith," 2–5. Books by Bryan were advertised in a full-page spread in *The Pentecostal Evangel*, 15 August 1925, 16.

19. J. R. Flower, interview by Menzies, 26 June 1967.

of the ACCC. The new group eventually rejected the idea of joining the ACCC and chose instead to work toward the formation of what came to be the NAE.[20]

The development of the NAE separately from the ACCC was due in large part to the strong rejection of Pentecostals by McIntire's group.[21] In fact, McIntire later forcefully attacked the NAE for including Pentecostals, calling speaking in tongues "one of the great signs of the apostasy."[22]

In 1943 the third and final meeting called to form the NAE—the Constitutional Convention of Evangelicals—was held in Chicago, this time attended by six hundred delegates, of which over one hundred were members of the Assemblies of God. By vote of the General Council held later that year, the Assemblies of God officially chose to join the NAE.[23] No representatives of the Council had been at the 1941 Chicago meeting, but "a number of brethren from headquarters" were among the one hundred and fifty who attended the second meeting in St. Louis in 1942.[24] If reservations had been expressed about involving Pentecostals, they were forgotten by the time of the second Chicago meeting where J. Roswell Flower was elected to be one of the nine executives of the new National Association of Evangelicals for United Action.[25] Ironically, Chicago, the very city in which Fundamentalists had so strongly repudiated the Pentecostals in 1928, was now the site of lasting reconciliation.

The idea of cooperative effort was more gradually accepted within the ranks of the Assemblies of God than is at first apparent. Flower, then in his eighth year as general secretary of the General Council, served as chief promoter of the NAE, using the platform of the General Council and articles in *The Pentecostal Evangel* to urge the constituency to accept

20. Shelley, *Evangelicalism in America*, 81.

21. This rejection plus the negative posture of the ACCC in general led to the rejection of the ACCC by evangelical moderates. Conn, *Like a Mighty Army*, 215–59.

22. McIntire, editorial, 8.

23. General Council minutes, 1943, 8. The previous year the General Presbytery had unanimously adopted a resolution supporting the NAE and authorizing the Executive Presbytery to appoint delegates to the Constitutional Convention in 1943 who would report back to the General Council. General Presbytery minutes, 1942, 2.

24. Flower, "The Basic Unity," 8. Official delegates from the Assemblies of God were general superintendent Williams, general secretary Flower, and missionary secretary Noel Perkin. Menzies asserts that for the Pentecostals this was the first time any evangelical body had extended them an invitation to participate. See Menzies's book, *Anointed to Serve*, 185.

25. "The Diary of a Delegate," 4.

affiliation.[26] Frodsham also wrote in glowing praise of the priority of evangelism and prayer at the 1944 NAE convention. He answered the oft-raised question regarding the danger of compromise with "an emphatic 'No,'" assuring his readers that cooperation and compromise were not necessarily one and the same.[27] The question was not put to rest until the end of the decade. Resolutions were presented at the 1947 and 1949 General Councils, the first one questioning the membership of the Assemblies of God in the NAE. Both Councils voted in favor of the affiliation, the second one by "a clear majority," and the issue finally seems to have been settled.[28]

The development of the NAE also led to cooperation among Pentecostal groups which had been severely fragmented, and soon the Pentecostal Fellowship of North America (PFNA) and the World Pentecostal Fellowship (WPF) were formed. Having already joined with evangelicals, affiliation with other Pentecostals proved to be a less controversial matter.[29]

In the decades following World War II, American evangelicalism itself underwent great change. In reaction to early fundamentalist tenets, proponents now dealt more openly with issues of social concern. From the 1940s to the 1960s there was within the movement an increasingly louder call for social involvement, and this gave birth in the latter sixties and early seventies to an ethical renaissance. This resurgence was most evident in 1973 at a Chicago conference of the Evangelicals for Social Action (ESA) and the subsequent Conference for Implementation in 1975. After that date, at least two quite divergent streams of social activism exhibited themselves within the movement: the radical evangelicals, represented in the ESA, and the Religious Right.

Coming out of the nineteenth century, the Fundamentalists did not have a stated social ethic. What heritage was to be gained from earlier

26. Flower, "Why We Joined the N.A.E.," 12.

27. Frodsham, "Days of Heaven upon Earth," 4–5.

28. General Council minutes, 1947, 24–25; General Council minutes, 1949, 28.

29. General Council minutes, 1949, 28–29. The PFNA held its Constitutional Convention in October 1948 at which time Flower was elected secretary of the Executive Board and general superintendent Williams was elected to the Board of Administration; "Pentecostal Groups Meet," 13. The WPF, created in 1947 on the initiative of European Pentecostals, was organized more informally, with reservations being expressed by the Swedish Pentecostals. J. R. Flower, interview by Menzies, 26 June 1967. The prior meeting in Europe provided the impetus for the formation of the American organization in 1948.

evangelicals had been lost in what Moberg called the "Great Reversal," in which the conservative evangelicals clung to theological purity but rejected the social activism of their predecessors. Such activism came to be associated with modernism and the social gospel—movements rejected for their repudiation of what Fundamentalists held to be essential.[30]

Although the Pentecostals were born in the midst of this Great Reversal, they never were involved in it and often evidenced some of the radical ethic of the earlier movements. In their subsequent search for respectability, moderate Pentecostals such as those Assemblies of God worked hard to shed this radical image while cautiously attempting to align themselves with their theological cousins—the Fundamentalists—who were at the same time rejecting them. When the Pentecostals finally were accepted by the NAE in the 1940s, some in the evangelical movement were just beginning to develop a fresh social concern which in time would influence a younger generation of Pentecostals with a new perspective on society and ethics.

The essence of this newer evangelical consciousness was never fully owned by the Assemblies of God of that day. The Council took note that awareness of social issues was important—even to evangelicals. Primarily, official statements such as the 1966 paper on social concern were in lockstep with the NAE alignment and, essentially, were statements made in response to what was most acceptable in the social climate at the time.

30. For more on the concept of the great reversal within American evangelicalism, see Moberg, *The Great Reversal.*

5

Building Blocks
of a Pentecostal Worldview

IN MANY WAYS THE origin and development of the Assemblies of God were unique in the history of Pentecostalism, a uniqueness which may well have contributed to its stellar rise as a worldwide phenomenon over the past century. But within these unique qualities were characteristics which also contributed to future challenges—challenges of an ethical nature.

At the micro level, the individuals who came together to form or join the Council were attracted by qualities in the fellowship, but they also brought with them their own orientations which influenced and, in turn, were influenced by the new community. Individuals in an organization might think or behave differently than the collective whole, but any individual member contributes to and is shaped by the collective worldview.

At the macro level, a whole range of contributors—theological (or philosophical) commitments, sociological factors, historic influences, cultural effects, and so on—produced the Assemblies of God. Together these combined to shape the fellowship's collective consciousness.

We have already considered some of the contributors to the formation and development of the General Council: world events such as the world wars, the changing American culture, and the evolving American church—in particular the modernist-fundamentalist divide within Protestantism, the rise of Fundamentalism, the evolution of twentieth century evangelicalism, and the impact of the charismatic movement.

We have also examined the influences of Wesleyanism, Christian Per-
fectionism, the Holiness and Keswick movements, and the New Issue, as
well as individuals such as Dowie, Parham, Seymour, and Durham. There
were theological and sociological elements as well that contributed to the
General Council's worldview, and more specifically, to its ethical posture.

Theological Elements

While the Council adheres to a sixteen-point statement of faith, Assemblies of God literature and sermons are sprinkled throughout with a four-
fold refrain of salvation, Holy Spirit, healing, and the Blessed Hope. Often
referred to as the four cardinal doctrines, these are a modification of earlier holiness teachings for which "Holy Spirit" replaced "sanctification."

Frequently, members of the Assemblies of God speak of their one
distinctive as speaking in tongues, the universal sign of the initial physical evidence of the baptism in the Holy Spirit. Sometimes this distinctive
is viewed, at least from a lay perspective, as being the most important
teaching—which should only be understood as an emphasis that distin-
guishes it from the rest of orthodox Christianity. For the initial evidence
teaching is nested within orthodoxy, the teachings on the nature of God
and salvation through Jesus Christ being higher in order and priority in
the organization's basic doctrines. But do these teachings, as essential as
they may be, help us understand why the fellowship behaves the way it
does? There are other lenses, not all cardinal doctrines, through which we
can analyze the ethical posture of the fellowship.

Eschatology

Eschatology, especially as evidenced in the belief in the imminent return
of Christ or the Blessed Hope, has played an important, if varying, role
over the years. The fellowship's self-understanding was shaped in the
beginning by the Latter Rain teaching. Moreover, the very existence of
the movement has been attributed largely to "the conviction that the
premillennial return of Christ was at hand."[1] This emphasis on end-time
prophecy was often accompanied by an otherworldly detachment. The
return of Christ was seen to be "the only possible solution of the present

---

1. Flower, "Fifty Years of Signs and Wonders," 6.

disturbing and unsatisfactory world conditions."[2] Such thinking was a major theme in the earlier pacifism and, though the eschatological focus changed somewhat, it affected later positions regarding civil rights and nuclear armament. While eschatological teaching remained highly revered into the 1980s, it no longer affected the attitudes and behaviors of Pentecostals as it once had; the end of the present age had somehow become compatible with the world as it is.

Authority of Scripture

In their strong belief in the authority of Scripture, Pentecostals identified with their Fundamentalist and evangelical cousins, even as each interpreted passages of that same Scripture differently. For Pentecostals, this belief was in tension with the moving of the Spirit—one would not contradict the other, so it was taught, but the dual leadings of Word and Spirit were occasionally complicated for mere mortals to decipher. Essentially, the adherence to Scripture did not always provide a uniform approach to moral matters, often creating conflicting positions.

Although belief in the authority of Scripture fostered an earlier tendency toward pacifism, it also helped move the denomination away from this same pacifism because of scriptural teaching on loyalty to government. Authority of Scripture likewise was a primary determinant in the formation of views on the women/eldership issue and on modern feminism. In another direction, it provided linkage of sorts with adherents of a general conservative social stance.

The Age of the Spirit

A significant theological concept among earlier Pentecostals was the focus on the power and anointing of the Spirit, often in contrast with the emphasis on Scripture. In the 1950s, Flower cautioned the Council: "We must be alert to the dangers of becoming so literal in our interpretations of the Scripture that, like some of the older denominations, we 'deny the power thereof.'"[3] The pioneers knew they were indeed living in the Age

2. From an advertisement of *The Return of the Lord Jesus* by R. A. Torrey, 14. The book was one of multitudes of second coming writings produced and/or distributed by GPH.

3. Flower, "Fifty Years of Signs and Wonders," 7.

of the Spirit, a time in which the transformative work of the Spirit could and would be felt in every aspect of life.

This belief created a greater openness toward women ministers as well as toward people of color in the earliest days. Though the Assemblies of God has always maintained its Pentecostal distinctive, this perspective of the Age of the Spirit lost breadth over time. One might even say that the Pentecostal distinctive became truncated, limited to the "initial evidence" doctrine, its fuller impact on the Assemblies of God much less thoroughgoing than in the beginning.

World Evangelization

The priority of missions and evangelism, or world evangelization, is what has propelled the Assemblies of God into a worldwide movement—and in turn has rescued the American General Council from stagnation and decline in the past quarter century as waves of its international adherents have migrated to the US. In the 1920s, the Assemblies of God perceived itself primarily as a missionary agency.[4] In midcentury, the declaration was "Evangelism is our supreme task!"[5] Frodsham wrote that because the present Pentecostal revival "has been so distinctively evangelistic hundreds of thousands of souls have been won for Christ."[6] This priority on world evangelization has stemmed directly from the Keswickian notion of enduement of power. Pentecostal power provides the power to proclaim.[7]

This emphasis on world evangelization has led to some contradictory positions. It was the excuse for a lack of initiative in reaching black Americans prior to the civil rights advances of the sixties; yet it fueled a greater openness toward people of color in more recent years. It led the sect away from pacifism in earlier years and away from social activism throughout most of the church's history. And it assisted in creating a more positive posture toward women in ministry both in the first generation and again in the latter part of the century.

4. In reply to the question, "What is the General Council?" it was answered, "It is a missionary agency." The 1927 General Council reported 277 foreign missionaries, compared to fifteen hundred ordained ministers total. "Twelfth General Council Meeting," 2–10.

5. Duncombe, "Pulling Them Out of the Fire," 4.

6. Letter from Frodsham to Eveleth, 29 July 1943.

7. Flower, "Fifty Years of Signs and Wonders," 6.

Ecumenism

The ecumenism of the movement also played a key role, bringing together a broad range of perspectives. The Greek root of the word ecumenical means "house" and comes to mean bringing everyone under one house.

The pioneers evidenced a strong restorationist vision; the desire of those who gathered at Hot Springs was not to create a new denomination, but a uniting fellowship.[8] In 1921, the General Council appointed a committee to organize a conference for the formation of an "Ecumenical Union of Pentecostal Believers," though this never materialized.[9] In the 1950s, unofficial overtures were made to other Finished Work Pentecostals to consider union. Donald Gee, general superintendent of the British Assemblies of God and highly revered as a statesman among American Pentecostals, did much to promote the concept of Pentecostal unity until his death in 1966. In 1973, the General Council passed and then rescinded a resolution to establish a study committee to explore possible union with other Pentecostal bodies.[10] The dream of Pentecostal ecumenism, though never realized, did much to shape the self-perception of the Assemblies of God as a movement or fellowship rather than as a denomination. It also aided in the rise of the Sisterhood Myth regarding the Church of God in Christ.

Much of the ecumenical spirit was fueled by the diversity of backgrounds of the founders of the General Council. Though the majority came from more traditional holiness churches, the first two chairpersons, Bell and Collins, were Baptist in origin. Another pioneer, S. A. Jamieson, was Presbyterian. Much of the Keswickian influence came through A.

8. "A Movement toward Unity," 1.

9. F. A. Hale, W. F. Carothers, Robert McAlister, Hugh Ulrich, and J. Narver Gortner comprised the committee. See Combined General Council minutes, 1921, 59. *The Pentecostal Evangel* again promoted the idea the following year ("A Movement toward Unity," 1, 7), until Hale, the chair of the committee, tried to pull together an unauthorized conference in October 1922. His efforts were not endorsed nor rejected outright by the Executive Presbytery. See "St. Louis Unity Meeting," 1. At the following council, Hale reported that the committee had not been able to meet in the previous two years because of great distances and nothing had been accomplished. Combined General Council minutes, 1923, 61.

10. General Council minutes, 1973, 66–69. Though the action was rescinded, a privileged motion later prevailed in the same council "that this General Council go on record as encouraging the Executive Presbytery to keep the lines of communication open with any Pentecostal groups interested in cooperating or possibly uniting with the Assemblies of God." General Council minutes, 1973, 69.

B. Simpson's Christian and Missionary Alliance, itself an ecumenical missionary movement, with a whole segment of that organization being swept into Pentecostalism to contribute a sizeable number of the founders of the Assemblies of God.[11]

Because the denomination was formed from people of many varied backgrounds, including independents, and because it saw itself as a unifier of Pentecostalism, it frequently showed a nonsectarian attitude on many issues. A competitive spirit with other Pentecostal churches, regardless of race, was not encouraged. As time went on this perspective brought the Assemblies of God into greater cooperation with non-Pentecostals and created a moderating influence on divisive distinctives.

Sociological Elements

As we have seen, more than theology determines the ethical mindset of a faith community. Several sociological elements also had an influence on the Assemblies of God.

Geographical Concentration

Although the Assemblies of God was organized in Arkansas, it had a nationwide constituency from the very beginning.[12] Yet it maintained its primary strength in the southcentral states of Texas, Oklahoma, Arkansas, and Missouri.[13] By the 1980s, nearly a fourth of all of its churches were still to be found in those four states.[14] Geography had special significance

11. Including leaders such as John W. Welch, Frank M. Boyd, D. W. Kerr, David McDowell, William I. Evans, Minnie Draper, A. G. Ward, W. W. Simpson, Noel Perkin, Alice Reynolds Flower, and J. T. Boddy. The Alliance had significant impact in other ways on the Assemblies of God, including doctrine, organizational patterns, and missionary vision. See Brumback, *Suddenly . . . from Heaven*, 94.

12. In 1925, the top states in number of subscribers to *The Pentecostal Evangel* were California (2,616), Texas (1,613), Missouri (1,235), Pennsylvania (1,138), Illinois (1,130), Oklahoma (1,128), Ohio (1,054), New York (996), Arkansas (890), Washington (610), and Kansas (608). "What State is the Most Pentecostal?" 7.

13. J. R. Flower, interview by Menzies, 26 June 1967.

14. Approximately 24.9 percent of all churches and 22.6 percent of all members, 1984 statistics. In 1955 the percentages were slightly higher for churches with 28.6 percent, the percentage of members remaining unchanged. "Ending December 31, 1984," "Assemblies of God Church Membership," "Membership by State, 1985," "Church Report—1955-1958," and "Report of Churches for 1955."

for modifying the denomination's stance on various issues, particularly regarding race relations and the move toward integration.

Anti-intellectualism

An anti-intellectual attitude also marked the Assemblies of God from its inception. The reaction against the "dead" seminaries of the turn of the century, the affinity with the lower class, and the focus on being "led by the Spirit" all helped create this posture of anti-intellectualism. Contrasting with the church's upward social mobility, higher education and theological study were long frowned upon.

From World War II on, the Assemblies of God constituency experienced a rapid upward social mobility. What was once a largely lower-class sect emerged as a predominantly middle-class denomination. Even so, the church membership remained a people non-literary in outlook. Serious attempts were made to alter this perception, but it took nearly sixty years for the Council to approve a seminary and another ten to call it such. The fellowship is still largely a movement of grassroots initiative, of pragmatic growth orientation and of verbal, more than written, expression.

Mainstreaming

As was discussed in chapter 2, mainstreaming became increasingly important in how the fellowship viewed itself. Attempting to accommodate in all "non-essentials" to prevailing fundamentalist/evangelical thought, the Council adopted neutrality on most issues of controversy, which led to alignment with social and political views espoused by other evangelicals. This alignment was made irrespective of unique perspectives Pentecostals might have to offer.

In her book, *God Forgive Us for Being Women*, Joy Andrich Qualls writes that she asked then general superintendent George O. Wood what factor contributed most to the challenges women have faced in the Assemblies of God. "Culture," he replied. "We tended to succumb to the prevailing culture."[15] The same could be said for the fellowship's change from its original commitment to pacifism, though the influence of social accommodation is most notable on the issue of race.

15. Quoted in Qualls, *God Forgive Us*, 19.

Wood echoed his statement to Qualls in 2014 in speaking on the fellowship's track record on the handling of race. "It's just tragic that there was that epoch in America where the church caved in to the culture rather than transforming the culture."[16] It was a very long epoch.

Three Prevailing Ethical Postures

All these historical, theological and sociological influences created a worldview lens through which the fellowship viewed moral considerations both within and without—and influenced what might be valued as of moral import. When decisions of an ethical nature had to be made, this lens brought perspective through which positions could be established.

Is it acceptable for Christians to smoke, drink, or gamble? Are believers allowed to marry someone from a different race? Should Pentecostals vote for a Roman Catholic to become President of the United States of America? Can believers engage in political protest? Can Christians go to movies or dances? Should Pentecostals fight in physical combat? Can women preach the gospel or serve as pastors? Should believers salute the flag in a worship service? Which takes priority—reaching the lost or being holy? What position should Christians take on capital punishment, abortion, or immigration? The answers to these and so many more questions have been incubated in a worldview mix of historic, theological, and sociological factors that have made up the collective consciousness of the American Assemblies of God.

What this worldview does not provide is a precise roadmap toward ethical decisions. Even cut-in-stone biblical commandments such as "thou shalt not kill" lead to differing interpretations. The collection of contributing factors provides a range of ethical options.

What options did the Assemblies of God draw on? In the thinking of the Assemblies of God constituency, three ethical options or approaches came to dominate during the first 75 years of the fellowship's history: dogmatic, pragmatic, and reactionary.

The first two options were often found in tension with each other. The dogmatic approach was expressed in a parroting of clichés and traditions in ideology, while the pragmatic approach was evidenced by a rapid shift in values and an indifferent attitude toward ideology. The dogmatic strain was linked to the past; the pragmatic was concerned with what

16. "Pentecostal Groups Confront."

produces results. A dichotomy of thought often resulted when official statements were developed according to dogmatic perceptions while actual procedures by the constituency (lay and clergy alike) were changing due to practical concerns. Ideas tended to be modified less by careful study than by actions and results. In the beginning, the denomination developed organically, and this caused much of the church's ethical stance to be a pragmatic one. "What people by their actions believe" was an attitude discernibly different from earlier perspectives and often causing considerable contradiction.

The third ethical option was the reactionary approach, in which attitudes were established primarily in response to other influences, such as changes in society at large or the church world. The addition of the word "verbal" to the statement of biblical inspiration in the Fundamentals is a case in point. Even much earlier, the very development of the Doctrines of Fundamental Truths was itself a reactive response to the New Issue. Essentially, theology, including moral theology, was often determined according to someone else's agenda.

The reactionary approach is most evident in how the Council has related to African Americans, while the fellowship has demonstrated a pragmatic approach concerning war and a dogmatic approach toward women in ministry. The question which will have to be asked in the end is what most adequately constitutes an ethical approach informed by Pentecostal theology, experience, and tradition.

6

Interracial Roots
(prior to 1914)

THROUGH MOST OF THE twentieth century, the Assemblies of God remained a predominantly white denomination in the United States, almost devoid of any American black constituency.[1] While it shares a heritage with black Pentecostals, as all Pentecostals draw from the same historical wellsprings, it has struggled uniquely with the race issue.

In the 1970s and 1980s, church leadership and rank and file alike were cognizant of the overwhelming lack of African Americans in membership. By acknowledgement of former general superintendent Williams, "The Assemblies of God began, of course, as a white denomination."[2] Even today, issues relating to race which arose at church and presbytery meetings lie nearly forgotten in official minutes. Until this study, no survey on the subject had ever been made of the contents of *The Pentecostal Evangel*.

Where facts remained buried, myth arose. One popular misconception that developed was that the Assemblies of God was in a unique

1. Side-by-side with other language branches, the Hispanic segment of the Assemblies of God had long been a distinct, though increasingly significant and growing element of the denomination, accounting for 8.9 percent of total membership and 10.6 percent of churches by 1984. "A/G Hispanics," 19 August 1986. However, this strength of the Hispanics had not yet been expressed in levels of denominational leadership. The present study on racism is limited to the American blacks because the development of the two ethnic groups within the fellowship has been very different. More study, though, is needed on the role of the Hispanics in the General Council.

2. Williams, interview by Tinney, 8 November 1978.

relationship with the Church of God in Christ, largest of the American black Pentecostal denominations. Though there were some early associations between the two, the contact was insignificant from the time Charles H. Mason, the church's long-term bishop, in some way affirmed the Hot Springs General Council. As a result, the Sisterhood Myth that the one was the black/white counterpart to the other was without basis.

The Church of God in Christ was founded as a holiness church by Mason and Charles Price Jones prior to the turn of the century. After Mason visited Azusa Street in 1906 and received the Pentecostal experience, he returned to Memphis, Tennessee, to bring the church into the fledgling Pentecostal movement.[3] Contact with future Assemblies of God constituency developed shortly after, but the roots of interracial relations were planted in Azusa Street and are part of the larger picture encompassing the whole Pentecostal movement.

The Founding Father Debate

One of the matters for concern in the subject of the racial origins of the Pentecostal movement is when it was launched. Was Pentecostalism born in Topeka, Kansas, with Charles Parham, a white, serving as midwife? Was it first a black movement in Los Angeles led by a black holiness preacher, William Seymour, which soon attracted whites? Or did it arise from disparate groups around the world with significant contributions from both blacks and whites?

Several people are prominent as major pioneers in the American Pentecostal movement, though historians have disagreed on their relative significance. William F. Bryant (1896) is suggested by Charles W. Conn (Church of God); Charles Parham (1901) by Klaude Kendrick (AG); and William Seymour and Azusa Street (1906) by Gee (British Assemblies of God), Frodsham (AG), and Vinson Synan (Pentecostal Holiness).[4]

Those who point to a twentieth century founding portray the "tongues speaking" incidents of the previous century as isolated cases. Yet direct links with later revivals were evidenced by the people involved

3. A split occurred in the Church of God in Christ, with the church's founder C. P. Jones reorganizing a non-Pentecostal holiness church, presently named Church of Christ (Holiness) U.S.A. See Cobbins, *History of Church*, 16, 52, 117, 149, 426–34.

4. Conn, *Like a Mighty Army*, 18–27; Kendrick, *The Promise Fulfilled*, 36; Gee, *The Pentecostal Movement*, 11; Frodsham, *With Signs Following*; and Synan, *The Holiness-Pentecostal Movement*, 95.

in such diverse locations as Rhode Island, Arkansas, Ohio, Minnesota, and Tennessee, as well as by Armenian immigrants. The Church of God was born out of one of these pre-Topeka experiences. While such cases of "tongues speaking" are known at present only of whites, there is no reason to believe that people of color did not have similar experiences prior to 1900.

What these incidents of tongues speaking did not include was an understanding that such was the initial physical evidence of the baptism in the Holy Spirit—a doctrine developed chiefly by Parham, a white holiness preacher whose growing group of followers were also white. Under him the movement expanded from Kansas and Missouri to Texas; however, when the movement spread to California, Parham's undisputed leadership was brought into question.

There is a definite link between Parham and the Azusa Street event. Seymour, the leader of the Azusa Street Mission, attended some of Parham's meetings in Houston, but Seymour did not receive the Pentecostal experience until he moved to Los Angeles. Although the Bible school in Topeka, Kansas, was responsible for linking baptism with tongues, the happenings at Azusa Street made the movement a worldwide phenomenon in less than three years. Most Pentecostal groups trace their origins to the Azusa Street Mission.

B. F. Lawrence, a pioneer in the Assemblies of God, made specific mention of the Azusa Street outpouring in a series he wrote in the *Evangel* about the early days of the movement. Although he focused more on the developments in Texas because of his own involvement and leadership there, he did pay tribute to the roles of Seymour and co-worker Lucy Farrow in advancing the Pentecostal movement. Lawrence saw Seymour's going to Los Angeles as an occasion which "changed the whole history of the movement."[5]

Though the teaching on Spirit baptism came through Seymour from Houston and Parham, Bartleman gives credit to the Welsh Revival of 1904–5 for being the primary catalyst of the Azusa revival. In any event, shortly following Seymour's arrival in California in the spring of 1906, the Pentecostal message spread from Los Angeles around the world.

Seymour was the unequivocal head of the Azusa Street Mission when it was in its prime.[6] The crowd may have been primarily black

5. Lawrence apparently did not share Parham's repudiation of the Azusa Street ministry. Lawrence, "Apostolic Faith Restored; Article VII," 4.

6. For more information on Seymour, see Nelson, "For Such a Time as This."

when it was at the Bonnie Brae house before it moved to Azusa Street, but the meetings grew increasingly integrated.[7] Although both Seymour and Parham tried to unify the new Pentecostal movement under their respective leaderships, neither succeeded. Parham tried to assert responsibility for the Los Angeles group when he thought the latter had been given over to excesses and fanaticism; however, his authority was rejected.[8] In September 1906, *The Apostolic Faith*, a paper produced by the Azusa Street Mission, referred to Parham as "God's leader in the Apostolic Faith Movement."[9] By December, the paper issued a disclaimer regarding Parham's role:

> Some are asking if Dr. Chas. F. Parham is the leader of this movement. We can answer, no he is not the leader of this movement of Azusa Mission. We thought of having him to be our leader and so stated in our paper, before waiting on the Lord. We can be rather hasty, especially when we are very young in the power of the Holy Spirit. . . . we saw that the Lord should be our leader. So we honor Jesus as the great Shepherd of the sheep. He is our model.[10]

On Seymour's invitation, Parham had paid a visit to the mission during the interim between those two issues of *The Apostolic Faith*.[11] Not long after, the Los Angeles fellowship separated completely from the original movement, "under circumstances which the present writer [W. F. Carothers] believes justified them, but about which it would be painful to write."[12]

Seymour then attempted to organize a church society on the local level and to tie in a new group growing rapidly in Portland and Seattle, known as Apostolic Faith. Even though in its inception this latter group's

---

7. There is some disagreement on this point in that Bartleman writes that blacks and whites were meeting together from the beginning. *How Pentecost Came*, 43.

8. See Goss, *The Winds of God*, 72; Bartleman, *How Pentecost Came*, 69; and Mack Jones, quoted in Lovett, "Black Origins," 133.

9. "Letter from Bro. Parham," 1. "Apostolic Faith" was a common designation in early Pentecostal circles, signifying the movement's restorationist perspective.

10. "Pentecost with Signs Following," 1.

11. Parham, *Life of Parham*, 154–55.

12. Lawrence, "Apostolic Faith Restored; Article VII," 4, quoting from an article by W. F. Carothers in the *Apostolic Faith* (Houston), October 1908. Carothers, a white minister, had been involved in Parham's Apostolic Faith group in Texas from the beginning of that movement. He would later help found the General Council.

leadership had been in the Azusa Street revival, Seymour's efforts were rejected.[13] "Apostolic Faith" was a name common to local assemblies led by Parham, Seymour, Florence Crawford (leader of the Portland group), and others, but there was no official connection. All of them had an aversion to organization, yet each moved separately toward a more structured ministry.

Parham's Attitude toward Black People

Black Pentecostal scholar Leonard Lovett has attempted to discredit Parham's leadership in the Pentecostal movement on the basis of racism, citing Parham as a "great supporter of the Ku Klux Klan" (KKK) in later years.[14] Indeed, Parham referred to the KKK's "high ideals about the betterment of mankind"[15] and later wrote for the racist periodical of Gerald B. Winrod at Wichita, Kansas.[16]

Parham included some strong racist sentiments in his writings and teachings. He averred that interracial marriage was the reason God caused the flood of Noah's day and decried modern-day marriages between whites, blacks and "reds" as a threat to the whole human race,[17] basing his beliefs on his understanding of Scripture and history.

He taught that Queen Victoria was directly descended from the Old Testament prophet Jeremiah;[18] that the descendants of Abraham are the Hindus, the Japanese, the high Germans, the Danes, the Scandinavians, and the Anglo-Saxons. The Gentiles account for the other Europeans, while the heathen are the blacks, the browns, and the reds. The ten lost tribes are to be found among the modern nations: England stands for Ephraim and the United States for Manasseh in which all the prophecies

---

13. Williams, interview by author, 18 March 1978; also, Bartleman, *How Pentecost Came*, 69.

14. Although Lovett does not support this statement with any evidence in this article, the opinion is in keeping with Parham's record. See Lovett, "Black Origins," 135.

15. *Apostolic Faith* (Baxter Springs, Kansas), March 1927, 5.

16. Parham, *Life of Parham*, 276.

17. Parham, *A Voice Crying in the Wilderness*, 83.

18. Parham, *A Voice Crying in the Wilderness*, 91–100. Parham weaves a whole genealogical history from Adam through the Kings of Israel (Judah) to the modern British monarchy.

concerning the sons of Joseph are fulfilled—"Thou shalt be the head and not the tail of nations."[19]

This British-Israelism helps explain Parham's paternalistic attitude toward other races. They were not excluded from ever receiving salvation, but the Anglo-Saxons were a chosen race of God selected for dominating the earth. Other races were inferior, and not to be intermingled with in marriage.

Parham's racial beliefs are evident in his attitudes and actions toward the black people he encountered in his ministry. He is said to have likened the excesses of the Azusa Street revival to the "Southern Darkey camp meetings."[20] In decrying what he calls the free love found in the Apostolic faith movement, Parham expressed his feelings quite strongly:

> In the Azusa mission in Los Angeles, (where all this counterfeit Pentecost power was born) in the Upper Room, men and women, whites and blacks, knelt together or fell across one another; frequently, a white woman, perhaps of wealth and culture, could be seen thrown back in the arms of a big "buck nigger," and held tightly thus as she shivered and shook in freak imitation of Pentecost. Horrible, awful shame! Many of the missions on the Pacific coast are permeated with this foolishness, and, in fact, it follows the Azusa work everywhere.... [Regarding a meeting in Oakland], an outsider would have said this was another bunch of nigger-lovers and free-lovers; but they were not, oh no, but were a very esteemable class of Christians. "Avoid the very appearance of evil."[21]

African Americans did have a part in Parham's revivals, even if it were within the limitations of the social norms of the day. For years Parham held integrated meetings, though he did expect black people to "keep their place" and respect the welcome extended them.[22] A black man, Mack E. Jones, who was part of the Azusa Street revival, commented on how Parham separated the races in Houston. "Well, it was in the

---

19. Parham, *A Voice Crying in the Wilderness*, 106–8.

20. Synan, *Holiness-Pentecostal Movement*, 99.

21. Parham, "Free Love," 4–5. Parham continued to attack the Los Angeles ministry for its excesses. See Parham, *Life of Parham*. 161–170; and Parham, *Everlasting Gospel*, 71.

22. Parham, *Life of Parham*, 246. See also, 302.

south, and people didn't believe in white and colored mixing, and going to the altar bowing together in prayer like that."[23]

There are some positive indications of black involvement in Parham's ministry. A Methodist minister who attended one of Parham's services in Wichita, Kansas, in 1909, left in disgust over the failure of those in charge to "keep niggers in their place." When this minister was "converted" to Pentecostalism fourteen years later, his baptism occurred in a predominantly black meeting in the same city. "I had to wade through a whole camp meeting of them when I got the Baptism . . . God surely broke me over the wheel of my prejudice."[24]

At least one black person was accepted into Parham's Bible school in Houston. That was Seymour who became a daily participant. Parham later admitted that he could not refuse Seymour admittance because of his intense interest in biblical instruction.[25] B. F. Lawrence later wrote that he remembered very clearly Seymour coming to the classes in the morning and later preaching with Parham to the black people of the city. Seymour was already a minister but was seeking the baptism.[26]

How far the whites accepted fellowship with blacks in Houston is not definitely known. It is likely that Seymour did not live at the school as did many of the whites because Howard Goss said he was not a full participant. Although whites were "nice" to blacks, there do not seem to have been any blacks active in the white Pentecostal churches of the time. "There was no association and they didn't eat together—ever."[27]

These white Texas Pentecostals did not seem to be entirely bound by the cultural attitudes that surrounded them. Lucy Farrow, a black cook at Parham's school, went to Los Angeles to work with Seymour, and Parham provided the money for her fare from the school's treasury.[28] When Farrow returned to Houston, she attended the August 1906 camp

23. Lovett, "Black Origins," 133.

24. Perkins, *The Pentecostal Evangel*, 22 March 1924, 6–7, quoted in Anderson, *Vision of the Disinherited*, 123.

25. Sarah Parham writes, "In Texas, you know, the colored people are not allowed to mix with the white people as they do in some of the other states; but he was so humble and so deeply interested in the study of the Word that Mr. Parham could not refuse him." Parham, *Life of Parham*, 137.

26. Lawrence, "Apostolic Faith Restored; Article VIII," 4. See also, Goss, *Winds of God*, 71.

27. Cadwalder, interview by author, March 1978. The Cadwalders were eyewitnesses of this early Texas movement.

28. Goss, *Winds of God*, 70.

meeting, preaching and sharing of the events of Azusa Street, and then laying hands on people to receive the Holy Ghost. Goss said that she was received as a messenger of the Lord to them, even though this was in the South.[29]

Not only was Farrow allowed to attend the white camp meeting, she was given opportunity to speak, a rarity for a black person. Even if Parham had sent her and Seymour to California under the impression that they were simply going to start a black mission,[30] he could never have predicted the far-reaching events that would transpire.

The Integrated Azusa Street Mission

Seymour went to Los Angeles on the invitation of a Nazarene woman.[31] Once there, he first went to preach in a black Nazarene church, but after his message was rejected, he was invited to a home meeting on Bonnie Brae Street. Bartleman visited this place on 26 March 1906 and found "both white and colored saints were meeting there for prayer." The Pentecostal experience came on 9 April. Ten days later the daily meetings were moved to Azusa Street to an old Methodist church—more recently used as a barn. Bartleman records that there were then about a dozen in attendance, some whites, some blacks, with Seymour in charge.[32]

Reports from the Welsh Revival had brought an atmosphere of expectancy to American believers in holiness and other groups. When word of the Azusa Street meetings began to spread through the same network of church papers and itinerant preachers, people began flocking in from everywhere, even from across the nation and from other countries. Azusa Street "started out mostly black folks, and then the white folks began to come in from all over."[33] In time, whites outnumbered blacks. "The 'color line' was washed away in the blood." Bartleman saw the explanation of the phenomenon in the fact that "great emphasis was

29. Goss, *Winds of God*, 96.

30. Parham expected Seymour to take the Pentecostal teaching to "his own people" in Texas" and was "rather surprised when he said he felt led to go to California." Nonetheless, Parham helped provide the fare for Seymour's travel as he would later do for Farrow. Parham, *Life of Parham*, 142.

31. "Pentecost Has Come," 1.

32. Bartleman, *How Pentecost Came*, 43, 48.

33. Catley, interview at Society for Pentecostal Studies, 1974.

placed on the 'blood,' for cleansing, etc. A high standard was held up for a clean life."[34]

The evidence suggests real fellowship existed between the two races. Lawrence Catley declares that Azusa was an interracial assembly—not just whites and blacks sitting together, but a real oneness. Even as late as 1910 the two races could be found eating, sitting, and praying together.[35]

"There were no differences in race or color; everybody was somebody."[36] "Services were conducted as we say, as the Spirit moved. . . . We never knew who was going to preach until we saw him give the Bible to so and so . . . white or black."[37] "Everybody went to the altar together. White and colored, no discrimination seemed to be among them."[38]

This perception was shared by others who visited Los Angeles during this time or who were familiar with what was happening there. Williams came into the Pentecostal movement at the Azusa Street Mission where he received the baptism in the Spirit.[39] G. B. Cashwell, a minister of the Holiness Association of North Carolina, went to Azusa Street in 1906. Cashwell later returned to the Southeast and was responsible for bringing a large wing of the holiness movement into Pentecostalism. Before then, however, while he was still in Los Angeles, his racial experience and understanding expanded.

> While waiting before the Lord, Cashwell was disturbed to notice that a young colored man was praying with him, and even more disturbed when he asked, "Do you want me to pray for you so that you will receive the Holy Ghost?" This was a little too much for this Southern Christian, and he was just at the point of telling the would-be-helper to help someone else, when the Lord whispered to him, "This young man is deeply in earnest, and I have sent him. How badly do you want to be filled?" Cashwell wanted God to manifest His power more than he wanted to manifest his racial prejudice, so he meekly consented. The result of this desegregation at the throne of grace? A proud Southerner

---

34. Bartleman, *How Pentecost Came*, 54.

35. Catley, interview at Society for Pentecostal Studies, 1974.

36. Catley, interview at Society for Pentecostal Studies, 1974; also, Cornelius, "Our Church History," 4.

37. Catley, interview at Society for Pentecostal Studies, 1974

38. Jones, quoted in Lovett, "Black Origins," 133.

39. Williams, interview by author, 18 March 1978.

was filled by the "Holy Ghost sent down from heaven" where there are no racial distinctions at all.[40]

This change in his personal perspective, however, did not translate into a more open racial stance among the churches Cashwell introduced to the Pentecostal message. Frank M. Boyd, an educator of great influence in the Council who came into the movement about this time in the Northeast,[41] admitted that black people were not accepted too enthusiastically, for the most part, and that Azusa Street stood out as "exclusive"—as unique.[42]

By 1909 the Azusa Street Mission had reverted to a mostly black congregation. Many other churches had already grown out of this center as early as four months within the birth of the revival with the separations apparently occurring over doctrinal and ecclesiastical differences.[43]

The birth of the Pentecostal movement is properly understood as happening in 1906. What occurred in Topeka was certainly a critical stage in the gestation of the movement which had begun well before 1901. However, Pentecostalism prior to Azusa Street was little more than a white-led, white-membered, and white-oriented regional phenomenon. At Azusa Street it became a full-born movement. Early Assemblies of God publications acknowledged 1906 as the starting point of the movement. One article noted that "the Pentecostal Movement has been existent since 1906 as a powerful factor for the evangelism of the world."[44] Another stated that "the Latter Rain began falling in 1906, in Los Angeles."[45]

The Latter Rain theory held high consideration among early Pentecostals in interpreting history, prophecy, and particularly their own identity as a movement.[46] This theory established the Azusa Street outpouring

40. Brumback, *Suddenly . . . from Heaven*, 84.

41. A product of the Christian and Missionary Alliance, Boyd was principal of Bethel Bible Institute in Newark, New Jersey, from 1918 to 1923, and subsequently principal of Central Bible Institute in Springfield, Missouri. Later he served on the faculty of Southern California Bible College (Vanguard University) and established the General Council correspondence program, originally known as the Berean School of the Bible.

42. Boyd, interview by author, March 1978.

43. Bartleman, *How Pentecost Came*, 83–84.

44. "Conscription Law," 4 August 1917, 7.

45. Doney, "The Gospel of the Kingdom," 2.

46. For further explanation of the Latter Rain theory and its significance in the Pentecostal movement, see chapter 3.

as the pivotal event in the birth of the Pentecostal movement. Thus, the interracial nature of the Los Angeles revival becomes significant.

Some scholars attest that the Pentecostal movement was a revival among whites from which blacks benefitted. If Azusa Street is as much a key as suggested here, this perspective is false.[47] Others, such as James Tinney, argue that the movement was first a black movement that whites later joined, citing Azusa Street as the beginning. Tinney raises several points that must be considered here.

First, he states that the Azusa Street Mission was all-black at first, not integrated. In opposition to this statement, Bartleman, Catley, Jones, and Williams all attest to the interracial complex of the mission before the move to Azusa Street.[48]

Second, whites came as "spectator participants whose family and other social relations remained outside the ghetto." Again, the sources cited above express the opposite point of view. The total picture presented in Bartleman's book is that there was a great deal of interchange between the races and a constant changing of church affiliations. No definite proof can be given that life outside the church was so separate among the early Pentecostals at this time. With services often going night and day, most social activity was either non-existent or church related.

Third, resegregation occurred almost immediately. Here Tinney cites Bartleman and draws a fairly accurate picture of how local congregations began to develop racial homogeneity. Catley, however, affirms the continued mixing of the races even as late as 1910; and it is significant that Bartleman, a white, continued to look to the black-led Azusa Street Mission as the mother church of his congregation,[49] although it is not entirely evident which race predominated in the Eighth and Maple group. Assuming Bartleman's perception was not uncommon, the issue

47. There is a revisionist school among some scholars of Pentecostal church history that argues that the times were so ripe for an event such as Azusa Street that it could have occurred elsewhere. Whether African Americans would have played as significant a role in Pentecostalism had Azusa Street not occurred is speculative. The fact is that Azusa Street did happen, that it did have a major impact on Pentecostalism, and that African Americans therefore did play a significant, historic role in the American Pentecostal movement.

48. Bartleman, *How Pentecost Came*, 43; Catley, interview at Society for Pentecostal Studies, 1974; and Williams, interview by author, 18 March 1978.

49. Bartleman, *How Pentecost Came*, 70. The reference by Parham earlier of the racially-mixed Oakland meeting occurred about 1910 and was linked with Azusa Street. See Parham, "Free Love," 5.

of division was as much ecclesiastical as it was racial.[50] The most credible perspective is that while the movement had, in its roots, developments with little or no mixing of the races, it was born in 1906 as an unequalled example of interracial interaction within the church.

The Apostolic Faith Mission in Portland

Healed of numerous ailments and filled with the Holy Spirit at Azusa Street, Florence Crawford engaged in extensive evangelistic ministry throughout the Northwest before settling in Portland, Oregon.[51] Even before Crawford's arrival in the region, a young girl, Laura Jacobsen, had received the baptism in a holiness mission on 24 December 1906. The experience of this girl, who later became the wife of E. S. Williams, prepared the people of the mission for Crawford's message. Crawford led the Apostolic Faith Mission[52] in Portland and opened others as far away as Seattle. A large number of missions looked to her for leadership. The Apostolic Faith also became a model of interracial fellowship. "Portland church made no distinction. There was great freedom . . . And God's blessing was upon them irrespective of their color.[53]

The literature of the Portland Apostolic Faith Mission reflects this attitude. Stories were printed of ministry among Southern "colored folks" in Houston, Birmingham, Florida, and New Orleans. The same paper boasted of Apostolic Faith's newest Sunday school, with a picture showing it to be integrated at all age levels.[54] Another periodical demonstrated a unique emphasis on social concern. Included were articles about atrocities in South America, the ill-effects of rubber plantation farming, and one entitled, "My Healing of Gentile Blindness Concerning Israel."[55]

50. Discussion of points made by Tinney, "Between Black and White Pentecostals," 36–37.

51. *A Historical Account*, 59.

52. See n. 95 regarding the term "Apostolic Faith."

53. Williams, interview by author, 18 March 1978.

54. *The Lower Light*, No. 7, 4, 6.

55. *The Latter Rain Evangel* (Portland, OR), November 1912, 6–7.

Dowie's Unity of the Races

Though Dowie himself never embraced Pentecostalism, the scattering of his flock at the time of the Azusa Street impact caused his influence to be felt far and wide in the new movement, particularly in the Assemblies of God. Pentecostal leaders may have gleaned more from his concepts of healing, but his teachings on race are noteworthy. Like Parham, Dowie was a British-Israelite; unlike Parham he advocated miscegenation, which he said was essential for restoring what he called the "primitive man."[56]

Dowie believed in the unity of the human race,[57] but he also believed in the superiority of the Anglo-Saxons, lineal descendants of the scattered Ten Tribes of Israel.[58]

> I believe the Anglo-Saxon race to be as Israelitish as the Jews. You Saxons are Israelites, Isaac's sons. You Danes are Dan's sons, who escaped to sea in ships, as the Book tells us. . . . If I was not, and if you were not, by inheritance, Israelites, the moment we became Christians we were engrafted into Israel, and we are Abraham's seed and heirs according to the promise.[59]

Out of his often-confusing theology came a deep commitment to racial healing which saw miscegenation as the only solution to the intractability of white prejudice. Though Dowie was not entirely free of prejudice himself, he called for equality in all areas of the Zion community. And his concern went far beyond his own city:

> If you in the South continue to allow him to vote, and mock him by not counting his vote; if you continue to say that there is one law for the white and another law for the black; if you permit countless rapes to be perpetrated by the white man on the black women—the proof of which is the color of one-fourth of the people in the South, which is neither black nor white, but the product of a licentious race that has raped the black woman for centuries—I pray, if you appeal to the sword to settle the racial question, that the great God in the heavens will deal with you scoundrels.[60]

56. Dowie, "God the Father of all Men," 801–7.

57. Dowie, "Zion College Lectures," 16–19.

58. Dowie, "Let Us Go Up to Zion," 498–501.

59. Dowie, "The Syrophoenecian Woman," 236–38.

60. Dowie, "God the Father of all Men," 803.

That his utopian ideas were lost in his own dreams of grandeur does not blunt the impact of his teachings. While Parham was allowing his British-Israelism to build walls between black and white Pentecostals in the South, Dowie was perpetrating a British-Israelite gospel of the unity of all races in the North.

The Church of God in Christ and Its White Branch

Largest of all black Pentecostal denominations, the Church of God in Christ was largely the work of one man, Bishop Mason, a son of former slaves who grew up in the Missionary Baptist Church in Tennessee. Mason joined the holiness movement after being licensed to preach in 1893 and helped C. P. Jones establish what was to become the Church of God in Christ in 1895.[61] Eleven years later he traveled to Los Angeles with two companions, D. J. Young and John Jeter.[62] During his five-week visit he accepted the Pentecostal doctrine of baptism and received the experience of speaking in other tongues. Upon returning to Memphis he discovered that Glen A. Cook of Los Angeles had already been there with the Pentecostal message. When in the next year a split occurred in the organization with Jones withdrawing with the non-Pentecostals, Mason then reorganized the Church of God in Christ as a Pentecostal body.[63]

From 1910 some white Pentecostals were affiliated with Mason's group. The First Assembly of God—then known as the Church of God—of Memphis, Tennessee, seems to have had a close relationship with the Church of God in Christ, apparently through Elder L. P. Adams, pastor of the white Church of God. Both Adams and William B. Holt, a deacon of the white church, were listed as overseers of the Church of God in Christ, and Holt was listed as secretary to the general overseer.[64]

61. Mason, Jones, and W. S. Pleasant had begun "associating" as holiness preachers under the name "Church of God" by 1895. It was not until two years later that the first church was established by Mason and Jones in Lexington, Mississippi. Eventually Mason became a pastor in Memphis, Tennessee, and when Mason and Jones parted ways, Memphis became the permanent headquarters of Mason's Church of God in Christ. See Weeks, "COGIC/Mason," [4–5].

62. Jones, quoted in Lovett, "Black Origins," 133–34.

63. See chap. 6, n. 3 on the split in the Church of God in Christ.

64. Letter from Carter to Warner, 16 February 1985; referring to the constitution and bylaws of the Church of God in Christ, as contained in T. L. Delaney, *History and Life Work of Elder C. H. Mason*, 1977, a rewriting of the book by George Bacon. Holt was also listed with the title of "secretary to the general overseer" as the recorder of a

Between 1907 and 1913 a growing number of Pentecostals had no affiliation with any established organization. These included the scattered followers of Parham with his Wesleyan teachings in the Midwest, the Finished Work followers of William H. Durham generally in the Midwest,[65] and the many former members of the Christian and Missionary Alliance churches most prominent in the Northeast. Even when these groups felt forced to withdraw from their previous affiliation, they had little interest in establishing another. Organization was nevertheless inevitable.

The early Pentecostal associations often grew out of the loyalty the younger ministers had for leaders such as Parham or Seymour. Many in the Apostolic Faith contingent who followed Parham later pulled away from their leader because of the Finished Work teaching or because of the "falling away" of Parham.[66]

Bell, who was then pastoring in Malvern, Arkansas, assumed editorship of the publication *Apostolic Faith* (affiliated with the Apostolic Faith movement in Texas). The term "Pentecostal" gradually replaced "Apostolic Faith" as the former began to dominate and form a strong nucleus in the southern Midwest.[67]

Other independent Pentecostals in the southeastern states began their own organizational efforts. H. G. Rogers called a three-day council at Dothan, Alabama, late in 1909, and the council adopted the name "Church of God," not knowing it was already in use by other organizations. Working closely with Rogers was Pinson, editor of *Word and Witness*.[68] Both Rogers's Church of God and the Apostolic Faith group in Texas were merely very loosely structured fellowships.

In order for ministerial credentials to be properly accepted, the Church of God made application to the Southern Clergy Bureau. The Texas group followed a different course, with Goss receiving permission from Mason in 1910 to borrow the name "Church of God in Christ."

---

sermon preached by Mason on 23 June 1918, "The Kaiser in the Light," 3–4.

65. Durham influenced a large segment of the Pentecostal movement toward a baptistic concept of sanctification with his Finished Work doctrine. See chapter 3 for a discussion of his teaching which had a profound influence on the pioneers of the Assemblies of God and in fact did much to lead to its founding.

66. An incident with police involvement in San Antonio, Texas, which to this day lies clouded in mystery and speculation. It supposedly involved a charge of moral indiscretion. *San Antonio Light*, 1.

67. Goss, *Winds of God*, 97.

68. Flower, "History of the Assemblies of God," 18.

There would be no organizational union, but the white Pentecostals would have a name in which to issue credentials and receive recognition from the clergy bureau.[69]

J. Roswell Flower later referred to a trip Goss made in 1907 to Arkansas, at which time he met with Mason. Flower comments, "Brother Goss accepted the courtesies of that organization and was issued credentials, which were recognized by the southern railroads. With the consent of Elder Mason, a white organization was formed, using the name 'Church of God in Christ' and credentials were issued to Bell and a few other ministers."[70]

Goss makes no mention in his book of this meeting with Mason and seems to downplay the actual association with the Church of God in Christ. Affiliation was apparently only for pragmatic purposes. "For some years now we had had no organization beyond a 'gentleman's agreement,' with the understanding for the withdrawing of fellowship from the untrustworthy. There was, however, an association of ministers called 'Church of God in Christ' to which a few of us belonged from 1910–1914, mainly for purposes of business."[71]

Donald Pierce Weeks presents a different picture, describing the Church of God in Christ as being biracial from 1907 to 1914. The church had "separate branches for 'colored' and 'white' brothers, due to the segregation laws of the south, which forbade joint assemblies of people of different races." According to Weeks, Mason appointed Goss to oversee the "white branch."[72]

Starting in 1912, the white branch began holding annual conventions listed as the Church of God in Christ. L. P. Adams seems to have been a leader in this work, and apparently did not wish to join the Assemblies of God in 1914 because of his connection with the other organization.[73] Only after Adams retired as pastor of the local white Memphis congregation in 1923 did that church join the General Council.[74]

---

69. Goss, *Winds of God*, 163. Such recognition was necessary for receiving discounts for rail travel and would be increasingly important for filing for conscientious objection status as World War I approached.

70. Flower, "History of the Assemblies of God," 17.

71. Goss, *The Winds of God*, 163.

72. Weeks, "COGIC/Mason," [7].

73. Letter from Carter to Warner, 16 February 1985.

74. Letter from Carter to Warner, 29 January 1985.

This minimal amount of affiliation between the white and black Pentecostals was enough to cause Mason some problems. In 1918 he was arrested by federal agents in Lexington, Mississippi. At the time Mason was the subject of federal surveillance regarding his views on conscientious objection, a view common among Pentecostals of the time, and was suspected of collusion with Germans during World War I. This information came to light in 1983 when Roy Dixon, an elder in the Church of God in Christ, obtained Mason's files from the Federal Bureau of Investigation under the Freedom of Information Act. Dixon cites a letter dated July 1918 from the Office of the Chief of Staff of the old War Department to the Chief of the old Bureau of Investigation in the Justice Department.

Note was made in the letter of a "white branch" of the church in Memphis, with federal agents suspecting the influence of a church elder, William Holt, a white man with a German background who was then the church's general secretary. Dixon theorized that the government's interest stemmed in part from the attraction Bishop Mason's Pentecostal fervor was having for whites, observing that the balcony of Mason Temple was built for whites and that the "predominantly white Assemblies of God were an outgrowth of the Church of God in Christ."[75]

Just how much interaction there was between these white Pentecostals and black Pentecostals is not easy to determine. A review of the issues of *Word and Witness* prior to the council at Hot Springs reveals minimal mention of "colored brethren." In 1912, Pinson reports on a ministry trip through Arkansas. At Little Rock he found "not much work among the white people, but quite a work among the colored folks."[76]

Word and Witness became a strong proponent of the loosely affiliated white Churches of God in Christ, urging its readers to use either of two biblical names for churches—"Church of God" or "Church of God in Christ," as opposed to "sectarian" or "nonbiblical" names such as "Mission" or "Baptist" or even "Apostolic Faith."[77]

---

75. Clark, "FBI File Reveals Endurance of Church Founder," [page number not identifiable]. Such suspicions on the part of the FBI led Mason, in a sermon preached 23 June 1918 to defend his own patriotism and to attack the Kaiser as being ungodly: "I cannot understand, after preaching the gospel for twenty years and exhorting men to peace and righteousness, how I could be accused of fellowshipping with the anti-Christ of the Kaiser." "The Kaiser in the Light," 4.

76. Pinson, "Trip to the Southwest," 1.

77. "Not Missions," 2. See the following issues for further evidence of organizational activity under the name, "Church of God in Christ": "To Preachers," 20 December 1912, 1; news item from J. M. Roe, 20 February 1913, 3; and "To Preachers," 20 December 1913, 4.

Though it is extremely difficult to ascertain the exact nature of affiliation of the white branch with its parent black church, close fellowship was enjoyed between the branch and Rogers's Church of God. When the white Church of God in Christ met in Dothan, Alabama, in February 1913, the two groups had apparently already merged. The 352 members listed included leaders from both fellowships. Goss suggests that there was no organization "beyond a 'gentleman's agreement,' with the understanding for withdrawal of fellowship for the untrustworthy."[78]

The *Word and Witness*, edited by Pinson, merged with Bell's *Apostolic Faith*, with Bell assuming editorship of the paper which adopted the former name. By the end of 1913 a "Bureau of Information" had been established with Bell as head. Others serving included Robert Brown of New York, Mrs. William Piper of Chicago, and A. H. Argue of California.[79] Thus, although the fellowship was heavily concentrated in the South, it had the appearance of a national organization, one quite distinct from the Church of God in Christ.

78. Goss, *Winds of God*, 163.
79. *Word and Witness*, 20 October 1913, 1.

7

Withdrawal and Separation
(1914–38)

Organization and Division

SOME LEADERS WERE REALIZING that a loosely organized white Church of God in Christ was wholly inadequate to coordinate missionary activity and to handle affairs at home. Goss, Bell, and D. C. O. Opperman engineered a conference for April 1914 in Hot Springs, Arkansas.[1] The call was issued to " . . . all the churches of God in Christ, to all Pentecostal or Apostolic Faith Assemblies who desire with united purpose to cooperate in love and peace to push the interests of the kingdom of God everywhere."[2]

The Council served to bring together the various independent Pentecostals from across the nation, although organizational structure was kept minimal and doctrinal refinement was not even attempted. The founders of the General Council of the Assemblies of God saw their efforts primarily as a unifying force for all of the Pentecostal movement, not just the non-affiliated churches and ministers. Their minutes reflect this intention:

> Therefore, be it resolved, First, That we recognize ourselves as a General Council of Pentecostal saints from local Churches of God in Christ, Assemblies of God, and various Apostolic Faith

1. Goss, *Winds of God*, 174–75.
2. *Word and Witness*, 17 November 1913, 1.

> Missions and Churches, and Full Gospel Missions, and assem-
> blies of like faith in the United States, Canada, and foreign
>   Finally, That we recognize all of the above said assemblies
> of various names, and when speaking of them, refer to them by
> the general scriptural name, i.e., "Assemblies of God" . . .[3]

Though their fuller intentions were never realized, they did bring together white Pentecostals of the Finished Work persuasion.

The Council also served to provide an alternative home for white
Pentecostals who had sought documentation with the Church of God in
Christ.

> The Conference Committee recommended that in view of the
> fact that the work which has been done hitherto in the Interstate
> Camp Meeting of the Churches of God in Christ, has been com-
> mitted to the General Council of the Assemblies of God, that
> the Council publicly recognize itself as the proper place for said
> business in the future.
>   On motion the Resolution was adopted.[4]

Of much speculation is whether African Americans in general or
Mason in particular attended the Hot Springs Council. From an official
standpoint, the Council involved the white branch of the Church of God
in Christ and not the parent black denomination.

Beyond official delegates, attendance records were not a deep concern of the founders of the Assemblies of God, so it is difficult to ascertain the exact racial make-up of the delegation. Significantly, no people
of color appear in the official photograph taken of the participants, but
there is some indication that black people were present. Hugh Cadwalder
is said to have remembered blacks seated in the balcony of the audito-
rium who blessed the council with their singing.[5]

Though the minutes do not mention Mason's being in attendance,
the *Word and Witness* did record Mason's engagement of some sort. In
reporting the actions of the council, it was stated that "Mason, a real
prophet of God, also in the power of the Spirit, blessed the council in
its action for God."[6] Thus, at once the writer of this article reported the

3. General Council minutes, 2–12 April 1914, 4.

4. General Council minutes, 2–12 April 1914, 4.

5. Aman, interview by author, 10 February 1978.

6. "Hot Springs Assembly," *Word and Witness*, 20 August 1914, 1.

involvement of Mason and demonstrated the kind of spiritual authority the white Pentecostals recognized in Mason.[7]

Mason could have blessed the actions of the Council from afar, but several people did confirm that he was there in person. According to Walter J. Higgins, Mason "brought a glorious message," adding that there were "a number of colored folks present at this meeting." Willie Millsaps confirmed that Mason preached an "anointed sermon from Acts 2:17–21." Some of his singers also ministered, possibly the same singers referred to by Cadwalder. Paul Carter wrote that Mason "attended [the Hot Springs Council] and gave one of the evening messages," information that was confirmed by Carl O'Guinn.[8]

Weeks asserts that Mason delivered the keynote address at the council and that Mason and Millsaps traveled together on a revival tour throughout Arkansas and Texas following the conference.[9] Although Mason's attendance has been highly corroborated, the notion that Mason preached the keynote address is contrary to other evidence. Thus, Robert Anderson is correct in stating that Mason and other African Americans were at Hot Springs and Synan is misinformed when he states that no Negroes were invited and none of Mason's group appeared.[10]

---

7. It is possible that the blessing of Mason came without his actually being present, but note the wording of the full paragraph, which may or may not indicate his actual attendance: "Nothing was ever more manifestly *approved by God*. See the steps of unity and approval. *First,* the body of brethren appointed to consider the matter prayerfully and carefully *unanimously* approved and recommended it to the council. *Second,* the General Council itself as a whole without one dissenting voice *unanimously* approved it. *Third,* then as all stood before God in consent, the power fell and the glory of God came down, praises, thanks and shouts went up as the sound of many waters unto God. When things were quiet enough to hear, a message in the Spirit came and the interpretation followed and the approving voice said, 'I have guided in all this, and my approval rests upon it.' *Fourth,* Bro. Mason, a real prophet of God, also in the power of the Spirit, blessed the council in its action for God." [emphasis in the original] This exact paragraph was repeated in the very next issue of *Word and Witness*, 20 September 1914, 1.

8. Higgins, *Pioneering in Pentecost*, 42; Willie Millsaps, "Willie Millsaps Remembers," 8; letter from Carter to Warner, 29 January 1985; O'Guinn, interview by author, 5 February 1986. Millsaps eventually served as the first superintendent of the Kansas District and later as superintendent of the Appalachian District. O'Guinn would serve as Illinois District superintendent and as a general presbyter 1923–42.

9. Weeks, "COGIC/Mason," [7].

10. Anderson, *Vision of the Disinherited*, 189; Synan, *The Holiness-Pentecostal Movement*, 270.

Perhaps the only other whisper of any interaction between the organizing Assemblies of God and the established Church of God in Christ is the story that there was some kind of gentleman's agreement between Mason and the newly elected leaders of the General Council. The agreement was supposedly to the effect that the Assemblies of God would leave the "colored people" to Mason's care, referring African Americans to the Church of God in Christ.[11] There is no documentation regarding this agreement and the idea lies shrouded in denominational folklore. Collins, who served briefly as chair of the General Council was appointed by the Executive Presbytery to attend a "colored" convention in Memphis in 1914. Nothing is reported of this trip.[12]

There is, however, some meager evidence that the Church of God in Christ continued to have an interest in a white branch. In 1926 August Feick, an Assemblies of God pastor in Indianapolis, Indiana, resigned his credentials from the General Council. In his letter of resignation, he wrote that his plans were to work with the Church of God in Christ whose leaders "have felt for some time that the white phase of the work should be set in scriptural order, and if agreeable to me, they would start with our Tabernacle as headquarters."

On the letterhead which read "The White Churches of God in Christ, incorporated February 24, 1926," Feick was listed as a general superintendent and W. B. Holt as national secretary. It was this officer of the Church of God in Christ whom Feick mentioned in his letter as having recently met.[13]

Following the 1914 Hot Springs meeting, no mention is made in the General Council minutes or *The Pentecostal Evangel* of either Mason or the Church of God in Christ until the 1937 General Council held in Memphis, Tennessee, headquarters of Mason's denomination. At this convention, Mason "brought words of greeting and admonition" following the communion service, and a Church of God in Christ delegation provided special music during one of the evening services.[14] Mason was

11. O'Guinn, interview by author, 23 May 1985.

12. Executive Presbytery minutes, 23 November 1914, 1; 25 November 1914, 4.

13. Letter from Feick to the General Council of the Assemblies of God, 6 April 1926. Feick was pastor of the Woodworth-Etter Tabernacle.

14. General Council minutes, 1937, 64; and "The Diary of a Delegate," 25 September 1937, 2.

included in a photographic review of the council, making him only the second black person to be pictured in the *Evangel*.[15]

Though silence dominated the public scene between the two churches, common understanding, among the Assemblies of God at least, was that the Church of God in Christ was the black counterpart of the General Council. Mason was considered a strong leader among "his own people" and an expectation was that the Assemblies of God would direct "the colored men" to Mason's organization.[16] Church of God in Christ leaders viewed the Assemblies of God as "an offspring," a perception that continued to be expressed into the 1980s.[17]

The Rare Black Minister

Official mention can be found of only two black ministers connected with the Assemblies of God prior to the New Issue schism of 1916. Three problems make it difficult to determine accurately whether more black people were involved in the Council at the time. First, records of ministerial credentials did not ordinarily reflect race. Second, pictures were rarely taken. Third, the organization was so loosely structured at the time that it is sometimes impossible to establish whether a person was indeed a minister with official General Council credentials.

Such is the case with G. T. Haywood, who early sided with and finally affiliated with the unitarian Pentecostals after the New Issue rift in 1916. His name is not to be found on any list of Assemblies of God ministers, nor is his church in Indianapolis, Indiana, registered at any point. Yet he obviously was recognized among the ranks of the Assemblies of God, even speaking on the Council floor as a "Jesus Only" proponent in a debate on water baptism.

This opportunity to speak came at the request of the Council committee which recommended him, along with such established Assemblies of God luminaries as William G. Schell, Collins, and Bell.[18] Flower,

---

15. "More Visitors at Memphis," 4. Photographs began appearing in the *Evangel* as early as 1916.

16. O'Guinn, interview by author, 23 May 1985.

17. Clemmons writes that "among the 15 largest [denominations in America] is a Church of God in Christ offspring 'The Assemblies of God' . . . " Clemmons, "Insidious Racism," 3.

18. General Council minutes, 1915, 4, 5. See also, Brumback, *Suddenly*, 201–8. A biography of Haywood, part of a series on Oneness pioneers, mentions Haywood's

previously acquainted with Haywood in Indianapolis, had taken pains to warn his friend by letter in 1915 of the spreading Oneness heresy, but by the time the letter was received, Haywood had already accepted the new teaching.[19]

His Indianapolis church, known as Apostolic Faith Assembly, was racially mixed and adopted the Oneness tenet along with Haywood. Though its actual affiliation with the General Council is uncertain, the church must have had some recognition, at least through Haywood, because it received front page coverage in the *Christian Evangel*. In fact, a story on the church took up the entire first column of one issue.[20]

At least one black minister was officially listed with the Assemblies of God in 1915.[21] Ellsworth S. Thomas, a bachelor from Binghamton, New York, was ordained in December 1913 by R. E. Erdman.[22] Thomas ministered in the Council until his death in 1936 at the age of seventy.[23]

In writing a letter of recommendation to Welch in 1917, Robert Brown, pastor in New York City, said that Thomas had wanted to pastor in Binghamton, but was not accepted by the white people. He was also ministering at the time in other places, largely among whites, though "some think he is very repulsive to white people."[24] Even so, he had the full recommendation of Brown, and his obituary was listed in *The Pentecostal Evangel*, an infrequent occurrence in those days.[25]

---

presence at the Saint Louis Council ("an outstanding spokesman for the Oneness movement"), but never specifically states whether he was officially a General Council minister. Dugas, *Haywood*, 23.

19. Dugas, *Haywood*, 19.

20. Haywood, "Pentecost at Apostolic," 1.

21. Prior to this research, it was widely understood that the Assemblies of God had not ordained any black ministers until the 1950s and had not appointed its first black missionary until the 1960s.

22. Erdman, who pastored a large Pentecostal congregation in Buffalo, New York, preached at the Hot Springs Council but did not join. See Flower, "A History of the Assemblies of God." In 1915 Erdman organized the United Pentecostal Association, a loose fellowship of churches in the New York area. This fellowship, still under Erdman's leadership, merged in 1924 with the Pentecostal Holiness Church, though the churches in the former association splintered away following Erdman's death in 1927. Synan, *Old-Time Power*, 176–77.

23. From Thomas, deceased ministers' file.

24. Letter from Brown to Welch, 20 February 1917.

25. 11 July 1936, 7; does not mention his race. The obituary was asked to be placed in the *Evangel* by Paul Westerdorf; letter to Frodsham, 19 June 1936.

Regardless of how many African Americans were affiliated with the Assemblies of God prior to 1917, the New Issue practically emptied them from the trinitarian Finished Work movement and particularly the Assemblies of God.[26] The absence of black people in the constituency is to be noted in the occasional appeal to the exceptions within the ranks.

The Northeast especially has numerous examples of people of color being accepted into white congregations. A black woman was a member of Flower's first pastorate. In Indianapolis, home of Haywood, no particular animosity was reported against black worshippers. Ernie Lloyd, a "Spirit-filled" African American, was a valued member of the Gospel Tabernacle and considered "just one of us."[27] Williams recalled black ministers being ordained in Oregon and Massachusetts.[28]

Specifically, only a handful of African Americans are actually known to have been ordained during this period. Another bachelor minister in the Northeast was James Edward Howard who pastored in Newark, New Jersey, and was ordained by the Eastern District in 1919. For no apparent reason he allowed his credentials to lapse from 1920 to 1924,[29] then withdrew in good standing in 1926 for lack of ability to maintain his financial obligations to the Council.[30] In a much later letter Flower wrote that Howard "withdrew from us a few years ago because he felt self-conscious over his position in our fellowship."[31]

Isaac and Martha Neeley, a black couple had been listed in a 1913 issue of the *Word and Witness* under the heading "Ordained Elders, Pastors, Ministers, Evangelists and Missionaries of the Churches of God in

26. The African Americans who left during the New Issue likely joined other Oneness Pentecostals. Anderson documents the dearth of African Americans among trinitarian Finished Work Pentecostals. At least by the late 1970s, no significant black or interracial denomination existed of this persuasion and only 1 percent of all black Pentecostals fell into this category. See *Vision of the Disinherited*, 169, 171, 187.

27. A. R. Flower, interview by author, 17 March 1978.

28. But their names were lost from memory. Williams, interview by author, 18 March 1978.

29. Howard was listed among the workers expected at Glad Tidings Tabernacle's Sixteenth Annual Pentecostal Convention in 1923, which means he continued to associate with Assemblies of God ministers and churches during this period. From a note in *The Latter Rain Evangel* (Chicago), November 1923, 13.

30. From Howard, deceased ministers' file; also, in a letter from Howard to Evans, 17 October 1926. The General Council renews ministers' credentials annually; ministers are obligated for a portion of their tithes to both district and General Council offices.

31. Letter from J. R. Flower to Williams, 13 July 1939.

Christ with Their Stations for 1914."[32] The Neeleys's station was Cape Palmas, West Africa. This issue of *Word and Witness* was the one in which the call was made for Pentecostals to gather at Hot Springs, Arkansas. Therefore, the Neeleys were black ministers who had affiliated with the white branch of the Church of God in Christ. Their names do not appear in any subsequent lists of ministers until 1920, when they were ordained from the historic Stone Church in Chicago, Illinois.

After returning from Africa, the Neeleys were actively associated with a "Colored Mission" on Langley Avenue and served as evangelists until Isaac became an associate pastor at Stone Church in 1923. During that year they were appointed by the missions department of the General Council to serve again in Liberia; however, Isaac died in 8 December 1923 before their departure from America.[33] Nevertheless, Martha proceeded to serve her missionary appointment in Africa, directing a receiving and rest home in Cape Palmas until returning in 1930.[34] Her husband's picture had appeared on the front cover of *The Pentecostal Evangel* along with other missionaries in 1923, thus making Isaac Neeley the first African American to be pictured in the periodical.[35]

Strange then that another African-American from Chicago was not so well received. Alexander Howard asked for missions appointment, also to Liberia, in 1917, and was denied on the basis of his race. Instead of working with the Assemblies of God, he went under the umbrella of a group of black churches in New England who in 1920 formed the United Pentecostal Council of the Assemblies of God.[36]

32. "Ordained Elders," 4.

33. The cause of death was listed as "paralytic stroke." Noel Perkin had earlier written that he was glad that the Neeleys would be taking charge of the work "at the Coast." See "With the Lord," 24 February 1924, 14. In a Sunday memorial service eulogy at the 1925 General Council, William M. Faux included Isaac S. Neeley of Liberia among seven missionaries "that laid down their lives for Jesus' sake to carry the Gospel to the heathen." General Council combined minutes, 1914–25, 62.

34. "From the Mission Field," 14, 15; also, Neeley, deceased ministers' file. The Executive Presbytery minutes refer to Isaac Neeley as a missionary supported by a colored congregation in Chicago, presumably the mission on Langley Street. Stone Church, a predominantly white congregation, was founded by William H. Piper, earlier a deacon in Dowie's work and introduced to the Pentecostal movement by William Durham in 1907.

35. *The Pentecostal Evangel*, 13 October 1923, 1. The picture, taken at the 1923 General Council in Saint Louis, is also in an E. S. Williams photograph album (See Isaac Neeley, missionary group).

36. Dempster, "Pentecostal Church Mission," 207–8.

How many other black ministers were given ministerial credentials in this time is difficult to know. Cornelia Jones Robertson, an eyewitness of Azusa Street, was ordained in California in 1922, pastoring in San Francisco and Oakland. She withdrew from the fellowship in 1935 to join "the colored organization."[37]

The denominational structure and the processing of credentials became more formalized in 1927. Even so, a black minister in the ranks continued to be a rarity. Such was Bruce Gibson, who appears in the church's history in two distinct periods and geographical settings. The first occasion was when he was granted credentials by the Northwest District in 1933. Having pastored in Winlock, Washington, he had already been in active full-time ministry for a decade.

Four years later he withdrew from the Council when "the Lord put it upon his heart to go to Virginia and work among his own people. Consequently, he feels he should join with the colored organization." (Presumably the district secretary who wrote the letter was referring to the Church of God in Christ.) There did not seem to be any conflict involved, and the secretary stated that Gibson was interested in renewing fellowship should he return.[38]

Gibson did rejoin the Assemblies of God eventually (as will be discussed later), but of interest at this point was that his ministry in Washington was to a racially mixed group of people in a church in "colored town," a half mile out of Winlock. He also preached in the Longview, Washington, Assembly on occasional Sunday afternoons to another integrated audience.[39]

Racial Perspectives in the Fellowship

In a strongly worded statement in *The Weekly Evangel*, W. F. Carothers, a member of the Executive Presbytery at the time, explained to the northerners in the fellowship why segregation in southern churches was good and necessary. Previously a Methodist preacher, Carothers came into Pentecost through Parham. Carothers justified southern segregation on

37. Robertson, Ministers' file.

38. Gibson, Deceased minister's file; Gibson's application for ordination certificate; and letter from Bogue to J. R. Flower, 15 November 1937. Bogue was secretary of the Northwest District.

39. Collins, interview by author, 20 October 1985.

his belief that God had divided the nations along colored lines, something that had gotten jumbled up because of the slave trade. God intended "racial purity and integrity of the different nations." Moreover, God himself was working through a "final effort to preserve the integrity of the races."

In the article, Carothers stated that prejudice did not exist among Pentecostals as it did in the southern society as a whole. Merely, Pentecostals were cheerfully conforming to the South's necessary "wholesome regulations." "A proper segregation of the races looking to the integrity of each is no more 'prejudice' than is a proper separation of the sexes. Both alike are but the dictates of common decency and of a wholesome regard for the decrees of the Almighty."[40]

Occasionally, white preachers ministered in black neighborhoods. One notable example was Aimee Semple McPherson, who in 1918 held numerous evangelistic meetings for both blacks and whites in Florida. Frequently, in whatever city she happened to be preaching, she would conduct a second meeting for black people in their part of town because "the dear colored people did not feel free to attend the white meeting."[41]

While in Key West, McPherson became "so burdened" for the black community that she publicly announced that she "had done my duty in the Lord toward the white population of the Island, and must risk their displeasure and disapproval now by going to the poor colored folk and telling them the same story."[42] Though whites did object at first, soon it was impossible to keep them away and McPherson had to reserve the center seats for blacks.[43]

The 1920s and 1930s were a difficult period for race relations in the United States. At the forefront in society's conflict was the fast-growing KKK. An ambiguous attitude toward the Klan is reflected in *The Pentecostal Evangel* where only one article mentioned the subject. Frank Boyd wrote a column concerning "Romanism." Though he feared the growing strength of Catholicism, he did not consider the Klan a viable counter force to this religious power. The General Presbytery had recently decreed against involvement in secret societies, thus ruling out membership in organizations such as the Klan. Boyd had more concern about affiliation than just that the KKK was a secret order. He considered the

40. Carothers, "Attitude of Pentecostal Whites," 2.
41. McPherson, *This is That*, 116.
42. McPherson, *This is That*, 118.
43. McPherson, *This is That*, 119.

Klan's negative approach toward individual Catholics and Jews as entirely wrong because it failed to positively present the truth of the Gospel, therefore making a person's witness to these people ineffective. No mention was made of the KKK's position toward African Americans.[44]

A. B. Cox was a member of the KKK for at least seventeen years beginning in 1906. A charter member of the General Council, he later served as a district official in the old Central District and has been called by Assemblies of God historian William Menzies a "giant of faith."[45] Cox claimed that no one could be a true American and not be a part of the KKK. "I have more respect for a man true to his country than [sic] with NO Religious profession at all, than for a weak kneed [sic] religious man." Though he mentioned nothing of the KKK's racial bigotry, he lauded its anti-Romanism.[46]

In response to one of Cox's parishioners who had written complaining of his promoting the Klan, general superintendent Welch suggested it was better to "stay free of entanglements in these last days no matter how good they look on the surface." Though he admitted to knowing little of the KKK, he said they had some good things to say. He did not suggest that his friend, Cox, was wrong in being a member of the KKK.[47]

Walter Higgins, a pastor in Illinois, faced persecution because his predecessor had been a leader of the KKK. The Klan tried to get him to join, even offering to pay his initiation fee. But Higgins refused, because "the purpose of the Klan in that time was to do away with Catholicism, outlawing the outlaws, and didn't believe in the colored people and the white folks mingling together." Higgins stated that even though there was a lot of fear regarding the society, he was not afraid to express "what I thought of the Klan."[48]

44. Boyd, "Romanism," 8.

45. Menzies, *Anointed to Serve*, 135, 169.

46. Cox, "America and Her Needs," 7 October 1923.

47. Letter from Welch to Schlemmer, 25 October 1923. Welch had been introduced to Pentecostalism through Cox in 1910. Menzies, *Anointed to Serve*, 134.

48. Higgins, *Pioneering in Pentecost*, 76–77, 78. This incident occurred around 1925.

Blacks in the Evangel

The Pentecostal Evangel reflected the whiteness of the fellowship's constituency with occasional articles, captions, and cartoons having a decidedly ethnocentric attitude. A strongly worded article on prophecy appeared in 1926, reflecting such a view. Quoting a London paper, it warned: "The shadow of a war-cloud in the East is falling darkly upon the hitherto sunny world-supremacy of the white race. . . . The white man's prestige will disappear when the savage, barbaric millions from Africa and Asia can defy the white man."[49] This great war cloud was centered over the Pacific, and its perpetrator was Bolshevism. The writer went on to warn of a "Black Peril" as well as a "Yellow Peril." On a rather pessimistic note the article ended by conceding no real solution existed to the impending conflict of the races.[50]

Overt paternalism was evident elsewhere in the weekly. A cartoon entitled, "Looking Our Way," appeared in 1933. Urging a greater African missions focus, the caption read, "The Ethiopian may not be able to change his skin, but God can change his heart."[51] This physical/spiritual color identification common to society in general during this era was frequently reflected in church slogans. The caption for a missions picture later in the same decade read: "Black faces—white hearts."[52]

A frequent feature over the years in *The Pentecostal Evangel* was a question and answer column begun by Bell and later continued by Williams. The column dealt with questions about the Bible, interpretation of Scripture, and other spiritual concerns. Questions of race were raised repeatedly, often of a nonsubstantive nature; for example, the question of whether Cain's mark was the source of the Negro race was asked of Bell in 1918 and again of Williams almost two decades later in 1937.[53]

During this period the only question dealing with race relations was raised in 1929 when a reader asked Williams if it were "right for white and colored to worship together," and suggested that the two races should be separated in their social and religious gatherings. Mentioning that the inquirer was from the South, Williams responded that "it would be much

---

49. "War Clouds," 7.

50. "War Clouds," 9.

51. "Looking Our Way," 10.

52. *The Pentecostal Evangel*, 27 June 1936, 8.

53. Bell, "Questions and Answers," 28 December 1918, 5; Williams, "Questions and Answers," 7 August 1937, 7.

better in the South for the two races to meet each in their own separate place of worship." No further elaboration was made.[54] The principle was obvious enough: do not tamper with the status quo.

Oddly, *The Pentecostal Evangel* began printing "colored" dialect stories in 1923 and throughout the next two decades. These ranged from black people being presented as spiritual heroes in stories which had a positive devotional point[55] to black people portrayed as simple, even silly, folks in stories with little or no purpose.[56] But one message all these articles inadvertently proclaimed was that the "colored" population was quite distanced from the everyday lives of the general readership of *The Pentecostal Evangel*.

The first of these stories to appear was about "Black Moses," a pillar in a black Boston congregation in the 1800s. A quaint yet positive tale, it predicted through Moses' distinct dialect the soon-coming outpouring of the Holy Spirit.[57] From the same author the story of "The Colored Auntie's Prayer" again presented a devout black saint in a very positive light as an effective prayer warrior, though this time no dialectal speech was used.[58]

Usually these stories hinged on a catchy phrase, dependent for humor on distinctive grammar and spelling. One such anecdote was about a recently freed slave who was being taught how to pray the Lord's prayer. When he came to the part on forgiveness, the man left his mentor, found his master, forgave him for grave wrongs committed, and returned to his teacher. "Now go on wid dat prayer," he said, the phrase serving as punch line and title to the tale.[59]

Most of these stories appeared as filler items or devotional pieces. Surprisingly, one was contained in a report on the 1933 General Council when J. R. Evans, secretary of the General Council, commented on what he considered a bad resolution.

> [Evans] spoke about a colored woman who brought her baby to be christened. The preacher asked what her name would be. She said, "Judas Iscariot." The preacher protested and said, "Don't

54. Williams, "Questions and Answers," 20 July 1929, 9.

55. Hill, "Is Yo' Wheat Good," 6; Knapp, "Old Nanny's Faith," 5.

56. "Nuggets from Black Susan," 8; "A Chariot of Fire," 9.

57. Gordon, "The Present-Day," 6.

58. "The Colored Auntie's Prayer," 13.

59. "Go on Wid Dat Prayer," 9.

you know that am a bad Name?" She said, "Sure, I knows it. But weren't it writ of him it would have been better for him if he had never been borned?" Brother Evans . . . said he thought it would have been better if these propositions had never been born.[60]

60. "A God-Blessed Convocation," 6.

8

The Struggle for Inclusion
(1939–62)

As WORLD WAR II got underway, a new chapter in race relations began within the Assemblies of God. Articles in *The Pentecostal Evangel* centered on the intense antisemitism of the age; simultaneously, a new type of Negro story emerged. This time a more positive black model was used, featuring men like George Washington Carver and lesser known persons of godly persuasion. More significantly, the church leadership began to take a new look at the relationship between the Assemblies of God and the American black.

Questions of Exclusion Initiated

The issue of what to do with black ministers in the Council began to surface quietly as early as 1939. In that year an ideal case developed. William Ellison, who with his wife, Ruth, had been saved and baptized in the Spirit at Glad Tidings Tabernacle in New York City, was ordained by the Eastern District predicated on his ministry as pastor of "a good congregation" in the Bronx.

Members of his regularly organized church—generally "educated" black people—had appealed to the district committee desiring the ordination of their pastor, and many in his congregation knew "nothing else but the Assemblies of God."[1] A. Newton Chase, then secretary of

---

1. General Presbytery minutes, 1939, 2. The people of Ellison's church had been brought up in Glad Tidings Tabernacle, the leading Assembly of God church in the city.

the Eastern District, advised the national office that the Eastern District brethren were willing to refer Ellison to the colored organization, namely, the Churches of God in Christ if so desired.[2]

Robert Brown, pastor of Glad Tidings, had been responsible for originally presenting Ellison's name to the committee, and Brown and his wife, Marie, had encouraged the Ellisons to enter the ministry in 1928. As pastor of one of the denomination's leading churches, Brown was an influential elder in the Northeast. He also had earlier been responsible for endorsing the ordination applications of two other black ministers, Thomas and Howard. Flower, general secretary in 1939, in presenting the matter to general superintendent Williams, incorrectly understood that these were the only black ministers to have been ordained up to this point—all Eastern District men endorsed by Brown. In addition, Flower pointed out to Williams that Ellison had been presented to the committee for a license to preach without the committee knowing he was black![3]

The General Presbytery took up the matter in its September meeting later that year. After some consideration, the Presbytery went on record disapproving the ordination of black men to the ministry: ". . . that when those of the colored race apply for ministerial recognition, license to preach only be granted to them with instructions that they operate within the bounds of the District in which they are licensed, and if they desire ordination, refer them to the colored organizations."[4] The primary issue was not racial prejudice, so it was stated, but the differing attitudes around the nation and how to handle ministerial recognition intersectionally.[5] Deference to the Church of God in Christ was also cited: "We felt it is better to have them in the Church of God in Christ as their organization."[6]

The action of the General Presbytery left the issue fairly ambiguous. No credentials of black ministers then in the Council were recalled. Nor, as will be seen, was this action used uniformly in processing the

2. Letter from J. R. Flower to Williams, 13 July 1939.

3. Letter from J. R. Flower to Williams, 13 July 1939.

4. General Presbytery minutes, 1939, 2. Of note, this is a singular occasion when the plural is used for black denominations, meaning more than just the Church of God in Christ. However the Church of God in Christ is the only organization listed.

5. General Presbytery minutes, 1939, 2.

6. O'Guinn, interview by author, 5 February 1986. A general presbyter in 1939, O'Guinn said he was supportive of directing blacks to the Church of God in Christ "because of the times."

credentials of black ministers in the future. It is best seen as an attempt to do away with an isolated, difficult question.[7]

Proposals for a Colored Branch

At the 1943 General Council, a resolution was presented, "that provision be made through our Missions Department in cooperation with our various District Councils to promote missionary activity among our American colored people." The matter was referred to the Executive Presbytery, following a discussion which centered on the advisability of undertaking such work with "the situation in the South with regard to the colored people" and whether such work would be placing the Council in competition with the Church of God in Christ.[8]

At the very next council, Bruce Gibson reappeared, this time from New York City. He had not as yet reaffiliated with the Assemblies of God but had been invited to speak to the council in session on behalf of the establishment of a colored branch within the denomination. Following Gibson's speech, this resolution was adopted: "That we encourage the establishment of Assembly of God churches for the colored race and that when such churches are established they be authorized to display the name, 'Assembly of God—Colored Branch.'"[9]

This action, taken the last day of the council, was not accompanied by any plan of action and was never implemented, though it was reported in *The Pentecostal Evangel* months later. That report stated that Gibson, "a man held in high esteem by our white brethren who know him, was asked to take the initiative in seeking to bring this about." Gibson also was said to have been conducting a Bible school "with the hope that it may provide colored workers who will become familiar with General Council principles and doctrine, who can go forth to evangelize those of their own race."[10]

---

7. Apparently, Ellison and his church continued to enjoy an association with Glad Tidings Tabernacle. In 1946, Ellison's congregation purchased a church on Jennings Street and later considerably enlarged the facility. The black pastor and congregation were prominently featured in the fiftieth anniversary celebration of Glad Tidings. See "Golden Jubilee," May 1957, 29. Ellison's church eventually became affiliated with the General Council as the Community Full Gospel Church.

8. General Council minutes, 1943, 13.

9. General Council minutes, 1945, 31.

10. "Our Colored Brethren," 12 January 1946, 12.

Many years later, Williams recalled that the Executive Presbytery had invited "a very fine black man" from New York to come for an interview to see if he would be willing to take the first step in organizing a black Assembly of God church or churches. "He seemed willing for that, but with all of his goodness, he did not have the strong leadership that such would desire. And it fell through; nothing came of it."[11]

The matter of a black affiliate, this time conceived in a different form, was again proposed and adopted at the 1946 meeting of the General Presbytery. The Presbytery went on record favoring the establishment of "a colored Pentecostal Church altogether separate and apart from the General Council of the Assemblies of God." It was further resolved that the Executive Presbytery act upon this proposal by lending assistance, counsel, and financial aid, and that a follow-up report be made to the General Presbytery in 1947.[12]

Nothing came of the 1946 action either, but on the last day of the Council the following year, one more resolution was proposed to establish a "Colored Branch of the Assemblies of God. "A spirited floor debate ensued until Williams, who was chairing the meeting, "poured oil on the troubled waters." John Richards, missionary to South Africa who had just returned from the field, later expressed the shock he experienced "at the attitude of the brethren when somebody introduced the idea of accepting black brethren into our fellowship."[13] This time the Council voted to set up a committee "of representative brethren from the North and the South," appointed by the general superintendent. The committee was to study the issue thoroughly and report its recommendations to the 1949 General Council.[14] Whether the committee was ever even appointed is not known; in any case, the 1949 minutes of the General Council are silent on the matter.

Years later Williams reflected on the debate over a proposed black branch:

> The executive brethren at Springfield presented the matter of a black organization within ours such as the Baptists had in the South, the Methodists had. . . . It met considerable opposition

11. Williams, interview by author, 18 March 1978. This reference is assumed to be to Gibson and his 1943 effort.

12. General Presbytery Minutes, 1946, 12. The proposal came from a Southern presbyter.

13. Richards, interview by author, 18 March 1978.

14. General Council minutes, 1947, 43.

> by certain leaders of the South. Their argument was if we ordain
> in our movement black men, we should recognize those men if
> they were to come our way. And if we were to permit a black man
> to preach in our churches it would never do. The people would
> not accept it at all. And so their fear was so pronounced as they
> felt in the interest of not creating division within their organized
> churches that it was dropped. It never got any farther.[15]

The Assemblies of God thus entered the civil rights era with a very ambiguous attitude toward African Americans, these Pentecostals expressing that they were struggling with more of a Southern problem than a
"colored" problem.

Changing Attitudes on Race

The national focus of the early 1940s was on the Second World War, and
the primary issue in race relations was anti-Semitism. The Assemblies of
God, which had carried into the First World War a somewhat ambivalent
attitude toward involvement in the conflict, now presented a much more
united support posture for the nation's war efforts. One motivating factor
was the denomination's concern over Nazi treatment of the Jews.

In the 4 January 1941 issue of *The Pentecostal Evangel*, Williams began a series on "The Jew and the Church." In the first article of the series,
Williams quoted extensively from a tract entitled "If I were a Jew." This
tract was a ringing defense of the Jewish people, citing their contribution
to the history of the world and to America in particular.

> If I were a Jew I should feel that I had a right to be proud of the
> part played by my people in the drama of history. If it is asked,
> "To what nation or race is humanity most indebted?" "Who has
> played the leading role of the centuries?"—for answer all eyes
> must turn toward the Jew.[16]

At the 1943 General Council, Williams expressed great concern over
the anti-Semitism of the day. He gave tribute to Myer Pearlman, a Jew
converted to Christianity who had become a respected leader within the
Assemblies of God. Williams urged the delegates "all to show great love
for Jewry."[17] That same Council passed a resolution strongly denounc-

---

15. Williams, interview by author, 18 March 1978.

16. Porter, "If I were a Jew," quoted in Williams, "What of the Jews?" 2.

17. "The Diary of a Delegate," 9.

ing anti-Semitism, and an editorial further expressing this sentiment was published in the *Evangel* later that fall.[18] This positive attitude toward the Jews came largely from a dispensational eschatology which considered the Jewish people as specially favored by God.

No such ringing attack was made on black-white racism or mention ever made of the extensive lynching of black Americans over the decades. However, the 1940s did bring an entirely different kind of focus on black people to the pages of *The Pentecostal Evangel*. The last of the colored dialect stories appeared in September 1943. Shortly before that, an article had appeared about a Jew, converted to Christianity, who was serving as a prison chaplain in Chicago. The news item told how Louis King, a former convict himself, was now ministering to the prisoners and directing a gospel band made up of black inmates. While the article was mainly about King's testimony, it also brought attention to ministry among African Americans, and even included a photograph of the prison band.[19]

That same year an excerpt from George Washington Carver's life was used as a front-page inspirational piece by the *Evangel*. Referring to Carver as "the great Negro scientist," the article was illustrated by a drawing from the *Chicago Daily News*.[20] Carver was presented to the readers of the *Evangel* as something of a hero, and his biography, advertised in the publication, was distributed through the General Council's Gospel Publishing House (GPH).[21]

Two other articles gave very positive roles to black people. One was a story about a black Jamaican doctor who was confronted with prejudice and paternalism while traveling on a train in England, but who used the situation for a gospel witness in an ingenious fashion. In fact, he was presented in the most positive light of all the characters in the story. However, the author also mentioned that the doctor was "unduly sensitive" to the issue of color.[22] A second story featured a black man in Chicago who voluntarily served many years as a full-time chaplain at Cook County Hospital.[23]

18. "The Editor's Notebook," 18 September 1943, 9.

19. Thomson, "Releasing Prisoners," 6.

20. Argue, "Do the Work of an Evangelist," 1.

21. See *The Pentecostal Evangel*, 23 October 1948, 16, for the advertisement of G. W. Carver's biography.

22. Schofield, "The Good Black Doctor," 6–7.

23. Simkins, "Man with the Battered Grip," 6–7. Both Chicago chaplains, this one and Louis King, were supported by the NAE.

Stories in this new mode were of outstanding black people who had made a mark on the world. The earlier exaggerated and stereotypical anecdotes had ended with "Nuggets from Black Susan" in 1943, but one final article of this nature was printed in 1947. Entitled "Our Colored Brethren," it listed twelve things, mostly of a "spiritual" nature, that the author believed the black man could do better than anyone else. For example, "He can be the most penitent sinner who ever bowed at the feet of a forgiving Saviour." "No one can rise higher in Christianity and at the same time maintain a keener respect for his heathen father." "No race can suffer more humiliation and at the same time remain a loyal friend to his abuser."[24]

Denials and Approvals

The first black minister to bring the issue of credentials for black ministers into prominence was a grandson of an eyewitness of the Azusa Street Meetings. Robert (Bob) Harrison was not well received by some Assemblies of God officials in the early 1950s, though later he was to minister with the Billy Graham Evangelistic Association and be ordained within the General Council. The first black person to attend Bethany Bible College[25] in Santa Cruz, California, he was denied preliminary ministerial credentials (licensing) with the Northern California-Nevada District in June 1951. According to Harrison, the reason given to him for this denial was that "it is not the policy of our denomination to grant credentials to Negroes."[26]

Harrison claims to be quoting the district superintendent, which would have been W. T. Gaston. Joseph L. Gerhart, the district secretary-treasurer under Gaston, said that the stated reason Harrison was denied credentials was that transferring Harrison's credentials would be a problem, for example, to Southern districts.[27] Gaston had earlier served as a general superintendent of the Assemblies of God (1925–29), and had grown up in the state of Arkansas. Gerhart was also a Southerner, as was Leland Keyes, the president of Bethany Bible College at the time Harrison

24. "Our Colored Brethren," 23 August 1947, 6–7.

25. Montgomery and Harrison, *When God was Black*, 19. Bethany Bible College was an Assemblies of God college until it closed in 2011.

26. Montgomery and Harrison, *When God was Black*, 29.

27. Gerhart, interview by author, 25 July 1986.

was enrolled. Harrison says he and Gerhart, the district superintendent later when Harrison was finally ordained, had a good relationship from the time of Harrison's original rejection by Gaston. Keyes, Harrison says, was "a blessed man" who was "very hurt at his [Harrison's] rejection."[28] Interestingly Keyes was chair of the district committee which rejected Harrison, while Gaston was president of Bethany. According to Willard C. Pierce, dean of the school, "in the committee meeting, both Brother Gaston and Brother Keyes the chairman of the committee were most gracious and kind, and due apology was given that he had not been properly advised of this ruling ahead of time."[29]

Ironically, Harrison's own grandmother, Cornelia Jones Robertson, had been ordained in the same district in 1922.[30] While this amazing fact was never brought to light in the ongoing debate over Harrison's credentials, his initial denial caused an immediate and strong response from Harry C. Warwick, an ordained prison chaplain with the fellowship. Warwick appealed to J. Roswell Flower regarding the district's action.

> We are a Christian church with high claims, but our practice in this point is found wanting. Our conduct has not been Christian. . . . Bob Harrison is both spiritually and academically qualified but not racially! I repeat, one failure of the American Church is that it follows when it should lead on this issue.[31]

Flower replied that he intended to bring to the Executive Presbytery the matter of "the breaking down of racial prejudice affecting candidates for the ministry from the colored race."[32] No further action apparently was taken at that time.

Pierce wrote to Warwick that he "felt terrible that they had to take this action in the case of Bob Harrison." In the future black students would be advised of the "custom" of the Assemblies of God.[33] Robertson, who had left the fellowship in 1935, assumedly for the Church of God in Christ, expressed shock at her grandson's rejection. Even athletes no

28. Harrison, interview by author, 3 March 1986.

29. Letter from Pierce to Warwick, 6 September 1951.

30. See chapter 7.

31. Letter from Warwick to J. R. Flower, 22 September 1951.

32. Letter from J. R. Flower to Warwick, 10 October 1951.

33. Letter from Pierce to Warwick, 6 September 1951.

longer act this way, she wrote. "I pray God will open their blinded eyes to see where they have let down in faith the compromise with Sin."[34]

It would be another decade before Harrison finally was ordained. In the meantime, he immediately began to minister in both white and black congregations doing evangelistic work.[35]

In 1952 Bruce Gibson applied for reinstatement of his ordination with the New York-New Jersey District.[36] His reinstatement was recommended by the district and was sent on to the General Council for final approval. R. J. Bergstrom, district secretary-treasurer, noted this recommendation came when Gibson was "carrying on a fine work in the Bronx," and that there were "other ordained colored brethren working" in the district.[37]

During the 1940s Gibson had continued to minister in Assemblies of God meetings, in places as far away as North Dakota.[38] The response from the General Secretary's office was quite favorable and Gibson was reinstated.[39]

Overtures to the Church of God in Christ

With the national debate on desegregation growing in the latter 1950s, the "colored question" became an issue of much internal discussion among executive and general presbyters. At the 1954 World Pentecostal Conference in Stockholm, Sweden, Ralph M. Riggs, Assemblies of God general superintendent, met with Lawrence Williams, vice-president of the Board of Education of the Church of God in Christ.[40]

This casual meeting led to a flurry of correspondence between Riggs and several Church of God in Christ officials over the next two years, primarily regarding a Sunday school literature publishing project. Though it was not uncommon for GPH to seek business from other denominations, the long-perceived unique relationship between these two

34. Letter from C. J. Robertson to Warwick, 18 September 1951.

35. Letter from Pierce to Warwick, 6 September 1951; letter from C. J. Robertson to Warwick, 18 September 1951.

36. The New York-New Jersey District had split from the original Eastern District.

37. Letter from Bergstrom to J. R. Flower, 26 February 1952.

38. Brandt, interview by author, 15 February 1986. Brandt had served as superintendent of the North Dakota District.

39. Letter from J. R. Flower to Bergstrom, 1 March 1952.

40. Letter from Riggs to D. L. Williams, 8 July 1955.

denominations led to some interesting interaction. Riggs offered "closer cooperation than we have known in the past."

> As you may realize, the Assemblies of God have been content in the past to allow the Church of God in Christ to be the counter part of our church in its dealings with the colored people in the United States. Since this relationship has been taken for granted and assumed in the past, it might not be out of order for there to be some friendly exchange between our organizations. This might lead to a closer relationship as it was mutually desired.[41]

The overture was continued with other leaders of the Church of God in Christ. Riggs wrote to one official that "the matter of the closer relationships between our organizations" would be discussed at the next meeting of the General Presbytery: "It is certainly high time in American living and in our church experience that we come closer together."[42] He added that the two churches shared the same Pentecostal doctrine and the same objective of the advancement of the kingdom of God. "We should walk closer together," he concluded.[43] Finally, Riggs wrote nearly identical letters to the five leading bishops of the Church of God in Christ under Mason. "Hitherto," he wrote, "we have been content to be conscious of each others' existence and merely to wish each other well in our respective tasks. It is now impressed upon me that it would be brotherly and spiritual if we got better acquainted."[44] He also confirmed his intentions of attending their national convocation in Memphis the following December.

The replies from these Church of God in Christ ministers and bishops were cordial, even enthusiastic. They variously affirmed the publishing concerns, the need for greater cooperation and Riggs's visit to the national convocation, but nothing was said of Riggs's observations of the unique relationship of the two denominations.[45]

---

41. Letter from Riggs to D. L. Williams, 8 July 1955.

42. Letter from Riggs to Battle, 29 August 1955. Battle was pastor of the Gospel Temple Church of God in Christ, St. Paul, Minnesota, and involved with the denomination's educational program.

43. Letter from Riggs to Battle, 26 September 1955.

44. Letters from Riggs to Patterson, Crouch, O. T. Jones, McEwen and Lyle, 31 October 1955.

45. Letter from Battle to Riggs, 31 October 1955; letter from Jones to Riggs, 5 November 1955; letter and from Lyle to Riggs, 15 November 1955.

Two years later mutual invitations to conferences and expressions of openness concerning publishing interests were still being discussed. But though Riggs and Zimmerman, then assistant general superintendent, attended the Golden Jubilee Convocation of the Church of God in Christ, a more concrete relationship never materialized.[46]

A New Proposal for a Colored Branch

The interaction between Riggs and the Church of God in Christ apparently had its origin when Nicholas B. H. Bhengu, a black evangelist from South Africa, visited the United States.[47] Bhengu had made contact with the black Pentecostals and had conveyed the idea to an Assemblies of God official that the Church of God in Christ was interested in closer fellowship.[48]

Bhengu later wrote that he had been approached by various American blacks about starting a black branch of the Assemblies of God and that leaders of the Church of God in Christ had expressed a need for a Bible college. While expressing the need for black missionaries to Africa from America, he declared his interest in returning "to the States for five years if our Church was prepared to start a Coloured wing."[49] Perhaps unaware of the changing American attitudes, Bhengu saw any attempt at integration as potentially disastrous.[50]

Based on optimism shown by members of the foreign missions department, Riggs expressed to Bhengu cautious interest about the idea, not being sure if it would aid or hinder the work of the Assemblies of God among African Americans. He invited Bhengu to "come over and spearhead" such a branch, even though he knew the matter would first have to be taken up by the General Presbytery in the fall.[51] Riggs's advi-

---

46. Letter from Riggs to Mason, 6 August 1957; letter from Riggs to Williams, 27 November 1957.

47. At the time, Bhengu was a member of the Assemblies of God in South Africa. Later he established his own Pentecostal denomination.

48. Letter from Riggs to Bhengu, 20 December 1954.

49. Letter from Bhengu to Riggs, 27 January 1955.

50. Bhengu wrote, "Any integration policy should be out of the question and it will come in its own time—a rather gradual process." Letter from Bhengu to Riggs, 6 March 1955.

51. Letter from Riggs to Bhengu, 23 February 1955.

sors were more optimistic regarding Bhengu's abilities than they were of the American constituency to accept the idea.[52]

The General Presbytery took no official action on the matter but told Riggs that the idea of a black branch was unwise. They felt that any scheme of integration would be disastrous at this time and that to "build up a separate church for our colored brethren would likewise run counter to the present trend in American life." Given the tenor of the times, maintaining the status quo seemed the best option.[53]

In response to a letter of inquiry regarding the Assemblies of God policy on segregation, Riggs articulated the posture of the Presbytery:

> We did not feel free to create a Colored Branch for this would be condoning segregation and even creating segregation when this can not be felt the right thing to do at this time. On the other hand, the intense social conflict, particularly in the deep South, makes it unwise to introduce integration at the present time. For these reasons we felt that it would be best for us to mark time at the moment until the matter had developed further in the public consciousness and practice.
>
> You may be assured that we are thoroughly alert as to the trend of the times and also what our Christian duty in this regard is. A number of the Executive Presbyters have visited the Church of God in Christ in Memphis and we are in the process of working out with them a united program in our Sunday school advance.[54]

Presbyters in Search of a Solution

However, the times were changing and a significant element in the denomination was not satisfied with maintaining the status quo on the issue. Riggs himself was very aware a new era was beginning: "But the matter, however, will not be this easily downed. It is clamoring for solution. Even the churches are going to be challenged concerning their attitude."[55]

In 1956, the New Jersey District ordained two black ministers under the leadership of R. J. Bergstrom, then district superintendent. At the

52. Memorandum from Phillips to Perkin, 16 February 1955.

53. Letter from Riggs to Bhengu, October 12, 1955.

54. Letter from Riggs to Roper, 16 January 1956.

55. Letter from Riggs to Lindquist, 12 September 1956.

1957 General Council, a resolution never got to the floor opposing the action taken by the district.[56]

In his autobiography, Harrison mentioned a national Assemblies of God convention, held in Springfield, Missouri, in 1956.

> The case of Bob Harrison, first Negro ever to apply for creden-
> tials in the denomination was brought to the floor. After an im-
> passioned debate, the problem of what to do about blacks was
> given a half solution. . . . It was decided that the granting of a
> license to preach was a district function and that the national
> body could not dictate this policy.[57]

Such discussion was not found in any official minutes, assuming Harrison was referring to a General Council, and there was no such council in 1956. There was discussion of the race issue in the General Presbytery meetings of 1956 and 1957, and perhaps one of these is the occasion to which Harrison was referring. Yet Harrison's name is not mentioned in any of the minutes of these meetings.

Whatever transpired, Harrison wrote, a black could now be granted a license from his district, if it so approved, but he still could not be granted ordination. This was to remain a function of the national office. In any case, the following year, with a new superintendent in office in the Northern California-Nevada District, Harrison was granted his ministe-rial license, but a much more complicated process was involved before Harrison was fully ordained.[58]

Though nothing is to be found in the official records of the decision to which Harrison refers, Riggs did appoint in the General Presbytery that year a committee to study the question of race relations, stating that the General Council had not declared itself on the subject but had gener-ally left such policy to local churches and districts.[59] Riggs was desirous that the committee study the relationships between the races—not only in terms of black and white individuals, but also in denominational terms of the Assemblies of God and the Church of God in Christ.[60]

After the committee submitted its report, "Segregation versus Inte-gration," to the 1957 meeting of the General Presbytery, the Presbytery

---

56. Reynolds, interview by author, 13 September 1985.

57. Montgomery and Harrison, *When God was Black*, 91.

58. Montgomery and Harrison, *When God was Black*, 92.

59. General Presbytery minutes, 1956, 26.

60. Letter from Riggs to Lindquist, 12 September 1956.

voted to adopt its recommendations.[61] Among these was one calling for a definite program under the direction of the home missions department with the aim of evangelizing the Negro population of America. "The mistake of the Assemblies of God is not in spending so much money to evangelize Africa, but in neglecting the negroes in our own country." One concrete suggestion was the possibility of establishing a Bible school for the training of black ministers to help them "reach their own people."[62] In addition, the committee urged that direction and all assistance possible be given "to young Negro ministers interested in establishing churches among their own people."[63]

Though the General Presbytery had voted in favor of the committee's recommendations, the issue of accepting black people in the Assemblies of God was still very unclear, and the matter came up again in the General Presbytery the following year. The Northern California-Nevada District appealed to the General Presbytery on behalf of Harrison for his ordination.

The Executive Presbytery apparently gave the district permission to pursue what course it chose, and what it chose was to await the favorable action of the General Presbytery. "Following that [choice] there was a unanimous vote registered to ordain Brother Robert J. Harrison as soon as favorable action is taken by the General Presbytery."[64] The district was also on record favoring the affiliation of "colored" assemblies. The Executive Presbytery did, in turn, refer the case to the General Presbytery, but nothing was really decided except that another committee was appointed to consider the advisability of establishing a "Colored Fellowship in the framework of our organization for the purpose of evangelization."[65]

61. General Presbytery minutes, 1957, 21.

62. "Segregation versus Integration," 9. Although ministerial training was recommended for persons preparing for ministry in the Assemblies of God, formal Bible school or seminary education was never a requirement. However, it was helpful to prospective ministers to complete such education at Assemblies of God colleges. Records have been difficult to obtain regarding when American blacks were accepted at the various Assemblies of God schools, but generally foreign-born blacks were accepted first.

63. "Segregation versus Integration," 10.

64. Letter from Palmer to Riggs, 5 February 1958. Palmer was the new district superintendent.

65. General Presbytery minutes, 1958, 36. This committee reported back to the General Presbytery the following year, but the report was tabled.

It was in that same year that Riggs reportedly made an offer to Harrison to lead a black or colored branch. The offer, made during the World Pentecostal Conference in Toronto, proposed that African Americans would be allowed to organize as a separate branch like the denomination's language branches. Harrison turned down the offer, citing a desire for normal access and status on the part of black ministers.[66] Yet Harrison still had not been able to obtain his ordination with the Assemblies of God.

Breaking the Color Barrier

In 1960, Harrison again applied for ordination with the Northern California-Nevada District. The response of the district was to appeal once again to the national office, stating that "there is no question whatsoever about his qualifications and ability except for the position taken by the General Presbytery [presumably its non-action in previous sessions]."[67]

Zimmerman, the new general superintendent, sent the following reply accompanied by a review of the recent Presbytery decisions:

> In spite of the foregoing some of the northern districts have ordained colored ministers for years. They have not made an issue out of it, but have quietly ordained those who have applied and who have met basic requirements for ordination. This is particularly true in the New York District and, I understand, in the Northwest. So far no problem has developed with the procedure. There is really nothing in the General Council constitution and Bylaws prohibiting the ordination of Negro ministers, and such applications have been honored by the General Secretary's office in the past, when they have been duly processed and recommended by the District Credentials Committee.[68]

The New Jersey District, for example, had passed a standing resolution in 1959 encouraging "the spreading of a sound full gospel ministry"

---

66. Harrison, interview, 3 March 1986. Other proposals reportedly were made at the same time by Riggs to the Open Bible Standard Churches and the International Church of the Foursquare Gospel for possible merger with the Assemblies of God.

67. Letter from Gerhart to Zimmerman, 2 November 1960. Gerhart was now district superintendent, while Zimmerman was serving his first term as general superintendent.

68. Letter from Zimmerman to Gerhart, 4 November 1960. See Olena, "I'm Sorry, My Brother!" 138–39, for further clarification on this correspondence.

to the state's black population. The district council affirmed the idea that its leadership had full authority "to recognize ministers and churches of any race."[69]

Events outside the Assemblies of God soon overrode all the General Presbytery discussions and actions of the previous two decades regarding ordination of black ministers. Harrison was invited to join the crusade team of evangelist Billy Graham in 1962, and shortly thereafter, the General Council headquarters cleared the way for Harrison to be ordained by the district.[70]

How many other applicants had been denied credentials because of their color is impossible to know. Such records are not kept. Contrary to Harrison's claim, he was not the first black minister ever to apply for and be granted credentials in the Assemblies of God.[71] Although his ordination was perhaps the most visible, there were others before him. However, in one sense Harrison might be considered to have broken a "color line," for his high-visibility ordination and ministry effectively ended once and for all the ongoing ambiguities of the General Council on the matter of the inclusion of black ministers. The issue had been effectively pressed by the larger evangelical community.

The Assemblies of God had chosen to allow time to change things. Inherent fears of becoming out of line with the mainstream of American society had been revealed. Concern had been expressed on the part of some of the presbyters that "in accepting colored people into our churches on the integration pattern we would probably discourage white people attending our meetings." The anxiety fostered was that this would cause the movement "to develop into a colored work exclusively."[72] The issue of integration of the Assemblies of God in the forties and fifties centered on two salient points: one, the whites were not ready for it; and, two, the blacks were not interested in a "colored" branch.[73]

69. 1962 Yearbook, New Jersey District, 44.

70. Montgomery and Harrison, *When God was Black*, 94.

71. Montgomery and Harrison, *When God was Black*, 91–93.

72. Letter from Riggs to Palmer, 11 February 1958.

73. Peterson, interview by author, 5 March 1986.

9

Adjusting to a Changing Society
(1955–75)

THE RACIAL UNEASINESS BEING expressed at leadership levels was also being felt among the constituency. The number of local Assemblies of God
churches which excluded people of color is unknown, but the practice
was common throughout the South. However, free-flowing tendencies
among Pentecostals often broke down barriers at least temporarily. While
preaching an evangelistic meeting at the Assembly of God in Prichard,
Alabama, Gayle Jackson prayed for a paralyzed black child outside the
church. The next night, after the boy was reportedly healed, "hundreds
of blacks and hundreds of whites" showed up at the service. Black people
were not allowed to come in, but did anyway, sitting in the Sunday school
rooms, where Jackson later prayed for them. Confronting the pastor,
Jesse Smith, about the prejudice, Jackson said, "You are going to pay for
this some day." The events apparently had no lasting effect on the racial
policy of the congregation.[1]

The "White" Evangel

With the growing national interest in the issue of civil rights, questions
about interracial marriages began to surface again in Williams's question-
and-answer column in the *Evangel*. What is surprising is that more similar questions did not arise and that those which did were all printed in

1. Jackson, interview by author, 1 May 1986.

1957. As in earlier years, the question of the origin of the black race was a popular concern. Williams was asked whether the "Ethiopian" wife of Moses was a "Negress," whether Ham was a Negro, and, more generally, "Where did the black man come from?"

He always answered these questions specifically: "It is generally considered that Negroes are descendants of Ham, one of the sons of Noah." Only once did he add comment of a broader nature. To the question regarding Moses's wife, he responded, "It [Miriam's criticism of Moses] also teaches us that racial and class spirit is not something new, but has always existed among people whose hearts are still carnal."[2]

One question that year dealt more directly with interracial marriages: "Does the Bible forbid a person of one race to marry into another race; for example, for an American to marry a Japanese?" His answer was twofold. First, the only time God specifically forbade intermarrying was because of the idolatry of the Canaanites. Second, there are possible sociological and biological problems to be considered.[3]

Although there was no official editorial policy during the 1950s excluding blacks from pictures in *The Pentecostal Evangel* unless they were "foreign" blacks, such seems to have been the case at least coincidently. After a picture appeared of Raymond Lilly, Cook County Hospital chaplain, in 1949,[4] another African American is not pictured until 1960—with one exception. That was when members of the Church of God in Christ were shown among delegates to the World Pentecostal Conferences and Advisory Committees of 1952 and 1958.[5] The American blacks who appeared in the 1960 picture were a couple of youths seated near the front row in a large tent meeting in Saginaw, Michigan.[6]

In a news review, *The Pentecostal Evangel* called 1957 "an ugly year indeed" in America, by which it implied that forced integration was the source of racial unrest in society. "It was the year of forced integration—when federal troops were called to enforce Federal law in Arkansas. Tensions in the conflict over racial integration in public schools reached a boiling point."[7] Even so, there was little other mention in the 1950s of

2. Williams, "Your Questions," 24 February 1957, 23, and 13 October 1957, 9.

3. Williams, "Your Questions," 2 June 1957, 5.

4. Simkins, "Man with the Battered Grip," 6–7.

5. "World Pentecostal Conference," 8; "Advisory World Conference," 5; and "Swedish Leader," 15.

6. *The Pentecostal Evangel*, 10 January 1960, 26.

7. Hitt, "Looking Back," 19.

the growing struggle in the nation over civil rights as the *Evangel* maintained an awkward editorial silence on the question of racial equality. For most of the two decades in which the civil rights movement was most visible, the General Council tended to follow quite closely the cautious responses of its evangelical and Pentecostal fraternal organizations, particularly the NAE.

African Americans in Other Organizations

It is helpful, perhaps at this juncture, to portray where the Pentecostal movement stood as a whole coming into the civil rights movement. Racial attitudes among white Pentecostals have covered a broad spectrum, but, on the whole, separation of the races was the norm from the 1920s for most Pentecostals and the 1930s for the Oneness Pentecostals.[8]

In the holiness branch of the movement, there were dissimilar examples of the mostly black Church of God in Christ, the all-white Pentecostal Holiness Church, and the Church of God, which had a separate black district until 1964. All three of these churches were in existence in one form or another prior to the beginning of the Pentecostal movement and later entered that movement as denominational entities. The Church of God bowed to Southern segregation policy and by 1926 black members had been separated under a white overseer.[9] The black Fire-Baptized Holiness Church of God of the Americas separated from the predominantly white Fire-Baptized Holiness Association of America in 1907 over racial difficulties. Soon after the white group merged with the Pentecostal Holiness Church, the few black persons in the latter organization left.[10]

The trinitarian Finished Work Pentecostals had always been almost entirely devoid of African Americans. Such is true of the International Church of the Foursquare Gospel and the Open Bible Standard Church,

---

8. For further discussion of racial separation patterns in the Pentecostal movement, see Anderson, *Vision of the Disinherited*, 188–93; and Synan, *Holiness-Pentecostal Movement*, 165–84.

9. Synan, *Holiness-Pentecostal Movement*, 173–74.

10. Synan, *Holiness-Pentecostal Movement*, 174–75.

as well as the Assemblies of God.[11] Moreover, there were no significant black denominations in this sector of the Pentecostal movement.[12]

Originally racially mixed, the unitarian Pentecostals divided into distinct denominations along racial lines by 1924 because of the Southern system of segregation. In the Pentecostal Assemblies of the World at the time, blacks predominated in the North and whites in the South. This made holding national conventions quite difficult, with black members having to accept segregated accommodations when in the south. The whites chose to leave, forming various splinter organizations along the way. By 1931 mergers temporarily reintegrated what was then known as the Pentecostal Assemblies of Jesus Christ, but the African Americans soon became unhappy with the arrangement and were gone by 1937. As of the 1980s, the primary black oneness church was the Pentecostal Assemblies of the World, which maintained a limited interracial character, while the leading white group was the United Pentecostal Church.[13]

Well before the 1940s, Pentecostal denominations had solidified as white, black, or segregated. The holiness churches, predominantly in the South, reflected the segregationist attitudes of the Jim Crow era, and significantly, the major black Pentecostal churches were also established in the South. The trinitarian Finished Work churches, headquartered in the West or Midwest and national in constituency, were almost exclusively white. Likewise, the unitarian Pentecostals could not keep from

11. Charles Edwin Jones notes that the Foursquare Gospel church included a small, significant black minority by the 1970s, although he mentions no statistics. He does add that the church's West Adams Boulevard branch in Los Angeles claimed lineal descent from the Azusa Street Mission and that the denomination's L.I.F.E. Bible College had hired an African American as an Old Testament teacher. *Black Holiness*, 140.

12. Jones lists the following predominantly black denominations as "Baptistic" trinitarian bodies: The Assemblies of the First-Born was founded in 1950 and is based in Jamaica; as of 1980, it had ten churches and five hundred members in the United States. The Bible Church of Christ was founded in 1961 with headquarters in New York; it had five churches and 2,300 members in 1981. The Deliverance Evangelistic Centers were founded in Newark, New Jersey, in 1966 and grew to one hundred churches. The International Evangelical Church and Missionary Association, founded in the 1960s, was the amalgamation of more than four hundred congregations worldwide, with seven or eight churches in the United States as of 1982. From 1972, it was led by John Levin Meares, white pastor of the predominantly black Evangel Temple of Washington, D.C. Jones, *Black Holiness*, 135-41.

13. Clanton, *United We Stand*, 27-28, 32-33, 68-69, 84-86, 111, 115.

separating racially. It should be noted that—nearing the end of the 1980s—the racial patterns had changed little in spite of the civil rights era.

Though the NAE was organized in 1942, it was not until nearly a decade later that the first black denomination affiliated—the United Holy Church of North America. By this time, the NAE had more than thirty member denominations, and congregations from thirty more.

While the World Pentecostal Conference had long enjoyed the fellowship of various African and American black denominations, the PFNA never included any of these, nor was the Church of God in Christ invited to participate in the formation of the PFNA in 1948–49.[14] Hollenweger, a European historian, suggested the reasoning for the ongoing omission lay in the discrediting attempts by mainline churches for "their lowly beginnings in a Negro church," and on the Southern laws prohibiting racially mixed meetings. "It would therefore be unfair to blame the white Pentecostals alone for this development. They have simply adapted themselves to what was considered at that time to be American Protestantism."[15]

The racial compositions of the WPF and the PFNA produced a sharp contrast. *The Pentecostal Evangel* made special note of the "hundreds of colored people among the delegates" at the WPF's Fifth World Conference of Pentecostal Churches held in Toronto in 1958. The lack of racial segregation in Canada made it possible "for blacks and whites to sit side by side in this great assembly of God's anointed people." Among the U.S. blacks represented was a choir from the Church of God in Christ.[16] However when the PFNA met five years later in another major Canadian city, there were no black denominations represented, not even the Church of God in Christ.[17] More than relaxed segregation laws accounted for the inclusion of African Americans at the earlier World Conference.

In that same year, 1963, black evangelicals from across the United States met in Los Angeles to form the National Negro Evangelical Association. The new organization did not consider itself to be in competition with the NAE or any other group. Its primary concern was how the

14. Jones, *Study of the Pentecostal Movement*, 1:315.

15. Hollenweger, *Pentecost between Black and White*, 49.

16. "Fifth World Conference," 8.

17. "Representatives of 16," 16–17.

"Negro church can do more in the field of foreign missions."[18] A former delegate to NAE conventions questioned the policies of the NAE toward black members, asking whether black people were made to feel genuinely welcome in the organization, noting that he saw no African American delegates at the 1963 annual NAE meeting. The editor of the *United Evangelical Action*, the official organ of the NAE, responded simply that NAE meetings and membership were open to people of all races.

Official Responses to the Civil Rights Movement

In 1956 the NAE adopted a declaration of human rights which affirmed the "inherent worth and intrinsic value of every man, regardless of race, class, creed or color," urging "all our constituency to use every legitimate means to eliminate unfair tactics by any individual or organization." The resolution stated that "evangelistic Christian groups have a moral responsibility to influence social attitudes," and that "the teachings of Christ are violated by discriminatory practices in many, if not all, sections of our society."[19] Calling for action yet followed by no specific resolutions aimed at overcoming discrimination, the declaration followed a neutral course mentioning neither segregation nor desegregation.[20]

The Pentecostal Evangel carried no response or report on the NAE resolution. However, that very year the General Presbytery approved the appointment of the Committee on Race Relations.[21] This committee, in reporting back to the General Presbytery the following year, affirmed the equality of all men in the eyes of both God and the law. It did voice several concerns, however, which it felt needed to be considered, as for example, in correcting injustices, care should be taken that new injustices not be created. It further expressed concern for the negative impact that total integration might have on both blacks and whites, primarily in the potentially reduced evangelistic effectiveness of integrated churches. The committee affirmed its belief that the main problem of existing integrated churches was stagnation.

The committee was ambiguous as to whether by "integration" it was referring to the merging of black and white denominations or simply

18. "Negro Evangelicals," 21.

19. *United Evangelical Action*, 15, 131.

20. Blackwelder, "Fundamentalist Reactions," 23.

21. General Presbytery minutes, 1956, 26.

to the opening of local white congregations to blacks. The report did not specifically address the question of whether the Assemblies of God should open its church and ministerial affiliation to African Americans, but it did state a willingness to assist existing Negro Pentecostal churches, to establish a Negro Bible school, and to help Negro ministers establish churches.

The recommendation was also made that "we should be ready to integrate our churches as soon as the general public is ready for such a move and it will not interfere with our progress and expansion as a movement." The stated concern was for maintaining a course of action which would most effectively aid the denomination in its primary task of evangelizing the unchurched. Thus, the existing approach of leaving such matters up to local and district leaders would best ensure this effectiveness, as "some areas of the country will be quicker than others to receive integration."[22]

The next round of responses to the civil rights movement began in 1963 when the NAE again passed a resolution on racial equality. Generally, it reiterated the content of the 1956 document. This time *The Pentecostal Evangel* gave a summary of the resolution in a larger report on the NAE convention.[23]

In the meantime, Zimmerman and Bartlett Peterson, general secretary, had been among two hundred religious leaders invited to a White House conference on civil rights. It turned into a strife-filled session, and Zimmerman and Peterson left, as did a third of those invited. Reporting on behalf of the General Council leaders, a "spokesman said the Assemblies of God has no national policy on integration; that some of its churches (including those in Springfield) are integrated and some are not."[24]

A more significant resolution was passed by the NAE the very next year, 1964, following a "heated floor debate." Important support for the measure was given by Billy Graham; Howard Jones, a black associate of Graham; and Frank E. Gaebelein, co-editor of *Christianity Today*. In the end the resolution received unanimous approval in what *Eternity* called a "history-shattering session."[25] For the first time the entire NAE body

22. "Segregation versus Integration."
23. "Evangelical Position," 21.
24. "Jack Seeks Church," 13.
25. "NAE Takes," *Eternity*, 14, 34.

committed itself to the principle that segregation as practiced in the United States was not consistent with the Christian faith. Of note, the landmark Civil Rights Act of 1964 had been passed by Congress earlier and signed into law by President Lyndon B. Johnson on July 2.

In this same season, it was strongly felt within the ranks of the Assemblies of God that the General Council needed to take some official action, if for no other reason than that the lack of a decisive stand on segregation might have negative impact on the denomination's primary objective of world evangelization:

> But if it is true that Negro students are not welcome at CBI [Central Bible Institute] (unless they come from overseas); if it is true that most of our districts are reluctant to ordain Negro ministers; if it is true that in many districts local congregations would be unwilling to accept Negroes into membership, our missionary work overseas may become a great deal more difficult than it is now.[26]

In August of 1964, the Executive Presbytery adopted the following noncommittal statement on integration, which was subsequently reported to the General Presbytery:

> Inasmuch as the Assemblies of God is a cooperative fellowship made up of sovereign churches which retain their right of self-determination and are affiliated on a voluntary basis in accordance with adopted Constitution and Bylaws, matters of procedure along these lines are left to local determination and are not established by organizational action.[27]

At its 1965 meeting, the General Presbytery amended and approved a resolution prepared three months earlier by the Executive Presbytery. This declaration was subsequently adopted by the 1965 General Council.[28] Incorporating the Executive Presbytery statement of the previous year, the resolution echoed earlier NAE affirmations. Following the paragraph on local determination, the passage declared that "the teachings of Christ are violated by discriminatory practices against racial minorities,"

26. Memorandum from Garlock to Zimmerman, 18 May 1964. Garlock was serving as an Assemblies of God missionary in Africa.

27. General Presbytery minutes, 1964, 33, 90.

28. General Presbytery minutes, 1965, 32–33; and General Council minutes, 1965, 60–61.

and that "the transformation of mankind through faith in the gospel of Jesus Christ breaks down prejudice and causes justice to prevail."

The resolution clearly stated that adherence to biblical teachings and the practice of Christian principles were relevant to the solution of all social problems. It further reaffirmed belief in Christ's teachings, particularly placing emphasis on "the inherent worth and intrinsic value of every man." Quoting word for word from the NAE statement, the resolution concluded by proclaiming that "we believe those in authority in political, social and particularly in evangelical groups have a moral responsibility toward the creation of those situations which will provide equal rights and opportunities for every individual."

The only change made in the General Council statement from the NAE document came in one phrase. In the final document, the constituency was urged "to discourage unfair and discriminatory practices wherever they may exist." The word "discourage" was less strongly worded than the NAE's "eliminate," and "wherever they may exist" had been added. Also, the phrase had been preceded by "to use every legitimate means" in the earlier document. Such modifications were made prior to the resolution's being presented to the General Council.[29]

Three years later, the General Presbytery followed within weeks the action of the NAE in issuing a statement on social action. Echoing closely an NAE resolution entitled, "The Crisis in the Nation," the General Presbytery declared that the Assemblies constituency would "as citizens make our influence felt where concrete social action is justified."

Yet the Presbytery reaffirmed its deep conviction that the spiritual condition of man must be considered foremost. "We labor to win men, not merely to move men. We are called to accomplish our objectives not by coercion, but by conversion." The most important responsibility of the Church to society is the proclamation of the gospel. Interestingly the statement also pledged "a renewed dedication to proclaim . . . the . . . gospel . . . both at home and abroad without respect to *color,* national origin, or social status."[30]

29. General Council minutes, 1965, 60–61.

30. Cunningham, "Social Concern Articulated," 5. Emphasis added. Also, "26th NAE Convention," 32.

Opposition to the Civil Rights Movement

Although the Assemblies of God and other evangelicals struggled to keep up with the progress of integration and civil rights, they were generally averse to the manner in which social change was carried out. In an NAE convention address printed in *The Pentecostal Evangel*, the question was raised, "If Paul went to Watts or to Selma or to Montgomery, would he go as a civil rights demonstrator or as a gospel preacher?" The answer in brief was that "Paul had one message. He simply preached Jesus Christ and Him crucified." Strangely, one example of such Pauline conviction used in the speech was Evangeline Booth, who was considered a social radical in her own day.[31]

Two years later, an article appeared which probed the various implications of the growing racial tensions. The author, an Assemblies of God minister, was reflecting on the funeral of Martin Luther King, which he had attended. He spoke of the need to keep the ministry centered on the evangelistic gospel, not on social action. He argued against the effectiveness of civil rights legislation and government spending in solving basic social needs. He decried civil disobedience. But he also affirmed with African Americans the historic exploitation of their race and the need for whites to repent. He had felt for some time, he wrote, that "we have done more to evangelize the black African than we have the black American."[32]

Generally, writers in *The Pentecostal Evangel* were ill at ease with civil disobedience and the methodology of civil rights leaders, especially ministers such as King. In an editorial dealing with the nation's growing crime rate, increased lawlessness was linked with encouragement of law-breaking under the guise of "allegedly justifiable civil disobedience." The editorial referred to a recent NAE resolution which criticized church leaders who defy the law instead of teaching people to obey the government.[33] An earlier editorial had expressed the idea that "it is just as wrong to advocate civil strife as it is to deny rights."[34] However, the *Evangel* continued to condemn the former much more quickly than the latter.

---

31. Sanders, "To Serve is Still Enough," 2–3.

32. Bacon, "Eyewitness at a Funeral," 20–21.

33. Cunningham, "Iniquity Abounding," 5.

34. Cunningham, "Wake Up, America!" 4.

Theoretically, nonviolent protest was acceptable; civil disobedience was not,[35] with the Pauline call to submit to those in authority frequently cited as the reason.[36] But in one article a differentiation was made. Civil disobedience was considered to be consistent with the gospel when it involved a law in conflict with God's law; but it was considered sinful when motivated by greed, selfishness, and avarice. "Permissible" civil disobedience was supported by two passages: "render unto God the things which are God's"; and "You yourselves judge which is right in God's sight, to obey man or to obey God." Unfortunately, the article never clarified right and wrong civil disobedience with contemporary examples.[37]

Diverse causes and solutions were occasionally debated in the discussion on social unrest and civil rights. The social upheaval was generally attributed to spiritual conditions, but social causes were occasionally mentioned, including racism and injustice. One author acknowledged that he knew that "the American Negroes had not been treated right." He even stated that whites had "exploited" blacks and called for "us" to "repent and begin to show our Christian love toward all our fellowman" and to do it quickly.[38]

Rarely was the problem of racism itself considered. One such exception was a later (1970) article which dealt with the turmoil then current on the nation's campuses. The absence of black studies programs was mentioned as an often-cited cause of campus riots, and prejudice was listed as an underlying cause of campus unrest.[39]

Other not overtly spiritual causes cited were drinking and communism. Drinking was said to have "set off the worst racial riot [Watts] in American history." The same editorial stated that the Scriptures link rioting and drunkenness.[40] Though other more radical fundamentalist publications continually traced racial tensions to communist influence,[41] the thought was raised only cautiously in *The Pentecostal Evangel*. C. M. Ward, national radio evangelist for the General Council as preacher for

---

35. Bacon, "Eyewitness at a Funeral," 20.

36. Bacon, "Eyewitness at a Funeral," 20; also, Johnson, "Civil Disobedience," 7.

37. Bacon, "Eyewitness at a Funeral," 20; also, Johnson, "Civil Disobedience," 7.

38. Bacon, "Eyewitness at a Funeral," 20.

39. Alexander, "Campus Unrest," 27, 6–9.

40. Cunningham, "Watts—a Year Later," 4.

41. See Blackwelder, "Fundamentalist Reactions," 56–70.

"Revivaltime,"[42] interviewed J. Edgar Hoover. Some of the questions and answers gave the implication that there was some Marxist-Leninist influence among American revolutionaries.[43]

The Root Cause

Without question, sin was considered to be the overriding cause of social and racial struggle. Commenting on the 1968 paper on social concern by the General Presbytery, Robert C. Cunningham, editor of *The Pentecostal Evangel*,[44] asserted that the paper "went to the heart of the matter by affirming 'that man is a sinner and inclined to evil by nature.'"[45] Another article declared that the basic causes of unrest were materialistic humanism and self-centeredness, that alienation or rebellion against God were the root cause.[46]

The theory was that if sin was the root cause, there had to be one solution: the gospel of Jesus Christ. Even though civil rights legislation and government spending could not meet the basic needs of the ghettos, the gospel could.[47] Robert Harrison stated in a General Council message: "I cannot help but emphasize that although political and economic pressure can help curb the racial problem, only Christ and his gospel can solve it."[48] Calling for an evangelical solution to the problems of Watts, an editorial stated that the gospel was the only remedy for the situation. People without moral responsibility needed a sense of importance and self-respect and this came "as a man is reconciled to God."[49]

Regardless of what needed to be corrected in society, the primary role of the church was to preach the gospel. Editorially *The Pentecostal Evangel* affirmed the General Presbytery's social concern document in its conclusion that "the first and foremost obligation of the Church to society is to preach publicly in every community the Biblical gospel of

42. "Revivaltime" was the denomination's official radio broadcast.

43. Ward, "J. Edgar Hoover," 10.

44. Cunningham had replaced Frodsham as editor of *The Pentecostal Evangel* in 1949 and continued in that capacity until his retirement in 1985.

45. Cunningham, "Social Concern Articulated," 5.

46. Alexander, "Campus Unrest," 9–10.

47. Bacon, "Eyewitness at a Funeral," 20.

48. Harrison, "These Things Shall Be," 2.

49. Cunningham, "Watts—a Year Later," 4.

the Lord Jesus Christ."[50] The same theme rang clear in an earlier editorial which declared, "Churches should lead people to God—not to jail, not to the courthouse, not to the state house, not to a housing construction project . . . "[51] The implication of these articles was that those in need of salvation were the members of the black community calling for freedom. Lacking was a call to repentance on the part of those who had caused or sustained the oppression.

Though the gospel was considered the primary solution, many constituents called for other more overtly social responses, especially when their own civil rights were threatened. *The Pentecostal Evangel* spoke out in favor of tougher law enforcement measures,[52] particularly the 1968 anti-crime bill.[53] "When the courts show greater concern for the criminal than for the victim of his crimes, who can hope for public safety?"[54]

Rarely, there were suggestions of a more drastic solution. A 1967 editorial proposed that a Christianity which would direct the "'haves' to share with the 'have-nots'" and to require an equal enforcement of the law among both "landlords and tenants" was the solution to ghetto violence.[55] Eight years later, editor Cunningham quoted the following call to action from *Decision* magazine: "Labor to eradicate the social conditions that breed crime, including poverty, unemployment, and racial discrimination."[56]

Yet in all the rising turmoil, the sovereign hand of God could be seen. Recalling apocalyptic themes of first-generation Pentecostals, contemporary developments were variously assigned to divine judgment and to the impending "end of the age." One author attributed the "spreading revolution and lawlessness" to divine judgment for lack of love toward others.[57]

C. M. Ward spoke of social unrest, whether in the United States or abroad, as being "a significant sign of the end time."[58] Cunningham

50. Cunningham, "Social Concern Articulated," 5.

51. Cunningham, "Wake Up, America," 4.

52. Cunningham, "Wake Up, America," 4; see also, Cunningham, "What Christian Citizens," 31.

53. Cunningham, "One Nation Indivisible?" 4.

54. Cunningham, "Iniquity Abounding," 5.

55. Cunningham, editorial, 4.

56. Cunningham, "What Christian Citizens," 31.

57. Bacon, "Eyewitness at a Funeral," 20.

58. Ward, "Signs of the End Time," 6.

added that no social measure could hope to alter the tide of history. "All the believer can do is to keep himself free from the worsening corruption—to let his light shine—and to exhort as many as possible to accept Christ and save themselves from the approaching judgment."[59]

Apparently, the church itself could not—and should not try to—alter the tide of history either. The underlying message was that it was best for the church to go with the flow as society changed, but to go slowly, leading from behind.

59. Cunningham, "Iniquity Abounding," 5.

10

Becoming a Church for All Peoples
(1960–80s)

WHILE THE ASSEMBLIES OF God was trying to cope with a quickly changing society on the outside, significant changes were slowly beginning to
occur within the fellowship. The sixties began with faltering steps to include black people, and a decade later they were receiving at least nomi-
nal attention. Not until the 1980s would solid advances be made beyond
token effort.

One event symbolically if quietly marked the changing of eras
within the movement. In November 1961, Bishop Mason died at the age
of ninety-eight. Though he had not had official contact with the General
Council since 1937, he had personified, for the Council at least, the legend that assumed a connection between the Assemblies of God and the
Church of God in Christ. Yet for nearly two decades the General Council
had been wrestling with the question of accepting African Americans
for the most part quite apart from any consideration with Mason and
when he died, his passing was not prominently featured in *The Pentecostal Evangel*. For the man who had in theory so dominated a major part
of the home missions policy of the Assemblies of God for fifty years, a
small obituary was all that was presented.[1] In the end, the notion of the
Church of God in Christ as the black counterpart to the Assemblies of
God was not very evident.

---

1. "Bishop Mason with the Lord," 27.

The Breakthrough Efforts

The most important catalyst within the Assemblies of God in breaking down the color barrier at the grassroots level was Teen Challenge, begun in 1958 by David Wilkerson as an outreach to New York City gang members. Recognition for such an accomplishment was slow in coming,[2] but Wilkerson did receive immediate notoriety for his work among the Hispanic, black and white youth. As he visited churches across the nation sharing his ministry, some of his young converts traveled with him. For many churches, Teen Challenge was their first experience in having black people ministering in their midst. Reaction often was mixed, but pastors generally responded favorably to successful evangelistic stories.[3]

The first article about Wilkerson's work among New York youth appeared in the *Evangel* during the summer of 1958.[4] Soon after that time, stories about Wilkerson and Teen Challenge became popular items in the periodical. In September 1960 the first of many articles featuring black people appeared. The story highlighted black worker Thurman Faison, a recently converted gang member who was helping Wilkerson reach other gang members. Described as a "Negro helper" to fellow ex-gang member-turned-preacher Nicky Cruz, Faison was one of three full time workers for Teen-Age Evangelism (later known as Teen Challenge).[5]

For a time, increasing numbers of black workers were involved in Teen Challenge, though a decline occurred in the early 1970s—partly due to the difficulty in finding black people to serve as directors. In fact, until the start of the new decade, Faison had been the only black person to serve as director in Teen Challenge despite the large number of black staff workers. Strict General Council regulations prohibiting ministers from remarrying after divorces had limited many street converts from entering the ministry, and most Teen Challenge workers who came from more traditional Assemblies of God church backgrounds were white.[6]

2. Charles W. H. Scott, assistant general superintendent, would later acknowledge the major role Teen Challenge had played in reaching into the black community. See his article, "Black Americans for Christ?" 7.

3. Reynolds, interview by author, 13 September 1985. Reynolds began working with Wilkerson in 1958 and served as the national representative of Teen Challenge 1973–87. For a more complete review of the beginnings of Teen Challenge, see Wilkerson, *The Cross and the Switchblade.*

4. "Pray for Youth," 20–21.

5. Coxe, "New 'Gang' Church," 4–5.

6. Reynolds, interview by author, 13 September 1985.

Most of the denomination was still dealing with reaching out to the black population on a level less sensational than inner city outreach. On rare occasions in the early sixties, photographs in *The Pentecostal Evangel* included black persons, at first limited to those being on the receiving end of a witnessing encounter.[7] An article on "Witnessing to Negroes" dealt openly with the hesitancy of a white couple in interacting with black people. "It might have looked a little peculiar, but . . . " The author went on to describe how God "laid a special burden on our hearts for the souls of colored people." It was specifically clarified that black converts were channeled to a black congregation.[8]

Shortly thereafter, news items began to mention black individuals who were involved in ministering. A nineteenth century black woman, Katy Ferguson, was featured in one article describing her work among poor black and white children.[9] But again it was Teen Challenge which most clearly offered people of color a viable contemporary place of ministry. Black people appeared in *Evangel* photographs as street evangelists and staff members for Teen Challenge.[10]

The first photographs of black persons appearing in *The Pentecostal Evangel* were generally pictures of children attending services with white congregations.[11] A 1963 photograph of an anniversary service at historic El Bethel Assembly, Staten Island, New York, included six black adults on the second row.[12] Though people of color were not necessarily common in attendance at Assemblies of God churches across the nation, the inclusion of such pictures in the denomination's official weekly meant that the practice was becoming increasingly acceptable.

As with Teen Challenge, special home missions efforts opened doors for the inclusion of black people much more quickly. Such efforts

7. For example, a photograph in the special outreach issue of *The Pentecostal Evangel* showed a black serviceman being offered gospel literature, 1960, 8. In another issue, a white woman was shown in a photograph offering an *Evangel* to a black man. 26 March 1961, 14.

8. Crosby, "Witnessing to Negroes," 7.

9. Bevis, "Aunt Katy's Sunday School," 13.

10. Wilkerson, "What God Is Doing," 10–11; Hall, "Teen Challenge Marches On!" 10–11; and Bartlett, "Teen Challenge Workers," 22.

11. The first photographs of a church service in which black children were highly represented were of a worship gathering at the Far East Servicemen's Home. Reid, "Our Servicemen Abroad," 16–17. Then in 1962 for the first time a black girl was pictured in a stateside Sunday school class. Beaver, "The Small Church," 12.

12. Davis, "Revivaltime Originates," 22.

were depicted in stories in the *Evangel* about ministries among servicemen, the deaf, "skid row" poor, and prisoners.[13]

Then in 1966, as part of an increasing awareness of the needs of the
inner city, a home missions story for the first time included a black pastor, his wife, and their congregation and gave an account of how the Lawrence Dalrymples were pioneering a mission in the Bedford-Stuyvesant
area of Brooklyn, New York.[14] Again the Northeast led the way when
Angela Muldrow of Elizabeth, New Jersey, won first place in the vocal
solo division of the denomination's 1968 Teen Talent program to become
the first black person to reach such a level.[15]

Prejudice Confronted

There is, of course, more to including black people in church affiliations
than just using them in pictures, though this development was a highly
visible sign that the denomination was relaxing its attitudes. However,
old attitudes still had to be dealt with. The sixties and early seventies were
years of struggling with the problem of how to relate to what was, at the
time, the largest American minority.

The sixties were difficult years for editors. Acceptable words and
stories were constantly changing as the general populace grew more
sensitive to black people and black American culture. Even as late as
1961 a tract, published by GPH and reprinted in *The Pentecostal Evangel*
contained a dialect story and referred to African Americans as "colored,"
an acceptable term of the day, but that was the last time such a story appeared.[16] In contrast, four years later the *Evangel* printed a tale in which
the heroine was a black woman and no dialect was spoken.[17]

The issue of the origin of the Negro race resurfaced at the beginning and the end of the decade as evidenced by the questions posed in
Williams's column. "Are they descendants of Cain? of Ham?"[18] And

13. Williscroft, "Victory in Retreat," 20–21; "Foreign News Digest," 26; and Pipkin, "Servicemen in Taiwan," 22–23; "Homefront Highlights," 20; Strobridge, "Deaf
Olympics," 7; "Skid Row Mission Supports," 22; Michael, "Collaborate in Prison Evangelism," 16–17; and "State Prison 'Gospelaires," 25.

14. Lyon, "Buried Treasure," 24–25.

15. Reed, "Winners Named," 22–23.

16. Olson, "Slavery Still Exists," 6.

17. Stafford, "Brown Sugar," 16–17.

18. Williams, "Your Questions," 26 March 1961,19, 23.

throughout the sixties readers continued to show their curiosity about whether certain biblical characters—Simon of Cyrene, Solomon, Zipporah, and Moses's Ethiopian wife—were black.[19] In response to the growing black movement, a new question arose: Was Jesus a black man? Williams replied in his usual terse manner: "Jesus was a Jew as to His humanity, a descendant of David."[20]

Prejudice was evaluated on a much more substantive and sensitive level in an article by Robert L. Brandt, who served as home missions secretary for the General Council in 1960. Though the article was specifically concerned with the Native American population, it dealt frankly with the subject of racial bigotry and acknowledged the often-sordid history of the treatment of Native Americans by whites. Quoting Lee Metcalf, a Congressman from Montana, he wrote:

> The way white men treated the Indians is truly a sorry page in the history of the United States. The American Indians were driven from their native lands like cattle, and were ostracized, paternalized, supervised, and finally victimized. . . . There is no satisfaction in our record of dealing with the American Indians from the beginning to the present.[21]

Racial tensions began to be felt early in the work of Teen Challenge and were reported in a matter-of-fact tone. Still the interracial work continued: "Racial tension was high and a feeling of unrest was evident on the streets as the teams began their work." Permits from the police department were now needed for street rallies. The authorities were concerned about large gatherings "because of the possible Black Muslim uprisings and racial demonstrations."[22]

But *The Pentecostal Evangel* did not begin to confront the issue of racial prejudice directly until 1968. Cartoonist Chris Ramsey in a drawing entitled "Crucifixion—1968" labeled the hammer which drove in the nail as "racial prejudice." The cartoon accompanied a Sunday school lesson on Peter's Gentile prejudice and his ministering to Cornelius; but the lesson itself drew no contemporary application as did the cartoon.[23]

19. Williams, "Your Questions," 2 April 1961, 13; 26 December 1965, 25; 15 October 1967, 7; and 25 February 1968, 12.

20. Williams, "Your Questions," 22 September 1968, 9.

21. Brandt, "Problems Encountered," 18.

22. Wilkerson, "Teen Challenge Marches On!" 24.

23. Ramsey, "Crucifixion—1968," 14; and Bishop, "Peter Preaches," 14.

Three weeks later an article related the story of a widow who, though she had considered herself above prejudice, found herself paralyzed by fear when a black family moved in next door to her. Her first reaction was that she needed to sell her house and move away. Despite her initial reaction, she gradually developed a friendship with her new neighbors whom she admired for their Christian convictions and family unity. In the end she attended a service with them at their church where she came to realize that "neither race nor color mattered at all." She said God's hand was in them becoming neighbors. How hard it would be for her if they were ever to move away.[24]

Julia Kirk Blackwelder noted the uniqueness of this article among evangelical periodicals: "Although several conservative journals printed letters of inquiry from whites who were troubled over how to deal with blacks, this was the only article published in the periodicals investigated which related an actual confrontation and resolution."[25]

The only printed response to the article was a letter of appreciation from a reader who, though he stated he did not believe it "our business" to become involved in civil rights marches and demonstrations, wrote that "we must take a Christian attitude in every situation of life," and this the article properly portrayed.[26]

Ambiguity would best describe how the *Evangel* continued to react to racial concerns. A news review of 1970 acknowledged that progress had been made in race relations, but implied that black people were too often overly sensitive to racial prejudice. "On the positive side: Biracial greeting cards were selling big as blacks relaxed and began laughing at themselves."[27] The same annual report the following year reacted negatively to the "barbed message" of black evangelist Tom Skinner.[28]

Seven years following its earlier appearance, the Sunday school lesson on Peter and Cornelius was reprinted, virtually unchanged. Notably, Ramsey again took the opportunity in his weekly cartoon to focus on the issue of racial prejudice in a drawing titled "No Place for Garbage."[29]

---

24. Jones, "The New Neighbors," 22–23.

25. Blackwelder, "Fundamentalist Reactions," 40.

26. Trimmer, letter to the editor, 27.

27. Rohrer, "Religion in Review," 17 January 1972, 25.

28. Rohrer, "Religion in Review," 5 January 1975, 31.

29. Ramsey, "No Place for Garbage," 14.

The Pentecostal Evangel effectively maintained a policy of limiting itself to issues overtly spiritual; thus, more "social" concerns such as race relations rarely surfaced. One exception was an article dealing with eternal punishment and likening it to a spiritual segregation. The opening paragraph stated, "The very thought of segregation is repugnant to most Americans. When we hear of discrimination against a particular race, class, or ethnic group, we bristle with indignation, for we cherish our American philosophy of equal rights."[30]

The year was 1982.

Interracial Engagement

Fighting interracial tensions and integrating neighborhoods may have become increasingly accepted, but interracial marriages were an entirely different concern. Throughout the sixties, Williams was asked his opinion on mixed marriages. His responses were generally from one of two directions. Sometimes he would focus on the social problems inherent in such relationships.[31] At other times, he would refer specifically to scriptural injunctions against mixed marriages. The Scriptures, he stated, seem to indicate that nations were to continue within national bounds as established in God's original plan (Deut 32:8, 9). Though this order had now long been broken, Williams did not see that as an excuse for disobeying God's plan. "If God set the bounds, we should not disregard them."[32]

Though the Assemblies of God had never issued an official position on interracial marriage, the general attitude had been tacit disapproval. Only in churches with large military constituencies were mixed marriages common. Probably the most direct statement on interracial marriages came in the form of an article in *The Pentecostal Evangel* in 1976. Written by a black Pentecostal minister from another organization, the article strongly advised against people marrying who were from very diverse backgrounds. He worked from the "unequally yoked" passage and said that this referred to more than just marrying non-Christians. At the heart of his concern were the tremendous social pressures such unions would surely face. Finally, he added, "In Pentecostal circles I do not know

---

30. "Segregation Today and Tomorrow," 15.
31. Williams, "Your Questions," 2 October 1960, 11; and 18 August 1968, 21.
32. Williams, "Your Questions," 13 February 1966, 11; 4 January 1970, 14.

a church where a black man involved in an interracial marriage can be a pastor successfully."[33]

In contrast at the same time, Frank Davis, a longtime black pastor in the denomination's headquarters city, was married to a white woman and they admitted in the mid-1980s that they had been well received at all levels.[34] Others were not. Interracial marriages continued to be frowned upon in certain areas of the country, especially in the South. In 1985, Bruce Sigmund, a white, non-credentialed Chi Alpha campus minister was told by a district official in Louisiana he would have to decide between his black fiancée and his position. He chose to marry his fiancée and had to resign.[35]

In the latter sixties *The Pentecostal Evangel* began focusing on the issues of interracial witnessing and reaching the American black population. A poem, "And the World Goes On . . . ," raised the question of looking beyond "us." A young boy of color comes to the door asking if he can mow their lawn. His mother had died by suicide just days before. No church misses this boy and his brothers, the writer lamented.[36]

Curtis W. Ringness, national home missions secretary in 1968, challenged the movement to focus on the spiritual needs of the inner city. Though no specific actions were suggested, he called on Christians to be "as concerned for black America as he is for those of any other color."[37]

Even so, emphasis in ministering to black people continued to be on channeling them into existing black congregations, which inevitably meant something other than an Assembly of God church. When one woman sensed God's leading her to witness to a nearby black family, she was filled with fear. As with the widow cited in the earlier *Evangel* article, she eventually overcame her fear. Soon she was able to lead the family to Christ and then to the local black church.[38]

---

33. Winley, "The Unequal Yoke," 6–8, reprinted from *Reach*, an official youth publication of the Pentecostal Holiness Church.

34. Frank and Nancy Davis, interview by author, 18 January 1986, Frank was pastor of Tampa Assembly of God.

35. Sigmund, interview by author, 31 December 1987. Chi Alpha is the Assemblies of God campus ministry to non-Assemblies of God colleges and universities.

36. "And the World Goes On . . . ," 17; no author listed except "by a Christian mother." Emphasis in the *Evangel*.

37. Ringness and Smith, "The Now Generation," 12–13.

38. Cox, "Interracial Witnessing," 5.

In the midst of violent racial demonstrations, a young female collegian wrote of her experience as the only white girl in her classes at a college of mostly black students. In a confrontation with a "Black Panther," she shared her commitment to Jesus Christ, and he later became a believer along with three other "Black Panthers." The article made no mention of what follow-up took place.[39]

A letter to the editor appearing in the *Evangel* expressed approval of the church's growing commitment to reaching black people. The writer shared news of her ministry in an interracial neighborhood Bible story time for children—"English-speaking and Spanish-speaking, white and black, Protestant and Catholic."[40]

Moving from "Them" to "Us"

Coming into the 1970s, *The Pentecostal Evangel* clearly gave the impression that the Assemblies of God was still basically a white denomination. There was little evidence of the burgeoning Hispanic wing of the church, and even less of African Americans. The *Evangel* photographs were still lacking black people in scenes of everyday life.

Then in 1971 for the first time "real life" black people began to be featured. North Central Bible College with an inner-city campus[41] had long been a leader among Assemblies of God colleges in enrolling African Americans. Its dean of education wrote feature articles for *The Pentecostal Evangel* on two of its black alumni: Linton Scott, an Assemblies of God minister who had developed a flight training program for black people;[42] and Robert Graham, who had just graduated from the college.[43]

Black families attending Assemblies of God churches were still uncommon enough to warrant a write-up in the *Evangel*. Such was the case of Mary Hines and her family, who attended the Patuxent River (Maryland) Assembly of God. They were very active in the church for five years until they moved away. Perhaps their greatest gift to the congregation,

39. Radumas, "A Smile Stopped," 2–3.

40. Borden, letter to the editor, 24.

41. The college, now North Central University, is located in downtown Minneapolis, Minnesota.

42. Nelson, "They Call Him 'Scotty,'" 5.

43. Nelson, "On His Own Feet," 6–7.

it was said, was "the love and understanding that reached beyond racial differences to prove that all people truly can be one in Christ."[44]

This Hines story—the only such article found in this survey of *The Pentecostal Evangel* of a normal black family attending an Assembly of God church—may have signaled a new era of wider acceptance. Perhaps black people were becoming more common in white congregations. But racial sensitivity was far from resolved. A couple of articles in the late 1970s and early 1980s drew strong reaction from readers for their references to black people as criminals. One story related the experience of a white Mississippi highway patrolman who was converted after being nearly killed by an assailant, a black youth.[45] A reader, a white Assemblies of God pastor, responded that "there was no reason to identify the man involved by color or race."[46]

A similar reaction followed the first-person testimony of a teenage girl who had been robbed at her family service station at gunpoint by a black man.[47] Reaction was again quick and direct from a reader who asked, "Would you have said a 'white man' had the . . . man with the gun been white?"[48]

No response came regarding a third article about a young woman living in a predominantly black part of Portland, Oregon, who found protection one night from some threatening gang members, the article implying they were white. Not only did it specifically state that her defenders were black, but it also held them up as heroes used by God to protect this white student.[49]

Famous African Americans had rarely served as heroes in Assemblies of God literature, except for the ever-favorite George Washington Carver, who was again eulogized in *The Pentecostal Evangel* as recently as 1983.[50] The in the following year, American Football Conference "Rookie of the Year" Curt Warner was the cover feature of the inaugural issue of

44. Bonnici, "A Lesson in Love," 8–9.

45. Horne, "Is This My Last Road?" 7.

46. Edwards, letter to the editor, 30.

47. Atkinson, "I Was Sure He Was Going to Kill Me!" 14.

48. Hansen, letter to the editor, 31.

49. Dunn, "Caught in the Middle," 32.

50. Hembree, "Peanut Man," 4–5.

Youth Alive, an Assemblies of God publication for teenagers. Warner had been active in the Assemblies of God for several years.[51]

With the exception of a photograph of a black postman in 1966,[52] black people had never been portrayed in the many "anonymous" pictures which regularly illustrated *The Pentecostal Evangel*. These were the photographs of people not specifically related to the article, used only for layout enhancement. But 1971 began a series of firsts: the first black family; the first black person in a cartoon (1975); the first black (a child) in the background on the front cover (1975); and the first black (boy with dog) as focus of the front cover (1976).[53] For the Father's Day issue in 1976, a black boy was pictured holding his father's hand. This same picture was so popular it was used in subsequent Father's Day issues![54] In 1979, a black family was portrayed on the front cover.[55] Then, finally, a black family was pictured on a page promoting Church Membership Day (1981).[56] All this would not seem significant, except that including that first black family picture in 1971, only fourteen "anonymous" pictures or drawings portrayed black people in positive role-model settings for the next decade through May 1981.[57] Unfortunately, one of the few times a black person "made it" onto the front page was the issue for National Prison Sunday in 1979.[58]

Black People in Leadership

The late sixties and early seventies were a time of great urgency within the church regarding the black community. As the civil rights movement

---

51. *Youth Alive*, Fall 1984, 1; advertised in *The Pentecostal Evangel*, 29 April 1984, 25.

52. Accompanying an article titled, "The Blind Hear," 16–17.

53. 11 July 1971, 5; 12 January 1975, 18; 21 September 1975, 1; and 21 March 1976, 1.

54. 20 June 1976, 2; 12 June 1977, 8–9; and 17 June 1979, 2.

55. 9 December 1979, 1; the same picture was used inside the 11 July 1971 issue. One might think there was a shortage of blacks in the city of Springfield, which is not far from the truth as blacks comprised approximately 3 percent of the city's population in the 1970s.

56. 22 February 1981, 17.

57. See, for example, other photographs, 31 March 1974, 6; 4 May 1975, 11; 11 May 1975, 6; 18 February 1979, 18; and 10 May 1981, 3.

58. 14 October 1979, 1.

exploded in the late sixties, white church leaders began to realize that they were ill-prepared for the times. Emphasis began to be placed on finding and encouraging strong black leadership to meet the need. As the 1970s developed, the church came to realize that mere tokenism was not enough.

Symbolic of the changing agenda were two conferences held in 1969 and 1970. The first was the Black Christian Literature Conference which recognized the need that the gospel witness to African Americans must be directed by black evangelicals. A principle speaker at the conference was George M. Perry, president of the National Negro Evangelical Association and an Assemblies of God minister.[59] The following year the Black Congress on Evangelism convened, directed entirely by black leaders.[60]

Perry represented a new breed of leaders in the Assemblies of God, black ministers who were making their mark on the evangelical world in general and on their denomination in particular. As this study has shown, there were black pioneers in the General Council forty years before 1960, but the black ministers that emerged now were much more visible within the Council. It was obvious that black people were receiving at least token acceptance, but it was equally obvious that improvements in relations were yet to be made.

Four trailblazers stand out in the sixties: Harrison, Edward and Ruth Washington, and Thurman Faison. As was mentioned previously, Harrison was ordained in 1962. His acceptance into the ranks of the Assemblies of God came primarily from his association with Evangelist Billy Graham. Accompanying an address by Graham that was printed in the *Evangel* was a photograph of Harrison with Graham and Howard Jones. The caption focused on Harrison, publicizing his recent appointment in the Graham Association and mentioning that he was a graduate of Bethany Bible College and a licensed minister in the Northern California-Nevada District.[61] Such association brought almost instant renown, especially as two years later he again appeared in the *Evangel* arm-in-arm with Graham.[62]

---

59. "Identity, Leadership, Involvement," 27.

60. "Black Congress on Evangelism Meets," 28.

61. Caption, *The Pentecostal Evangel*, 10 June 1962, 22.

62. Photograph, *The Pentecostal Evangel*, 15 March 1964, 13.

The *Evangel* began tracking Harrison's missionary journeys, such as to British Honduras in 1964 and West Africa in 1965.[63] In 1967, he was asked to speak for a morning service at the General Council in Long Beach, California.[64] In his address Harrison noted that "one of the most explosive problems [of this age] is the racial situation." He declared it to be clearly a sign of the times as predicted in Scripture. Yet he challenged the Council not to shrink back from the task, affirming that while political and economic pressure could help curb the racial problem, only Christ and His gospel could solve it.[65]

At the 1972 Council on Spiritual Life, he addressed an evening rally on the subject "The Believers' Relationship to the World."[66] In response to the 1971 General Council which called for a concentrated effort to minister to the needs of the inner city, Harrison was appointed as a consultant on inner-city evangelism beginning in 1973.[67] Identified as "one of America's leading black ministers," he served in this capacity as a resource person to the Divisions of Home and Foreign Missions.[68] He continued to play an active role in the denomination's national conferences, ministering in music at the 1975 General Council and as a featured speaker at the 1980 Annual Evangelists Seminar,[69] and also serving as vice-chair of the Inner-City Conference.[70]

Edward "Eddie" and Ruth Washington, also from the Northern California-Nevada District, were appointed as missionary-evangelists to Europe in 1964. They served as frequent guest ministers at various conferences throughout the continent, including the Overseas Teachers Christian Fellowship and servicemen's retreats.[71] In 1968, they spent eight weeks in Senegal, West Africa, holding evangelistic meetings.[72] The

63. *The Pentecostal Evangel*, 15 March 1964, 13; and "Welcome in West Africa," *The Pentecostal Evangel*, 6 June 1965, 8–9.

64. "General Council Speakers Announced," 28.

65. Harrison, "These Things Shall Be," 2–3.

66. "Heard at the Council on Spiritual Life," 6–9. See also, "Format, Speakers Announced," 27.

67. Gannon, "Division of Home Missions," 1973, 26.

68. "Bob Harrison Named Consultant," 28.

69. "New Heights at Denver," 30; "Annual Evangelists Seminar Focuses," 24.

70. Harrison, interview by author, 3 March 1986.

71. Braxton, "Overseas Conference Inspires Teachers," 27.

72. "The Washingtons," 34.

Washingtons were the first African Americans[73] to serve under regular missionary appointment with the Division of Foreign Missions since the Neeleys in the 1920s. All other black ministers, such as Harrison, had served on short-term assignment only,[74] but unlike Harrison, the Washingtons did not receive extensive visibility due to their race. Nor were they, as has been clarified, the first black people to be appointed, contrary to previous belief.[75] Even so, they did serve as a symbolic marker for increased involvement of African Americans within the Assemblies of God. Significantly, their ministry since Edward Washington's ordination in 1963 was not to the black community alone, but to a broad cross-section of Assemblies of God constituency.

Referred to as "kind of a showcase" for the Council,[76] Thurman Faison gained quick recognition through the ministry of David Wilkerson in New York City. By 1960 a full-time staff member with Teen-Age Evangelism (Teen Challenge), he served as co-pastor with fellow convert Nicky Cruz of a "gang" church in Brooklyn under the supervision of Wilkerson.[77] Later he pastored Emmanuel Chapel in Bronx, New York.

In 1965, Faison was asked to speak at the Friday night home missions service of the General Council.[78] Although not the primary speaker of the evening, he became the first American black minister to address a General Council session since Gibson in the 1940s. He challenged the Council not to neglect the black community, saying that "full-scale evangelism among the Negro people has been sadly lacking." Faison's report that night was in conjunction with the launching of an "Urban Missions" ministry in the home missions department. Gayle F. Lewis, then executive director of the department, responded to Faison's challenge, noting that "we stand indicted that we have not done more."[79]

---

73. Edward Washington's race was listed as Colored-Indian-English. Washington, ministerial credentials.

74. Information confirmed with the Personnel Office, Division of Foreign Missions, 17 January 1986.

75. See Blackwelder, "The Assemblies of God appointed its first black missionary for foreign work in 1964." Blackwelder, "Fundamentalist Reactions," 111–12.

76. Pirtle, interview by author, 6 January 1986.

77. Coxe, "New 'Gang' Church Grows in Brooklyn," 4–5.

78. "General Council Speakers Announced," 29.

79. Lyon, "Focus on Home Missions," 12, 13, 27.

Within two years, Faison opened the Assemblies of God Revival Center in Harlem under the supervision of the home missions department.[80] Then in 1968, he was invited with much fanfare by the Illinois District to begin "a Negro church" in Chicago, a first for the district.[81] Southside Tabernacle was established, and Faison continued as its pastor until 1972. He was in demand as a popular speaker on inner-city ministry at various conferences,[82] but in 1985 Faison resigned his credentials with the General Council for undisclosed reasons.[83]

Other black leaders began to share the platforms at General Councils and other conferences. Harrison was not alone at the 1967 Long Beach General Council. Black gospel singer Andrae Crouch, then director of music for Southern California Teen Challenge, directed four combined choirs (including many black members) which sang during the home missions rally.[84]

Infrequently, African Americans addressed the interdenominational Pentecostal conferences. Junius Blake, then an assistant bishop in the Church of God in Christ, preached at the Ninth Pentecostal World Conference (1970) in Dallas, Texas. This rare event was chronicled in *The Pentecostal Evangel* with the printing of his address.[85]

In the late sixties and early seventies, invitations to black speakers were of strategic importance to conference planners. Almost as if it had been a fad, such invitations became much less frequent in the latter 1970s, but then in the 1980s African Americans again served as conference speakers. James Johnson, former Assistant Secretary of the Navy, spoke at the first National Men's Convention in 1980.[86]

Non-Council black ministers were invited to be main speakers at two Conferences on the Holy Spirit. Billed as transdenominational gatherings sponsored by the Assemblies of God, the conferences convened in Springfield, Missouri, in 1982 and 1984, and each was attended by

80. Buchwalter, "Revival Center to Open in Harlem," 10–11.

81. Knight, *Ministry Aflame,* 104, 156.

82. For example, he addressed the Seminar for Evangelists (1968); "The Church and Urban Problems," Evangel College Summer Seminar (1969); and the annual convention of the Evangelical Home Missions Association in conjunction with the NAE convention (1970).

83. Information confirmed with the Office of the General Secretary.

84. Pictures and captions, *The Pentecostal Evangel,* 15 October 1967, 11, 12.

85. Blake, "The Undying Flame of Pentecost," 8–10.

86. "Speakers and Themes Announced for First National Men's Convention," 26.

nearly ten thousand delegates. Harold Carter, pastor of the New Shiloh Baptist Church in Baltimore, Maryland, addressed the first conference on "The purpose of the Holy Spirit."[87] At the second conference on opening night, E. V. Hill, pastor of the Mount Zion Missionary Baptist Church in Los Angeles, preached on "The Holy Spirit, our Helper."[88]

Moving Beyond Tokenism

In late 1969 a move was made toward more substantive changes when several black Council and non-Council ministers were invited to meet with the Executive Presbytery. The expressed purpose of the conference was to "prayerfully seek ways and means by which the Assemblies of God can reach the black community in America."[89] Chaired by Zimmerman, black ministers included Harrison, Faison, and Perry. The continuing ambiguities of the denomination are evident with these opening remarks from the minutes of the conference: "We have avoided, and continue to desire to avoid any effort which might be competitive with the Church of God in Christ. At the same time we feel our responsibility to reach people of all walks of life and all colors."[90] It was primarily a brainstorming session. Suggestions made included providing full scholarships for black students through Assemblies of God schools; selecting more black leaders for important positions at headquarters; and revising the statement of social concern with African Americans included on the rewrite committee.[91]

This conference was followed by a "Feasibility Study Committee" which met in February 1970 and included Zimmerman, Faison, Harrison, and two assistant superintendents, G. Raymond Carlson and Charles W. H. Scott. The stated purpose of the committee was to consider more specifically how the Assemblies of God could become more meaningfully involved in its ministry to black constituents. One particular item debated was the need for the shaping of new concepts within the

---

87. Carter, "The Purpose of the Holy Spirit," 5–7.

88. Hill, "The Holy Spirit, Our Helper," 4–6.

89. "Church Leaders Meet," 29.

90. Conference with Blacks, minutes, 15–16 December 1969.

91. Conference with Blacks, minutes, 15–16 December 1969.; other black conferees were Ralph H. Houston, Louise Whittingham, Donald Green, Wendell H. Wallace, and Douglas S. Bass.

fellowship through publications and the consequent necessity for greater use of black writers.

Other issues discussed included increased training possibilities for black youth;[92] planting new churches; broader use of black personnel in Assemblies of God colleges, headquarters administration, and overseas missions; and the retention of present churches in transitioning areas.[93]

The recommendations of the committee were received with favor by the Executive Presbytery. The Presbytery later appointed an in-house committee to be responsible for determining writers, subject matter, and use of articles. The committee to set up guidelines for publications to reach the black race suggested various black writers in the Assemblies of God and topics for articles.[94]

At the time of the first conference in 1969, Cunningham interviewed Zimmerman, Harrison, and Faison in an article entitled "How can we reach black Americans for Christ?" In the interview Harrison and Faison urged a change of attitude toward black people, saying that a compassion was needed which sees no color. They were firm in declaring that any efforts had to be made without a paternalistic approach, with whites willing to work with blacks and allow black people to assume leadership.[95]

A 1970 editorial in a student paper at Evangel College,[96] reported that the General Council administration had in recent weeks made commendable efforts "to correct some of the failures of yesteryear by consulting the few leaders the denomination does have in the black community." Commenting on the absence of any black faculty and the paucity of American black students at the college, the writer endeavored to explain the historical reasons for the current situation. People had come to the fellowship with their prejudices, and eventually these people became dominant in the Assemblies of God. "As a result, the General Council

92. It was suggested regarding college scholarships that requirements should be stipulated in advance of inquiry so that students would not receive funds simply because they happened to have a certain skin color.

93. Feasibility Study Committee, minutes, 10 February 1970.

94. Letters from Zimmerman to Harrison and Faison, 27 March 1970. See also, Executive Presbytery minutes, 16 April 1970, 18; and Feasibility Study Committee minutes, 11 May 1970. G. Raymond Carlson served as chair; also, on the committee were Zimmerman and Gannon.

95. Also interviewed was C. W. H. Scott, executive director of the home missions department. Cunningham, "How Can We Reach Black Americans for Christ," 6–8, 20.

96. Evangel College, now Evangel University, was then a four-year liberal arts college, as now owned and operated by the Assemblies of God in Springfield, Missouri.

of the Assemblies of God has intentionally neglected the needs of the American Negro."[97]

As mentioned earlier, Harrison was appointed in 1972 to serve as a consultant on inner-city ministries. The following year the Home Missions Board invited Harrison and two black pastors to a conference on reaching the inner city.[98] In 1969, Zimmerman had stated that there were at least twenty-five black ministers in the Assemblies of God.[99] He focused on this small but growing group in his 1971 Biennial Report:

> There are no boundaries, home or foreign, set for our mission.
> . . . A number of black pastors and their congregations have recently joined our ranks. Inner-city churches and evangelistic centers with black leadership have been opened in major cities. Similar projects are planned for other cities as qualified workers, suitable locations, and funds are available.[100]

Many ministers, both black and white, had a growing concern that the Assemblies of God had done much to reach every major population group in the world with the obvious exception of the American black. Curtis Ringness spoke out on the issue in his column "Viewpoint." He noted that African Americans were searching for a new identity, that the basic problem in race relations was spiritual. It was a theme sounded before, but now the focus was also on white prejudice. "Assemblies of God church doors must be open to all regardless of race, national origin, or station in life."[101] This was the strongest statement yet in calling for the Assemblies of God to become inclusive.

The Pentecostal Evangel printed an address Faison gave at the Pentecostal Evangelism Conference sponsored by the PFNA. Faison asked, "What are we going to do about our cities?" and "How are we going to reach the blacks who live there?" He challenged Pentecostals not to ignore the inner city, to keep the priority on evangelism, and he asserted

97. Black students comprised less than .5 percent of the campus community. "Predominant Prejudices against Black Community Must Be Corrected," 2.

98. The pastors were Irvin Hopkins, of the Assembly of God, Linden, New Jersey; and Michael Patterson, of the Assembly of God Mission, Gary, Indiana. "A/G Looks to Inner-city Ministry," 27.

99. "How Can We Reach Black Americans for Christ?" 20.

100. "The General Superintendent's Report," 14.

101. Ringness, "Reaching Black Americans," 23.

that the central problem facing the inner city was sin—be it prejudice or adultery.[102]

Establishing a New Norm

Whether it was white leaders or black leaders giving the challenge to reach the inner city and the black community, the message was becoming increasingly clear that it was time to move beyond the patterns of the past. T. E. Gannon, national home missions director, challenged the Assemblies of God to be unrestricted in its concern.

Gannon's challenge was not simplistic. He acknowledged the many barriers facing the church's outreach among African Americans. "The church has been identified with the system that has imposed and perpetuated these ills, and partly because the church has been slow to raise its voice against these wrongs when and where they exist." He addressed the barriers of ministering from a platform of the "white man's culture," of the need for compassion which motivates action, and of a restricted compassion which has neglected only the American black population in all of the missions strategy of the Assemblies of God. Then he called for specific action, namely, a three-fold response: (1) support inner-city evangelism (new works); (2) make room in existing churches nearby; and (3) support the black student scholarship fund to train new black ministers.[103]

Increased focus had already begun to be placed on training black ministers, especially through Assemblies of God colleges. It was a much different stance from that of the forties and fifties when the denominational leadership had at times considered a separate Bible school for African Americans. While Harrison had been admitted to Bethany Bible College in 1948, most Assemblies of God colleges were slower in their admittance procedures by as many as two decades. In these schools, foreign blacks paved the way and then the government opened doors throughout the entire American educational system.[104]

Denominational leadership was now responding to the recommendations of black conferees and pushing for increased black enrollment through scholarships for black students. When the scholarship fund was

---

102. Faison, "What Are We Going to Do about Our Cities?" 8–9.

103. Gannon, "Unrestricted Compassion," 20–21.

104. Peterson, interview by author, 5 March 1986.

begun in 1970,[105] only three or four black students were studying for the ministry in Assemblies of God colleges. By school year 1973–74, the Division of Home Missions had awarded twenty grants to black students. Eligibility was based on being an American-born black student with a call to the ministry and expected to serve within the Assemblies of God.[106]

In 1975 Bethany Bible College, Harrison's alma mater, became the first Assemblies of God school to include a black student in its *Evangel* advertising.[107] During that time, about 40 percent of the recipients of the black student scholarships were enrolled at North Central Bible College.[108] One award-winner, Lemuel Thuston, was chosen as commencement speaker for Central Bible College in 1979.[109] In 1984, *The Pentecostal Evangel* published an article on four Assemblies of God students training for the ministry.[110] James Lee, a black student attending Southeastern College in Lakeland, Florida, was one of those featured. Like many other African Americans in the Assemblies of God, Lee had come up through the ranks of Teen Challenge.

The idea of internship and the Black Internship Fund grew out of the various conferences on black ministry. The intern program, spearheaded by Spencer Jones, provided young ministers the opportunity to serve under established ministers before opening new churches. As of 1983, six young men had already trained under Jones and gone out as ministers to inner-city churches,[111] but black students attending Assemblies of God colleges were still few in number. A case in point, in 1986, the Assemblies of God Theological Seminary had only two American-born black students out of an enrollment of 320.[112]

105. "The General Superintendent's Report," 14.

106. "Scholarships Available for Black Students," 21. Twenty-five scholarships were awarded in 1977. See Gannon, "Division of Home Missions," 1977, 26.

107. 22 June 1975, 32.

108. "1975–76 Black Scholarships," *The Pentecostal Evangel*, 29.

109. "Kansas Youth," 15. A second-generation Church of God in Christ minister, Thuston would go on to serve as chair of the General Assembly of the Church of God in Christ. He also served for a time as Professor of Urban Ministries at North Central University (Assemblies of God). Rodgers writes, "He successfully navigated the worlds of both the Church of God in Christ and the Assemblies of God, becoming a pioneer bridge-builder between white and black Pentecostals." Rodgers, "New COGIC leader," para. 5.

110. Gentzler, "Assemblies of God Ministers-to-be," 8–9.

111. Enyart, "Special Ministries Are on the Move!" 12–13.

112. Information confirmed with the Assemblies of God Theological Seminary Registrar's Office, 17 January 1986.

The 1970s saw great strides in the development of churches—both inner-city and rural—ministering to the black community. Some were pastored by black ministers, others by whites; and there were even models of black-white co-pastors. In 1970, two graduates of North Central Bible College pioneered an inner-city church in Minneapolis. Louis Walton, black, and Dwight Palmquist, white, served as co-pastors in the heart of the black community.[113] Palmquist eventually left for other ministry, and Walton assumed the sole role as pastor.[114] A second inner-city church was begun in 1971, this time in Saint Paul by North Central Bible College graduate Robert Graham.[115]

Black ministers were usually desired for pastoring "black" churches. Part of this perspective stemmed from the attitude that it was better for blacks to minister to "their own people" than to whites, but it also came from the expressed need to reach the black community and the realization that such a goal would require black leadership. When there was a shortage of American-born blacks within the ministry ranks, foreign-born—especially Guyanese—ministers were called upon. Such was the case with two inner-city churches in Missouri. The Southern Missouri District opened Progressive Assembly of God in the black community in Saint Louis in 1970 and invited Allen Hendricks to pastor the church.[116] Then in 1974, Sydney Ramphal started Grace Assembly in Kansas City. Within two years this congregation was averaging nearly 150 members, about 95 percent black.[117]

The Saint Louis church had been billed in the *Evangel* as "the first black church in the history of the Southern Missouri District."[118] However, students from Central Bible College in Springfield, Missouri, had begun an outstation called Tampa Assembly of God in a black neighborhood in 1966. It was later pastored by Spencer Jones, then a Central Bible College student, and he, in turn, was followed in 1971 by Frank Davis.

Though the pastors at Tampa Assembly had been black, the congregation was highly integrated. It was not known in the city as the black Assembly of God, but rather as Tampa Assembly, where Frank Davis—who happened to be black—was pastor. The church's black constituency

---

113. Nelson, "Inner-City Church," 18–19.

114. "Inner-city Problems," 18–19.

115. Olson, "Remembering the Urban Man," 16–17.

116. "Opens Black Church," 16–17.

117. "Inner-city Problems," 19.

118. "Opens Black Church," 16.

was actually a small percentage of the total congregation (12 percent), but that was well above the community's racial proportion. Davis and his wife, Nancy, were one of the few interracial couples among Assemblies of God ministers. Married after they had both graduated from Central Bible College in 1972, he found no problem obtaining ministerial credentials in the Southern Missouri District, and reception from the community and area pastors, though hesitant at first, improved for the couple over the years. It had also helped that in 1984 Tampa Assembly had the fastest growing Sunday School in the district.[119]

In a far less urban setting, John Husbands, another native of Guyana, began the Mississippi District's first outreach to the state's black population in the rural town of Shelby. Community Assembly, pioneered in 1972, was the fulfillment of a desire district superintendent F. L. Langley had earlier expressed: "I must see that someone goes to the black man in Mississippi with the full gospel, or stand in judgment before God."[120]

Ministry in black and interracial communities was not limited to black ministers alone. Several inner-city churches were successfully pioneered by whites. Evangel Temple Christian Center of Springfield, Missouri, for several years maintained an aggressive program of "parenting" new congregations in the Northeast. The church's second such project was what was known as Bronx Christian Center, a racially diverse congregation pioneered in 1966 by co-pastors Mark Gregori and Jose Rodriguez.[121]

Coney Island Gospel Assembly in New York was a congregation of several hundred, much more dominantly black. Known respectfully in the community as "Brother Jack," Jack A. San Filippo, a white, pastored the church from 1958 until his death in 1985.[122] A very different inner-city church was pioneered in Brooklyn in 1979 by another white minister. Bill Wilson, who grew up an orphan, pastored Metro Assembly of God—basically a Sunday school of four thousand children. Black workers served on his administrative staff and the Sunday school was extensively interracial.[123]

119. Frank and Nancy Davis, interview by author, 18 January 1986; also, Frank Davis, interview by author, 12 February 1986.

120. Quoted in "Mississippi: A Venture," 10–11.

121. "New Church in Manhattan," 16–17; and Johansson, "A 6-year Prayer," 6–7.

122. Carlson, "Salt in the Inner City," 11; and San Filippo, "There Is Hope," 8–10.

123. Causey, "Bushwick Miracle," 8–9. See also, "'The Most Unusual Sunday,'" 16–17.

Ministry by white pastors in black communities also took place in the South. One notable example is in Atlanta, Georgia, where James G. Mayo pioneered Park Street Assembly in 1977. For thirty years he had pastored Atlanta's Assemblies of God Tabernacle, one of the largest churches in the denomination. Though it proved a difficult task for this man in his late sixties who had helped start nearly thirty other churches, he expressed his commitment to the black community: "Although we have some tremendous black churches in America and a number of black organizations that are doing a good job in evangelization, yet we as a church and denomination have left the responsibility of getting the gospel to the black people to the blacks."[124]

A new Assembly of God opened in Bay Springs, Mississippi, in 1975. Such an event would not be so unique except that the congregation was almost entirely black, and the pastor was a white highway patrolman. The church grew out of opportunities O. W. Eubanks had to witness to members of the black community. A Bible study started, and later regular church services began to be held. Opposition came, more so from whites, but the Mississippi District proved supportive.[125]

One other group of pastors should be mentioned, though it was quite limited in number. Although there were still relatively few black Assemblies of God ministers as a whole, there were almost no black women ministers. One exception was Marguerite Hannah who pastored Holy Light Church of Jesus Christ in Burlington, New Jersey, from its beginning in 1975 with membership growing to around two hundred by 1983.[126]

A second was Wanda R. Carter, a graduate of the Assemblies of God Theological Seminary who co-pastored with a white woman minister a new church in Philipsburg, also in New Jersey. Unlike Holy Light, it was not primarily oriented toward the black community.[127] Fellow black pastor Zollie Smith would later describe Carter as "a defender for equality and justice, because she directly aligns her position to the will of God."[128]

Another milestone for African Americans in the Assemblies of God was the 1984 appointment of the first black minister to active military

124. "Reaching Blacks in Atlanta," 20.

125. Eubanks, "Highway Patrolman," 8–9.

126. Hannah, "Milestones in My Life," 8.

127. Carter was ordained by the New Jersey District, May 1987. *New Jersey District Advance*, June 1987, 5.

128. Kennedy, "Still Bugged," para. 19.

chaplaincy duty—Olric R. Wilkins, a native of the British Virgin Islands.[129] This discussion of black ministers and churches ministering to the black community is important because it shows the increasing, if gradual, openness of the Assemblies of God to black Americans. Though difficult to document, by the mid-1980s hundreds of other established Assemblies of God churches had black church and Sunday school members, sometimes in significant numbers.

Two keys to the increased openness in the sixties were Billy Graham's backing of Harrison and the work of David Wilkerson and Teen Challenge. But into the 1980s, leadership for the development of inner-city and black ministry fell to Spencer Jones. A graduate of Central Bible College in 1972 where he was the first African American to enroll,[130] Jones first served as pastor of Tampa Assembly of God in Springfield before following Thurman Faison as pastor of Southside Tabernacle in Chicago. While others talked of "parenting" other inner-city churches, Jones provided the vision and structure to accomplish the task. As a member of the national Home Missions Board, he became far more than a figurehead for black people within the Assemblies of God.

In 1981 he coordinated the first Inner-city Pastors Conference, which grew into an annual event for black ministers. Overall purposes of the conferences were to challenge ministers and lay persons in outreach to American cities and to make it possible for church leaders to recruit ministers for new churches.[131] The conference developed into an informal fellowship of black ministers in the Assemblies of God.[132]

In the late 1970s Jones began to organize recruits for inner-city ministry. His stated goal was to start fifty inner-city churches by the end of the 1980s, including one church per year in Chicago. In the first four years of the decade ten new such churches were established, bringing the number of such inner-city churches in the Assemblies of God to approximately seventy. Southside Tabernacle, which itself averaged over

129. "Olric Wilkins," 31.

130. Jones, interview by author, 3 March 1986. Jones, who enrolled at Central Bible College in 1968, grew up in a Methodist church in Poplar Bluff, Missouri.

131. "Second Inner-city Pastors," 28.

132. Pirtle, interview by author, 6 January 1986. In 1990, the National Black Fellowship became an approved ethnic fellowship (one of 23 ethnic fellowships in 2018) within the General Council comprised of ministerial and congregational members with elected officers and biennial meetings. See http://nbfag.org/home and https://ethnicrelations.ag.org/Fellowships/National-Black-Fellowship.

six hundred in Sunday morning attendance, provided many of the new workers for the task, thanks to the training program for young ministers that Jones initiated.[133]

A White Church Embracing a Diverse Future

As of 1985, seventy-three churches in the Assemblies of God were ministering primarily to and/or were pastored by black ministers, with another ten fellowships not yet having attained church status. Total membership in these churches stood at 6,212, with adherents around 8,400. Only 109 black ministers held credentials with the Assemblies of God.[134] This compared with a total Assemblies of God constituency of over two million in eleven thousand churches and over thirty thousand ministers.[135]

Although 10 percent of Assemblies of God adherents in the United States were Hispanic, the denomination remained a white church. This perception was reinforced in the denominational headquarters in Springfield, Missouri, where only one black person was employed in the maintenance department and one Hispanic was serving at an administrative level. No native Americans served in an administrative capacity, though the Assemblies of God had a sizeable home missions force working among native Americans.[136]

What was needed? "We need someone prominent who will care" was the cry of the black Assemblies of God minister.[137] On the district level, leaders were groping for help, but "a lot of ignorance is out there," said Robert W. Pirtle, the national director for the church's home missions program. The primary key for the future, he said, was that the Assemblies of God fellowship keep its "hands and arms open to black ministry."

133. By 1984, Jones and Southside Tabernacle had planted churches in Minneapolis, Minnesota; Atlanta, Georgia; Houston, Texas; Chicago, Illinois; Little Rock, Arkansas; and Hampton, Virginia. Jones, "America's Inner-city Churches," 22–23. Information verified with Jones, interview by author, 3 March 1986.

134. As of 31 December 1985, except for the number of ministers, which is for 1984. Information obtained from a telephone call to the Intercultural Ministries office of the Division of Home Missions.

135. "A/G Annual Church Ministries Report; Vital Statistics Summary, 1985," 16 April 1986; and "Number of Ministers by District," 31 December 1986.

136. Kessler, interview by author, 6 March 1986. At the time, the headquarters employed a work force of over nine hundred.

137. Frank and Nancy Davis, interview by author, 18 January 1986.

White ministers at district and local levels needed to become more supportive of black people in their meetings, such as the inner-city pastors
conferences.[138] Black people desired to be a part of the white church, but
whites did not reciprocate. People in the United States had the attitude,
"let them come through the normal channels." That was not the situation
"overseas, where we've reached out," according to James Kessler, director
of the Intercultural Ministries Department of the General Council.

This attitude was not intentional or premeditated, suggested Kessler,
who served as a missionary in Africa for twenty-eight years. He attributed the attitude to geographical reasons, noting that the denomination's
headquarters is in the Bible Belt in a community notably lacking in ethnic groups. Also, Assemblies of God churches were predominant in the
Bible Belt, while not numerous in the Northeast where ethnic groups
were strong.[139] In other words, resistance to engaging others is strong
where others are less likely to be encountered.

Within the Division of Home Missions, there was an expressed
concern that more black people be trained for ministry. "Our black
brethren feel they are better qualified to reach blacks than anyone else."
Because there was a sense that black students tended to lose their ethnic
effectiveness at Assemblies of God colleges, intern programs such as the
one directed by Jones were critical. The black fellowship and the goal of
planting new churches were also vitally important. This fellowship had
no direct link with the Division of Home Missions, but the division did
provide some funding to establish churches and to endow educational
scholarships,[140] although the Black Scholarship Fund existed only as a token amount, according to Pirtle, and, therefore, exerted little influence.[141]
No study had been made to determine the effectiveness of this scholarship fund in the previous decade or its perception among the black
community.[142]

138. Pirtle, interview by author, 5 March 1986.

139. Kessler, interview by author, 6 March 1986. The black population of Springfield at the time was approximately 3 percent.

140. Kessler, interview by author, 6 March 1986.

141. Pirtle, interview by author, 5 March 1986.

142. Among recipients, the scholarship program had often been viewed as tokenism. Frank Davis, interview by author, 12 February 1986.

11

Race Relations: A Reactionary Ethic

THROUGH THE 1980S, FOUR distinct periods were evident in the approach the Assemblies of God had toward African Americans. The first period was the pre-organizational era during which there were varied affiliations with black Pentecostals. Williams received his ministerial credentials from Seymour's Azusa Street Mission.[1] Bell and others were affiliated for a time with the white branch of the Church of God in Christ.

The second period, spanning the years 1914 to 1938, was a time in which the ordaining of black people was mostly a non-issue. A few black ministers held credentials, with most of them having departed in the New Issue schism, apparently for theological reasons. Others were turned away because of their race, but such cases did not reach the national level. The Assemblies of God was almost completely white, but the racial composition and perspective of the fledgling movement was generally not a matter of discussion.

With the Ellison case coming before the General Presbytery in 1939, the third period began, lasting until 1962. During this time the issue of black people in the fellowship was a source of conflict. The relationship with the Church of God in Christ was pondered; the idea of a black branch was hotly debated; and the question of ordaining black ministers was answered with conflicting responses. Some black individuals such as Gibson were ordained and even asked to address the General Council; others such as Ellison and Harrison were denied ordination, sometimes repeatedly.

1. Williams, interview by Tinney, 8 November 1978.

Finally, with Harrison's ordination in 1962, the fourth period of more open acceptance began. The notion of a black branch of the church body was shelved permanently with the desegregation of American society. Instead of expressing unease over being in competition with the Church of God in Christ, Assemblies of God leaders became increasingly concerned with why they had neglected the American black. The question of ordaining black ministers was never officially answered, but the 1939 resolution of the General Presbytery was quietly forgotten—neither being fully carried out nor repudiated.

Three phases might be observed in this final period. From the mid-sixties there was a growing interest in relating to African Americans and reaching the inner cities; the denomination was looking to Faison and Harrison for help. Then in the mid-1970s the Assemblies of God followed the national trend and gave less overt attention to the issue of race, though attitudes of its members were gradually and quietly shifting. But with the beginning of the 1980s, under the leadership of Spencer Jones and others, a renewed thrust was made regarding reaching the American black community.[2] However, it must be admitted that by the end of the 1980s the denomination continued to lack a black constituency of any statistical significance, remaining in self-perception a church for whites.

Predominant Views

Attitudes to be found within the Assemblies of God on the race issue spanned the spectrum. It would be safe to say that the official positions of the Council and the personal views of the membership generally tended toward an accommodation of cultural standards. Although large segments of the fellowship's constituency may have fed on the racist fodder of the likes of Gerald Winrod, Father Charles Coughlin, and Gerald L. K. Smith,[3] such virulent material were never endorsed or promoted in Assemblies of God publications or by other official action.[4]

2. Spencer Jones shared the perception that there had been these three phases since the mid-1960s. Jones, interview by author, 3 March 1986.

3. Pirtle, interview by author, 5 March 1986.

4. However, the files of Frodsham do allude to some association with Winrod. A letter from Frodsham to Winrod, 12 August 1941, indicates they knew each other on friendly terms. A letter from Frodsham to F. D. Davis, then Texas District superintendent, 30 May 1942, included a cautionary note: The Federal Bureau of Investigation had said that Winrod must desist with his anti-Semitic campaign. The concern of the

It is possible to identify six predominant perspectives which influenced racial attitudes in the course of the development of the Assemblies of God: one, Anglo-lsraelism; two, the Age of the Spirit; three, social accommodation; four, social stability; five, the overriding commitment to world evangelization; and, six, the Sisterhood Myth.

Anglo-Israelism was a prevalent concept in early fundamentalist and Pentecostal circles, although this doctrine has largely been forgotten and had influence apparent only in the first few years of the young movement. Proponents who had great effect on the Assemblies of God included Charles Parham and Alexander Dowie. Ironically, the same belief in Anglo-lsraelism led Parham to maintain deeply racist views, while Dowie promoted miscegenation.

Short-lived also was the concept that the first-generation Pentecostals were experiencing the birth of the age of the Spirit. It was indeed the time of the latter rain, a time for bold new possibilities as the Spirit was being poured out on all flesh. But with consolidation of Pentecostalism into denominations, rigidity replaced any innovation inspired by the Spirit.

A stronger influence than organization in moderating the radical flair of the pioneers was the pressure of social accommodation. Facing rejection on all sides for their emphasis on charismata, particularly tongues, Pentecostals sought to jettison any belief or action which otherwise created a wall of separation between them and their evangelical cousins. One result was the almost immediate resegregation of white and black Pentecostals within a decade of Azusa Street.

Hollenweger saw the main reason for segregation being "the very heavy criticism of the traditional white denominations against the Pentecostals who disqualified Pentecostalism by pointing to its humble Black beginnings. . . . They just adapted themselves to what was considered decent American Protestantism . . ."[5] Such social accommodation is most obviously apparent by how quickly the General Council changed regarding the ongoing struggle over ordination of black ministers when Harrison became an associate of Billy Graham.

Few champions of civil and human rights were to be found within the ranks of the Assemblies of God. Violence by African Americans

letter seems to be more with the rhetoric which was "unAmerican and furthering the cause of the enemies of the United States," and less with the issue of anti-Semitism itself.

5. Hollenweger, "A Forgotten Chapter in Black History," 27.

was condemned though violence by whites against blacks was left un-
mentioned. When civil disobedience was an issue in the civil rights
movement, the Pauline injunction in Romans 13 to obey governmental
authorities was consistently preached. However, when the government
itself pressured society to desegregate or later to integrate, the response
changed. Government was overstepping its bounds. Morality could not
be legislated; the heart must be changed first. The implication, therefore,
is that social stability for the white majority—not obedience to the state—
was the priority.

In the end, however, the challenge of world evangelism played the
greatest part in winning the constituency to the idea of including persons
of color in the American church, even as, ironically, world evangelism
had also been the major excuse for the denomination not to include black
people in the forties and fifties. At the grassroots level, Teen Challenge
proved to be the greatest single factor in breaking down the color wall. In
1970, Charles Scott, assistant general superintendent for the fellowship,
acknowledged the major role Teen Challenge had played in leading the
way in reaching into the black community.[6]

For many years before and after 1960 amid the persevering efforts of
David Wilkerson, the cry of many Council missionaries and leaders was,
we have reached the world but have ignored the American black. The
question that remained unanswered was Why?

The Sisterhood Myth

The answer to that question lies in the Sisterhood Myth. Except for the
perspectives of social accommodation and world evangelization, other
concepts had only brief periods of influence. This one theory, however,
dominated the racial attitude of the Assemblies of God for most of its
history and lingers today as the excuse for past sins now repented.

The Sisterhood Myth was the popular idea that the Church of God
in Christ was the black counterpart of the Assemblies of God, that it was
the black General Council. While the white denomination had a fraternal
relationship with various other Pentecostal organizations, the myth gave
rise to the idea that this particular relationship between the two denominations was unique.

---

6. "How Can We Reach Black Americans for Christ?" 7.

Such a view was never publicly acknowledged by the Church of God in Christ. Although scholars within the Church of God in Christ affirm a special relationship with the General Council, they view the relationship inversely. Weeks, for example, pictures the Church of God in Christ as the "mother" church of the Assemblies of God.[7]

Nor was the black counterpart notion ever officially endorsed by the Assemblies of God. Yet this relationship was the primary justification for the whiteness of the General Council, being the publicly affirmed notion of all but one general superintendent from 1925 to 1993 (and likely of those before),[8] and found expression in the minutes of the General and Executive Presbyteries at various times.

And yet, this special relationship was never valued from the perspective of the historian with the exception of Weeks who saw it as a mother-daughter relationship rather than as a sister relationship. Most surprisingly, J. Roswell Flower never once referred to the Church of God in Christ in his short review of the first fifty years of the General Council. In listing some of the "larger" Pentecostal denominations in the United States, he made no mention of any predominantly black denominations, although he did include two less significant white groups numbering fewer than ten thousand members each.[9]

A combination of factors was involved in the rise of the Sisterhood Myth. First, the Assemblies of God had a particularly cooperative attitude about its evangelistic work. In foreign missions, the "partitioning of mission fields" was the policy in earlier years among missions agencies. These geographical missional districts were divided between churches almost like colonial territories. Often this was done officially by the governing country or, unofficially, by the churches themselves when they refused entrance of other groups into territories they had already claimed.[10]

Partitioning of fields also was practiced to a certain extent in the United States. A one-church-per-city mentality often prevailed and was generally extended to ethnic communities within cities. There were a number of examples of cooperation with black people in the earliest days of the Assemblies of God. In 1920, when the headquarters of the General Council was in Saint Louis, a Church of God in Christ was already

7. Weeks, "The History of the COGIC/Mason," [1].

8. The perspective of one general superintendent who served a very brief tenure and died in office, Wesley R. Steelberg (1949–52), has not been determined.

9. "Fifty Years of Signs and Wonders," 4–5.

10. Richards, interview by author, 18 March 1978.

established in the black community. Evening services were held late to accommodate the working people, so the whites were able to attend both their own church and the black church. J. Roswell and Alice Flower often visited the Church of God in Christ, especially when "Elder" Mason was present.[11]

Anderson asserts that this "fellowshipping" is historically common among black and white Pentecostals, who "have always had the custom of visiting one another's services and joining together in revival campaigns, conventions and camp meetings." He concludes that "Pentecostals have probably retained as much contact and friendship between racial and, it might be added, ethnic groups as have the adherents of any other religious community in America."[12]

Oddly, this partitioning of mission fields was never applied in the United States to other white Pentecostal groups. The deference to the Church of God in Christ on the part of the General Council is singular.

Second, as has been demonstrated, many of the Assemblies of God pioneers had been associated—admittedly loosely—with the Church of God in Christ prior to 1914. Mason held a unique place of respect among earlier Council leaders, though this esteem had dimmed by the time of his death. As a result, there was a feeling among the whites that if the black Pentecostals had their own organization, black people should be a part of it instead of the white Pentecostal church. If they did not have that option, "as far as I know," said Mother Flower, "we always gave them welcome."[13]

Third, the Assemblies of God was not aware of, or at least was disinterested in the fact that its doctrinal positions on sanctification and the trinity as well as its church polity separated it from existing black Pentecostal churches. Historian Charles Edwin Jones writes that the memory of the earlier association between the Church of God in Christ and the Assemblies of God caused the latter organization "for many years to regard itself as the white counterpart of the Memphis-based body, despite the doctrinal gulf which in fact separated the two groups."[14] When the General Council was formed, doctrinal uniformity and church administration were simply not important. All theological variations of Pente-

---

11. A. R. Flower, interview by author, 17 March 1978.

12. Anderson, *Vision of the Disinherited*, 192, 193.

13. A. R. Flower, interview by author, 17 March 1978.

14. *Black Holiness*, 135.

costals were present at the organizational meeting in Hot Springs. It was only after the New Issue that theological conformity began to be of value and that the fellowship gradually took on the nature of a denomination.

After the consolidation period of the 1920s and 1930s, the Council increasingly struggled with the problem of consigning a certain ethnic group to a denomination quite distinct from itself. Although there had once been a loose affiliation between the General Council and the Church of God in Christ, the two had now in effect become strangers. Riggs, who had visited the Memphis Assembly when Adams was pastor, was aware of that former relationship and made some attempt to renew contact, but his hopes were never realized.

Whatever unique relationship might have existed was no longer remembered by members of the Church of God in Christ. They did not consider themselves the black version of anything. By the 1970s they were the largest Pentecostal church in America, either black or white.[15] Furthermore, they were one of several white and black denominations from the holiness wing of the Pentecostal movement whose emphasis on sanctification was understood in terms of a distinct crisis experience, quite unlike Finished Work Pentecostals such as the Assemblies of God.

In fact, African Americans were to be found in only two of the three major divisions of Pentecostalism—the holiness Pentecostals and the unitarian Finished Work Pentecostals. It was to this latter division that those black people who were among the trinitarian Finished Work Pentecostals went after the New Issue arose. Therefore, in effect, there was no black counterpart to the Assemblies of God among the trinitarian Finished Work Pentecostals. Other such denominations, including the Church of the Foursquare Gospel and the Open Bible Standard Church, were even "whiter" than the Assemblies of God.

What is intriguing is that no one seriously asked why the early white brethren did not simply choose to join the Church of God in Christ, which has never excluded whites, instead of forming another organization. Aside from purely racial considerations, perhaps they saw other

15. Conservative estimates in 1970 put the membership of the Church of God in Christ in the United States at one million members in approximately eight thousand churches. Hollenweger, "A Forgotten Chapter in Black History," 27. By comparison, the Assemblies of God in 1976 claimed 850,000 members in 9,140 churches. "Churches on the Official List," 1 May 1977; "Comparison of Church Membership," 1 May 1977. In 1983, Church of God in Christ officials claimed a worldwide membership of 3,709,661 in 10,211 congregations, presumably the majority of which were in the United States. Clemmons, "Insidious Racism in American Religious Statistics," 3.

important distinctions. Significantly the first sermon at the Hot Springs Council was on the "Finished Work of Calvary." A doctrinal reason for separation is confirmed by at least one historian in the Church of God in Christ. According to Weeks, ministers from the white branch of the Church of God in Christ joined with other Pentecostals from the Christian and Missionary Alliance and independent groups at Hot Springs, Arkansas, to establish the General Council. "They diverged doctrinally toward the belief in sanctification as the result of growing in grace rather than a result of a specific experience."[16]

In any case, by the 1980s, the Sisterhood Myth had long outgrown whatever usefulness it might have had in the past for the fellowship. Though it had not been expressed openly since the early 1970s, the legend was still accepted among Assemblies of God constituency, especially among the generations which predated the civil rights advances of the sixties.

Gradually the newest generations of leadership began reconsidering the "whiteness" of the Assemblies of God. Fred Cottriel, Southern California District superintendent, wrote in 1986 that "We dare not franchise any people or ethnic group to anyone else; they are our task."[17] While he was speaking specifically of immigrants, others came to see his intention as inclusive as his language. The question is whether newer leaders were truly having a change of heart or merely once again accommodating to a culture now changing.

A Reactionary Ethic

The denomination's ethical approach to racial policy was reactionary. It determined its course by what the status quo of society—and particularly the expression of status quo values found in mainstream white Fundamentalism/evangelicalism—directed. Its major concern was with what white America would find acceptable and it acted only when imitation appeared safe or when forced to do so by circumstances beyond its control.

What is disturbing about this entire scenario is that no careful study was ever made to determine historical or theological ramifications of the Council's actions or inactions. The studies of the forties, fifties, and

16. Weeks, "The History of the COGIC/Mason," [7].
17. Cottriel, "The Immigrants Are Coming," 14.

sixties were stopgap operations, reactionary measures which attempted to accommodate official policy to a quickly changing world. Occasional thoughtful insights appeared, but rarely did they dictate or alter standard practice. In reality, the 1939 decision of the General Presbytery to ban black ministers from ordination was never repealed—though fortunately it was made irrelevant in the decision to ordain Harrison. Meanwhile the myth of a black twin named the Church of God in Christ continued to overshadow the racial history and policy of the General Council and still serves to excuse the whiteness of the Assemblies of God prior to its very recent and increasingly dramatic diversification.

Another realization equally disturbing is that the fellowship's utmost commitment to world evangelization at first held back black involvement, then opened wide the doors of acceptance. This observation demonstrates that, in the movement's hierarchy of values, social accommodation has been accorded a higher priority than evangelism.

If General Council members ever wonder why they have been so slow to incorporate African Americans, perhaps they are unaware of the culturally static path the fellowship long chose to follow. The fellowship proved willing to accept people of color only when such action involved little or no risk to its palatability among its white constituency and external white observers. Even more, segregation ended in the American Assemblies of God only when it was no longer legal; de facto segregation lingered on much longer.

12

Women Forerunners
(prior to 1914)

WITHIN THE RANKS OF the Assemblies of God, women ministers have been much more prominent than black preachers. From the very beginning, the Assemblies of God has recognized the role of women preachers, but not without reservation. It will be helpful to examine the issue of women in ministry from three perspectives: the official General Council actions and statistics related to women credential holders; women ministers of prominence in the fellowship; and opinions expressed about the role of women by denominational and other influential leaders.

Women who Pioneered

The significance of women in ministry in the Pentecostal tradition began well before the founding of the General Council. Women played an important role in the early years of the Pentecostal movement and were instrumental in its founding and subsequent growth. It was a woman, Agnes Ozman, who is said to have been the first person in the twentieth century to experience the baptism in the Holy Spirit, as evidenced by glossolalia. Two Pentecostal denominations were founded by women: The Apostolic Faith by Florence Crawford, and the International Church of the Foursquare Gospel by Aimee Semple McPherson. Christine Gibson, an Evangelist, founded Zion Bible Institute in Rhode Island, while the editor of the *Latter Rain Evangel* (Chicago) for many years was Anna Reiff. And it was a woman from New England, Alice Belle Garrigus, who brought the Pentecostal movement and the Assemblies of God to New-foundland. Countless other women served as teachers, ministers, associate ministers, evangelists, and missionaries.

The earliest Pentecostal periodicals were filled with reports of women ministers. The *Christian Evangel* rarely printed an issue without a report of some woman's activities. For example, Mrs. Fannie Reif, an evangelist from Great Bend, Kansas, wrote a report of her ministry.[1] Another letter the following week told of Sarah White and Mrs. Susan Chester, missionaries to India.[2] Miss Celia Smock and a Sister Hall were reported to be opening a Pentecostal Rescue Home in Los Angeles, California.[3] Sister Bertha Mackay, a former nun, and Sister Melvia Bocker, of Minneapolis, reportedly would be speaking at the Assembly of God in Indianapolis the following spring.[4] These were typical news items about the women who, for the most part, were hardly more than anonymous footnotes in history, but who were all pioneers in the Pentecostal movement in the United States and around the world.

Several women had great influence on the fellowship in its earliest days, as well as on the larger Pentecostal movement, even though they never joined the General Council. Minnie T. Draper, for example, served, until her death in 1921, as president of the Executive Council of the Bethel Pentecostal Assembly in Newark, New Jersey. This agency, led by Draper, directed a missionary society and a Bible school, both of which were closely related to General Council institutions.[5]

Prior to her work with the board, Draper served many years as an associate with A. B. Simpson, assisting him with meetings on divine healing at various conventions. She also served as a member of the executive board of the Christian and Missionary Alliance until it was reorganized in 1912.[6]

---

1. Reif, letter, 7 September 1913, 8.

2. Letter, *Christian Evangel*, 14 October 1913, 8.

3. Letter, *Christian Evangel*, 26 October 1913, 8.

4. *Christian Evangel*, 9 May 1914, 4.

5. The church itself, while not entering the Council until 1953, was pastored in these earlier years by Assemblies of God ministers Williams and Allen A. Swift. Missionaries sent by the society included Ralph and Lillian Riggs and Edgar and Eleanor Pettinger. Administrators and teachers of the school included William W. Simpson, Frank M. Boyd, William I. Evans, and Ralph Riggs.

6. McGee, "Three Notable Women," 3–5.

By far the most important woman preacher of these early days was Maria Woodworth-Etter. Born Maria Beulah Underwood near Lisbon, Ohio, in 1844, Woodworth-Etter was perhaps one of the greatest female evangelists of all time. Unfortunately, her legacy is nearly forgotten. But she is beginning to receive the recognition long overdue her as one of the premier pioneers of Pentecostalism.[7]

Maria's parents were not very religious, though they did join a Disciples of Christ church in 1854. Her father died an alcoholic two years later, forcing her and her older sisters to go to work and abandon any hope for further formal education.[8]

At the age of thirteen she had a conversion at the Christian church,[9] although she later made an adult commitment at age thirty-five which led her into the preaching ministry.[10] Prior to this second experience, she married a farmer and Civil War veteran, P. H. Woodworth, a union which proved to be an unhappy match. At the time he had no inclination toward spiritual matters, though he later was converted. Five of their six children died by 1880. Only Lizzie, her firstborn, lived to maturity, dying one month before her mother.[11]

Her call to the ministry was accompanied by a serious struggle that climaxed with the death of her fifth child. The Disciples of Christ had taught her that women belonged in the home, not behind the pulpit. But the commission to preach she had received as a teenager would not fade from her memory.

> I heard the voice of Jesus calling me to go out in the highways and hedges and gather in the lost sheep. Like Mary, I pondered these things in my heart, for I had no one to counsel with. The Disciples did not believe women had a right to work for Jesus. Had I told them my impression they would have made sport of me. I had never heard of women working in public except as missionaries, so I could see no opening—except as I thought, if I ever married, my choice would be an earnest Christian and then we would enter upon the mission field.[12]

7. The first complete and scholarly biography of Woodworth-Etter was written by Warner, *The Woman Evangelist*. Warner affirmed the view of her supporters that she "broke the male domination of the pulpit and paved the way for other women," 292.

8. Warner, *The Woman Evangelist*, 4.

9. Woodworth-Etter, *Holy Ghost Sermons*, 3.

10. Warner, *The Woman Evangelist*, 1–2.

11. Warner, *The Woman Evangelist*, 7–8.

12. Woodworth-Etter, *Marvels and Miracles*, 3–4.

Such circumstances did not materialize, and her call persisted. Whereas the contemporary church lacked models of women responding to calls, the Bible was filled with them. "The more I investigated, the more I found to condemn me. . . . I had one talent, which was hidden away."[13]

She would later criticize the idea of the ministry being reserved for men with this observation: "If some women had to depend on their husbands for knowledge they would die in ignorance."[14] God is calling women all over the nation to work in various places in the Lord's vineyard, she proclaimed. Frequently referring to Joel's prophecy, she said that the modern-day anointing was for men and women alike.[15]

Following this long struggle, Woodworth began preaching around 1880 in Ohio. At first, she remained close to home, a concession she made to her husband. She preached in revival meetings and pioneered churches wherever she went. Her method for the next two decades was to preach a series of meetings in a community, organize a church out of the converts, and place someone in charge of the new congregation. In her first year-and-a-half of preaching, she held nine revivals, organized two churches (one starting with seventy members), organized a Sunday school of about a hundred members, preached in twenty-two meeting houses, and delivered two hundred sermons.[16]

Warmly received by various denominations, including the Friends, Woodworth joined the United Brethren Church for a brief period,[17] but left it in 1884 and was granted a license to preach by the 39th Indiana Eldership of the Church of God,[18] which also appointed her as an "eldership evangelist." Regardless of her affiliation, she tended to operate independently in her evangelistic crusades. By 1885 she began to receive national attention.

Woodworth's husband had finally consented to her traveling farther afield. He accompanied her, handling the business operations, taking charge of erecting the tents and operating the food and book stands. But his presence had its drawbacks. His mind and health had been affected

13. Woodworth-Etter, *Marvels and Miracles*, 13–14.

14. The quote is from a sermon by Woodworth-Etter, "Women's rights in the Gospel," which was published in Woodworth-Etter, *Signs and Wonders*, 211.

15. Woodworth-Etter, *Signs and Wonders*, 215.

16. Warner, *The Woman Evangelist*, 15.

17. Woodworth-Etter, *Marvels and Miracles*, 19.

18. The Church of God, General Conference, was founded by John Winebrenner, a German Reformed minister, in 1825.

in the Civil War, he lacked social graces, and he was later discredited by reports of "sexual indiscretions." However, Maria never spoke negatively of her husband and publicly accepted him until the last.[19]

Her meetings were marked by physical demonstrations, similar to earlier frontier revival meetings. Trances or "falling in the Spirit" were not uncommon. What made her ministry so appealing to the masses was the participation they were allowed as much as the emotional expression. Maria gave extensive opportunity for testimonies of healing and conversion, which in turn whetted the appetites of seekers for more demonstrations.[20]

By 1888, Woodworth had traveled as far west as Illinois where thousands were converted. In one meeting in Ohio, she preached to a single audience of 25,000 people. Then in 1889, she ventured to Oakland, California, for a four-month campaign. She attracted as many as 8,000 people, but the meeting proved disastrous on many counts as she was plagued by mob violence, prophecies she and others had made which did not come true, and the desertion of her husband. She left the West Coast quite frustrated.[21] At a subsequent meeting in St. Louis attempts were again made to discredit her, but friends and Church of God leaders came to her defense.[22]

In 1891, Maria and her husband were divorced, a year before he died. She continued to have a highly successful ministry during the rest of that decade, traveling back and forth across the nation. In 1902 she met and married Samuel Etter, hyphenating her name. Etter was a great contrast with P.H. Woodworth, believing strongly in Maria's ministry and supporting her until his death in 1914.[23]

While some Church of God leaders defended her in St. Louis, she was attacked by other leaders on many occasions. Her relationship with the church was at best stormy. In 1904 church elders asked her to return her credentials. The tension came because of the charismatic features of her ministry, especially healing. Her openness to the poor and

<hr>

19. Warner, *The Woman Evangelist*, 152–62.

20. Warner, *The Woman Evangelist*, 59.

21. Warner, *The Woman Evangelist*, 74–129, for a thorough study of what Warner terms the low point in her ministry. It was here also that she met and was supported by Elizabeth Sisson and Carrie Judd Montgomery. See Montgomery, *Under His Wings*, 130–31. Woodworth-Etter also had the endorsement of two influential black pastors.

22. Warner, *The Woman Evangelist*, 160–61.

23. Woodworth-Etter, *Signs and Wonders*, 384, 396–98.

concentration on the cities distanced her socially from the mainstream of the Church of God—a rural, middle class constituency.[24]

Although Woodworth-Etter's gifts were not well received by the Winebrenner group, she soon found herself highly honored in the Pentecostal movement. Of the great divine healing preachers at the turn of the century, only she would embrace the Pentecostal experience.[25] In fact, her simple but powerful preaching helped prepare cities across the nation for the Pentecostal movement. Many of her followers experienced speaking in tongues at her meetings long before the events at Topeka, Kansas, in 1901,[26] and several other manifestations of early Pentecostalism were already found in her meetings.

> Throughout the 1890s Maria's preaching contained many of the elements that marked the Day of Pentecost: prophetic preaching, healings, speaking in tongues, an experience of power subsequent to salvation, people under the influence of the Spirit, unbelievers under conviction of the Holy Spirit, water baptism, churches established, wide publicity, persecution—but always evangelism. For Maria, the bottom line of everything she did was evangelism.[27]

It is not known exactly when she embraced Pentecostalism, but she found herself a welcome adherent in the movement. By 1912, she was not only fully accepted but regarded as a prominent leader as well. Any hesitation at first was on her part, for she was concerned about some people in the new movement going to extremes, such as on the issue of tongues. She claimed to have received the gift of tongues herself years before 1901, and very early she had embraced the doctrine of initial physical evidence.[28] She noted many instances of speaking in tongues in her meetings of 1904 and 1905.[29]

24. A conciliatory response was heard more recently in the church's official periodical. See Neeley, "Maria B. Woodworth-Etter," 2–7. He wrote that she was "a powerful and persuasive evangelist," but the church failed in not building on her efforts.

25. Warner positioned her alone, in embracing Pentecostalism, among five such well-known preachers of this era: John Alexander Dowie, A. B. Simpson, A. J. Gordon, and Charles Cullis.

26. Unlike the Pentecostal movement which began at Topeka, Woodworth-Etter and her followers had not yet associated tongues-speaking with the "initial physical evidence" teaching.

27. Warner, *The Woman Evangelist*, 150.

28. Woodworth-Etter, *Marvels and Miracles*, 500.

29. See for example, Woodworth-Etter, *Acts of the Holy Ghost*, 342.

Then in 1912 at the age of 68, she took a leading position in the Pentecostal movement and never relinquished her role until her death in 1924. The breakthrough came when F. F. Bosworth invited her to Dallas in 1912. During her five-month campaign there, thousands came to hear her night and day. Many established and future leaders of the Pentecostal movement found their way to Dallas during those months.[30] Of this gathering, Wayne Warner writes, "The Pentecostal movement 'discovered' Maria B. Woodworth-Etter in this 1912 Dallas meeting, and she would remain a leading evangelist the rest of her life."[31]

The following year, a second major campaign produced fewer satisfying results for Woodworth-Etter. This was the Arroyo Seco meeting in California and to which she was invited by R. J. Scott. Scott planned the meeting as a great unifying conference for the fragmented movement, but it led to even deeper divisions. It was here that the Oneness or "Jesus Only" teaching surfaced and spread. During the meeting itself, however, impending divisiveness was not evident, and the camp meeting was heralded as a tremendous success. Hundreds of people were reported saved, healed, and baptized in the Holy Spirit.

But Woodworth-Etter felt repressed in her ministry there. She had gone to Arroyo Seco expecting to have free rein during the services as usual. Instead she was given the morning services only, while others preached in the afternoon and evening. Later she wrote that she believed hundreds more would have been converted had she not been so confined.[32]

Perhaps Frank Ewart was one of those responsible for restricting her appearances to the early part of the day. Soon to be a proponent of the new Oneness doctrine, he wrote later that Woodworth-Etter had a limiting influence. "Early in the meetings the preachers rebelled against turning the meetings over to Mrs. Woodworth-Etter." They were anxious to receive a new message, which indeed came.[33]

Overall, however, Woodworth-Etter's role expanded in the Pentecostal movement, and during the next two years she preached at numerous meetings across the nation.[34] Although many of her followers joined

30. Bosworth, "The God of All," 1.

31. Warner, *The Woman Evangelist*, 168.

32. Woodworth-Etter, *Signs and Wonders*, 251.

33. Ewart, *The Phenomenon of Pentecost*, 76.

34. The author's grandmother, Edith B. Osgood, received the Pentecostal experience as a girl at Woodworth-Etter's meeting in Long Hill, Connecticut, in June 1913.

the Assemblies of God upon its formation in 1914, Woodworth-Etter never united with this or any other Pentecostal group. Warner attributes this to her greater interest in spiritual unity than in organization; also, she may have sensed some resistance to women in leadership positions. David Lee Floyd, who was involved in her meeting in Hot Springs, Arkansas, in 1913, stated that local leaders of her meeting appreciated her ministry but were hesitant to "give her too much authority."[35]

She continued to traverse the nation, enthusiastically received by the masses, but often persecuted by religious leaders and city authorities alike. The Pentecostal periodicals, including *The Pentecostal Evangel*, followed her ministry closely and reported on it with great respect.[36]

Although she had pioneered countless churches since 1880, she had pastored none of them. Then in 1918, she founded the Woodworth-Etter Tabernacle in Indianapolis, while continuing her travels. The Tabernacle was built—as with other decisions made in her ministry—in response to a vision she received, and it became a center for people to be ministered to from all over the country.[37] She continued to pastor the church until her death on 16 September 1924, seldom preaching, but still exhorting and praying for the sick during the last few months of her life. Later known as Lakeview Church, the former Tabernacle eventually affiliated with the General Council and became one of the leading churches in the fellowship.

Men Who Opened Doors

Three men played key roles in opening the door to ministry for women in pre-Pentecostal circles: Adoniram J. Gordon, John Alexander Dowie, and A. B. Simpson. Each of these leaders also channeled the language Pentecostals would later use to validate the ministry of women.

One of the fathers of Fundamentalism in the late 1800s was Gordon, founder of Gordon College in Boston. By 1876, he and other leaders had established the "Believers' Meeting for Bible Study," which became known as the Niagara Bible Conference and which continued until 1898,

---

35. Floyd, interview by Wayne Warner, 26 February 1981.

36. Hardly an issue of the *Evangel* was printed without a report of Woodworth-Etter's meetings.

37. Warner, *The Woman Evangelist*, 254.

three years after Gordon's death. Gordon has been described by several writers as a significant forerunner to the Pentecostal movement.[38]

In an article reprinted in *The Alliance Weekly* more than a half-century after his death in 1895, Gordon outlined his biblical basis for the ministry of women, using Joel's prophecy as his foundational text.[39] He quoted the Apostle Peter who had declared the prophecy fulfilled on the Day of Pentecost:

> These men are not drunk, as you suppose. It's only nine in the morning! No, this is what was spoken by the prophet Joel:
> > "In the last days, God says, I will pour out my Spirit on all people.
> > Your sons and daughters will prophesy, your young men will see visions, and your old men will dream dreams.
> > Even on my servants, both men and women, I will pour out my Spirit in those days, and they will prophesy.[40]

For Gordon, all scriptural statements regarding women had to be interpreted in light of this passage. Thus, no text in Scripture could be found denying women their "divinely appointed rights in the new dispensation."[41] This prophecy was, for Gordon, "The *Magna Carta* of the Christian Church," giving women a status in the Spirit never before known. It became a classic Pentecostal argument. According to Gordon, the Day of Pentecost ushered in a "new economy," therefore we are now living in the dispensation of the Spirit—a new age that differs radically from that which preceded it.

Gordon described four classes of people named, according to the prophecy, as being brought into equal privileges under the outpouring of the Spirit: Jew and Gentile, male and female, old and young, and bondmen and bondmaidens. The Apostle Paul, Gordon wrote, later based his equality teaching on this prophecy, referring to three of these classes, including male and female.[42] He explained that women were given equal

38. See, for example, Marsden, *Fundamentalism and American Culture*, 79, 94, 249 (n. 37). Also, Bruner, A *Theology of the Holy Spirit*, 44–45, 340; and Menzies, *Anointed to Serve*, 23, 26. According to Menzies, Gordon's theology, particularly of sanctification, had great impact on A. B. Simpson. See Menzies, "Non Wesleyan Origins," 88.

39. Gordon, "The Ministry of Women, 277–78, 286.

40. Acts 2:15–18; New International Version (NIV).

41. Gordon, "The Ministry of Women," 277.

42. 1 Cor 12:13: Jews and Gentiles, bond and free; Gal 3:27: Jew and Gentile, bond and free, male and female.

warrant with men to proclaim the gospel when Joel declared, "Your sons and your daughters shall prophesy." To prophesy meant not merely to foretell future events, but also to communicate religious truth under divine inspiration.[43]

Gordon then devoted the rest of the article to the Pauline "problem" passages. First Gordon considered 1 Tim 2:8–11 which, he argued, really contains an exhortation to the orderly and decorous participation of women in public prayer. Paul was not forbidding women to pray or to prophesy but was only exhorting them to do so in proper order.[44]

Similarly, Gordon refuted the popular interpretation of 1 Cor 14:34–35, where the injunction to silence is given twice to men and once to women. He asserted that in every case the command was conditional, not absolute, that Paul was not suppressing the decorous exercise of spiritual gifts either by men or women; but was dealing only with various forms of disorder and confusion in the church.[45]

Gordon argued that 1 Cor 11:5 indicated that Paul was not objecting to public response by women but was "only finding fault with what was considered an unseemly attire for women thus publicly engaged." Gordon's conclusion was that "there is no Scripture which prohibits women from praying or from prophesying in the public assemblies of the Church." In fact, they were affirmed in the practices.[46]

Dowie's influence on the beginnings of the Pentecostal movement has already been discussed. His beliefs with regards to women in ministry were as countercultural as were his ideas on race. While in England around 1900, he ordained his wife, Jane, as an overseer.[47] Soon after, he boasted that for the first time he was ordaining more women than men. On the particular day he spoke of, he ordained four elders (all women), nine evangelists (six of them women), thirty-eight deacons, and forty-four deaconesses.[48]

In his address to these ordination candidates, he declared the event to be a fulfillment of Ps 68:11: "The Women that publish the Tidings are

43. Gordon prepared the way for the Pentecostal movement in affirming "the Holy Spirit's perpetual presence in the Church—a presence which implies the equal perpetuity of his gifts and endowments." "The Ministry of Women," 277.

44. Gordon, "The Ministry of Women," 277–78.

45. Gordon, "The Ministry of Women," 278, 286.

46. Gordon, "The Ministry of Women," 286.

47. "The General Overseer Sets Sail for America," 356.

48. Dowie, "Address to the Candidates," 624–26.

a Great Host." Convinced that this verse had been purposely obscured by the translators of the King James version, he proclaimed, "It is high time that this Great Host of Women Preachers of the Tidings of a Full and Free Salvation for all, were in evidence."[49]

On another occasion, Dowie rebuked various religious traditions—namely, the Lutheran, Presbyterian, Episcopalian, Roman Catholic and Greek churches—for preaching that women must be silent and must not preach or teach publicly. Arguing that Paul did not say or practice this idea, but, on the contrary, that God was wanting to use women mightily for the extension of his kingdom, Dowie determined to assist God with that desire: "I intend to set a whole host of women upon the Devil this year."[50]

Dowie's commitment to the role of women was not limited to ministry. He made scathing denunciations of employers ("God have mercy on the mean wretches") who paid women less than men for their work. "I think it is a perfect abomination that a woman should get less than a man because she is a woman."[51]

While the Christian and Missionary Alliance has through most of its history restricted the ordination of women, A. B. Simpson, its founder, appears to have had a much more open attitude. Numerous women speakers were included in his conventions and tours.[52]

Simpson also incorporated women into his leadership ranks, and at least two of these women—Minnie Draper and Carrie Judd Montgomery—later joined the Pentecostal movement. In the earliest structures of the Alliance, women were found among its managers, its highest board,[53] and Minnie Draper continued in leadership until the CMA was reorganized in 1912. Four years later, just two years before Simpson's death, only one woman—his wife—remained as a manager.[54]

In 1914, the CMA drew up regulations providing for the issuing of a deaconess' certificate to women workers. This certificate was for "women feeling a distinct call of God to special Christian work in the Home field,

49. Dowie, "Address to the Candidates," 625. Dowie was quoting from the Revised translation.

50. Dowie, "Having the Seal," 686–91.

51. Dowie, "Let Us Go Up to Zion," 498–501.

52. Thompson, *A. B. Simpson*, 106, 109.

53. Women members on the board numbered four of thirteen in 1889, three of twelve in 1890, and two of twenty-four in 1897. *Manual of the Christian*, 12, 13, 14.

54. *Manual of the Christian*, 16.

and who are qualified for the same by a knowledge of the Scriptures, and the gifts of the Spirit."[55] The more institutionalized the CMA became, the less receptive it was toward the idea of women in ministry. Yet its earlier open-minded attitude would have had the stronger impact on the Pentecostals who left the CMA prior to 1914.

A Place for Women

From the very beginning women were prominent in the Pentecostal movement itself. Parham seems to have been more open to women ministers than to black people, even having women who helped with the preaching. One such woman was Anna Hall, who preceded Parham to Texas in 1905 and laid the groundwork for the great Houston outpouring.[56] Under his ministry and that of others, women and men alike were called to preach in these Houston meetings. Goss listed several women who were called through Parham's efforts: Rosa Cadwalder, Hattie Allen, Millicent McClendon, and others.[57]

Bartleman recalled the equal prophetic role given to women and men in the Azusa Street Mission, whether "a child, a woman or a man."[58] Barfoot and Sheppard have observed that as the center of "Prophetic Pentecostalism," the Azusa Street Mission was very important for "it readily recognized the charisma of women, and even children, as well as men."[59]

In the loosely formed organizations which led to the founding of the General Council at Hot Springs, women made up a sizeable percentage of the ministerial ranks. Listed among the 352 ministers of the white branch of the Churches of God in Christ in June 1913 were 87 women, 53 of these having husbands also listed as preachers. Thus, one-fourth of the ministers were women.[60]

While Bartleman may have approved of women prophesying, he himself did not readily accept women in leadership roles. He saw woman striving for mastery over man as one of the signs of the end times and declared that God never intended women to rule because women act from

---

55. *Manual of the Christian*, 40.

56. Menzies, *Anointed to Serve*, 46.

57. Goss, *The Winds of God*, 30.

58. Bartleman, *How Pentecost Came*, 58–59.

59. Barfoot and Sheppard, "Prophetic vs. Priestly Religion," 8.

60. "Ordained Elders," 4.

impulse, not from reason. Bartleman decried a Christianity gone effeminate, what he described as a "Flapper Evangelism." He agreed that women had their place in ministry but argued that according to the words of the Apostle Paul, it was not in the office of bishop or deacon. God had made man the head; he "never ordained petticoat government for either church or state."[61]

On the whole, however, women seem to have been easily accepted in leadership roles in the fledgling associations of Pentecostals which were forming prior to the Hot Springs Council of 1914. One such "organization" connected the Pentecostal assemblies of the Indiana area. Kate Driscoll, a missionary to the Sudan, was a primary speaker at the association's Convention and Camp Meeting, at "Gibeah," in Plainfield, Indiana, 15–22 June 1913.[62]

At a public meeting held in the camp tabernacle, Saturday afternoon, 21 June, there was a general discussion regarding the need for more cooperation in the Latter Rain Pentecostal movement in that part of the country. A committee of twelve members—four of them women—was appointed to consider the issue. They recommended that the name of the movement be the Association of Christian Assemblies, and that an advisory council be formed, composed of representatives of local assemblies in Indiana and the central states. Out of twenty-four persons named to the council, nine were women, although no women were among the three officers or nine members of the Board of Trustees. After the report was unanimously adopted, Alice M. Flower, wife of J. Roswell, was called on to lead in prayer.[63]

61. Bartleman, "Flapper Evangelism," 3.

62. "A Closer and Deeper," 1.

63. "A Closer and Deeper," 2.

13

The Formative Years
(1914–26)

Organizational Developments

AT THE FIRST COUNCIL in 1914, women were granted the right to preach. However, they were denied positions of eldership, a restriction which would not change, at least concerning eldership in the denominational hierarchy, until recently.

When the Council roll was formed early in the Hot Springs organizational meeting, all missionaries, ministers, evangelists, and delegates were requested to hand in their names to the conference committee. At this point no gender distinction was made. However, the very next motion provided that "all male Ministers and Delegates be eligible to vote in this Assembly,"[1] thus bringing the first segregation by gender.

Later the same Council unanimously made provision for the ordination of women, "not as elders, but as Evangelists and Missionaries, after being duly approved according to the Scriptures." The provision came on the recommendation that "the hand of God is mightily upon many women to proclaim and publish the 'good tidings of great joy' in a wonderful way." Four scriptural bases were given for women being able to minister and being restricted from eldership: (1) there is no distinction in Christ for salvation on the basis of gender; (2) women are commanded to

1. General Council minutes, 2–12 April 1914, 3.

be in subjection to men and not to usurp authority over them; (3) women are called to prophesy and preach the Gospel; and (4) they are also able to be helpers in the Gospel.[2]

In reporting the action of the Council, the *Word and Witness* added that women, called of God, had been given the right to be ordained, "not as Elders *with authority.*" So, the issue of distinction was clearly one of authority. Four ministerial offices were recognized at the Council: Elder, Evangelist, Exhorter (a licensed unordained preacher on test) and Deacon.[3] Since women could not hold positions of eldership, they were generally ordained as evangelists.

In the second 1914 General Council, this time held in Chicago, women were given a token recognition on the floor when a resolution was passed that women be received as advisory members of the Council. Several passages from Scripture were cited for the action.[4] Then for the next council in 1915, a special call was sent out inviting "the sisters to be present and take part in the deliberations," noting that "the brethren need their presence and their prayerful assistance."[5]

Of the 531 ministers on the roll in November 1914, a total of 150 were women, with 66 married to male ministers, 31 listed as single, and 53 not cited as to marital status.[6] Therefore, in the first year of organization nearly one-third of all recognized ministers in the Assemblies of God were women. A year later, at the November 1915 Council the roll showed 585 ministers, of whom only 82 were women, though the list did not give the names of licensed ministers or home missionaries who would probably account for a large share of women clergy. Only ordained ministers had been tabulated—those who were "authorized to perform the marriage ceremony, to administer the ordinances, bury the dead and all other functions which pertain to the regular ministry of the Gospel in accordance with the laws and customs of the State in which they reside."[7]

2. General Council minutes, 2–12 April 1914, 7, under the section entitled, "Rights and Offices of Women."

3. "General Council Session," 1. Emphasis added.

4. Rom 16:1–3; 1 Cor 11:7–11; and Col 4:3. General Council combined minutes, 9.

5. "General Council Meets," 1.

6. General Council combined minutes, 13–15.

7. Designations used and number of women for each category were as follows: evangelist, twenty-two; evangelist and deaconess, one; minister, nine; missionary and evangelist, two; missionary, thirty-eight; home missionary, one (somehow one was

However, the status of women regarding these various ministerial functions was quite restricted. The Executive Presbytery did make an exception for women foreign missionaries when a man was not available who could fulfill such functions as baptism, marriage, burial of the dead, and communion. A certificate was attached to such women's credentials "as special privilege in case of emergency only." This action came in response to the request of two missionaries in India—Miss Hattie Hacker and Miss Jenny Kirkland.[8]

At the 1916 General Council, women were granted the right to speak on the council floor. In fact, one woman minister, Elizabeth Sisson, gave the opening message, preaching on "the building of the body of Christ."[9] The council deliberated over the issue of whether women should be "requested to vote," but the final decision was to leave matters as before—namely, for women to serve as advisory members, with the privilege of participating in all discussions."[10] Women were appointed to two committees, however: Laura Radford was one of three ministers named to the Missionary Nominating Committee and Miss S. C. Easton was elected to the seven member Foreign Missions Committee that was to act as a governing board for the foreign missions work of the Assemblies of God.[11]

Other issues had been uppermost during the General Council sessions of 1917 and 1918, but at the meeting in 1919, the chair again made it clear that women could have the privileges of the floor, but not the privilege of voting.[12] Then in 1920, the same year that women received the right of suffrage in the American Constitution, they were granted voting privileges in the General Council. The motion bringing the change read simply:

> Whereas, There is a strong sentiment among us in favor of granting our women a larger share of responsibility and privilege in our work, be it

---

listed); not designated, nine; pastor, zero; and elder, zero. General Council minutes, 1915, 9–16.

8. Executive Presbytery minutes, 23 November 1914, 1.

9. General Council minutes,1917, 5.

10. General Council minutes, 1917, 9.

11. General Council minutes, 1917, 16, 23.

12. It is interesting to note that in this same council, four people were ordained, three of whom were women. General Council minutes, 1917, 7, 25.

> Resolved, That all restrictions upon the privileges of women on the General Council floor be removed from the Minutes and records of the Council, and that they be given equal privileges with the brethren in voting upon all questions at the Council meetings, as well as in speaking. Carried.[13]

In 1922, the Executive Presbytery took up the thorny issue of the differing credentials for men and women. The Clergy Bureaus, which determined eligibility for clergy rates on the railroads, had refused to recognize women's ordination certificates from the General Council on the basis that such certificates did not grant women the right of pastoring, marrying people, and administering the ordinances of baptism and communion. The executives responded that ordained women had the power to perform such acts when necessary. The Clergy Bureaus in turn replied that, if this was indeed true, then the ordination papers should say so.

Thereupon the Executive Presbytery authorized the Credential Committee to issue new certification to all ordained women "who are fully qualified preachers, and who give their full time to ministry, and who have appointments to preach separate from their husbands, and who give the main message from the Word at these services, whether their husbands are present or not." But it carried the following limiting phrase regarding ordained ministry functions: "when circumstances make it really necessary for them to do so."[14]

A letter accompanying the new credentials described the reasons for the new certificates and pointedly noted this limitation, adding that it was not the intention of the Presbytery to encourage women to do "these things" in the future any more than in the past. They would be expected to do such things "only when ordained men are not present to do them or when some real emergency makes it necessary for them to do so."

Women were further warned to be careful not to boast about having such authority, and they were forbidden "to stir up opposition in places where they are opposed to women doing such things." Finally, this letter was not to leave their personal possession.[15]

---

13. General Council combined minutes, 1920, 48.

14. Executive Presbytery minutes, 5 July 1922.

15. Undated general letter addressed to "Dear Sister" from the Credential Committee. The letterhead is from the Executive Office of the General Council, Assemblies of God, and lists Bell as chair and Welch as secretary, which would likely date it prior to June 1923.

Because of the inquiries of the Clergy Bureaus who were demanding more accurate information from credentialing organizations, further stipulations were placed on wives of ministers who wished credentials. For a minister to qualify for reduced rail rates, he or she had to devote his or her entire time to the ministry. For a minister's wife to qualify as a minister for the same reduction, she had to preach the gospel also, with her preaching appointments separate from those of her husband, and she had to receive separate collections. Therefore, the credential renewal forms included special questions for women ministers. For example, "How much time is given to household duties?" and "Do you actually expound the Word the same as do men?"[16]

Early Female Pioneers

Quite a few women not only did "expound the Word" but were highly recognized for their preaching. Roxie Hughes Alford was the Friday evening speaker at the St. Louis General Council in 1921, with her message later appearing in *The Pentecostal Evangel*.[17] Amy Yeomans spoke at a Tuesday morning session of the 1923 General Council on the topic of "Giving to God," and at that same council, ten ministerial candidates were ordained—two of them women: Laura Radford and Ada Pollard.[18]

By 1925, there were 207 women out of 1,115 ordained ministers (or 18.6 percent). Among missionaries (who were not included in the previous category), 157 of 235 (or 66.8 percent) were women. Though the total percentage of women in ministry had declined somewhat, they were yet a sizeable group. The even larger percentage of women missionaries was significant in a fellowship where there was one missionary for every four ministers.[19]

As a rule, the women ordained prior to 1935 were women who had already been ordained either by another denomination or by individuals or churches related to the new fellowship. Mary C. Brown, of Martinsburg, West Virginia, was ordained as a minister in 1911 and then was issued a certificate by the Assemblies of God in 1915 as a pastor (a rare designation, indeed). By 1918, she was being designated as an assistant

16. See Alford, Minister's renewal questionnaire.

17. Alford, "He Shall Baptize You," 3, 7; also, "Holy Ghost and Fire," 18–20.

18. General Council combined minutes, 64, 65.

19. General Council minutes, 1925.

pastor, and from 1922 until her death ten years later, as an evangelist.[20] The change to evangelist accompanied a new certification, probably in response to the changes required by the Clergy Bureaus.

Roxie Hughes Alford was typical of the women preachers of the day, carrying on evangelistic work while at the same time assisting with her husband's church. Ordained as an evangelist 10 July 1914 by Collins, she was issued a General Council certification in 1920.[21] Her husband, Henry E. Alford, was pastoring in Dallas, Texas, at the time. He later ministered in California, and for brief periods in Denver and again in Dallas. For the most part, Henry served as pastor,[22] while Roxie did evangelistic work, though for a year they both were teachers at Glad Tidings Bible School in San Francisco,[23] and she later officially co-pastored with her husband. They had no children, and Roxie stated on her 1922 credential renewal that she gave no time to household duties and had preached 235 times during the previous year.[24]

In 1924 the Alfords were asked to leave the Council because of a conflict with the Texas District, which claimed Roxie had "not shown a true Council spirit."[25] This was not the first controversy involving Roxie. In 1919 her credentials had been held up over differences related to unity and cooperation.[26] Later they moved to California, where they appear to have associated with Aimee Semple McPherson and the Church of the Foursquare Gospel. Finally, they were both reinstated in the Assemblies of God fellowship in 1930.[27]

In general, Pentecostal pioneers were an independent lot, and the women among them were no exception. Not all were wives of pastors, as was Roxie Alford. Elizabeth Sisson and Lillian Yeomans were single;

20. Mary C. Brown, Ordination certificate. There seems to be some discrepancy in her file as to the exact date of her certification by the General Council, either 6 July 1915, 1 July 1916, or 10 April 1917.

21. R. H. Alford, Credential record card.

22. H. E. Alford, Credential record card.

23. Letter from Havemann to Ringness, 21 November 1958.

24. It was a criterion of the Clergy Bureau that the wife of a minister devote herself entirely to ministry in order to be eligible for clergy rates. See Alford, credential renewal form.

25. R. H. Alford, Credential record card.

26. Letter from [Welch] to Alford, 9 August 1919.

27. Letter from Osterberg to Evans, 28 August 1930, recommending reinstatement of the Alfords. Osterberg was superintendent of the Southern California and Arizona District.

Carrie Judd Montgomery was married to a layman; and Aimee Semple McPherson had a rocky married life at best.

Born in 1843, Elizabeth Sisson was already at retirement age by the time the Assemblies of God was being organized, but she was accepted as an honored voice in the early days of the movement.

Converted at age twenty in New London, Connecticut, Sisson joined the Second Congregational Church, then left for India as a missionary in 1871. After returning to the United States in 1887 to work in Chicago, she developed friendships with A. B. Simpson, Carrie Judd Montgomery, and Maria B. Woodworth-Etter, the last occurring in Woodworth-Etter's meeting in Oakland where she had gone with Carrie Judd.[28]

Woodworth organized a congregation under the leadership of a Dr. Sidney Smith, with Sisson assisting.[29] The Bay Area newspapers soon named Sisson the "Shaking Matron" because of her unique shaking motions.[30] Unfortunately, she became part of the company which followed Woodworth in proclaiming what proved to be an inaccurate prophecy regarding the destruction of the Bay Area. Years later she confessed that she had fallen for Satan's deception during this period, leaving her "ecclesiastically beheaded."[31] Nevertheless, her friendship with Woodworth remained firm and when Woodworth left for Saint Louis, Sisson accompanied her,[32] although for a time, the struggles in Oakland took Sisson into what she later described as "comparative obscurity."[33]

Sisson returned to California about 1905 and was working in San Francisco when she began to hear reports of the Welsh Revival. Her desire to see a world-wide revival come to pass took her to Los Angeles, but she left before the Azusa Street meetings began,[34] although in the next few years she joined the Pentecostal movement.

Sisson often shared the preaching and ministry with Woodworth-Etter, such as in the latter's meetings in 1913 in Long Hill, Connecticut, and Framingham, Massachusetts, and it was in the Massachusetts

28. Sisson, *Faith Reminiscences*, 41, 43, 46, 92.

29. Warner, *The Woman Evangelist*, 108–9.

30. Warner, *The Woman Evangelist*, 105.

31. Sisson, "The Holy Ghost and Fire," 9.

32. Warner, *The Woman Evangelist*, 105.

33. Sisson, *Foregleams of Glory*, 140.

34. Sisson, *Faith Reminiscences*, 98, 101.

community, too, that she was called upon to defend her friend against false charges.[35]

She had been brought up in a church which said, "Let your women keep silence in the churches." Though Sisson believed such teaching, she kept obeying the Lord's prompting to speak, to testify: "Oh, how the devil did contend that point of speaking in meeting, and if I had yielded, taking it easy and just been a proper young lady, respected by my pastor, the life I have had for nearly fifty years, would never have been."[36]

Her call to preach led her to the mission field, into the holiness movement and eventually into Pentecostalism. In 1916, Elizabeth Sisson was the keynote speaker at General Council, the first and only woman so honored.

One of the greatest women ministers ever to affiliate with the Assemblies of God, Carrie Judd Montgomery lived to see the day when the Pentecostal movement was denominationally structured, but her life more clearly reflected the transdenominational mood of the first-generation Pentecostals. Her ministry lay primarily in teaching, publishing, and administration, and her influence spanned the globe and the renewal movements of her day. In sixty years of active ministry, from 1880 to 1940, she participated in the rise and development of the holiness, faith healing, Christian and Missionary Alliance, Salvation Army, and Pentecostal movements. Ironically, the knowledge of her life work came to be largely forgotten.

Born Carrie Faith Judd in Buffalo, New York, 8 April 1858, she grew up in a devout Episcopalian family which provided her with an extensive education as a young girl. In January 1877 she suffered an attack of spinal fever, which left her deathly sick for more than two years.[37] Then she was instantaneously healed and gradually recovered her complete health.[38]

The healing attracted immediate attention from the community, and as Judd began to write and speak, her story spread far beyond Buffalo. Around 1880, she wrote and printed *The Prayer of Faith*, later published in the United States by Revell, published in England, and translated into at least four European languages. Although she had had almost no contact with the new divine healing movement, her thinking was influenced

---

35. Warner, *The Woman Evangelist*, 218.

36. This is from an address given in the Stone Church, Chicago, at a Convention in May 1912. See Sisson, *Faith Reminiscences*, 97.

37. Albrecht, "Carrie Judd Montgomery," 15.

38. Montgomery, *Under His Wings*, 67.

by fellow Episcopalian Dr. Charles Cullis, a leading figure in the interdenominational holiness movement.[39]

In January 1881 she began to publish a magazine, *Triumphs of Faith*, subtitled "A Monthly Journal for the Promotion of Divine Healing and Christian Holiness," which would continue to be published for nearly a century.[40] She also began to write and publish tracts on the same themes. She and her family turned what had been her sick room into a "Faith Sanctuary," where meetings were held every Thursday evening. In 1882 they established a "faith home," known as Faith Rest Cottage, which served as a place for short stays by out-of-town visitors. Ever the organizer, Judd eventually assumed a leadership role in the faith home network of Western New York.[41]

With the widespread dissemination of her writings came many opportunities for speaking. One of the most significant early invitations was from William E. Boardman. Having read her book, he asked Judd to speak at an "International Conference on Divine Healing and True Holiness" to be held in London in 1885.[42] Though she was not able to accept, it demonstrated how quickly her influence had spread.

By this time, she had met A. B. Simpson, whom she came to view as a father figure. Instead of traveling to England, she spent much of the following two years assisting Simpson as a member of a team of speakers in many of the conventions he organized in the Northeast. The various themes of these conferences were integral to her overall teaching ministry and to the higher Christian life movements of the era: The Holy Spirit, the living Christ, divine healing, Christian work, and the coming of the Lord. Her own focus in teaching at these meetings was on "The Living Christ as Savior."[43]

Judd's association with Simpson also led her to be a part of a prayer meeting at Old Orchard, Maine, called by Simpson concerning the founding of the Christian Alliance. This association, eventually known as the Christian and Missionary Alliance, was later organized in New

39. Albrecht, "Carrie Judd Montgomery," 27. She had also had some contact with others in the movement as well as with some Quakers. See Montgomery, *Under His Wings*, 69, 72.

40. Montgomery, *Under His Wings*, 77. Carried on after her death in 1946 by her son-in-law, it ceased publication in the mid-1970s.

41. Albrecht, "Carrie Judd Montgomery," 39.

42. Montgomery, *Under His Wings*, 120–21.

43. Albrecht, "Carrie Judd Montgomery," 48, 49.

York City, with her a charter member and appointed the First Recording Secretary.[44]

In the 1890s Judd began to shift the base for her endeavors to Oakland, California. On 14 May 1890, A. B. Simpson assisted in marrying Carrie Judd to George S. Montgomery of Oakland. Montgomery had also experienced a healing, his of diabetes. A successful businessman,[45] he shared her spiritual commitment and was willing to allow Carrie to concentrate on her ministry.[46]

The Montgomerys soon became involved with General William Booth and the Salvation Army—starting a rescue home for girls in San Francisco, being inducted into the Army, and ministering for the Army in the Northeast where they met General Booth who made them "National Specials."[47]

Carrie also continued her work with the Christian and Missionary Alliance, pioneering the Alliance organization in Northern California and establishing an Alliance group in Oakland. However, her most enduring achievement in Oakland was founding the "Home of Peace" in 1893 in the area she called Beulah Heights. Related endeavors begun in the 1890s were the Shalom Training School for missionaries, a children's home for orphans, and an annual camp meeting in a redwood grove at Cazadera.[48] The four-fold gospel, as espoused by Simpson, became the backbone of the teaching sessions.[49]

Simpson's fourfold message of Jesus Christ as savior, sanctifier, healer, and coming Lord was laying the foundation for the Pentecostal movement. George visited the Azusa Street meetings in 1906 and returned with a positive review. Carrie was at first cautious,[50] but began to publish reports of the worldwide outpouring and she herself received the Pentecostal experience in 1908.[51]

44. Montgomery, *Under His Wings*, 101.

45. An article in the *Douglass Daily Dispatch* called him a millionaire. "Millionaire Healers in Douglas," n.p. The Salvation Army listed his fortune at a more conservative figure of $60,000. "Mr. and Mrs. Geo. Montgomery," *War Cry* (n.d.), 12.

46. Montgomery, *Under His Wings*, 132.

47. "Mr. and Mrs. Geo. Montgomery," 12.

48. Albrecht, "Carrie Judd Montgomery," 82, 89, 92, 97, 100; and Montgomery, *Under His Wings*, 154–55, 157, 163.

49. Montgomery, "Cazadera Camp Meeting," 172.

50. Montgomery, "The Promise of the Father," 145–49.

51. Montgomery, "Wonderful Days," 228–29; Montgomery, "Miraculously Healed," 4–10; and Montgomery, *Under His Wings*, 165.

Prior to joining the Pentecostal movement, Carrie and George had had a growing interest in missions. Carrie had used her journal and faith home to further the cause of foreign missions. George had become a successful fund raiser and had used his business trips—such as checking on his mining interests in Mexico—for ministry. Their plea for funds was more than matched by their own generosity.

After receiving the Pentecostal experience, their fervor for world evangelization accelerated. In 1909, they began an around-the-world missions trip which took them to Japan, China, India, and finally to England, where Carrie spoke at the Pentecostal Conference in London.[52] Back in the States before returning to Oakland, she addressed a Christian and Missionary Alliance meeting on the East Coast, delivering a Pentecostal message without any impairment to her friendship with Simpson.[53]

Subsequent trips took the couple back to Europe, to Mexico, and to the East Coast, there again ministering with the Alliance. Carrie continued her healing ministry, now coupled with a Pentecostal flavor. Several weekly meetings were held at Beulah Chapel in Beulah Heights and at two different places in San Francisco.[54] The Cazadera camp meetings, lapsed for a while, were reestablished in 1914, this time known as the "World-Wide Camp Meeting." Pinson, of the Assemblies of God and formerly of the white Church of God in Christ, superintended the meeting that year, with notables such as Smith Wigglesworth participating.[55]

On 11 January 1914, Carrie Judd Montgomery was ordained by Pinson into the white Churches of God in Christ. Other Assemblies of God pioneers who approved her ordination were Bell, Goss, D. C. O. Opperman, and Collins.[56] There is no evidence that she attended the organizational meeting in Hot Springs, but she is listed as a charter member. It is likely that her credentials along with others were brought into the General Council wholesale from the Churches of God in Christ. In any case, she continued as an active minister until she became ill in 1943, and then was inactive until her death on 26 June 1946.

In 1917, three years after her ordination, she was asked her special calling on an application form. In reply, she listed "Evangelist, Bible

52. Montgomery, "Letters from Mrs. Montgomery," 115, 116; "Letters from Mrs. Montgomery," 121–26; and "Pentecostal Conference, Sunderland, England," 152–54.

53. Montgomery, *Under His Wings*, 180.

54. Albrecht, "Carrie Judd Montgomery," 167–69.

55. Montgomery, *Under His Wings*, 213, 215.

56. Montgomery, Ordination certificate.

Teacher, and Editor of religious monthly called *Triumphs of Faith*." But on her minister's card she was considered a pastor and evangelist for most of her ministry in the Assemblies of God. The pastoral designation came because of her supervision of the Beulah Chapel in Oakland.[57]

Even after she joined the General Council, her affiliation profile remained low. Until her death, she was a minister for all evangelicals. Her home in Oakland was used by missionaries from over one hundred missions boards and denominations.[58]

Except at the very beginning of her ministry, Carrie Judd Montgomery does not seem to have been confronted with any problems about being a woman preacher. Perhaps this was because her scope of activity lay mostly outside of local church and denominational settings and came before the 1930s when women ministers were less favored. Interestingly, her administrative role was never questioned and, instead, was highly respected.

Only at one of her first speaking engagements shortly after her healing did she receive minimal reaction towards her being a woman and speaking.[59] After ministering for several years, she published an article from the China Inland Mission, setting forth a positive biblical view of women in speaking roles.[60]

Although she did not campaign for the right of women to minister, her connections with other women ministers were extensive. When she first moved to Oakland, she established a working association with Woodworth-Etter. Her devotion to missions and divine healing was fueled by a lifelong relationship with Sisson. And she maintained a fruitful relationship with Dr. Lillian Yeomans.

Would Carrie Judd Montgomery have played as significant a role in the Pentecostal and evangelical movements had she been born fifty years later? The answer is doubtful because few women have been granted as much leadership and influence in either the Christian and Missionary Alliance or the Assemblies of God since their founding years. One of these women was Aimee Semple McPherson.

A much more sensational person, McPherson held credentials for five years as an ordained minister in the Council, though she does not

---

57. Montgomery, Application Form.
58. Montgomery, *Under His Wings*, 149–56.
59. Montgomery, *Under His Wings*, 71.
60. "Should Women Prophesy?" 270–73.

refer to it in her writings.[61] She was a native of Canada who became a Christian through the efforts of Robert Semple, the evangelist she eventually married.[62] He died 9 August 1910 soon after they went to China as missionaries and she returned to the United States with her infant daughter, marrying Harold McPherson in 1912.[63] After building a nationwide evangelistic ministry, she established a permanent headquarters in Los Angeles, California. Angelus Temple was erected, the first service being held 1 January 1923.[64] The Temple became the center of a new denomination, the International Church of the Foursquare Gospel, Inc., an organization doctrinally akin to the Assemblies of God.

The facts related to McPherson's association with the Assemblies of God are sketchy at best. Her first ordination had come through the Full Gospel Assembly in Chicago, 2 January 1909, prior to her going to China.[65] She was ordained as a General Council minister on 4 September 1917,[66] resigning these credentials in January 1922.[67] Subsequently she was ordained by the First Baptist Church of San Jose, California, though the local Baptist association was divided over the issue and did not recommend the action.[68] In an earlier meeting in San Jose, she had been warmly received by Dr. W. K. Towner, pastor of First Baptist, who at that time embraced her Pentecostal message.[69]

Even while affiliated with the Council, McPherson's meetings always involved people from many church backgrounds. Her own heritage

61. See McPherson, *This is That*; and McPherson, *The Story of My Life*.

62. They married in 1908. McPherson, *The Story of My Life*, 34.

63. McPherson, *The Story of My Life*, 72. They were later divorced.

64. McPherson, *The Story of My Life*, 126.

65. "Historical Data," 1.

66. McPherson, Credential record.

67. Letter from McPherson to Bell, 5 January 1922. The letter alludes to a disagreement with the General Council over the propriety of her building a headquarters in Los Angeles with funds from her national campaigns. No doctrinal differences were at issue, nor was her ministry as a woman.

68. Mathews, *Hubert: Here, There & Yonder*, 48–49. Mathews in his memoirs writes unfavorably of McPherson and her ordination by the Baptists. The 4 April 1922 issue of the *San Francisco Call and Post* refers to her as a Baptist minister, so the ordination service would likely have been held prior to this date. McPherson, Minister's file. Another undated newspaper article in the same file records that the presiding officer for California of the Northern Baptist Convention was present at her ordination, thereby sanctioning it.

69. McPherson, *This is That*, 304–10. The chronological order of the book is confusing at this point, but the immediate context puts this meeting in 1920 or 1921.

included Methodist ministers and a Salvation Army captain.[70] It was her Methodist father who encouraged her with the idea that women could preach and even pastor. He challenged her to search the Scriptures to find where it forbade such ministry by women. The passage about women keeping silent in the church, he argued, had to do with women calling out questions to their husbands in the early church services.[71]

McPherson's gifted speaking ability soon guaranteed her an international following, and "she gradually broke down prejudice toward women preachers" among people from traditional church backgrounds, at least as far as her own ministry was concerned. In 1922 she reportedly became the first woman to broadcast a sermon.[72] At the time of her death in 1944, her organization boasted over 400 churches in the United States and Canada with 200 mission stations abroad and approximately 22,000 members. Over 3,000 ordained ministers, missionaries, and evangelists had graduated from L.I.F.E. Bible College in Los Angeles, which she founded in 1923.[73]

By her own testimony, Aimee Semple McPherson was called to the ministry at the age of seventeen. The title for her first book was taken from Acts 2:16–18, which refers to daughters prophesying and handmaidens receiving the Spirit.[74] The passage through which she was called was Jer 1:4–9, "Before thou camest forth . . . I sanctified thee and I ordained thee a prophet unto the nations."[75] But it was not until she was in the midst of her second marriage that she wrestled with the idea of going into full-time ministry. For a woman, it could mean a severe struggle against prejudice, and she had no support from her husband who was not interested in such a vocation for her. At this point in her story, she confronted the question of women in ministry: "Oh, don't you ever tell me that a woman cannot be called to preach the Gospel! If any man ever went through one-hundreadth [sic] part of the hell on earth that I lived in, those months when out of God's will and work, they would never say that again."[76]

---

70. "Historical Data," 3.

71. McPherson, *The Story of My Life*, 26–27.

72. "Historical Data," 3.

73. "Historical Data," 5.

74. McPherson, *This is That*, 3.

75. McPherson, *This is That*, 13.

76. McPherson, *This is That*, 78.

Describing her response to this second call of God, McPherson compared herself to Jonah finally going to Nineveh. She left her husband, took her two children, and returned to her mother. Shortly afterwards, she began the preaching campaigns that quickly catapulted her into national fame.

In Defense of Women Ministers

From the very beginning of the fellowship, there were leaders and writers who declared the legitimacy of women in ministry. A. G. Jeffries, of Peniel, Texas, wrote in 1916 that a significant feature of the present outpouring was the "Apostolate of women." "Men have hypocritically objected to women making themselves conspicuous in pulpit work, but thank God, this conspicuousness is of God Himself." Women had not pushed themselves into ministry; God had pulled them into it.[77]

His defense of women in ministry was mainly grounded in examples. If a woman gave birth to our Lord, he reasoned, why could not her daughters partake in His great work? Jeffries also cited women from the last century: Fidelia Fisk in Persia, Eliza Agnew in Ceylon, Mary Whately in Cairo, Matilda Rankin in Mexico, Mary Graybell in India, Clara Cushman in China, and Mary Moffat in Africa. Still, this number was nothing compared to the number of women now being called. More than half of the missionary force in 1916 was female, he wrote, and stateside, "they are in almost every village preaching and working in every way conceivable." This great movement of women was a sign of the end times.[78]

In 1921 the *Evangel* printed a defense of women in ministry in an article written by a Baptist minister, W. M. McArt, who had apparently embraced the Pentecostal experience. McArt provided extensive illustrations from the Gospels, the book of Acts, and the Pauline Epistles. Regarding the story of the Upper Room, he wrote, "Women were with the apostles on equal terms in the prayer meetings and in the business meeting."[79] He affirmed the role of women in prophetic ministry and in the proclamation of the gospel and declared that he had found nothing in the Bible which would restrict women's work to women alone. Touching only lightly on the controversial passages of Paul, McArt stated that 1

---

77. Jeffries, "The Limit," 6.
78. Jeffries, "The Limit," 7.
79. McArt, "Woman's Place," 14.

Timothy 2 had to do with the marriage relationship and also with headship and rulership "which belongs exclusively to men."[80] He stopped short of making a public statement as to whether this last point would exclude women from eldership in the church, but the implication existed that such was the case.

In a question-and-answer column in 1923, another writer discussed the subject of Philip's four virgin daughters who prophesied. A reader had asked whether this prophesying took place only at home and thus could not be considered as preaching. The reply given was that this was an incorrect and unprovable assumption. Reference was made to 1 Cor 11:5 where "the apostle distinctly authorizes the praying and prophesying of women in the church." Also, the writer continued, prophesying was more than uttering predictions; it also took the form of edification, exhortation, or comfort, with the speaker serving as a mouthpiece of the Holy Spirit.[81]

Even so, a mandate for women to preach stopped short of endowing them with blanket authority. Woodworth-Etter's ministry was accepted by some leaders because it would benefit the movement, but Goss, Bell, and others were cautious of her leadership role. "They saw to it that she didn't get too much authority."[82]

Bell's Reservations

In the early days of the fellowship the most prolific writer on the subject of women in ministry was Bell, who pondered the issue on the pages of the *Evangel* for nearly a decade. Though expressing an open-mindedness toward women's participation in the fellowship, he also reflected opinions held by members of his Southern Baptist Convention and the mores of his own middle-class background by his hesitation in giving complete support to the matter of women's role.

In 1914, Bell addressed some of the problems currently being faced "on the field." One of the complaints was that certain women were

80. McArt, "Woman's Place," 14–15.

81. W. R. M., "Questions Answered," 8.

82. Floyd, interview by Warner, 26 February 1981. Floyd, a charter member of the Council and responsible for housing arrangements at the 1913 meeting in Hot Springs where Woodworth-Etter ministered, was wary of her willingness to "grab the authority over everything." His reservation extended to all women preachers who were too inclined to make judgements by "sense" and not by facts.

traveling from mission to mission alone, thereby "bringing reproach upon the cause." Bell's position was that women should be permanently connected with some mission under proper supervision of some "good brother whom God has placed in charge of the work," maintaining that women were recognized by Paul only as helpers in the gospel.

He did acknowledge that some women had gone out and established works on their own, but these were not "busy-bodies." In fact, they were above the norm in character and settled habits. Even so, he professed that "there is no scriptural precept or example for such independent leadership by women."[83]

Of primary concern was the question of women in eldership. Bell considered the question in two lengthy articles in 1914 and 1915. While he accepted the preaching ministry of women, he emphatically objected to women in positions of authority. In his own mind he was striking a balance between those who would silence women altogether and those who would give them opportunity for every office. The criterion for decision was not expediency, he held, but the authority of Scripture.

To his way of thinking women might testify to the grace of God in their lives and might exhort "according to the gift of grace which God has given them," but neither act amounted to a specific calling to forsake all else and minister full-time. He did agree that women were also able to prophesy. "No one should think for one moment of forbidding such sisters from declaring and giving witness of God and to His glory when God has unmistakably called them thereto."

Yet, Bell continued to write, Scripture contained no instance of any woman being placed in a position of "authority to rule, govern or teach in the authoritative sense." No women had been known to have been appointed by the Lord as an elder or apostle; however, Bell did not see this as a restriction on women. Instead, he believed that God was taking "these heavy responsibilities off their shoulders" since men were better adapted through natural ability than women for such loads. Even so, Bell admitted, on occasion women might be given the ability for temporary leadership of a church or mission, but this did not require her ordination as an elder.[84]

In 1915, Bell editorialized that he knew of no movement where women had been more highly honored or given more freedom than in

---

83. Bell, "Some Complaints," 20 January 1914, 2.
84. Bell, "Women Elders," 2.

this particular fellowship. He was responding to the question, "Do you not forbid women to speak or make an address or give counsel at or in the General Council meetings?" His reply was that women had been granted the right to be ordained, to preach, to witness, to give advice, to be an evangelist, and to be a missionary. "The only thing not thrown unscripturally upon her weak shoulders is the making of her a Ruling Elder."

In Bell's opinion women were superior to men in some things and men superior in others; ruling eldership was definitely one area in which men were superior. But again, Bell did not rule out God's sovereignty in giving special calls to women "under exceptional circumstances." When appropriately gifted and called, a woman could pastor a church, run a rescue home, or a faith home. Still, the implications were that there were limits as to what positions she could fill. Authority outside of a local church or ministry was beyond the limits. Bell concluded the editorial by serving notice that he would oppose any further discussion of woman's rights at councils, noting that there was not enough time for such non-essential matters of business.[85]

However, even Bell could not stem discussion of the issue, either at Council or in the *Evangel*. The questions kept coming. If women could not serve as elders in the church, what were they permitted to do? Bell answered in his column that while he found no example in the New Testament of women pastoring, Philip's four daughters (Acts 21:8–9) provided a precedent for women becoming evangelists, workers, and missionaries. They could also serve for a time as supply pastors; but when men qualified to be elders or pastors were present, women should give way.[86] Bell seemed to allow for women pastors in temporary settings only where they were not "usurping authority," or, in other words, where they were granted the position by rightful authority.[87] He wrote that if women were wise, they would encourage men, when they are prepared, to bear "the burdens in management and government which God has especially designed for stronger shoulders."[88]

However, Bell warned, while women must not strive for authority, men must not stop a woman who has been raised up by God:

---

85. Bell, "Women Welcome," 2.
86. Bell, "Questions and Answers," 17 May 1919, 5.
87. Bell, "Questions and Answers," 29 January and 5 February 1916, 8.
88. Bell, "Questions and Answers," 2 September 1916, 8.

> If God will raise up now some Deborah who can give rest and
> peace to the Pentecostal people for forty years, I will only praise
> Him and leave God to attend to His own business. God is sov-
> ereign and can raise up or put down whom he will. If men fail
> God and don't take care of his flock in any place, and God does
> actually raise up a capable woman and make her do it for Him
> to their good and His glory, then we had better let God alone.[89]

Such privilege of leadership also applied to women who had pioneered
assemblies, he contended, and any woman, or man for that matter, would
have a right to remain with such an assembly as long as the people of that
assembly felt it agreeable and profitable.[90]

In 1921, Bell wrote that while women could not, on the basis of
Scripture, be authorized to baptize in water, neither could they be prohibited on the basis of Scripture from doing such. Therefore, where an
ordained man was not available, then an ordained woman could perform
baptism and communion, if such were acceptable to the congregation.

Actually, custom more than Scripture dictated that these ordinances
be administered by a minister.[91] A year earlier, Bell had written that if
a woman administered church ordinances or performed marriages, she
would do so contrary to the authority of the Assemblies of God. While the
ministerial certification made no distinction between men and women in
regard to evangelizing and preaching the word, the difference came in the
exercise of authority and ministerial acts of an official nature.[92]

As an official "voice" of the General Council, Bell made it clear that
women were permitted to hold the position of trustee in a local assembly
because such a position is not mentioned in Scripture, and that it would
also be fitting to have deaconesses where women were qualified and capable for such an office. Yet, Bell continued, it had to be realized that a
"deaconess" was by no means a "deacon." Women were not permitted to
serve as deacons, even if suitable men were not available. In such cases,
deaconesses could be appointed.[93]

Frequently Bell was asked to clarify the passage regarding women
keeping silent (1 Cor 14:34–36). Bell explained that women were not
to take part in the business affairs of the church independently of their

89. Bell, "Questions and Answers," 2 September 1916, 8.

90. Bell, "Questions and Answers," 25 January 1919, 5.

91. Bell, "Questions and Answers," 3 January 1921, 10.

92. Bell, "Questions and Answers," 6 March 1920, 5.

93. Bell, "Questions and Answers," 10 March 1917, 9.

husbands. Man, not woman, was to be the head of the house,[94] and when the husband was a believer, the wife was to defer to her husband in such matters. However, he wrote, this applied only to governmental matters in the church, and not to worship, prayer, prophesying, witnessing, or exhortation. "In these women are as free as men."[95] The issue was clearly one of authority (1 Tim 2:12), for Paul accepted women praying and prophesying in other passages (1 Cor 11:5). Women were only restricted from teaching in official matters—they could not make official decisions regarding doctrine or interpretation.[96]

In a later article written in 1921, Bell applied a cultural context to Paul's silence passage and alluded to the changes taking place in modern society. The previous year women had been given the right to vote by both the U. S. Constitution and the General Council. How far such changes would justify women officer seekers in society Bell hesitated to speculate. But he saw no room for women ruling in the church.[97] When asked if it was "right and proper for a woman who believes in holiness to register and vote," he avoided the male/female issue, replying that it was good to vote for good candidates, but it was best for saints to keep out of party politics.[98]

Rights of Women in Society

The constituency of the Council was generally pro-feminist on the issues of the day. Women's suffrage, though not lobbied for by the Assemblies of God, was quickly accepted by the fellowship. *The Latter Rain Evangel*, a Pentecostal periodical in Chicago produced by Stone Chapel, lauded women's liberation victories in other nations. It reported that the women of Turkey were abandoning the ancient veil and were even taking part in politics and business. In reporting the story, the periodical editorialized, "The missionaries in India who have been praying for years for the liberation of the purdah women will rejoice" to learn of the events taking place in a neighboring Asian nation.[99]

94. Bell, "Questions and Answers," 26 May 1917, 9.
95. Bell, "Questions and Answers," 14 June 1919, 5.
96. Bell, "Questions and Answers," 29 November 1919, 5.
97. Bell, "Questions and Answers," 11 June 1921, 10.
98. Bell, "Questions and Answers," 6 January 1923, 8.
99. "Turkey's Women Unveiled," 20.

The same article further reported that China's women were entering a new era as they were becoming involved in the professions, business, and philanthropy. Such a change was reportedly due to the influence of missionaries and their organizations. The article concluded by stating that the gospel is proving to be a truly liberating force in the world. "There is no doubt that within a few years the women of other heathen lands will be set free from the superstition and cursed customs that have bound them for centuries. Wherever Gospel light shines it drives away the darkness."[100]

100. "Turkey's Women Unveiled," 21.

14

The Exclusive Establishment
(1927–76)

WHEN THE GENERAL COUNCIL approved a major reorganization of its constitution and bylaws in 1927, all scriptural and other reasonings regarding women ministers were deleted. What remained was that "women may be ordained in any degree except eldership and be licensed to preach as provided for men." Thus, women were forbidden only the role of eldership.[1]

The Council's Fluctuating Position

Then in the General Council meeting of 1931, the ordination of women was again discussed and this time severely limited. The subject came up immediately following a debate on the ordination of divorced ministers, an issue which plagued the Assemblies of God for much of its history. Just prior to the issue on women in ministry being introduced, Williams, then general superintendent, turned the chair over to Welch. When the resolution was presented, Welch turned to Williams and said, "You must have known what was coming up."

Welch then announced that the women had the right to speak first on the question. Those women who started the discussion declared themselves to be "old fashioned" and stated that "women should keep their place in the ministry," which meant not performing the marriage ceremony. Rebuttal came from other women in the form of exceptional

1. General Council constitution and bylaws, 1927, 16.

cases, such as women pastors and missionaries who had no men to do the task. Finally, Robert A. Brown, who was married to one of the most respected women ministers in the fellowship, stated that he could not help noticing that, "In the Scriptures there was no woman in the priesthood and none in the apostolic ministry. God chose men. . . . his wife always refrained from 'the acts of priesthood.' . . . he hated to see women put on a white garment and try to look like angels, and go into the baptismal pool to baptize converts."[2]

This sentiment carried the Council and a motion was passed which read that "the Scriptures teach that there is a difference in the prerogatives of the ministry of men and women in the church." Hereafter, ordination certificates of women would clearly state that women were ordained only as evangelists. The words "bury the dead, administer ordinances of the church, and perform the rite of marriage, when such acts are necessary," were to be omitted from women's certificates, both for ordination and for licensing.[3]

The limitation did not last long, however, and in four years the full right of ordination to women was restored. The new resolution repeated the statements used in 1931 that there was a scriptural difference between the ministry of men and women, and that the Scriptures also stated that divinely called and qualified women might also serve the church in the ministry of the Word. Therefore, the new resolution proclaimed, women could be licensed to preach and, if at least twenty-five years of age and proven in ministry, could be ordained as either evangelists or pastors.[4] Moreover, the right to administer the ordinances was also restored. This 1935 resolution was made retroactive, likely to 1931. With the age restriction, it is interesting to note that at this time no minimum age requirement had been placed on men.

The restrictions on ordaining women had not significantly decreased the number of such women since 1925. By 1935, there were 522 women out of a total of 2,606 ministers. The percentage of ordained women had increased to 20.0 percent from 18.6 percent a decade before. While few of the women in the mission field were ordained (37 out of 174 compared to 63 of the 89 men), women were still a dominant group. Comprising 66.2

---

2. "Editor's General Council Notes," 10 October 1931, 5. Brown's wife, Marie, would be one of the primary speakers at the next General Council.

3. General Council minutes, 1931, 17–18.

4. General Council minutes, 1935, 111–12.

percent of the missions force, their percentages had remained unchanged in the previous decade.[5]

Other than Marie Brown in 1933 and 1951, only two women appeared as speakers at General Council services until the late 1970s. The exceptions were both at the 1939 Council: Esther Harvey, a missionary to India, preached at an afternoon service, and Zella Lindsey spoke on a Tuesday morning.[6]

Even before then, a few women were able to assume positions at the district level in youth ministry. As early as 1933, Evelyn D. Becker served as president of the Christ Ambassadors (youth program) in the Potomac District.[7] In the 1940s Sadie L. Johnson was the first district youth director of the West Florida District and Margaret Miller served in Louisiana.[8] In the 1950s, Eunice Lindvall was district youth president in North Carolina, the same position held by Beulah Brasker Bayless in Minnesota.[9]

In New Jersey, Iola Smith was appointed as the full-time District Treasurer, a post she held for many years starting in 1958.[10] But when she was first elected, it caused a furor because of her gender. She was not an Assemblies of God *man*. The question was raised as to why she should be given the job unless there were no men qualified to fill the position.[11] Even into the 1980s, she remained the only woman to fill the post of district treasurer in the entire fellowship.[12]

A common perception during the thirties, forties, and even fifties was that there was a shortage of men in the Assemblies of God. While two-thirds of the missions force in 1935 had been women, four out of five of all ordained ministers were men. Even so, three articles in the *Evangel* appealed for more men. One article focused on the need for men to go to the mission field;[13] another expressed disappointment at seeing so

5. General Council minutes, 1935.

6. General Council minutes, 1939, 50.

7. See the editorial box, *Potomac District*, 2. Two of four of the vice-presidents were women as was the secretary-treasurer.

8. *The Pentecostal Evangel*, 25 September 1943, 8.

9. Obituary, *The Pentecostal Evangel*, 17 April 1977, 25.

10. Paproski, interview by author, 18 March 1987. Paproski served as superintendent of the New Jersey District.

11. Reynolds, interview by author, 12 September 1985.

12. Paproski, interview by author, 18 March 1987.

13. Peters, "Help Wanted—Male," 2.

few young men responding to altar calls. The writer noted his dismay at seeing only a sea of female faces.[14]

The first of these articles to be printed was by Ralph M. Riggs, at the time a pastor. Acknowledging the great role women had played in the Bible and in "these last days" because of the outpouring of the Spirit, Riggs insisted that the "dominant" scriptural teaching was that "men are the God-ordained leaders in the home and in the work of God." Not only did Scripture declare this truth, God had endowed men naturally with certain qualities of leadership, such as physical strength and an analytical intellect. Riggs wrote of the need for "a strong, dominant male element in our churches," and cited a dearth of men in the Assemblies of God. He reported in 1938 that 60 percent of the fellowship's Bible school students, 67 percent of its church members, and 75 percent of its missionaries were women.[15]

There were appeals for women to serve, also, as, for example, when Noel Perkin described a need for women in a particular mission field.[16] Perhaps the most balanced plea came in an advertisement for Central Bible Institute. "Men and Women Wanted," the caption read, and the text declared, "Preachers with willingness to sacrifice for God are needed in thousands of churchless communities in America."[17]

The man-woman ratio in the Assemblies of God constituency in 1936 was indeed predominantly female. There were only 58.7 males for every 100 females. In contrast, the International Church of the Foursquare Gospel, led by Aimee Semple McPherson, had 65.5 males for every 100 females. Meanwhile, the Church of God in Christ, led by Bishop Mason, had 39.1 men per 100 women. The male-female ratio did not necessarily correlate with gender-oriented leadership.[18]

Women of the Establishment

In contrast to Montgomery and McPherson, the new generation of women ministers tended to find their place in the local setting. There were still traveling evangelists such as Zelma Argue, but generally speaking, the

14. Keys, "Where Are the Young Men?" 6.
15. Riggs, "The Place of Men," 16.
16. Perkin, "An Appeal for Lady Missionaries," 8.
17. Advertisement, *The Pentecostal Evangel*, 8 July 1939, 12.
18. Barfoot and Sheppard, "Prophetic vs. Priestly Religion," 3, table 1.

leading women of the period were pastors and ministers' wives, fulfilling their calls through work in local congregations.

Marie Estelle Brown was the founder of the Glad Tidings Tabernacle in Manhattan, New York, and pastor/co-pastor there for 64 years. When she died 2 June 1971, she was the holder of the longest single pastorate in Council records. A native of Wisconsin, she was born Marie Burgess in 1880, grew up as a Congregationalist, and then attended Moody School (later Moody Bible Institute) in Chicago. When sickness struck her family, she moved with them to Alexander Dowie's city of Zion.[19] There in October 1906, she joined the growing Pentecostal movement and began conducting meetings in Chicago, Toledo, and Detroit.[20]

In January 1907, she was invited to New York City where in May she opened a mission on Forty-Second Street. There she met Robert A. Brown, a native of Ireland and a Methodist lay preacher, and invited him to give the dedication message for the new church. A short time later he embraced both Pentecostalism and Marie, and the couple were married 14 October 1909 in Zion City.[21] Robert had received the Pentecostal experience on 11 January 1908 immediately after he had preached a sermon on Acts 2:4.

Robert seems to have helped Marie at the mission early on, not taking the role of pastor until after their wedding. Then the two co-pastored for the next forty years until his death on 11 February 1948 at the age of 75.[22] While he officiated more as the pastor during their marriage, he alternated preaching duties with his wife.[23] Their style of delivery differed so greatly that one observer commented, "Pastor Robert A. Brown is a real evangelist of the militant type, wheras [sic] his wife is devotional, and most efficient as an expositor of the Holy Scriptures."[24]

After her husband's death, Marie Brown took his place at the helm of the church, but eventually asked her nephew, R. Stanley Berg, to assist her. Berg, who had been the first Assemblies of God chaplain to serve overseas, then assumed many of the pastoral and administrative duties, though she continued to share the preaching.

19. "In Loving Memory," 4–5.
20. Schuster, "World Missions Giving," 16.
21. They had only one child, who died at birth.
22. "A Pastor 40 Years," 21.
23. "Rev. R. A. Brown Dies," n.p.
24. McAlister, "Other Side," 23.

For two decades, Glad Tidings Tabernacle led the denomination in giving to missions. Finally, in 1952, Marie had the opportunity to take a missions trip herself. Accompanied by Hattie Hammond, she traveled to the World Pentecostal Conference in London, and afterward, the two women ministered throughout Europe.[25]

Ever popular, Marie's Sunday afternoon sermons were always preached to a full house.[26] She was also a favorite speaker at General Councils over the years, addressing the Memorial Service at the 1933 Council and speaking at a Monday morning council service in 1951.[27] In 1967 the chair of the Council, Thomas F. Zimmerman, called on her to bring greetings, recognizing her as having been pastor of Glad Tidings for the past sixty years.[28]

Following her death on 3 June 1971, her body lay in state at Glad Tidings Tabernacle from Saturday until Monday morning during four memorial services. Among the many who preached was retired general superintendent Williams.[29]

Perhaps the best-known minister's wife among the Assemblies of God constituency was Alice Reynolds Flower, co-founder in 1913 with her husband of the *Christian Evangel*. J. Roswell was in almost continuous leadership in the fellowship from its inception until his death in 1970 and she came to be known as "Mother" Flower, reflecting her unofficial role as matriarch of the Assemblies of God. Their home produced three district superintendents, a missionary,[30] and Joseph, a general secretary like his father.

Born in Indiana on 21 November 1890, Alice Marie Reynolds had a strong religious heritage. Her paternal grandfather, Samuel Reynolds, a Quaker, smuggled slaves to freedom from his station on the Underground Railroad. Her mother was healed through the prayers of a Quaker minister a decade before Alice was born.[31] Though her parents were

25. "In Loving Memory," 8.

26. Cortese, interview by author, 18 March 1987.

27. General Council minutes, 1933, 105; and General Council minutes, 1951, 23. See also, Brown, "Pentecost, the Calvary Road," 3, 12.

28. General Council minutes, 1967, 34.

29. "Marie Brown with Christ," 7; and Williams, "A Personal Tribute," 7.

30. All six of their children became Assemblies of God ministers, except one who died while a student at Central Bible Institute. See Earle, "Her children," 4. Earle was a daughter.

31. Overstreet, "Mother Flower Remembers," 4B.

Methodists, they became charter members of the Gospel Tabernacle in Indianapolis, a Christian and Missionary Alliance church.

It was at the Tabernacle in 1907 that Alice received the Pentecostal experience during revival meetings with Glen Cook. During those same meetings, Roswell, then a young law student, was converted, and they were married in 1911. Beginning her ministry as a teenage evangelist, the young bride was first ordained by D. W. Myland and other Indiana elders in June 1913, the same month the *Christian Evangel* began publication. Her husband traveled to the first General Council in Hot Springs the following year where he was elected secretary; during that time, she stayed home and published the *Evangel*.

In 1926, shortly after her husband left the Springfield, Missouri, headquarters to take a pastorate in Pennsylvania, Alice was ordained by the General Council. Her certificate listed her as an assistant pastor until 1929 when she was designated as an evangelist until she was superannuated in 1960.[32] Her primary ministry was in a supportive role. Speaking of her life with her husband, she once explained, "We were a team." They were in the ministry together, and she assisted her husband "in every undertaking in which he participated."[33] Her most consistent ministry posts were at Central Assembly of God, in Springfield, Missouri, where she taught an adult Sunday school class for nearly fifty years and led a prayer group for almost as long.[34]

By the time of her death in 1991, Mother Flower had authored 16 books, 100 poems, and numerous Sunday school lessons and other devotional writings.[35] Though she had been a prolific communicator, her writings reflected few of her views on women in ministry. Her husband's response to one couple may at least reflect the official family position. A minister wrote Roswell in 1947 requesting a clergy certificate for his wife to be used for rail discounts. In his letter he noted that his wife was of the belief that "as long as one's husband is ordained it is unnecessary for women" to be ordained. The exception would be single women who were pastoring churches or women who were serving as missionaries.[36] Flower replied that the woman's convictions were appreciated and he

32. A. R. Flower, Ministers' file.
33. Kleeman, "Mother Flower," 48–49.
34. Shedd, interview by author, 4 February 1987.
35. Overstreet, "Mother Flower Remembers," 4B.
36. Letter from Rahner to J. R. Flower, 18 January 1947.

"would be happy if a good many more of our married ministers would have the same view."[37] Flower wrote that response knowing that his wife had been ordained continuously for two decades at the time of that correspondence; however, she never sought the limelight, preferring to play a secondary role to her husband.

Zelma Argue began her evangelistic campaigns as a young girl, assisting her father, A. H. Argue, in meetings throughout Canada. She and her brother, Watson, forged a long-lasting ministry team in those early years. Launching campaigns on her own, she gave herself to evangelistic work from 1920 to 1947. Then she co-pastored in Los Angeles until 1957 when she returned to the evangelistic field, retiring in 1964.

Though Zelma was considered a Canadian, she was born in North Dakota, and received her ordination from the General Council since the Pentecostal Assemblies of Canada did not ordain women until 1986. Afterwards, her ministry took her throughout the United States and Canada, as well as to the South Pacific, Australia and New Zealand. A prolific writer, she died at the age of eighty on 29 January 1980.[38]

The most controversial woman minister in the Assemblies of God after Aimee Semple McPherson was Myrtle D. Beall, pastor of Bethesda Tabernacle in Detroit, Michigan. Her involvement in the fellowship was a short-lived ten years, but her impact was meteoric.

At the age of forty in 1937, Beall was ordained by the Central District. Married and the mother of three, she had already been active in ministry since 1930. Interestingly, she was ordained to the ministry as an evangelist although she was a pastor.[39] By 1945, her church, which she had founded, reported an average attendance of five hundred at the Sunday morning service and Sunday school and an even greater eight hundred at the evening service, a sizeable congregation for the day.[40]

During the period of 1947–52, there was a general evangelical awakening, evidenced in part by renewed emphasis on divine healing and the emergence of Billy Graham. In one movement which arose during this time, stress was placed on the imminent return of Jesus Christ, to be preceded by the outpouring promised in Joel 2:23, and thereby giving rise to the movement's name, the "New Order of the Latter Rain."

---

37. Letter from J. R. Flower to Rahner, 28 January 1947.
38. "Zelma Argue with Christ," 7.
39. Beall, Application form.
40. "Annual Report for 1945," Bethesda Missionary Temple.

Originating within the Pentecostal Assemblies of Canada, the movement emphasized a strong congregationalism with local authority committed to a restored order of apostles.[41] Dispensation of gifts came through the laying on of hands.[42]

The movement did not gain widespread notice until it entered the United States, primarily through Beall's efforts. She visited a meeting of the Canadian group in Vancouver in 1948, and then invited some of the leaders to come to her church to preach. After several months of inter-action and visits, Beall came to accept their teaching. In January of the following year, Frodsham, by then retired as editor of *The Pentecostal Evangel*, visited her church and came away convinced that this was a new movement inspired by God. Subsequently, he resigned his credentials with the Council.

Quickly the new teaching was seen as a major threat to the stability of the fellowship. In April 1949, the *Quarterly Letter* of the General Council sent to ministers described Beall and Detroit as a hub of ministry for the new doctrine.[43] At the same time, general superintendent Williams wrote to Beall expressing concern about the teachings of the Latter Rain movement, especially the bestowing of gifts by the laying on of hands and the emphasis on personal prophecy.[44]

By August 1949, denominational leadership had taken official action against Beall for her role. Perhaps realizing that she was no longer welcome, she wrote a letter to the Executive Presbytery resigning her credentials:

> Having received a fresh revelation of the Body of Christ, and knowing that all saved people everywhere belong to the Body, I feel it is the will of God for me to be free to serve and fellowship all members of the church which is His Body. This of course would necessitate my withdrawal from any denominational group. in view of this revelation I hereby tender to the General

41. The designation "apostle" as a position or office in the church had been considered by the Assemblies of God and most other American Pentecostal denominations to have ended with the New Testament church. However, some contemporary groups, such as the Latter Rain movement, have acknowledged the offices of apostle and prophet as well as evangelist, pastor, and teacher, as found in Ephesians 4.

42. Riss, "The Latter Rain Movement," 32–45.

43. "Quarterly Letter," 28 April 1949, 2.

44. Letter from Williams to Beall, 28 April 1949.

> Council of the Assemblies of God my resignation as an ordained
> minister.[45]

She was immediately informed by Flower that she could not resign because the district presbytery had already dropped her from the fellowship
on 20 August, four days before. The ground for such action was her extremely critical and antagonistic attitude toward the Assemblies of God
on the issues of gifts and prophecy.[46]

In September, Williams brought the issue to the annual meeting of
the General Presbytery. He recommended that *The Pentecostal Evangel*
reprint a series written by R. E. McAlister of Canada that had run in the
Truth Advocate and that was a vigorous defense against the teachings of
the new movement. The presbytery agreed, and the series was published
shortly afterwards.[47]

At the General Council, which immediately followed the presbytery
meeting in Seattle, a resolution was adopted that denounced some of the
practices of the Latter Rain.[48] Two years later, Flower reported that the
fallout from the controversy had been minimal, with few ministers and
churches withdrawing from the denomination.[49] The controversy had
ended quickly and quietly. Meanwhile, Beall and her church, later known
as Bethesda Missionary Temple, continued to remain a center for the new
teaching.

Attitudes in the Establishment

A cartoon appearing in the *Evangel* in 1952 depicted a preacher thunder-
ing from the pulpit, "And women have no right to a public ministry!"
Over his head the artist had drawn the hand of God holding several biblical characters identified as Miriam, Deborah, the daughters of Philip,
Priscilla, and Huldah. The caption read, "He had better look again."[50]

The defense of liberty for women was directed outward toward other
denominations. While the cartoon was in keeping with the perspective of

---

45. Letter from Beall to the Executive Presbytery, 24 August 1949.
46. Letter from J. R. Flower to Beall, 30 August 1949.
47. General Presbytery minutes, 1949, 5.
48. General Presbytery minutes, 1949, 26–27.
49. General Council reports, 1951, 8–9.
50. Ramsey, "Look Again," cartoon, 8.

church leadership in defending the role of women in ministry, a double standard was evident regarding matters of authority and headship.

In his many years as editor of the Evangel, Frodsham wrote little on the subject of women in ministry. Still, his earlier openness to Woodworth-Etter's ministry in 1912 and his eventual receptivity to Beall spoke strongly of his respect for women in leadership.

His views on the subject were expressed in a 1933 editorial on the Old Testament character, Barak. Frodsham called on his readers to treat women ministers with respect. "Barak had respect for the anointing that rested upon this woman of God [Deborah], and I believe the Lord would have us also have respect for God's anointing whether it rests on man or woman."

Frodsham stated that Paul had no objection to women praying or prophesying in the assembly (1 Tim 2:11–12). He appealed to Joel's prophecy for the validity of women ministering and echoed Dowie's reference to the Revised Version of Ps 68:11: "The Lord giveth the word: the women that publish the tidings are a great host." He concluded, "Don't let us, in zeal for the letter of Scripture, attempt to stifle this God-given ministry of Spirit-filled women."[51]

For Williams, the doctrine of headship was the primary consideration on the issue of women in ministry. Basing his belief on the writings of Peter and Paul, he wrote that "God has placed headship in the man." Women are commanded to be obedient (1 Cor 14; 1 Pet 3:1). While women are not to assume authority over men either in the home or in the church (1 Tim 2:11–14), they can be of much assistance. If they teach, they do so under male leadership. Philip's daughters spoke under the anointing of the Spirit, but they recognized that their headship was in their father.[52]

Referring to the Old Testament prophetess, Huldah, Williams defended the role of women in spiritual ministry under proper authority. "We see no reason why women should be denied the blessing of spreading the established doctrines of the church in the power of the Spirit of God."[53]

In 1929, *The Pentecostal Evangel* devoted almost an entire page to Williams's question-and-answer column, with all queries referring to the

---

51. Frodsham, "The Editor's Notebook," 10 June 1933, 4.

52. Williams, "May Women Preach?"

53. Williams, "Sunday's Lesson," 8.

conduct of women in the church. Scripture, Williams wrote, does not record any woman being appointed to be an elder, meaning pastor. However, if a woman were serving as pastor, she should reserve herself for such ministry as preaching the Word. Qualified men should be found to take care of communion, baptizing, burying, and marrying.[54] Two years later, the status of women ministers in the General Council would be restricted more than at any other time in the movement's history. Eldership and ministerial functions would be the central concerns.

The issue of women keeping silent continued to be a popular one, Williams observing that several *Evangel* readers had written in concerning the matter. First, taking up the passage in Paul's letter to Timothy, he noted that teaching and preaching were not the same, implying that teaching carried an authoritative connotation. Basing his answer on Young's Concordance, he wrote that to preach was to bear good news, and he continued by linking preaching and prophesying, citing various passages as references (Luke 24; Rom 16:12; Acts 18:26; Ps 68:11; Philip's daughters). While proclaiming that women were forbidden to have authority over men, he declared that women working in cooperation with men in the ministry were not usurping authority. Williams dismissed the 1 Corinthians passage on silence as being an admonishment regarding the practice of women calling across the aisle to ask questions of their husbands in assembly.[55]

For the next forty years, Williams continued to answer questions on the silence issue, contending always that Paul was appealing for order and not confusion. He argued that women should be modest and should recognize man's dominant position, stating that women were out of place when they sought to govern or advance new doctrines. According to Williams, Paul was not restricting women from preaching under male authority.[56]

A less common question was whether women could anoint with oil when praying for the sick. At issue was Jas 5:14, which connected this responsibility with the elders of the church. Williams restricted eldership to men but saw no reason to restrict women from anointing with oil because of this one passage.[57]

---

54. Williams, "Questions and Answers, 20 April 1929, 9.

55. Williams, "Questions and Answers, 20 April 1929, 9.

56. Williams, "Questions and Answers," 21 July 1934, 7; "Your Questions," 3 July 1960, 11; and "Your Questions," 19 April 1964, 20.

57. Williams, "Questions and Answers," 11 March 1939, 4; and "Your Questions,"

Whether in ministry or in secular work, Williams taught that a woman's first responsibility was to her home if she was married or a mother. "Home needs mother"; therefore, women should not have to work outside the home. Williams deplored day-care options and the idea of children coming home from school to a house devoid of parents.[58]

In a short undated treatise entitled "Women's Ministry," renowned Pentecostal scholar Frank Boyd rebutted the arguments of those who would use 1 Corinthians 14 and 1 Timothy 2 to silence women from participating in any public ministry. He wrote that such persons do not fully subscribe to what they officially forbid.[59]

Four women—all prophetesses from the pre-church period—are presented as models of women in ministry: Miriam, Deborah, Huldah, and Anna. Deborah, he declared, especially demonstrated two virtues that were beautifully blended: prophetic gift and womanly subordination.[60]

From both the Old and New Testaments, passages were cited that confirmed the testimony of women of faith, but Boyd's main concern was with 1 Corinthians 14. He contended that far from prohibiting women from speaking, Paul affirmed that "all may prophesy." According to Boyd, Paul was not silencing, but regulating. He was attempting to bring order out of disorder, and his statement regarding women was related to their lack of subordination to male headship.[61] Earlier in 1 Corinthians 11, Paul had recognized women's right to pray and prophesy.[62]

Boyd next considered Paul's injunction to Timothy: "I permit not a woman to teach." Here again the issue was one of authority. The teacher in this passage was one who exercised authority in the church. "Hence, the passage only teaches 'that a woman shall not usurp a place of rule in the church, or arrogate to herself any position which would involve leadership, such as accompanies the administration of the ordinances and the enforcing of the discipline of the church,' or the formulation of doctrine or church practice."[63] He also explained that submission of the woman

---

19 April 1959, 13.

58. Williams, "Your Questions," 27 August 1961, 11.

59. Boyd, "Women's Ministry," 3.

60. Boyd, "Women's Ministry," 6.

61. Boyd, "Women's Ministry," 8.

62. Boyd, "Women's Ministry," 11.

63. Boyd, "Women's Ministry," 13.

applied only to her husband or near male relative. Paul did not give "any promicuous [sic] privilege to other men to lord it over her."[64]

Boyd concluded his treatise by reminding his readers of the promise of Joel's prophecy and pointing out what ministry positions were available to women: missionary, Bible reader, Scripture teacher of children, evangelist, deaconess, helper, and servant in the church. "Every Bible-taught, lovely handmaiden of the Lord will joyfully recognize man's headship, while at the same time be gratefully aware of her joint-heirship with him in Christ."[65]

64. Boyd, "Women's Ministry," 12.
65. Boyd, "Women's Ministry," 15.

15

Decline and Thaw
(1977–80s)

General and District Councils

FROM 1935 THROUGH THE 1980s, no changes were made in official national policy, with the exception of the 1977 General Council. Much of the wording of the 1935 resolution had been deleted at some earlier point bringing requirements for men and women into greater uniformity. The statement prior to the 1977 change read: "The Scriptures plainly teach that while there is a difference between the ministry of men and women in the church, divinely called and qualified women may also serve the church in the ministry of the Word. Women who may have demonstrated a distinct ministry of evangelism and who have met the requirements of district councils may be licensed to preach the Word."[1]

Functionally, nothing was altered at the 1977 Council, but in the bylaws all wording that had made a distinction between men and women ministers was eliminated. In addition, the Council incorporated a stronger statement on the scriptural basis for women in ministry: "The Scriptures plainly teach that divinely called and qualified women may also serve the church in the ministry of the Word (Joel 2:29; Acts 2:19; 1 Cor 11:5)."

Although the ordination of women gradually became less restricted in practice, only exceptionally did women serve as senior pastors, and

1. General Council minutes, 1975, 95.

they were not granted the privilege of denominational "eldership."[2] Restriction on women receiving credentials lay not with the General Council bylaws, but with their interpretation by individual districts, which were more directly responsible for the credentialing process. For example, in the old Eastern District (New York, New Jersey, Delaware, and Pennsylvania prior to the 1950s), pastors' wives were responsible for interviewing women applicants for ministerial recognition.[3] The district was led in those days by conservative men such as Robert Brown, Joseph Tunmore, and Williams.

For a considerable time, the New Jersey District maintained an official policy more restrictive than that of the General Council. Ordination for women could be prompted and granted only by the initiative of the executive committee.[4] In the mid-sixties, a section on "Instructions to Candidates" was added to the district yearbook. It included this statement: "Women may be granted recognition in any degree in the ministry with the exception of eldership."[5]

While the actual bylaws were not changed specifically regarding ordination of women, a change in 1969 in the General Council wording replacing the generic term "elders" with "ordained ministers" led to a whole new interpretation by the New Jersey District.

Now women candidates were instructed that they could be granted recognition at any level except ordination. They were also specifically told that they would be allowed to "serve as evangelists or pastors to the extent that their qualifications warrant and their ministries are acceptable to the churches."[6] No such special stipulation was directed toward male candidates. Ironically, the bylaws still allowed for ordination of women, though only through executive committee initiative. In 1975 and 1976, special statements on women were deleted from both the bylaws and the instructions to candidates.[7] Policy exercised in the New Jersey District,

---

2. Denominational eldership in the Assemblies of God organization refers specifically to the positions of officer and presbyter at any level above the local church—sectional, district, and general (national).

3. Joseph R. Flower, interview by author, 10 January 1986.

4. 1962 Yearbook, New Jersey District Council, 15 (Bylaws article V, sections 1:4 and 2:1).

5. 1965–66 Yearbook, New Jersey District Council, 40.

6. 1970–71 Yearbook, New Jersey District Council, 41.

7. 1975–76 Yearbook, New Jersey District Council, 32–33, 60–61; and 1976–77 Yearbook, New Jersey District Council, 33, 61.

its members suggested, should conform more closely with the wording of the General Council bylaws. Some minimal, though powerful, sentiment against ordaining women continued in the district leadership. Then at the 1981 district council women were ordained for the first time in more than two decades.[8]

The Ohio District continued through the 1980s to use restrictive language in its bylaws. Women were allowed to be ordained and serve as evangelists or pastors, whichever their qualifications warranted. "The right to administer the ordinances of the church, when such are necessary, shall be included in the ordination." But the same paragraph specifically stated that women "may not hold executive office."[9]

Comparison with Other Organizations

In the forty-year period of 1930–70, the percentage of women clergy in the United States increased only from 2.2 percent to 2.9 percent, according to United States census data. A National Council of Churches survey in 1977 found that women comprised 2.2 percent of the total clergy force in the nation, compared to 1.9 percent a quarter century before. Of the 211 church bodies included in the survey seventy-six ordained both men and women, eighty-seven ordained men only, and ten placed women in special categories. Among the groups ordaining both men and women, women comprised 4 percent of the clergy, and nearly two-thirds of these women were in Pentecostal groups or service organizations, which had ordained women for years. The Salvation Army alone accounted for 29 percent of all ordained women in the country.[10]

American women ministers might have been more prevalent in Pentecostal and service organizations than in other groups; however, Pentecostals did not make it easy for women to be ordained. The limitations on women by the Assemblies of God were akin to those established in other Pentecostal bodies. More restrictive in its stand, the Church of God (Cleveland, Tennessee) ordained men only, and only ordained ministers could vote in the General Council. Women could be licensed and as such

---

8. The author's mother, Anita R. (Osgood) Kenyon, was one of the women ordained. Perhaps the previous lone exception, Sarah Bergstrom had been ordained in the 1950s about the time her husband was serving as district superintendent. Paproski, interview by author, 18 March 1987.

9. 1981 Yearbook, Ohio District Council, 23.

10. "Very Few Women," 9.

pastor a church; however, unlike licensed men, they could not perform baptisms, communion, marriages, or other ceremonial functions, and they served as pastors only under the supervision of the district pastor.[11]

The Open Bible Standard Churches had their roots in the Apostolic Faith group led by Florence Crawford. Somewhat in reaction to her leadership, the splinter group accepted women ministers, but refused for them to hold executive positions in the denomination.[12]

The Pentecostal Church of God, a white oneness group headquartered in Joplin, Missouri, carried a nearly identical restriction to the General Council, though its constitution was much more explicit. Basing its statement on Joel 2 and Acts 2, it acknowledged that daughters as well as sons shall prophesy. Women, duly called and anointed by God, could serve as helpers, pastors, and evangelists. However, because of 1 Timothy 2, "all executive positions in the district and the national movement shall be occupied by men."[13] What the Assemblies of God unofficially practiced, the Pentecostal Church of God legislated.

Fellowships related to the Assemblies of God in other countries varied in how they accepted women in ministry. Generally, cultural mores played a dominant role. In Latin America, even American missionary women had a difficult time finding acceptance. Such was not the case in East Asia. Oddly, the Pentecostal Assemblies of Canada did not ordain women until 1986.

Three mainline churches—the American Baptist Churches, the Christian Church (Disciples of Christ), and the United Church of Christ—had predecessors who began ordaining women in the nineteenth century, and in 1978 they together accounted for 52 percent of the ordained women in the ten major Protestant churches which ordained women.[14] The American Baptist Convention ordained women as pastors since at least the 1890s, although women made up only 1.8 percent of all ordained ministers in the convention. In the Disciples of Christ and the United Church of Christ, the percentages were somewhat higher at 5.7 and 4.2 percent respectively. However, in the Disciples, women served on

---

11. Case, *Church of God Polity*, 181–85.

12. Mitchell, *Heritage and Horizons*, 47–48.

13. Constitution and bylaws, 1981 Minutes, and Directory, Pentecostal Church of God, 35.

14. "Very Few Women," 9.

all the governing boards of the major units of the church and on regional boards, with as much as a 50 percent representation on some boards.[15]

The Methodist church licensed women to preach from its earliest days; however, it was not until 1956 that all ordination restrictions regarding gender were officially removed and the General Conference voted "full clergy rights for women." By the early 1980s, the United Methodist Church had more than a thousand ordained women, 67 percent of whom served as pastors in local churches. In 1980, the denomination elected its first woman bishop.[16]

Also, in 1956, women were approved for ordination by the General Assembly of the United Presbyterian Church, U.S.A. In 1978, this denomination counted 410 women out of a total ministry force of fourteen thousand, with most of those women being ordained in the 1970s. Of the 5,431 ordained clergy in the Presbyterian Church, U.S., 145 were women.[17]

Lutheran and Southern Baptist churches were even slower at including both genders. While the American Lutheran Church and the Lutheran Church in America had less than a hundred ordained women each by 1981, this figure was expected to increase rapidly due to a sharp rise in women seminarians.[18] The Lutheran Church—Missouri Synod continued to be opposed to women in ministry. Likewise, the Southern Baptist Convention refused credentials to women, although since local churches are responsible for ordaining ministers, some exceptions were made. Out of 33,000 ordained pastors and a total of 55,000 ministers, only about a hundred of these were women in 1982.[19]

Even if a denomination ordained women, they were not necessarily welcome into pastoral positions. According to a National Council of Churches survey, only 1,600 of 10,470 clergywomen were serving as pastors of local churches by the late 1970s.[20] The most rapid increase in women clergy seemed to come in denominations which had only recently relaxed restrictions. Meanwhile, Pentecostal groups such as the

15. "Very Few Women," 9; and Howe, *Women and Church Leadership*, 139–40, 146–48.

16. Howe, *Women and Church Leadership*, 153–55.

17. Howe, *Women and Church Leadership*, 156–58.

18. Howe, *Women and Church Leadership*, 148–52. The two denominations later merged to form the Evangelical Lutheran Church of America.

19. Howe, *Women and Church Leadership*, 142–46.

20. Kunz, "Women and the Evangelical Movement," 161.

Assemblies of God who had had a long history of ordaining women experienced a decreasing role for such ministers in their ranks.

Women in the General Council 1970s–1980s

While women were officially less restricted from entering the ministry in the 1980s than in previous years, the percentage of credentialed women in general and women pastors in particular had decreased. In the decade of 1976–1986, the number of ordained and licensed ministers[21] in the Assemblies of God grew by 26.8 percent to a total of 26,439.[22] During approximately the same period, the number of women ministers grew by only 14.4 percent to 1,588.[23]

The most surprising statistics were evident when only ordained ministers were considered. In the same decade, the total of ordained women grew by only sixteen in number or 1 percent, compared to a total growth of ordained ministers of 23.7 percent.

What growth there had been in women ministers came at the licensed status. The total of ordained women actually decreased between 1984 and 1986 to its lowest level since 1977,[24] with much of the decline accounted for by comparing the median age of female versus male ministers. Aging women ministers, granted credentials in the earlier years of the fellowship, were not being replaced. In 1986, the median age for women ministers was sixty-four, compared to forty-four for men.[25]

In 1977, 15.5 percent of all ministers were women. By 1986 the percentage was 13.9 percent.[26] Of the 3,718 women ministers, 18 percent had never been married, 41.3 percent were married to another minister, and 19.6 percent were widowed.[27]

---

21. Unless otherwise stated, statistics refer to ordained and licensed ministers. Christian workers or exhorters are not included.

22. "Analysis of Rate Gain," 11 March 1986.

23. "A/G Female Ministers Report, 1977–1986," 22 January 1987.

24. The statistics were compiled by the writer from the two reports just cited from the Office of the Statistician.

25. "A/G Ministers by Age and Sex, 1985," 17 July 1986.

26. Compiled from "A/G Female Ministers Report, 1977–1986" and "Analysis of Rate Gain in Number of Assemblies of God Ministers—1976–1985."

27. Other categories are "married otherwise," "divorced," or "marital status unknown." "A/G Female Ministers Report, 1977–1986."

Other 1986 reports indicated that only 2.6 percent of all senior pastors were women, out of a total of 11,141.[28] The actual number of women pastors, home missionaries, and foreign missionaries had declined over the previous decade. Pastors decreased by 16 to 276 and home missionaries by 21 to 74. The most significant drop occurred among foreign missionaries, with a net decline of 100 to a new total of 209.[29]

In contrast to 1936 when there was one ordained female minister for every four males, by 1986 there was only one ordained female for every eight males. Similarly, the percentage of male adherents in the denomination had increased. Whereas in 1936 there were thirty-seven men for every sixty-three women in church attendance, the 1980 ratio was 45.7 men to 54.3 women, only 3 percent less than the 1980 ratio of the general United States population.[30]

In 1977, Gloria Jean Orengo became the first woman granted ecclesiastical endorsement for the military chaplaincy by the Assemblies of God Commission on Chaplains. At the time, there were only nine other women chaplains in the Armed Services. A graduate of Bethany Bible College, Orengo received her Master of Divinity degree from Southwestern Baptist Theological Seminary in Fort Worth.[31] Her ministry took her to Korea and the United States Air Force Academy in Colorado.[32]

By 1987 women still did not serve in any eldership roles beyond the local church. While there were a few women district youth presidents in the pioneering days of the youth program, such positions had been given almost exclusively to men in the thirty years prior to 1988. Three exceptions in the 1980s were Robyn Williams, who served the Northern California-Nevada District 1981–85, Brenda Baker (1982–86) of the tiny German District, and Jonna Gonzalez (1982–88) of the Southeastern Spanish District.[33] Otherwise, women had served at the district or national level only in women's ministries and programs, with Iola Smith, still district treasurer in New Jersey, being the outlier.

28. Compiled from "A/G Female Ministers Report, 1977–1986" and "Ministers Ministry Status, 1985," 10 March 1986.

29. These statistics do not include missionary wives who are not licensed or ordained. "A/G Female Ministers Report, 1977–1986."

30. "A/G Men-Women Ratio," 13.

31. "First woman chaplain," 29.

32. Orengo, "Serving God and Country," 4.

33. Confirmed with the office of the National Youth Department Secretary. 10 March 1988.

The number of prominent women ministers also declined. Gone were women evangelists of the caliber of Woodworth-Etter or McPherson who could attract thousands. One exception was Marilyn A. Hickey of Denver, Colorado, who garnered an international following as a radio and television personality. While she was only a licensed minister in the 1980s, her husband was ordained. Rare indeed was there a woman pastor of a sizeable church, like Beall in the 1940s.

One exception was Aimee Garcia Cortese. The first woman to preach in an evening session of a General Council since 1921, Cortese addressed the Saturday evening service at the 1979 Council in Baltimore, Maryland.[34] She had been licensed to preach with the Spanish Branch, New York, of the Assemblies of God in 1951, and was first ordained by the Wesleyan Methodist Conference of Puerto Rico in 1962 where she was serving as conference evangelist. For sixteen years (1951–62, 1965–68), she was associate minister with her father, Raphael Garcia, pastor of Thessalonica Christian Church (AG, Spanish Branch) in Bronx, New York.[35]

Then for three years, Cortese assisted her brother, State Senator Robert Garcia, as a legislative aide, working as a community liaison with housing, welfare, drug, and rehabilitation programs. In 1973, she became the first female chaplain for the Department of Corrections for the State of New York.[36] For the next decade Cortese ministered at Bedford Hills, Ossining (Sing-Sing), Taconic, and Bayview Corrections Facilities. Her work with both male and female inmates included teaching, counselling, special services, family involvements, and preaching. She also assisted the inmates after release during the time of reentry.[37]

A desire to help with preventive work led Cortese back into local church ministry. In 1983, she founded Crossroads Tabernacle in the Bronx[38] and served as the full-time pastor of the church which by 1987 grew to an attendance of over six hundred.

Her husband, Joseph Cortese, licensed with the Assemblies of God in 1983, helped her found Crossroads Tabernacle, assisting with administrative responsibilities; however, his primary interest was music. When

34. General Council minutes, 1979, 42.
35. Cortese, interview by author, 18 March 1987.
36. Pakkala, "Confident in Christ," 3.
37. Letter from Cortese to author, 1 February 1987.
38. Pakkala, "Confident in Christ," 4.

his wife traveled, he was her minister of music, accompanying their musically talented daughters on the piano.[39] In the sixties, both served with the Billy Graham Evangelistic Team in South America.[40]

Aimee Cortese traveled extensively, appearing frequently on Christian television, and preaching in churches, women's groups, colleges and conventions. She served as a delegate to the first Congress on Evangelism in West Berlin in 1966, where she was one of only eight women among twelve hundred male delegates.[41] In 1984, she was a plenary speaker at the Second National Conference on the Holy Spirit in Springfield, Missouri.[42]

Her desire to preach followed shortly after her conversion as a teenager which took place at a meeting conducted by Dr. Charles Fuller in the old Madison Square Garden. She knew little about preaching, having grown up in a traditional church. However, her mother had told her of a meeting she had attended at the Garden shortly before Aimee was born when the speaker had been Aimee Semple McPherson. Aimee Garcia's mother had named her daughter after the famous evangelist and consecrated her to the Lord's service.

When Cortese was appointed a chaplain in 1973, her district—the Spanish Eastern—did not ordain women. General Council officials heard about her chaplaincy appointment and requested that the New York District ordain her which it agreed to do. In 1974, she was ordained by Joseph R. Flower, then district superintendent.[43]

Attitudes in the Fellowship

Overall in the 1980s, there tended to be a positive attitude expressed towards women in ministry. In 1984, *The Pentecostal Evangel* ran an article on Pastor Audrey Lee Hobson of Woodville, California. Growing up in a Free Will Baptist church in Oklahoma, Hobson had felt the call of God on her life, but it was not until age fifty-nine that she entered the ministry. Married to a layman, she often preached in missions and was active in her local church. Her three sons all became Assemblies of God pastors.

39. Cortese, interview by author, 18 March 1987.

40. Pakkala, "Confident in Christ," 4.

41. Cortese, interview by author, 18 March 1987.

42. "Speakers Announced for Conference," 25.

43. Cortese, interview by author, 18 March 1987.

Eventually, she applied for credentials herself and was ordained. After her husband took early retirement, she assumed a pastorate. The congregation was very receptive with attendance increasing "dramatically."[44]

In the early 1970s, radio evangelist C. M. Ward, wrote an article extolling the validity of women serving in the ministry.[45] The response was mixed. One California reader applauded the article but questioned why the voices of women were "so strangely silent in our Movement today?"[46] Another reader from Maryland attacked the "half-truths" he found in the article. "Everything I find in my Bible places man in authority over women." He wrote that God has a chain of command, and man is one step higher in that chain than woman.[47]

A month later another reader responded to the first letter which had deplored the lack of women in the ministry. He wrote in great praise of his woman pastor, Helen Wight, who had co-pioneered and co-pastored their church until her husband had died, whereupon she had continued as pastor. "Men and women alike are included in the outpouring of the Holy Spirit in our New England area," he wrote.[48]

Other readers later responded affirming women ministers. One woman, for example, questioned why a news article had appeared in the *Evangel* entitled, "Bishop gives reason not to ordain woman." Such an article was inappropriate inasmuch as the Assemblies of God ordained women. The reader concluded that if God made no distinctions ("neither male nor female"), "why should we?"[49] Another reader responded to the first reader, not discounting women in ministry, but affirming that men "should stand up and take the authority God has given them before we women perish."[50]

In 1977, *The Pentecostal Evangel* carried a review of a book entitled *The Magna Carta of Woman.* Originally published in England in 1919, it was authored by a Pentecostal woman minister whose life had been linked with F. B. Meyer, Andrew Murray, and D. L. Moody. The message of the book was that women should not sit idle, but that they should

44. Hobson, "'Sister Pastor,'" 19.
45. Ward, "His Handmaidens," 2.
46. Pfrimmer, letter to the editor, 16 July 1972, 24.
47. Lester, letter to the editor, 16 July 1972, 24.
48. Towler, letter to the editor, 27 August 1972, 25.
49. Rabe, letter to the editor, 27 April 1975, 30.
50. Rohlinger, letter to the editor, 22 June 1975, 30.

respond to the call of God on their lives. The reviewer stated that it was not a new message for Pentecostals because women had had a vital role in the church, but it did have merit for reading by those who questioned such a role.[51]

Three women ministers were featured in a 1984 *Evangel* article on singles which attempted to present positive role models of Christian singles in ministry. None of the women chosen were senior pastors, but two of them were ordained. Lynn Carter was responsible for youth and children's ministries at the Arlington (Virginia) Assembly of God. Debbie Menken, assistant professor of Greek New Testament at North Central Bible College in Minneapolis, later earned a PhD degree from Fuller Theological Seminary. A teacher in colleges and seminaries in the United States as well as the Far East, she had also served as a singles pastor and youth pastor. Cheri Colquhoun, a licensed minister, was then minister of Christian education at Calvary Temple in Wayne, New Jersey.[52]

Various Assemblies of God colleges highlighted women in ministry from time to time. Southeastern College, for example, conducted a week-long seminar, focusing on single and married women in various settings of ministry.[53]

Joseph Flower's Paper

By far the most extensive and definitive study on the role of women in the church by a denominational leader in the Assemblies of God prior to 1990 was an unpublished paper by Joseph R. Flower, general secretary of the General Council.[54] In his paper, dated 1983, Flower attempted to consider the issue from as many aspects as possible. He surveyed the official Council position, the actual number of women ministers in the fellowship, psychological and physiological differences, social customs, Old Testament perspectives, considerations from the Gospels and the book of Acts, and, particularly, the writings of Paul. While the paper was not an official denominational document, it came as close to an official

51. Penn-Lewis, *The Magna Carta of Woman*, 30.

52. Reddout, "Focus on Singles," 6–7.

53. "Southeastern Salutes Women," 28.

54. Flower, "Does God Deny." The unpublished paper went through several editions over several years, beginning in 1978. Each edition, through the 1980s, was updated for most recent data, but remained substantively unchanged. The copy presented this author by Flower is dated 1983.

interpretation as anything else written to that date on women in ministry simply because of Flower's position in the Council.

He began by positing the premise that "there is harmony and consistency in God's revealed truth." Flower then affirmed that there had been from the beginning of the modern Pentecostal movement "a recognition that God does call women to various aspects of ministry to the church."[55] With these two premises as bases, the paper's goal was to establish a perspective on the issue.

Early in the paper, Flower appeared to be defending the approval of women in General Council ministry against its detractors. There is no way any of these women ministers could be accused of "an arrogation of powers or usurpation of authority over the man" (1 Tim 2:12), since they minister under the authority of the Council and at the free choice of those whom they serve. He then presented the scriptural position of those who deny women a ministry role.[56]

Before responding directly to the question of authority, Flower elaborated on various other considerations, such as that men and women are created in God's image even though they are physically and emotionally different. Emotionally, women are disposed to being more receptive, intuitive, protective, and capable of sympathy and compassion. Flower wrote that while women are referred to as the weaker vessel (1 Pet 3:7), they are not necessarily inferior intellectually or morally. If anything, they would rate higher than men in morality and adherence to revealed truth.[57]

Flower noted that the conjugal relationship is clearly defined in Scripture. A woman's desire is to her husband and he will rule over her (Gen 3:16). Wives are to submit to their husbands as to the Lord (Eph 5:22; Col 3:18). Such submission is a voluntary act of the will, and because of this Flower strongly emphasized the responsibility of the husband. But his primary argument is that it is the husband-wife relationship which is the subject of these and other passages (including 1 Corinthians 11 and 14; and 1 Timothy 2).[58]

The social status of women was next considered. Flower noted that most nations and cultures have given women a second-class status, and

---

55. Flower, "Does God Deny," 1.
56. Flower, "Does God Deny," 2.
57. Flower, "Does God Deny," 3.
58. Flower, "Does God Deny," 4.

that this has often been true even in the religions of Judaism and Christianity. He believed that women have been particularly demeaned by the founders of Buddhism, Hinduism, Islam especially, as well as in such cultures as that of ancient Greece.[59]

The Old Testament appears to favor the male, but even here, Flower wrote, the woman is granted certain honors, rights, and privileges. He also made it clear that a distinction must be drawn between the picture gleaned from Scripture and the traditions which have accumulated through the years; that it is important to understand that woman's submission as connected with the curse after the Fall be contrasted to that role planned for Eve at creation; and that while the curse will be completely lifted in the future, believers benefit even now from Christ's redemption. "Christ's coming was like a breath of fresh air to the liberation of womanhood and the restoration of her dignity."[60]

> This . . . includes the release from male domination and subjugation of female under male headship and restores the mutual and complementary relationship which Adam and Eve shared before the Fall. . . . [Male headship] is based upon the order and design in creation rather than the consequences of the Fall, for man was first created, and the woman created to complement him and to be an helpmeet for him . . .[61]

Thus, authority is of the husband over the wife, not of men over women in general. It is not the extensive domination as depicted by some. The restrictions on women by the law of Moses in the Old Covenant were superseded by the New Covenant. Flower noted that women were included in the Spirit's outpouring on the Day of Pentecost just as Joel had predicted. "What became a fact on that day was designed as a pattern for all believers until Christ's return."[62] (Acts 2:33, 38, 39) Flower also mentioned that the New Testament contains numerous examples of women active in public proclamation, including Philip's four daughters.

With regard to Paul's writings in 1 Cor 11:16–18, Flower asserted that Paul did not dispute the right of women to pray and prophesy, but rather that his concern was that things be done properly. Paul's prohibition against women speaking at Corinth (1 Cor 14:34–35) did not relate

59. Flower, "Does God Deny," 5–6.
60. Flower, "Does God Deny," 6.
61. Flower, "Does God Deny," 7.
62. Flower, "Does God Deny," 9.

to ministry, Flower affirmed, but instead to women's practice of calling aloud to their menfolk about church affairs and events. Order, not silence, was Paul's concern.[63]

Flower continued his paper by writing that although it appears to some that Paul entertained a bias against women in his epistles, Paul recognized women in ministry roles and singled out a number of them for commendation. Flower affirmed the interpretation that Junia (Rom 16:7) was a woman and an apostle.[64] In affirming the apostleship of Junia, he made a clean break from all that had been written previously by Council leadership.

The general secretary then gave extensive documentation to prove that Paul's instruction to Timothy (1 Tim 2:11–15) was not designed to deprive women forever of a public ministry in the church and that, in fact, the context dealt with men and women praying. Verse eleven in the same chapter changed to a statement on the husband-wife relationship and the admonition that wives were to be subject to their husbands. Flower then firmly declared, "Wherever in the Scriptures women as a distinct class are indicated to be subject to men, it is always in the context of the marriage relationship."[65]

Concerning a woman not qualified to teach, Flower wrote that the woman of whom Paul spoke was arrogating to herself a position of authority to which she was not entitled and a function in teaching for which she was not equipped. Flower interpreted this to be entirely different from a recognition by the church of a woman's God-given ministry where she is indeed entitled and qualified, and contended that it is impossible to support the notion that "to teach" applies to an authoritative teacher.[66] Here Flower contradicted previous Assemblies of God writers such as Boyd, who assumed that Paul was prohibiting authoritative teaching by women.

As to the question of silence cited in the passage, Paul applied it to men as well as to women. According to Flower, it referred not to muteness, but to attitude. Paul's instruction to Timothy did not pertain to women with a God-given ministry, "but to bold women who are unqualified and who wrongfully attempt to teach and domineer over their

63. Flower, "Does God Deny," 10–12.

64. Flower, "Does God Deny," 13, 14.

65. Flower, "Does God Deny," 15.

66. Flower, "Does God Deny," 16.

husbands and others, but who instead need to learn with respectful and modest decorum."[67]

Regarding possible cultural implications, Flower wrote that Paul, when rightly understood, "gave a clear witness to the liberating principles of the gospel."[68] However, at times the apostle sought to bring an effective, if somewhat accommodating, witness even when he knew he could not by himself overturn the prevailing social order.

According to Flower, one of Paul's greatest statements was his "all one in Christ Jesus" proclamation, including "neither male nor female." Joel's prophecy also specifically included both genders. Spiritual gifts, in Paul's writings, were to be distributed to all members of the body. "There is no good reason to exclude spiritual gifts and ministries from the 'spiritual privileges' accorded Christian women."[69]

Flower refuted the notion that Paul's "husband of one wife" statement precluded the ordination of women, and he affirmed the interpretation of 1 Timothy 3 to include deaconesses. Attesting that one of the greatest contributions of the Protestant Reformation was the restoration of the truth of the priesthood of all believers, he wrote, "All believers, both men and women, are priests, and therefore all believers have a ministry to the entire body of Christ.[70]

Flower agreed that much progress had been made in the struggle for the liberation of women, but, quoting Theodore Weld, he stated, "the devil of dominion over women will be one of the last that will be cast out" of man. Still, Flower was not in accord with every act or all of the philosophy expressed by modern liberation proponents. He contended that true liberation will be scripturally sound, and that the goal should be to restore woman to the complementary role Eve had with Adam before the Fall. This would be the positive expression of Christ's redemptive work, of headship without domination. In conclusion, Flower urged, "The Christian church should be in the vanguard of any movement promoting true scriptural liberty for womanhood."[71]

Of all the writings by Assemblies of God leaders and scholars to that date, Flower's study most openly demonstrated an accepting attitude

67. Flower, "Does God Deny," 19.
68. Flower, "Does God Deny," 19.
69. Flower, "Does God Deny," 20.
70. Flower, "Does God Deny," 21.
71. Flower, "Does God Deny," 22.

toward full ministry by women. Certainly, he was no egalitarian. But, while his paper was not officially endorsed, he presented an alternative to what had become the dominant view in the church in recent years and even countered the restrictions established in 1914 regarding eldership.

Although Flower affirmed an eldership role for women, he saw no change in the denomination in his lifetime. No gender distinction is made from "headquarters" regarding eldership, but, he admitted, prejudice exists. Officially, there were no restrictions or prohibitions against women serving in the General Presbytery, but again he conceded, a woman achieving such a position in the foreseeable future was unlikely.[72]

Other Opinions

Two other articles reflected varying trends in the fellowship. One, by Joyce Wells Booze, provided an almost radical interpretation of Jesus's attitude toward women. The other, by *Evangel* editor Cunningham, displayed an open, if somewhat more traditional, approach to women in ministry.

In a 1987 article entitled "Let Georgia do it," Cunningham posed the question, "Why are there not more women in places of leadership in our churches?"[73] Demonstrating that women are not officially restricted from ministerial recognition by the General Council, he presented statistics to show that women are a small and declining force in the ranks of the clergy. At one time the movement championed the cause of women's ministry when women's participation was not popular with other churches. In the late 1980s, Assemblies of God women found it difficult to be accepted in public ministry.

While Cunningham acknowledged that women themselves were partly to blame for being "complacent and unwilling to take spiritual responsibility,"[74] he was also quick to point out that the greater issue was prejudice at the local level.

Cunningham's own writing exemplified the ambivalent attitude current at the time on the issue. He wrote that where men take the lead, women should follow since men have been granted headship by God. Yet, he declared, if men hold back, then women should be quick to obey the

---

72. Joseph R. Flower, interview by author, 10 January 1986.

73. Cunningham, "Let Georgia do it," 4–6.

74. Cunningham, "Let Georgia do it," 4.

Holy Spirit.[75] However, he also stated that if a woman is better qualified for a church position than any available man, "the fact she is a woman should not hold her back, nor should it keep the church from confirming her calling."[76]

Capping these ambiguous sentiments, Cunningham affirmed the unifying nature of the work of the Holy Spirit in the contemporary Pentecostal movement. "All of us must serve according to our gifts, not according to our gender.[77]

Joyce Wells Booze, an assistant professor of English at Central Bible College, took a very different tack by examining Jesus's attitude toward women as presented in the gospel of John. She wrote that it is evident that "John has portrayed Jesus as revolutionary in His attitude toward and treatment of women,"[78] and continued by stating that in a society where women were considered inferior, Jesus gave them equal, even superior treatment. Booze illustrated her point by using numerous examples, such as the woman of Samaria and Mary and Martha, the sisters of Lazarus.[79]

In the apostle's book, women occupy a prominent role; therefore, Booze wrote, it cannot be argued that women should be considered inferior to men in religious matters or relegated to minor roles of ministry in the church. "These revolutionary roles of women in John's Gospel provide a powerful delineation of ministry roles for women today."[80]

The Role of Women in Society

In general, the fellowship was moderately opposed to the modern women's liberation movement and particularly to the Equal Rights Amendment (ERA). Fully a year before the Supreme Court's historic decision on abortion, an article in the *Evangel* warned that society might soon grant women the right to abort or abandon their children. The primary warning of writer Ruth Copeland related to the push for equality. Copeland urged that some reform was needed, such as equal pay for equal work. What she deplored was the drive for erasing distinctions between men and women,

75. Cunningham, "Let Georgia do it," 5.

76. Cunningham, "Let Georgia do it," 6.

77. Cunningham, "Let Georgia do it," 6.

78. Booze, "Jesus and Women," 4.

79. Booze, "Jesus and Women," 5.

80. Booze, "Jesus and Women," 6.

especially in the home. "Their aim is to have complete social, economic, and sexual equality with men, with legalized abortion, and government-sponsored daycare centers provided for children of workers."[81]

This would produce undesirable results, Copeland argued. God had assigned specific roles to men and women. Some additional distinctions had come about as a result of the Fall, although women had been elevated through Christ. Nevertheless, she stressed, there were still definite spheres for men and women in which to act. "Children need both a father and a mother—not two 'unisex equal individuals.'"[82]

The following year the *Evangel* published a very positive review of a book entitled, *Woman Liberated*.[83] The theme of the book was that "Christianity as presented by Jesus Christ is never male-oriented nor female-oriented; it is person-oriented." The tenet expressed was that true liberation does not deny the inherent differences between man and woman but accepts them as given by God for fulfilling his purpose. The author of the book called for an end to discrimination against women in the church and for recognition of these complementary God-given roles.

In another article, C. M. Ward thundered that God's order was not to be tampered with. He affirmed the belief that Christ had elevated the position of women and that the Assemblies of God had recognized from its inception that God calls women into his service. Noting that many other groups had heretofore held women in inferior positions but now that the pendulum was swinging to the opposite extreme, he saw in these same groups a trend to place women in positions of supreme authority. Quoting Mary Daly, he wrote, "Radical femininity is not concerned with an equal slice of the pie but with *power*."[84] For Ward, it was this revolutionary contention which threatened to change every phase of society.

In responding to the ERA, the Assemblies of God tended to follow the judgement of the NAE in the issue, which was generally negative.[85] Constituents were quick to point out any apparently contrary opinions. An *Evangel* editorial on the subject of praying for the peace of Jerusalem called President Jimmy Carter "an outspoken Christian believer." One reader reprimanded the editor, objecting most to Carter's backing the

---

81. Copeland, "Wish to Be Equal," 6.

82. Copeland, "Wish to Be Equal," 7.

83. Clemens, *Woman Liberated*, reviewed by Hoover, 17 September 1972, 26.

84. Ward, "Women's Lib—Whither?" 5. His emphasis.

85. "NAE Women's President Says," 24.

ERA, and queried how the President could be such a great believer when he stood for such unbiblical ideas. Obviously, the reader indignantly declared, the *Evangel* editor could not have listed a person's stand on the amendment in his criteria for being a believer![86]

Another reader decried the focus on the feminist movement and its extensive criticism at the hands of Christians. Her concern was that the church had neglected the problems of rape, sexual harassment, and other indignities suffered by women. Instead, secular feminists, not Christians, had carried the banner for attention to such matters, imperatively calling for immediate redress.[87]

While the *Evangel* responded minimally to those concomitant sociological issues, Ward attacked what he called the new "bedroom evangelism." He deplored the notion that women should win their husbands over to their views through total submission, even seduction, arguing that such a mentality assumes that every believer-husband is essentially unfaithful, so wives must keep them interested. "Marriage, to survive, has to be built on something more than sex and servility," Ward wrote, and called for partnership in marriage, not ownership.[88]

Reader response was mixed and strong. One woman defended what she perceived was Ward's main target—*The Total Woman*—stating that the book had saved her marriage to her husband, an Assemblies of God minister.[89]

Other articles were published centering on man's responsibility in headship. Raymond T. Brock counseled husbands to be more sensitive, more communicative in their relationships with their wives.[90] Then in 1982 an article by the late A. W. Tozer of the Christian and Missionary Alliance was reprinted. In it, Tozer challenged husbands and wives to follow the rule of Scripture as the only way. He declared that neither is to be dominating, but both are to live in cooperation with each other and with the husband serving as head of the home. Tozer gave no place for harsh male rulership in a Christian home. but at the same time, he held that the wife must show consistent godliness and cooperativeness.[91]

---

86. Wilson, letter to the editor, 21 January 1979, 30.

87. Malmberg, letter to the editor, 27 January 1985, 30.

88. Ward, "The New 'Bedroom Evangelism,'" 12–13.

89. Letter to the editor, 25 April 1976, 30.

90. Brock, "When Is a 'Head' a Head?" 6–7.

91. Tozer, "Love and Obey," 7–8.

Rhonda J. Rusk opinioned that the world is trying to turn the home upside down. In her article she said that the man should be the spiritual leader of the home, but that this authority involves great responsibility. A husband must love his wife as Christ loves the church.[92] Elsewhere, Ross Byars affirmed the value of the mother in the home. "Children are what they are because mothers are what they are," he wrote.[93]

The *Evangel* was hesitant to discuss the issue of women working outside the home. In fact, by the time it did present an article related to working mothers, over half of the nation's mothers were employed. "This Mother's Day might be a great time to say a word in behalf of sincere Christian mothers who have to be employed outside the home," wrote Pastor E. S. Caldwell in 1981.[94] Citing the Old Testament mother Hannah as role model, Caldwell suggested that working mothers should not be condemned for placing their children in good child care settings. While the Bible nowhere extols a mother for refusing employment, Proverbs 31 praises an industrious woman. "So today we salute the godly Christian women who do their best to be the to be the kind of mothers their children need even while carrying the responsibility and burden of employment away from home."[95]

Response was emphatic and divided. One reader was surprised that such an off-balance article was published.[96] Others disagreed with Caldwell's exegetical use of Hannah and the woman of Proverbs 31 as role models.[97] Another reader affirmed the need to honor working mothers, but hoped that Pentecostals would not encourage women to work or "these trends which seem to be weakening the family life of our nation."[98] Two working women, who had each been in the job market for at least twenty years, wrote that they had been looking for such a good article for a long time.[99]

92. Rusk, "Will the Man," 4–5.

93. Byars, "Children Are," 3.

94. Caldwell, "Let Us Honor," 12.

95. Caldwell, "Let Us Honor," 13.

96. Impellizzeri, letter to the editor, 26 July 1981, 31.

97. Geiman, letter to the editor, 26 July 1981, 31; and Smith, letter to the editor, 26 July 1981, 31.

98. Owen, letter to the editor, 26 July 1981, 31.

99. Newman, letter to the editor, 26 July 1981, 31; Hahn, letter to the editor, 15 November 1981, 31.

A year later an article was printed about a young woman's conversion to Christ. While it never referred directly to her job, the pictures with accompanying captions depicted her at her desk at the *News-Press* in Fort Myers, Florida. Here was a career woman set in a positive light.[100]

100. Gentzler, "Being Born Again," 4–5.

16

Women in Ministry: A Dogmatic Ethic

THROUGH THE 1980S, FOUR periods may be identified in the approaches the Assemblies of God made to women in ministry. The first period was the pre-organizational era during which there were varying degrees of openness. Some of the influences which led to Pentecostalism were characterized by a general acceptance that God could and would call women to declare his Word. Women as famous as Woodworth-Etter or as obscure as Melvia Bocker were warmly received in pulpits all over the land. Even in some pre-Council organizations such as the CMA and the Indiana fellowship, women were given executive positions.

Then when the Council organized at Hot Springs, a second phase began. From the outset the General Council said "yes" to women ministers being accepted into the fellowship and "no" to women voting on business and serving in leadership. While the doors were opening to women voting in business sessions, they were closing to women preaching in Council services. In 1921, the first Council in which women could vote, Roxie Hughes Alford became the last woman to preach an evening Council meeting for the next sixty years. Women preachers and missionaries were still acceptable at the grassroots level, but women with extraordinary skills found themselves most useful outside the denomination. Carrie Judd Montgomery's greatest role was in interdenominational ministry. Aimee Semple McPherson founded her own denomination. While J. Roswell Flower may have been open and agreeable to having his wife ordained, the hesitations of Bell and others eventually swayed the movement against the ordination of women.

The third period began around 1927 with the reorganization of the General Council. Williams, general superintendent for the next two decades, maintained a very conservative attitude toward women in ministry. That perspective was expressed officially when ordination was not allowed for women during the early 1930s. But the greatest impact came after 1935 as the ranks of women ministers gradually dwindled. The role models then became pastors' wives such as Marie Brown and Mother Flower. Myrtle Beall and McPherson became shining examples of boisterous and insubordinate woman ministers. Officially, the Council approved the ordination of women in all types of ministry from 1935. Practically, women were severely restricted in seeking ordination and were never considered for denominational leadership.

When the fourth period began is difficult to pinpoint; 1977 might be a suitable year. The changes made in 1977 and the invitation to Cortese in 1979 at least symbolized a new attitude, though that attitude did not immediately translate into increased numbers of ordained women in the ranks. Looking at the pages of the *Evangel*, women ministers seemed to have been more accepted from the early 1970s on. However, by far the most significant "event" of this period was the appearance of Joseph Flower's paper. It was first prepared in 1978 with revised forms being distributed in the 1980s. Whether it would ever be endorsed by the Council or accepted by the rank and file was anybody's guess as late as 1988.

How the denomination would treat women in ministry in years to come was difficult to ascertain, but even someone as open as Joseph Flower thought it unlikely to change drastically from the policy of the time. On one side, pressures were building to make token accommodations to the growing role of women in society. On the other side, deep convictions urged guarding against any moves which might further weaken the family unit.

If Flower was correct—and he turned out to be—the door to executive leadership in the denomination would not open for the next generation. This door would probably have to open first at lower ecclesiastical positions, but resistance seemed to be stronger at the district level than at the national. Trends of the time indicated that fewer churches were accepting women as senior pastors, but other opportunities for ministry were growing. These included various staff positions inside the local church such as pastors for senior citizens and, outside, specialized ministries such as chaplaincy and campus ministry. In addition, some local churches were granting women lay eldership roles, specifically the office of deacon.

Predominant Views

Two fundamental and official positions toward women ministers remained basically unchanged from 1914. The first was that God will anoint and call women into service. The second was that the role of eldership is to be reserved exclusively for men. Variations in application of these two tenets had come in attempting to interpret the word "elder." For some, eldership included the roles of pastor and deacon; for others, it was limited to denominational executive leadership. Flower seemed to stand alone in considering that perhaps Paul did not exclude women from eldership at all.

At least four perspectives contributed to these two positions: The Age of the Spirit, strict allegiance to particular interpretations of Scripture, social accommodation, and institutionalization.

Gordon was prophetic in linking the Day of Pentecost and Joel's prophecy with greater freedom for women to preach. The holiness and Pentecostal movements, which proclaimed the Age of the Spirit, ushered in a whole new era for women. Soon there were women preaching in every town and hamlet. This emphasis on "the Age of the Spirit" has never enjoyed as much popularity as it did in the pioneer days, but it has been closely connected with how women have been accepted in ministry. Of the four, this perspective stands alone in opening doors to women.

Whereas Scripture was often ignored by the movement in defining racial policy, it was strictly adhered to in determining the role of women. The bottom line was what the Bible—particularly Paul—had to say on the topic. While Scriptures have been heavily referred to in making room for women, they have been mostly used to restrict women. Lengthy exegetical discourses have been held on the subject.

Barbara Brown Zickmund has written that these two perspectives, the Spirit and the Word, are fundamental in understanding the struggle for the right of women to preach in the nineteenth century. She suggested that the issue was divided into two camps. On one side, groups and individuals emphasizing the power of the Holy Spirit tended to call for increased female leadership. On the other side, groups and persons determined to preserve the authority of Scripture worked to maintain the status quo—to keep pastoring a male province.[1] Both camps maintained their adherents throughout the history of the Assemblies of God. As the fellowship shifted from a focus on the Holy Spirit to one on the authority of Scripture, it lost its vision of Gordon's "new economy."

The third perspective, social accommodation—brought on by an upward social mobility—is less obvious in its influence. No major shifts in position can be directly linked with social change. Subtly, however, the growing middle-class mentality made its impact. Women preachers found greater acceptance in the beginning of the movement because of its lower-class orientation. As the movement strove for status and acceptability, male leadership was preferred. Local churches might have been pioneered by women, but they "crossed the tracks" with men in the lead. Nancy Hardesty documented this trend in holiness and Pentecostal circles. She wrote that when Pentecostals move into the middle class, socially-defined status replaces Spirit-endued power. When classism develops, women lose their place.[2]

Barfoot and Sheppard have suggested that institutionalization has contributed most to shutting the door on the ordination of women. As with the CMA and other Pentecostal and holiness groups, increased organization in the Assemblies of God meant that women would have to accept a diminished role. During the 1920s, "routinization and regimentation of community relationships set in."[3] Barfoot and Sheppard noted that prophetic women were central to the birth and growth of the Pentecostal movement, but when the symbolic role of Pentecostal leadership shifted in the 1920s from "prophet" to "priest," the number of women in leadership positions rapidly declined.[4]

Institutionalization and social accommodation brought on by upward mobility go together. Max Weber proposed that "the religion of the disprivileged classes . . . is characterized by a tendency to allot equality to women." This equality tends to be divided, with women allowed a prophetic role and men dominating the priestly functions. Even so, such "equality" rarely lasts beyond the first generation.[5] Barfoot and Sheppard

1. Zickmund, "The right to preach," 193.

2. Hardesty, "Holiness is Power," 11.

3. Barfoot and Sheppard, "Prophetic vs. Priestly Religion," 9–10.

4. Barfoot and Sheppard, "Prophetic vs. Priestly Religion," 2.

5. Weber, *The Sociology of Religion*, 104–5.

effectively demonstrate that Weber's insight is valid in interpreting the role of women in the Pentecostal movement.[6]

A Dogmatic Ethic

Did this portrait mean that the denomination would never open its leadership doors further to women? If Barfoot and Sheppard are correct, prophetic voices are unwelcomed in institutional halls. Are there any instances of decreasing institutionalization in denominations?

Perhaps Flower's paper offered a ray of hope for those who wished to see change. The genius of Flower's argument on the subject is that it was based on sound exegetical study, the most comprehensive in the movement to that date. In any case, the pressures of accommodation, organization, and ingrained ideology were strong, and the emphasis on the role and power of the Spirit was sharply diminished.

The denomination's approach to ethics in this issue is best described as dogmatic. The primary source for appeal had been to the Scriptures, specifically to Paul's letter to Timothy, to an interpretation rarely opened to question. What made the impact of Flower's paper questionable is that leadership at various levels had been deeply reluctant to reconsider long-held beliefs. When fresh interpretations came to light, the tendency had been to maintain the "tried and true." Unfortunately, the tried is not always true.

6. Barfoot and Sheppard, "Prophetic vs. Priestly Religion," 4–15.

17

The Pacifist Years
(through 1919)

OVER THE YEARS, MAJOR shifts in the denomination's attitudes toward war were far-ranging, with debates within the fellowship's ranks occurring in high visibility. This subject had the distinction of being the second most hotly discussed social issue in the first 75 years of the Assemblies of God, with only the matter of divorce and remarriage disputed more.

The generally held belief that the denomination has maintained a consistently positive attitude toward Christians participating in war is inaccurate. At the same time, modern Pentecostal pacifists can claim only a limited precedent for their commitment to a noncombatant or absolute pacifist position.

In the five years following the Hot Springs organizational council, the debate over war participation was covered extensively in the *Evangel*, although there is comparatively little discussion to be found in official deliberations. The controversy was precipitated by the advent of World War I during the formative years of the General Council. Because the new organization was in the throes of determining its position on important issues, there was little attempt to curtail any display of differences of opinion.

In 1917 the Executive Presbytery went on record declaring the Council to be opposed to the participation of Christians in military combat. When the 1917 resolution was printed, the *Evangel* asserted that the resolution was in keeping with the overall attitude of all of Pentecostalism.

> Every branch of the movement, whether in the United States, Canada, Great Britain or Germany, has held to this principle [of non-violence]. When war first broke out in August of 1914, our Pentecostal brethren in Germany found themselves in a peculiar position. Some of those who were called to the colors responded, but many were court-marshalled and shot because they heartily subscribed to the principles of non-resistance. Great Britain has been more humane. Some of our British brethren have been given non-combatant service, and none have been shot because of their faith.[1]

This same editorial made claim that the Pentecostal movement had from the very beginning been characterized by Quaker principles. Such influence likely came through the holiness movement, in which the Pentecostal movement was rooted. Robert Pearsall Smith and Hannah Whitall Smith were Quakers, as was Robert Wilson, one of the founders of the Keswick Convention.[2] There were other pacifist influences in the nineteenth-century roots of Pentecostalism, but the more direct influence came from persons on both sides of the Atlantic in early years of the twentieth.

The Initial Debate (1901–1916)

One key predecessor of the Pentecostal movement was John Alexander Dowie of Zion City. As noted in chapter 3, many of Dowie's followers later joined the Assemblies of God. Adhering to a literal view of Scripture, Dowie attempted to apply the teachings of Jesus directly to society. His straightforward pacifism was impressed directly on his following. In 1902 he stated that "no person who went into the army to shoot and kill would remain a member of the church."[3]

Using the Sixth Commandment as his basis, he argued that both capital punishment and killing in war were wrong. "Appeal to the sword, and you appeal to brute force and superior power, and whoever has the best sword and the best gun will win. . . . All that is foreign to Christianity."[4] However, Dowie was no absolute pacifist. While he

---

1. "The Pentecostal Movement and the Conscription Law," 6.
2. Dieter, *The Holiness Revival*, 159, 187.
3. *Zion Banner*, n.p.
4. Dowie, "Zion College Lectures on Prayer," 210.

denounced war in general, saying that Zion does not believe in war,[5] he made one distinction. He declared that war is always wrong, except for a "war for protection." He made no elaboration on the difference other than to label wrong all "wars of aggression." It is better, he said, to let God and time settle many wrongs than to attempt to settle them by the sword. Calling war ungodly and unchristian, he said it was painful for him "to think that instead of missionaries carrying the Gospel from England, England is sending out hundreds of thousands of men to murder."[6] Perhaps it was this loophole of distinguishing between wars of protection and wars of aggression which made way for the later pacifist inconsistency in Pentecostalism.

Parham also had much to say on the topic of war and pacifism, being influenced by Dowie and his ministry in Zion,[7] and also by his wife, Sarah Thistlewaites, who had come from a Quaker family.[8] In a 1914 sermon preached in Zion City, Parham condemned the nations of Europe for their commercial interests in the war and for their imperialistic expansion. Warning of the coming destruction of the United States, he noted the necessity of premillennialism and the hopelessness of the peace conferences. He contrasted the call to arms with the call to be a missionary:

> We hang our heads in shame to see Christian nations and individuals yield themselves to the embrace of the Molech God, Patriotism, whose principle doctrine was honor, there to have consumed in the death struggle the feeling of philanthropy and humanity; spending millions to build the first for the consummation of these virtues, while the cause of Christ languishes, heaven loses, hell opens her jaws, and so-called Christian nations feed (by war) to satisfy her gluttonous appetite. . . . Yet while thousands of men will volunteer and suffer the hardships and privations of an earthly war for glory, few, indeed, will volunteer and endure the slightest privations for the Master's kingdom and eternal glory.[9]

5. Dowie, "God and Father of All Men," 805.

6. Dowie, "Zion College Lectures on Prayer," 212.

7. Brumback, *Suddenly . . . from Heaven*, 72–73, on further contacts by Parham with Zion City.

8. See Anderson, *Vision of the Disinherited*, 49.

9. Parham, *Everlasting Gospel*, 78.

During the war, Rolland Romack, Parham's office editor and manager for his paper, the *Apostolic Faith*, was inducted into the service and filed for exemption, which was not granted. Parham commented that it was hard for those who believe that the end of this age is nearing "to fight for the perpetuation of these nations, which we know will fall as the Gentile age will close and the millennium come."[10]

A great deal of Parham's teaching dealt with themes of eschatology, and in bold apocalyptic terms at that. Nearly every biblical passage had some eschatological significance. "The opening of the war, in 1914, marked the descent of the Devil from the heavens. . . . It is now at the opening of the midnight hour."[11] Like other Pentecostal pioneers, Parham saw himself a citizen of a new world. Therefore, he did not hesitate to chastise the churches for their alliance with the state and their opposition to the poor:

> The past order of civilization was upheld by the power of nationalism, which in turn was upheld by the spirit of patriotism, which divided the peoples of the world by geographical boundaries, over which each fought the other until they turned the world into shambles. The ruling power of this old order has always been the rich, who exploited the masses for profit or drove them en masse to war, to perpetuate their misrule. The principal teachers of patriotism maintaining nationalism were the churches, who have lost their spiritual power and been forsaken of God.[12]

For Parham the struggle had far greater dimensions than merely a war between European nations. Soon the old order of governments, the rich, and the churches would be aligned against those who believe in "the universal brotherhood of mankind and the establishment of the teachings of Jesus Christ as a foundation for all laws, whether political or social."[13]

Due to his declining influence in the Pentecostal movement in general and in the Finished Work wing of Pentecostalism in particular, Parham's opinions on the Great War did not directly affect the pacifist debate within the General Council. But Parham's views, including the rich-poor prophetic theme, were common among Pentecostal pioneers.

10. Parham, *Life of Charles F. Parham*, 274.

11. Parham, *Everlasting Gospel*, 28.

12. Parham, *Everlasting Gospel*, 27.

13. Parham, *Everlasting Gospel*, 28.

Bartleman was deeply involved in the Azusa Street meetings and his writings played a major role in the pacifist debate within the Assemblies of God although he never joined the denomination. Many of Bartleman's ideas about the European situation came from a visit he made to England and the Continent just prior to the war. On that trip he visited Pentecostal missions in Russia, Germany and England, decrying the war spirit wherever he went. He was not always well received. At the Central Pentecostal Mission in London, meetings opened with a "War Hymn," and when Bartleman spoke a strong message against the war spirit among Christians, his message "dropped like a bomb in the camp."[14] This mission, led by A. A. Boddy, was attempting to be a renewal movement within the Church of England which was itself unashamedly pro-war.[15]

The American received a very different and warm welcome for his message at the mission of Pastor Saxby, who had come into Pentecostalism with his congregation from a Baptist church.[16] One of Saxby's adherents was a young man named Donald Gee, who later became a conscientious objector and a foremost leader in the British Assemblies of God.

Englishmen played a dominant role in the Pentecostal pacifist debates. The first of these was Arthur Sydney Booth-Clibborn, whose primary influence was due to his book *Blood Against Blood*,[17] a statement of absolute pacifism. In fact, this book was undoubtedly the most influential piece of literature among early pacifists in the Assemblies of God. Booth-Clibborn, son-in law of William Booth, wrote the treatise "in a complete opposition and protest against war and the shedding of blood."[18]

Born into a family with a 250-year Quaker heritage, he early became a Quaker minister and was educated in France and Germany, learning to speak the languages of both countries fluently. In 1881 he went as a missionary for the Salvation Army to France and Switzerland where he met and married Catherine (Katie) Booth, daughter of the Army's founders, William and Catherine Booth.[19] During his career he faced much persecution, even prison terms, and became involved in civil disobedience when not allowed to preach the gospel.[20]

14. Bartleman, *Two Years Mission Work*, 54.

15. See Abrams, *Preachers Present Arms*, 31, who documents the Church of England's role in the war.

16. Bartleman, *Two Years Mission Work*, 55.

17. There is no date for the original edition.

18. "Pentecostal Saints Opposed to War," 1.

19. Thus, like other sons-in-law, he took the name Booth.

20. Booth-Clibborn, *Blood Against Blood*, 166.

Booth-Clibborn never claimed the Pentecostal experience for himself, though Pentecostals greatly admired him and claimed him as one of their own.[21] The *Evangel* called him "an English Pentecostal brother,"[22] and he himself spoke of his experience of the "Baptism of the Holy Ghost,"[23] though such terminology was also prevalent in holiness circles of the day. Regardless, the early Pentecostals considered him a leader in their ranks, and his influence was extended through his sons who became Pentecostal preachers.[24]

The inspiration for writing *Blood Against Blood* came during the Anglo-Boer War, while Booth-Clibborn was a commissioner in Holland and Belgium. What greatly influenced him were the many classic Quaker arguments against war from both Scripture and reason as well as figures in church history who opposed war. He understood there to be two kinds of blood shedding: one, carnal as in war; the other, spiritual as with Christ and the martyrs. These two kinds were never to be confused, so that, logically, Christianity was the only antidote to war. According to Booth Clibborn, the loss of pacifism in the church occurred at the time of Constantine, totally the result of great apostasy. He wrote that the greatest reforms advocated pacifism as part of returning to New Testament Christianity, a viewpoint likely to appeal to the restorationist mentality of the Pentecostals.[25]

---

21. William Booth-Clibborn writes, "To the questions so often asked me whether Father and Mother claimed this experience my answer is no! yet all their sympathies were with the Outpouring, even from the beginning. How could it be otherwise when nine of their children had received their Pentecost." Booth-Clibborn, *A Personal Testimony*, 74.

22. "Pentecostal Saints Opposed to War," 1.

23. Booth-Clibborn, *Blood Against Blood*, 15, 21, 23.

24. Eric Booth-Clibborn died as a young missionary for the Assemblies of God. Brumback, *Suddenly . . . from Heaven*, 339. William Booth-Clibborn was listed as a charter member of the General Council. General Council minutes, 1914, 13. He later joined the oneness faction, first in the Pentecostal Assemblies of the World, and later was a founder of the Apostolic Churches of Jesus Christ (later merged with the United Pentecostal Church). S. H. Booth-Clibborn (a son or was he the same Arthur Sidney?) wrote two articles for the *Weekly Evangel*, "The Christian and War: Is It Too Late?" 28 April 1917, 5, which called for an absolute pacifism and used much of the material from *Blood Against Blood*; and "The Christian and War," *Weekly Evangel*, 19 May 1917, 4. (William Booth Clibborn, in *The Baptism in the Holy Spirit*, 17, lists the names of the ten children and a Herbert is included.)

25. Booth-Clibborn, *Blood Against Blood*, 55–57.

Three theological factors provided the framework for his pacifism: a focus on missions, a biblical literalism, and a premillennial pessimism. Within his focus on missions, he understood it to be the Christian's place to declare the insanity of earthly war and to participate instead in the war for men's souls.[26]

His biblical literalism was directly linked with his view of eschatology, a pessimistic premillennialism. War could not be abolished by Christianity at its present rate of progress, nor was such a goal a part of the individual believer's duty. The end was too near to be so concerned. "One of the most glorious and solemn parts of the programme of Christianity is that the King is soon coming to claim the Throne of the World. . . . We appear to be now well into the Saturday Night of the world."[27]

Since this was the end time and the solution to wars would come only with the second advent of Christ, he had no desire to work with secular pacifists in the cause of peace. He also was antagonized by the working-class opposition to war, seeing this antiwar movement as contention in another form, "a war between the masses and the classes," and thus having nothing to do with Christianity.[28]

Booth-Clibborn eventually broke with the Salvation Army, partly because General Booth did not go far enough in his pacifist position. One biographer of Evangeline Booth links three factors with Booth-Clibborn's departure: pacifism; divine healing and his association with Dowie; and premillennialism.[29]

Early Editorial Controversy

The earliest articles in the *Word and Witness* and the *Christian Evangel* tended to present the impending world crisis in apocalyptic terms. The debate over participation in the conflict was more a matter of observing the unfolding of prophetic, dispensational eschatology rather than of determining personal ethics. A typical dispensational perspective is found in this statement from *Word and Witness*:

---

26. Booth-Clibborn, *Blood Against Blood*, 32.

27. Booth-Clibborn, *Blood Against Blood*, 123–24.

28. Booth-Clibborn, *Blood Against Blood*, 139.

29. Wilson, *General Evangeline Booth*, 138–39. See also, Booth-Clibborn, *The Baptism in the Holy Spirit*, 12–13.

The Rulers of this age realize the totterings of their man-made governments. No nation is decreasing his armies, but with armies of hundreds of thousands of able bodied men, they are still increasing them as rapidly as possible. Navies are being increased, and $2,000,000,000 per annum will not pay the world's army bill in these times of apparent enlightenment and peace. The arms factories are running to the limit, powder mills are busy, army and naval academies are full of students learning the arts of war, which is only legalized killing. (God says "Thou shalt not kill") The air has a new occupant, the war air ship, (foretold by the prophet Habakkuk in Chap. 1 verse 8.).[sic][30]

War was seen as direct judgement from God. Such is the case in an article by an Englishman who was praying that God would use the war to humble the British. According to him, his homeland, the "friend of the slave and the downtrodden," was now fighting for Belgium, "whose king ten years ago was held up before the whole world because of his inhuman treatment of the poor natives of the Congo." He predicted that England was helping her chief opponent in the future "Armageddon."[31]

Generally, the articles focused on the imminent return of Christ: "Be ready, for in such an hour as ye think not, the son of man cometh. Don't be too much absorbed in watching the daily papers for war news but keep looking up with enraptured gaze for the return of the Lord!"[32]

In December 1914, the *Christian Evangel* published an article entitled "Is European War Justifiable?" A series of editorials taken from *Confidence*, a British Pentecostal magazine, one editorial acknowledged national and individual transgression overshadowing the conflict; another focused on the need for evangelism, even in the prisoner-of-war camps. The remainder were all pro-British and/or written to illustrate a citizen's obligation to his country in time of war. "It is not the Church of God that has gone to war, but the British Empire, and both are fulfilling divine purposes, though those purposes are not the same." A Christian, with connections with both the church and the empire, has the duty "as citizens to suppress intemperance, to wage war against immorality, to protect children, to provide for the aged and hopeless, and to prevent wanton cruelty to animals."[33]

30. Hall, "The Great Crisis," 1.

31. Gray, "A Voice from England," 1.

32. "War! War!! War!!!" 1.

33. "Is European War Justifiable?" 1, 3.

This article served as a springboard for the debate. One month later, a rebuttal written by Burt McCafferty of Fort Worth, Texas, appeared on the front page of the *Evangel*. "Our citizenship is not of this world, our citizenship is in heaven," he wrote. His was an absolute pacifist stance, using arguments drawn entirely from Scripture, appealing particularly to the teaching and example of Jesus as a basis for the doctrine. Christians were not to fight in personal self-defense, let alone go to war. Instead of contending with flesh and blood, the Christian's warfare was to be waged against the host of spiritual darkness.[34]

An editorial written by J. Roswell Flower appeared in the same issue and expressed the *Evangel's* intention to keep the controversy under control, to maintain a sense of balance and neutrality, while at the same time allowing broad discussion on the topic of pacifism. The editorial became in effect a disclaimer of McCafferty's article, questioning the Texan's use of Jesus as the Christian's example in this matter.[35]

Avoiding friction on the subject of pacifism was a goal not to be achieved. Soon an article appeared in the *Evangel* which declared that the present war was retribution for the moral offenses of western "Christian" civilization. Stressing the fact that these countries were unchristian, it stated that only nations which followed the peacemaking principles of Jesus could be labeled Christian.[36]

Then the first of three articles by Bartleman appeared. His first article, "Present Day Conditions," was also printed in *Word and Witness* and produced by GPH as a tract. Occasioned by the sinking of the Lusitania, the piece was a scathing condemnation of all those implicated in the war, including—and not least—the United States. Bartleman accused the nations of materialism and moral degradation and predicted that judgment had begun with the end near at hand.[37]

Two weeks later, two articles with contrasting viewpoints appeared on the *Evangel's* front page. One news story told of the evangelistic work of A. A. Boddy and others among the soldiers. Boddy, a well-known non-pacifist British Pentecostal and publisher of *Confidence*, had been voluntarily serving with the Chaplain of the Expeditionary Forces on the

---

34. McCafferty, "Should Christians Go to War?" 1.

35. Flower, editorial, *Christian Evangel*, 16 January 1915, 3.

36. "Civilization Breaking Down?" 3.

37. Bartleman, "Present Day Conditions," *Weekly Evangel*, 5 June 1915, 3; also, in *Word and Witness*, June 1915, 5.

continent.[38] But to offset the possibility that anyone might think that the church's attitude toward participation in combat had changed, an editorial disclaimer followed the Boddy story headlined "Pentecostals Opposed to War."

> The Pentecostal people, as a whole, are uncompromisingly opposed to war, having much the same spirit as the early Quakers, who would rather be shot themselves than that they should shed the blood of their fellow-men. Because we have given this bit of war news is no reason that we are in favor of war, but rather that our readers may have some knowledge of how the war is actually affecting our own people, who, through force of circumstances are compelled to be in the midst of the terrible conflict. Indeed, some have already urged us to arrange for a great peace council among the Pentecostal saints, to put ourselves on record as being opposed to war at home or abroad.[39]

This short article was followed with a promotion of Booth-Clibborn's book, *Blood Against Blood*, then being distributed through GPH. The volume would be advertised extensively in the coming months in both *Word and Witness* and the *Evangel*.

During the ensuing summer, two other articles by Bartleman appeared. The first continued the theme of his previous essay, but it reserved particular chastisement for England. In condemning the injustice done to the lower classes by the rich and/or landed aristocracy in that country, he wrote, "God is done with the class system in England."[40] This theme was carried to its extreme in the next piece (the last in the series), in which Bartleman presented Germany as a victim of England's propaganda in the American press. Defending Germany, he wrote that though the sins of Germany be many, "she has accumulated what she has largely by hard labor. She is in a wonderful state of organism and cultivation. Such a nation cannot be destroyed."[41] An advertisement for *Blood Against Blood* followed the second article.

In the very next issue, Flower, the office editor, issued an apology for having published this last essay. He had printed it, he wrote, in the interest of fairness and balance, but it was indeed too strongly worded and much too excessive. He went on to explain that Bell, the editor-in-chief,

38. "Goes to the Front," 1.
39. "Pentecostal Saints Opposed to War," 1.
40. Bartleman, "The European War," 3.
41. Bartleman, "What Will the Harvest Be?" 1, 2.

had been away at the time, intimating that Bell had been opposed to the printing of the piece. Flower then quoted from the letter of a reader who criticized the article for its bias and almost total lack of spiritual application and closed with an appeal for Christians to lose their national preferences and prejudices: "We are not citizens of this world, but citizens of a better country and our interests are all for that country to which we all hope to go."[42]

Pentecostal pacifism was doubly marked by a deep concern for evangelism and a preoccupation with eschatological expectation. This dual evangelistic/other-worldly approach, so characteristic of the early Pentecostal mind-set, was to be visibly demonstrated barely a month later in the 11 September 1915 edition of the *Weekly Evangel*. Centered on the front page a boxed headline read, "Are you off to the front?" It was a reproduction of a tract being distributed among the soldiers in Europe, an appeal to the troops to consider their eternal destiny. It began by stating, "We are all proud of our soldiers and our sailors, and of all those who have so nobly responded to their country's call to arms . . ."[43]

Two pages later a strongly pacifist article entitled "Our Heavenly Citizenship"—by future editor Frodsham—appeared. Reprinted a month later in *Word and Witness*, Frodsham's article adopted Flower's idea that Christians are citizens of another world. Exhorting the movement to something deeper than an attitude of strict neutrality, Frodsham referred to the song, "This world is not my home," and wrote that the Christian's attitude to all the nations of the earth should be the same as that of Ruth to Moab. He reminded his readers that national pride like every other form of pride was an abomination in the sight of God and that pride of race had to pass away when one became a new creature in Christ.

While less vehement than Bartleman, Frodsham condemned war also, declaring that Christians should side with the Prince of Peace rather than with the bellicose kings of earth. "Is any child of God going to side with these belligerent kings?" Those who choose the sword will perish by the sword. He argued that the duty of Christians was to place their affections in things above. "It is important for the saint of God to realize that his citizenship is in heaven, and that here he has no continuing city." Human warfare is not the business of those who wage spiritual battles.[44]

42. Flower, editorial, 14 August 1915, 2.

43. "Are You Off to the Front?" 1.

44. Frodsham, "Our Heavenly Citizenship," 11 September 1915, 3; also in *Word and Witness*, October 1915, 3.

The debate over pacifism was to be overshadowed by a much more intense struggle within the fledgling denomination during the following year. In fact, the "Jesus Only" debate dominated all other concerns and consumed an immense measure of spiritual and intellectual energy. Only one article and a poem appeared on the issue of war during 1916. The poem, entitled "War 'Profits,'" posed the question of war's worth to the makers of war:

> You may boast of the wealth you've obtained by this war,
> You may count it in billions and more.
> You may tell of the hours that you gave to the strife
> In obtaining the precious ore.
> But,—those women who mourn the loss of their dead,
> The thousands now under the sod,
> Will one day with you at a judgment bar stand.
> Then—what will you answer to God?[45]

Later in the year Englishman Leonard Newby sought to answer some questions in regard to the war in Europe. To the question, "Is it not an awful thing for one Christian nation to be fighting against another Christian nation?" he emphatically replied, "There is not, and never has been, such a company of people as a CHRISTIAN NATION, and never will be until the Lord comes."[46]

Newby saw the nations as great antagonistic world powers, acting at the instigation of Satan. The people of God and the Gentile nations were not to be confused. As to the true Christians who are engaged in the war, they "are simply doing their duty in that state of life in which God has called them." Yet, though engaged in war, they hate bloodshed.[47]

Newby went on to depict the judgment of God on all involved nations, declaring that God was punishing the nations for their iniquities. The article was easily acceptable to most Pentecostals. It presented a prophetic theme. It spoke against war but not against Christians in the war. It demonstrated fallacy in choosing sides because all nations are evil.

---

45. Sisler, "War 'Profits,'" 7.

46. Newby, "Light on the Present Crisis," 6, 7, 9; emphasis in the original.

47. Newby, "Light on the Present Crisis," 6, 7, 9.

The War (1917–1919)

Once the Assemblies of God had begun to recover from the taxing New Issue controversy, attention again was centered on the question of wartime participation. This time however the issue was less academic as the United States moved toward a direct role in the conflict. An article in January 1917 emphasized the effects of war on the minds of men. The *Evangel* quoted Baron D'Estournelles de Constant from *La Paix par le Droit*, a French publication: " . . . They have grown accustomed to do evil unconsciously . . . . To kill has become their duty, their sole object and purpose of life." Though the article was not anti-war in intent, it did decry the immoral consequences of war. Concluding with a resume of the effects war has on soldiers, it read, "Their hearts are hardened; moral reaction takes place in the same proportion as scientific progress discovers new means of killing and causing destruction."[48]

A story appearing in the *Evangel* in March under the title "An Ambassador in the Trenches" was accompanied by opposing comment. It was the story of a onetime soldier who had been ignominiously discharged from the British Army but who later rejoined the service at the beginning of the war. Having become a Christian before his re-enlistment, he served with honor the second time and died a valiant death on the battlefield. Two statements in the article revealed the ambivalent attitude prevalent in Pentecostal circles at the time. Commenting on the huge influx of recruits in Britain at the beginning of the war, the writer took a pacifist position when he noted that "very few seemed to remember what Jesus said to us when He preached the sermon on the mount." Yet the same writer concluded by praising the enlistees, stating, "Let us pray that God will raise up many such ambassadors in the trenches."[49]

In April and May, the Assemblies of God leadership moved to an official position on the war issue, prefacing the action by extensive pacifist writings in the *Evangel*. Newby's article of the summer before was reprinted in a "Special Second Coming Edition," with the headline this time focused on the prophetic content of the article.[50]

One issue later, Bell, again the *Evangel's* editor-in-chief after his brief absence during the "Jesus Only" controversy, addressed the issue of whether a Christian could go to war and "hold his experience." Though

48. "Education of War," 3.
49. "Ambassador in the Trenches," 6–7.
50. Newby, "The Great War," 1–2.

hardly pacifistic in his response, Bell was not pro-military either, declaring that war is wrong and that "no Christian should go who can honorably and lawfully keep out of it." Admitting that it was difficult to serve God in the army, he said it could be done; in fact, there were Pentecostals serving in both the British and German armies. However, because of the problems involved, he wrote that he would not join "until compelled to do so, either by law or in defense of our mothers, wives, and children."[51] Bell dealt solely with the issue of whether joining the army was "spiritually safe" and never touched the question of whether taking part in combat was right or wrong.

A brief excerpt from *Blood Against Blood* appeared the following week under the title "What is War?" Quoting pacifists and generals, preachers and politicians alike, the excerpt decried war as of hell and opposed to "every principle of Christianity."[52]

In the same issue, an unsigned article posed the question of what the Scriptures say concerning participation in war. Building upon the theme of the Christian's citizenship being in heaven, it called for disciples of Jesus to consider the way of peace, implying that they were not to delight in battle.[53]

A week later the first of two articles by S. H. Booth-Clibborn[54] appeared. In it, Booth-Clibborn developed a careful scriptural defense of pacifism and limited himself to answering two popular criticisms of Christian non-resistance. The first dealt with God's sanctions of the militarism displayed in the Old Testament. Booth-Clibborn's defense was from a dispensationalist perspective. He explained that the Jews had been living in the age of law and judgment, whereas Christians were living in the dispensation of grace and mercy. Christ sent his followers out "to save men—not to butcher them like cattle."[55]

The second criticism of the pacifist belief came in the query, "Suppose a brute in human form attacked your wife and children." His response was that this war involved not a willful attacker, but "poor harmless people . . . driven like cattle and quite against their will by godless governments into butchering each other." Furthermore, he continued, countless Christian homes had not been broken into, and if they had been "Matthew 5 and

51. Bell, "Questions and Answers," 14 April 1917, 9.

52. Booth-Clibborn, "What is War?" 2.

53. "The Crisis," 7.

54. This is either a son or a different nomenclature for Arthur Sydney.

55. Booth-Clibborn, "The Christian and War?" 5.

Romans 12 would still remain true, and God's Word would still have to be obeyed."[56]

The article by Booth-Clibborn was followed two pages later by the testimonial of an English conscientious objector, an ideal story reflecting both the individual's integrity and his circumstances. It was printed in the hope that it would "help many of our young men in the stand they will take at this time."[57] Beaman, in his thesis on Pentecostal pacifists, noted that this article did not recognize that the noncombatant in the United States, contrary to the British situation, was not always easily distinguished from other soldiers in assignment. Absolute pacifists who refused noncombatant service were still placed in the army camps as a form of coercion.[58]

Among Assemblies of God leaders, much discussion on conscientious objection was taking place behind the scenes. The Executive Presbytery decided to issue an official pacifist statement in order to meet a federal government deadline. The leadership was apparently not unified in the action, however, and this is reflected in the pages of the *Evangel*.

The 19 May 1917, issue has been called "a study in editorial equivocation."[59] On the cover page, a headline was printed "To All Their Due," followed by a quotation of Rom 13:1–7. Inside was the second of the Booth-Clibborn articles, again a carefully stated exegetical piece which drew a firm pacifist conclusion. Here Booth-Clibborn raised the issue of Jesus cleansing the temple by force. He maintained that Jesus never did use physical force against human beings. The "little" whip he plied was the physical tool used to drive out the cattle; it was Christ's spiritual power which drove out the money changers. "The idea that he actually pushed that great crowd of men out of the Temple by physical force is absurd, seeing that they could easily have overpowered Him." Booth-Clibborn, then noting that the Temple was now spiritual and did not need to be defended by force, concluded by asking, "Could anything be more pitiable than the slaughter of thousands of gallant young Frenchmen in the vain attempt to save the old Roman Catholic cathedral of Rheims?"[60]

56. Booth-Clibborn, "The Christian and War?" 5.

57. "Compulsory Military Service," 7.

58. Beaman, "Pentecostal Pacifism," 90.

59. Robbins, "Attitudes toward War and Peace," 28.

60. Booth-Clibborn, "The Christian and War," 4.

An even more significant article was to be found on page eight of that same issue. It was an explanation by Welch, chair of the General Council, regarding a resolution by the Executive Presbytery that had been recently sent to all Assemblies of God ministers. The resolution itself, not actually printed in the *Evangel* until August, read as follows:

> Resolution Concerning the Attitude of the General Council of the Assemblies of God Toward any Military Service which involves the Actual Participation in the Destruction of Human Life.
>
> While recognizing Human Government as of Divine ordination and affirming our unswerving loyalty to the Government of the United States, nevertheless we are constrained to define our position with reference to the taking of human life.
>
> WHEREAS, in the Constitutional Resolution adopted at the Hot Springs General Council, April 1–10, 1914, we plainly declare the Holy inspired Scriptures to be the all-sufficient rule of faith and practice, and
>
> WHEREAS the Scriptures deal plainly with the obligations and relations of humanity, setting forth the principles of "Peace on earth, good will toward men." (Luke 2:14); and
>
> WHEREAS we, as followers of the Lord Jesus Christ, the Prince of Peace, believe in implicit obedience to the Divine commands and precepts which instruct us to "Follow peace with all men," (Heb. 12:14); "Thou shalt not kill," (Exod. 20:13); "Resist not evil," (Matt. 5:39); "Love your enemies," (Matt. 5:44); etc. and
>
> WHEREAS these and other Scriptures have always been accepted and interpreted by our churches as prohibiting Christians from shedding blood or taking human life;
>
> THEREFORE we, as a body of Christians, while purposing to fulfill all the obligations of loyal citizenship, are nevertheless constrained to declare we cannot conscientiously participate in war and armed resistance which involves the actual destruction of human life, since this is contrary to our view of the clear teachings of the inspired Word of God, which is the sole basis of our faith."[61]

Though the resolution was a straightforward pacifist statement, Welch's editorial served to put it in its proper perspective. Welch explained that the resolution was not intended to hinder anyone from fighting in war; rather, it was designed to aid those "real conscientious

---

61. General Council combined minutes, 1914–1917, 11–12. This was an Executive Presbytery resolution but was incidentally listed at the end of items.

objectors" who desired exemption from military service. He commented that this did not represent a change in any degree from the view always held by the "company of believers," declaring that the Council always had and always would stand on the simple teachings of the Word of God. Further, he made it clear that the Assemblies of God was not opposed to the government and that church members were "not unwilling to serve in any capacity that will not require the destruction of life."[62]

Welch concluded his article with an excerpt from the War Department's letter regarding receipt of the resolution. The letter implied that the status of conscientious objector was at that time being considered by Congress. Actually, the presbytery had been working under an early deadline set by the War Department itself. Such declarations by denominations had to be on the record by 18 May;[63] therefore, there was no time to wait for the upcoming General Presbytery or General Council to act. The five-man Executive Presbytery included Welch, Frodsham and Flower, as well as D. W. Kerr and D. B. Rickard. Frodsham had strong pacifist leanings, and Flower had some pacifist sympathies. Bell, who did not share the sentiment of the Pentecostal pacifists, was not a member at the time.

No further articles appeared on the subject until 4 August when the resolution itself was published in its entirety, prefaced by an editorial as well as significant correspondence that had passed between the War Department and the office of the General Council. The editorial stated that from the beginning the Pentecostal movement, as a whole, had been characterized by Quaker principles. The laws of the Kingdom, as espoused by Jesus in the Sermon on the Mount, had been unqualifiedly adopted, and as a result, the movement had been opposed to "the spilling of the blood of any man, or of offering resistance to any aggression."

---

62. Welch, "An Explanation," 8.

63. See Bell: "The draft law exempted those from war service who belong to some well recognized religious body, whose organization was in existence before the time of the passage of said law May 17 last, and whose creed or principles forbad its members to engage in war in any form." "Questions and Answers," 24 November 1917, 8. The 4 August Evangel took pains to note that the pacifist declaration was not a quick decision of conviction on the executives' part. "The principles of the General Council were in opposition to war from its very beginning which was considerably prior to May 18th, 1917." "Conscription Law," 4 August 1917, 7. Though this may have been stated to ensure the validity of the decision, the assertion is correct.

Thus, the resolution was rooted historically in the Peace Church movement and, more recently, in the mainstream of Pentecostal persuasion.[64]

Concern for Loyalty and Evangelism

The General Council of that year was held in September. In the council records, no mention is made of the resolution coming up for further discussion nor that it was ever approved for being included in the minutes. That was unusual because the resolution had been acted upon only by the Executive Presbytery. The 1917 General Council resolutions committee was composed of Bell, D. W. Kerr, and Raymond T. Richey. Only Kerr was a member of the Executive Presbytery which produced the original statement. His perspective on pacifism is unknown. Bell would prove to be a loyalist with only casual interest in the pacifist issue. Richey's primary concern lay with the evangelism of soldiers. Therefore, the council resolutions reflected concern for loyalty and evangelism. Two items of business did arise, however, at the Council that illustrated this great balance within the movement: concern for nonviolence on one hand, and commitment to evangelism and loyalty to government on the other.

The first item of business concerned the need for evangelism among the soldiers. Richey was asked to speak before the council about such efforts and of his involvement to date. Afterward a resolution was passed to "adopt every available means consistent with Scriptural teaching and example to co-operate with every approved agency for revivals among the soldiers. To this end it is recommended that saints everywhere determine, like the apostle Paul, to become all things to all men that by all means we may save some."[65]

The resolution stipulated that all such missionary endeavors had to be conducted under the supervision of the Y.M.C.A., but the council recommended the United Prayer and Workers' League, represented by Richey, as the specific agency with which to deal. Because of the way in which the resolution was worded regarding the Y.M.C.A., Beaman notes that concern may have been raised because of the liberal tendencies of the Y.M.C.A. and also the fact that it had become a conspicuously military organization.[66] One Y.M.C.A. physical director is said to have supplied

---

64. "Conscription Law," 4 August 1917, 6.

65. General Council minutes, 1917, 16.

66. Beaman, "Pentecostal Pacifism," 75.

the soldiers with a manual on hand-to-hand fighting, in which the chief points of attack were explained minutely. The Y.M.C.A. also was involved in recruiting men for the military, as well as indoctrinating them as to the Christian purpose of war.[67] The organization was further known for harassment of the conscientious objectors who were interned in military camps.[68]

Moreover, Richey was one of the Council's own. Several comments were made by delegates pointing to the tremendous evangelistic opportunity at hand.[69] Earlier in 1917 Richey, highly motivated with missionary zeal, had begun work in the military camps under the required auspices of the Y.M.C.A. while the *Evangel* had started reporting evangelistic work of Pentecostals among the soldiers.[70]

This concern for evangelism was noted in the 4 August Executive Presbytery announcement that opened, "From its very inception, the Pentecostal Movement has been a movement of evangelism, studiously avoiding any principles or actions which would thwart it in its great purpose."[71] From this it might be interpreted that the Assemblies of God was reluctant to take a stand on the war issue because of its commitment to evangelism. But another paragraph in the August statement implied that the position of nonviolence and the church's priority of evangelism were equally fundamental. "Inasmuch as the principles of the General Council were in opposition to war from its very beginning . . . we have therefore sought further recognition from the War Department."[72]

Another item of business at the council, following almost immediately after passage of the evangelism resolution, was a declaration of loyalty to the government. Members spoke forcefully on the importance of faithful allegiance to the powers-that-be, since they were ordained of God. "So-called" Pentecostal preachers were alluded to, who, it was said, thought they were doing honor to God by insulting the flag. Collins, then a member of the General Presbytery, avowed that the Council was on biblical grounds in honoring the government, and noted that the Texas

67. Abrams, *Preachers Present Arms*, 67.

68. Meyer, *"Hey! Yellowbacks!,"* 106–7.

69. General Council minutes, 1917, 16–17.

70. These articles specifically reported evangelistic efforts and made no comment on the morality of war: Doney, "Salvation for the Soldier," 2; and "Amongst the Soldier Boys," 2–3.

71. "Conscription Law," 4 August 1917, 6.

72. "Conscription Law," 4 August 1917, 7.

District Council had purposed to cancel the credentials of any preacher who spoke against the government. Whether this was a reaction against fellow Texan Burt McCafferty's *Evangel* article in January 1915 is not certain, but the General Council was obviously more occupied with patriotic allegiance at this point than it was with conscientious objection. The minutes read that the council in session "agreed that such radicals [as those with whom the Texas Council was concerned] do not represent this General Council."[73] A formal resolution expressing loyalty to the government would have to wait for the next council a year later.

With the United States now fully involved in the war and the Assemblies of God having made the necessary declaration on conscientious objection, the Council and the *Evangel* seem to have been content to leave the issue of military involvement up to the conscience of each individual. Bell wrote a lengthy response to the General Council's position on exemption in the *Evangel* in November 1917. He stressed that Pentecostal principles as held by the Assemblies of God, though always against killing, had not forbidden other types of military service; consequently, he took the position that the 28 April resolution did not apply to complete exemption. Furthermore, he stated that the General Council supported the President in the war effort and that duty to the flag must be upheld. "We should, even if exempted, do all in our power, consistent with our faith in God, to sustain our President in this great conflict."[74]

Approximately six weeks later, the resolution on conscientious objection was reprinted one more time in the *Weekly Evangel* desiring "to state what we have already set forth . . . the principles that have governed the General Council since its inception at the first Council meeting at Hot Springs. Ark., April 2, 1914, and which were crystalized in the resolution" of 1917.[75] Again, the resolution was considered a reaffirmation of all that the Assemblies of God had stood for since the beginning. Perhaps the clearest statement was a commitment to scriptural authority.

The concern for loyalty to the government had not yet run its course, however, and as editor of the *Evangel*, Bell became the banner carrier for fidelity to the government's cause. In one column, he focused directly on the issue of whether it would be right to help in the war effort. His answer was two-fold. Stressing that it was the duty of all to uphold the authority

73. General Council minutes, 1917, 17–18.
74. Bell, "Questions and Answers," 24 November 1917, 8.
75. "Conscription Law," 5 January 1918, 5.

of the government and, if drafted, to respond in an orderly way to such authority, he went on to say that if a person belonged to a well-recognized religious body which could not conscientiously engage in actual warfare, such a person should make appropriate plea to his exemption board.[76] Conscientious objection was proper, according to Bell, as long as it was practiced within the law. Keeping the law was the higher command.

This expression of necessary allegiance to authority may have had more to do with the Espionage and Sedition Acts than any theological stance. The Espionage Bill, passed by Congress 15 June 1917, was part of a growing endeavor to bring all dissident elements into line with the war effort. It had the effect of denying free speech when such speech was in opposition to America's participation in the conflict and called for the prosecution of anyone who should "willfully cause or attempt to cause insubordination, disloyalty, mutiny, or refusal of duty in the military or naval forces . . . or shall willfully obstruct the recruiting or enlistment services of the United States."[77] The Sedition Act, passed the following year to amend the Espionage Act, was even more repressive. Anyone who would oppose the war was seen as a German-collaborator or traitor.[78] Even quoting from the Sermon on the Mount could be considered treasonous.[79]

Thus, many of the earlier writings printed by GPH were now potentially illegal. Likely this accounts for the almost total silencing in the *Evangel* of pacifist views and attacks on participation in wartime service after May 1917. In contrast, the editors took great care to emphasize the need for registration for military service during June of that year. First, they announced the fifth of June as the day set aside by the government for registration.[80] Then, they warned about those who had been jailed for failing to register, explaining both times that exemptions could only be granted to those who registered.[81]

In any case, Bell felt it necessary to warn his readers on the matter. Stating that the General Council had always stood for law and order, he affirmed the strong stand taken at the previous council session "for

76. Bell, "Questions and Answers," 25 August 1917, 9.

77. Peterson and Fite, *Opponents of War 1917–1918*, 17.

78. Peterson and Fite, *Opponents of War 1917–1918*, 215–21.

79. See Abrams, *Preachers Present Arms*, 66, 128.

80. "Concerning Registration," 8.

81. "Failure to Register," 8.

Loyalty to our Government and the President and to the flag." Personal conscience had its limitations:

> It is one things [sic] to be in our faith opposed personally to taking human life, even in war, but quite another thing to preach against our Government going to war. It is unlawful to do so. It is none of our business to push our faith as to war on others or on the Government. Preachers who are excused from war . . . are under double obligation to show their gratitude to God and the Flag for such religious liberty and prove this by extra service and sacrifices to the good of mankind, to the Government and to God.[82]

Patriotism was also to be demonstrated in the economic sphere. Already tremendous pressure had sometimes been exerted through mob violence and bond salesmen to force pacifists to buy liberty bonds, and even Mennonites and Dunkards were being coerced into purchasing them.[83] Thus, Bell argued in favor of proving loyalty through financial means, and in his question and answer column, he spoke favorably of buying liberty bonds, declaring that buying a postage stamp contributed to the war just the same. He wrote, "If we appreciate the religious freedom we have under the stars and stripes, we will not want to bow our necks to the Prussian yoke or the Kaiser."[84] He added that those who did not want the bonds could give them to missions and "thereby kill two birds with one stone, help their country and spread the gospel too."[85] On the issue of being asked to support with taxes those who were doing the killing, he replied that if Jesus paid taxes and did not worry about how the Romans would spend it, the Pentecostals should do likewise.[86]

In sharp contrast to the *Evangel's* earlier emphasis on Christians being citizens of heaven, Bell was now stressing commitment to national, earthly citizenship. In June 1918 he wrote of his being pleased to see that nearly every copy of the minutes of the various district councils in the past year contained an expression of loyalty to the President and the government during the present crisis. He reminded his readers of Peter's admonitions to honor the king, and to "submit yourself to every ordinance

---

82. Bell, "Preachers Warned," 4.

83. Abrams, *Preachers Present Arms*, 188.

84. Bell, "Questions and Answers," 26 January 1918, 9.

85. Bell, "Questions and Answers," 28 December 1918, 5.

86. Bell, "A Tremendous Day is To-Day," 23 February 1918, 6.

of man for the Lord's sake."[87] On the question of saluting the flag, Bell replied that it is not worship, but only indicates love for the country and an acceptance of its rightful authority. Why should any loyal citizen desire to withhold such recognition?[88] In his writings he even went beyond the issue of loyalty, justifying the American war effort from a theological perspective: "Let us hope for every oppressor our country has to kill it may save a thousand others from slavery to the Kaiser, and while the country is trying to save the world from physical, mental and commercial slavery, let us save the souls from slavery to sin and bondage to Satan."[89]

The 15 June 1918 issue carried two more articles in support of the war. On the front page was an account of the work of GPH, describing it in analogous terms to the American war effort, affirming that just as the latter needed total cooperation from everyone, so did spiritual warfare require a united front.[90] Then in the second article on page three, Bell identified the Kaiser as antichristian, though he did not consider him to be the Antichrist or the Beast referred to in the Book of Revelation. Still, Bell asserted, the Kaiser was doomed to fail.[91]

For the *Evangel's* editor, the spirit of anti-Christ was the spirit of anarchy, and this included the spirit of unfaithfulness. Bell wrote, "Any spirit of disloyalty is certainly not of Christ, for his own blessed Word shows from beginning to end that 'the powers that be are ordained of God,' and if we resist them we 'resist God.'"[92] In warning the preachers the preceding January about treasonable acts, he had cautioned that "many utterances allowable in times of Peace may be Treasonable in Times of War, such as the present."[93] Shortly, Bell was to discover evidence of such anarchy and treason right in GPH, which he also was managing.

In an August editorial, he announced that he had destroyed all copies of Bartleman's "Present Day Conditions" in tract form and called on all readers to do likewise and to support the Government. Even when Bartleman's article had first appeared in print, it had proven quite a sensation with its defense of Germany. Now it was both dangerous and

---

87. Bell, "Loyalty Bonds," 8.
88. Bell, "Questions and Answers," 12 July 1919, 5.
89. Bell, "A Tremendous Day is To-Day," 7.
90. Bell, "Your Publishing House and Ours," 1.
91. Bell, "The Beast of Berlin," 3.
92. Bell, "Loyalty Bonds," 8.
93. Bell, "Preachers Warned," 4.

abominable. The problem, in Bell's view, centered on the lawfulness of having such an article still in circulation now that America was officially at war with Germany. What was acceptable in peacetime was "entirely too radical for war times,"[94] he wrote. It was definitely contrary in letter and spirit to the Espionage and Sedition Acts.

Bell does not seem to have at all shared the Executive Presbytery position on conscientious objection. In one column he had upheld the military's duty in combat, and in the same article had opposed membership in labor unions. A reader of obviously strong nonviolent sentiment had asked how Christian soldiers could kill. Bell replied that such soldiers "are not going to war with personal hatred or murder in their hearts, only out of loyalty to their country and to rescue those who are being oppressed."[95] He had earlier written that a soldier could only be safe in binding himself to obey his commander.[96] But when asked if a person could still be absolutely true to God while belonging to a labor union, he replied that he himself could not because he would have to be in obedience to the rule of sinners, and they sometimes command things contrary to the Word of God. "How can we obey two masters? "he asked.[97] Bell never did explain the difference between military and labor authority.

This growing commitment to the government's war efforts, so aggressively expressed by Bell but also shared by many in the general constituency, culminated in an official expression of loyalty at the 1918 General Council, held 4–11 September in Springfield, Missouri. The Council went on record declaring "its unswerving loyalty to our Government and to its Chief Executive, President Wilson, and that we hereby restate our fixed purpose to assist in every way morally possible, consistent with our faith, in bringing the present 'World War' to a successful conclusion."[98]

At the previous General Council, the commitment to evangelize the troops had been taken, and throughout the year Richey had continued to report on his work among the soldiers.[99] He was invited to speak at the

94. Bell, "Destroy This Tract," 4.

95. Bell, "Questions and Answers," 11 January 1919, 5.

96. Bell, "Questions and Answers," 27 July 1918, 9.

97. Bell, "Questions and Answers," 11 January 1919, 5.

98. General Council minutes, 1918, 9.

99. Richey, "Amongst the Soldiers," 13 October 1917, 15; and Richey, "Amongst the Soldier Boys," 16 February 1918, 1, 7.

Sunday evening session of the 1918 General Council and gave a stirring address on the work of the United Prayer and Workers League among the troops. Later at that same council, a resolution was passed "urging all the saints to pray earnestly for their [the soldiers'] evangelization by every scriptural means" and to cooperate with the British Pentecostals in ministering among the soldiers in France.[100] The same month, the *Christian Evangel* published a special issue "in honor of our soldiers and sailors." On the front page was a drawing with the headline, "Christ in the Trenches."[101]

A greater openness in supporting the war effort did not mean that the Assemblies of God had lost its emphasis on prophecy and eschatology, although the fervor of such concern was gradually eroding and would abate, for all practical purposes, with the end of the war. However, observing current events and studying prophetic passages went hand-in-hand for the early Pentecostals. In the heat of world conflict, the *Evangel* made a front-page appeal "to the Pentecostal People Throughout the World to Observe Sunday, Nov. 3rd, and Monday, Nov. 4, 1918 in United Prayer Inviting Jesus, Our Heavenly Bridegroom, to Come Back." Bell and Frodsham, two of the three signers of the appeal, asserted their belief that the time had come for Jesus to return. "The last days are being fulfilled in a very literal manner." The war itself was the means by which God was shaking the nations.[102]

The Voices of the Conscientious Objectors

Although General Council members contributed little to pacifist literature after publishing the 1917 resolution, one American Pentecostal, Bartleman, continued his crusade against Christian military involvement. Bartleman published much during the war, including the three articles in the *Evangel* that became notorious for their pro-German sentiments. Perhaps in reaction to the later rejection of his tract by GPH, he published another tract after the war accusing the Pentecostal people of failing to stand by the Lord. Using the example of a conscientious objector being persecuted by Pentecostals for his position, he implied that he himself had been under surveillance during the war. "To be a Christian meant

100. General Council minutes, 1918, 9, 11.

101. *Christian Evangel*, 21 September 1918.

102. *Christian Evangel*, 24 August 1918, 1.

to be denominated 'pro-German.' Spies haunted every little Pentecostal meeting."[103] The Great War was over, but Bartleman was still calling for a renewed stand against all warfare.

Two passages of Scripture played an important part in Bartleman's understanding of the Christian's role in society. Both were Jesus's own words: "My kingdom is not of this world" (John 18:36) and "because ye are not of the world . . . therefore the world hateth you."[104] His ethic was focused on the reality of an "other worldly" kingdom.

Shortly after World War I, he published another tract that pictured the Christian caught in between two conflicting systems—socialism and the apostate church, identified with the "autocratic, ruling, capitalistic classes." It is evident Bartleman had not altered his stand on the Christian's citizenship, for he wrote, "A Christian has no more to do with the politics of this world than an American has with the politics of Europe."[105] He questioned what place a Christian had in world politics when it was all corruption, hypocrisy and debasement, and held that a man of belief was a man without a country. He emphasized that a Christian renounced his earthly citizenship when he was converted, just as he would his citizenship in the United States should he swear allegiance to a foreign nation.[106]

Conscientious objection seems to have had a much more visible profile among British Pentecostals than among their American counterparts. Undoubtedly the most influential British Pentecostal in the American General Council constituency was Gee, an invincible pacifist. He came into the movement in 1913, later pastoring in Edinburgh before assuming denominational leadership in the Assemblies of God in Britain. From 1934 to 1944 he served as vice-chair and then from 1945 until 1963 as chair. He also became, until his death in 1966, an ambassador at large for the Pentecostal movement worldwide.[107]

Possessing a keen sense of ethical duty, Gee pushed Pentecostals toward ecumenical relationships, saying: "We may find excellent reasons for rejecting the idea of communism, but those professing to be filled with the Spirit of Christ have the responsibility of showing a realistic alternative."[108]

103. Bartleman, "War and the Christian," 3.

104. Bartleman, "Not of this World," 296–97.

105. Bartleman, "Christian Citizenship," 1.

106. Bartleman, "Christian Citizenship," 2.

107. Whittaker, *Seven Pentecostal Pioneers*, 83, 87, 94–98.

108. Quoted in Hollenweger, *The Pentecostals*, 212.

By his own admission Gee was heavily influenced by Arthur S. Booth-Clibborn and may have been impressed by Bartleman on his visit to England as well. He spoke highly of Booth-Clibborn's influence on Pentecostals in his widely read book, *Wind and Flame*.[109]

During the First World War the Assembly of God in Harringway where Gee was a member "let it be known that, as followers of Christ, its members could not participate in war and bloodshed."[110] This was about the time Bartleman visited the church where his message was so warmly received by Gee's pastor, the Reverend Saxby.[111]

Gee himself filed for conscientious objector status and gained exemption from military service to do "work of national importance" in agriculture. "The severe spiritual strain and stress this involved, including not only the fiery trial at the tribunal, but later the months and years of continual obloquy and petty persecution, meant a growth in character and conviction that would have come much more slowly under peaceful circumstances."[112] That was the opinion of Gee as expressed by Howard Carter, fellow leader in the British Assemblies of God and a man who shared similar pacifist beliefs.

Gee's influence on the Pentecostal movement regarding pacifism would not be felt until after World War I, but by that time his pacifist appeal was all but lost in the patriotic din of the American Assemblies of God. Even so, his writings on the subject continued to be accepted in *The Pentecostal Evangel*.

Gee was not the only prominent British Pentecostal to suffer for his pacifism during World War I. Brothers John and Howard Carter both filed for exemption. John at first received total exemption, but later served time on a farm milking cows. Howard was sent to prison and then did rehabilitation work with troubled teenagers in a farm colony.

The Carter brothers were two of the founders of the Assemblies of God in Great Britain and Ireland,[113] with Howard serving as one of the first executive members. He eventually became vice-chair in 1929 and then chair from 1934 to 1945. Thus, the chairs of the British Assemblies for three decades had served as conscientious objectors during World

---

109. Gee, *Wind and Flame*, 102.
110. Carter, *Donald Gee*, 18.
111. Bartleman, *Two Years Mission Work*, 55.
112. Carter, *Donald Gee*, 18.
113. Carter, *Man of the Spirit*, 39–47, 75, 78.

War I. Others who were imprisoned for conscientious objection were Ernest T. Mellor, Thomas Moggs, and Wilfred Richardson.[114]

In the United States, no provision was made in the draft laws for absolute abstention, although provision was made for the religious objector who was a part of a church which prohibited members from participating in war in any form. This was a limited measure, however, for the law stated that "no person so exempted shall be exempted from service in any capacity that the President shall declare to be noncombatant."[115] Thus, the Assemblies of God encouraged its members to comply and go noncombatant.[116]

During World War I when pacifism was strongest among Pentecostal leaders, the statistical evidence of the number who claimed to adhere to this position is almost nonexistent.[117] Of all personnel inducted, 20,873 claimed noncombatant status, the only position recognized by the government. Slightly less than four thousand of these "persisted in their position after reaching camp because of the extraordinary harshness with which objectors were treated."[118] An Assemblies of God historian wrote that he was acquainted with a few [Pentecostal men?] who were "taken to military installations and stripped of all their clothing excepting their underwear and forced to go this way for days or else don the uniform which was laying close at hand."[119]

One thousand of the conscientious objectors were catalogued according to religious affiliation. Of these, thirteen were listed as Pentecostal, another twenty were likely to have been, and also some of the 206 from lesser known sects.[120] Of the 450 court-martialed, seventeen were Pentecostals, compared to thirteen Quakers, but hundreds of other Quakers were sent to the Friends reconstruction unit in France.[121] Exactly how many of the Pentecostals were affiliated with the Assemblies of God is impossible to determine. Interestingly, no American Assemblies of God personage of prominence took as visible a stand as did Gee and the Carters.

---

114. Gee, *Wind and Flame*, 39–49.

115. Schlissel, *Conscience in America*, 162–63.

116. "Compulsory Military Service," 7.

117. Beaman, "Pentecostal Pacifism," 83.

118. Lynd, *Nonviolence in America*, xxxiv.

119. Harrison, "A History," 151.

120. French, *We Won't Murder*, 85–87.

121. Thomas, *Is Conscience a Crime?*, 48.

18

Transitional Years
(1920–38)

WHILE THE BRITISH PENTECOSTALS continued to evince a strong pacifism long after World War II, the American Assemblies of God essentially
slid away from such leanings during the period between the two great
wars. Pacifism was an all but forgotten issue by the outbreak of World
War II, though the denomination never systematically examined its
stand during the interim.

Constitutional Changes

With the close of the First World War, any debate on the subject was
primarily academic and therefore of little interest within the movement.
The General Council was more preoccupied with organizational matters
during the 1920s. But the constitutional revisions of 1925 and 1927 inadvertently affected the resolutions of 1917 and 1918. Resolutions calling for major revisions were first made at the 1925 Council, though not
passed until 1927. The 1925 proposals included only the "pacifist" section
under the heading "Resolution Concerning the Attitude of the General
Council of the Assemblies of God toward Any Military Service which
involves the Actual Participating in the Destruction of Human Life."[1]
The "loyalty" section was not included.

1. "The Interpretation of the Constitutional Agreements and Essential Resolutions;
recommended by the Executive Presbytery 1925," 24–25; General Council combined
minutes, 1914–1925, 38–39.

In the 1927 Council major organizational changes were finally passed, creating a uniform constitution and bylaws. In the final report of the revisions committee, this time only the "loyalty" paragraph appeared, listed under the heading "Expression of Loyalty to the Government."[2] Even this section was recommended not to appear in the constitution and bylaws. However, in the final document there is included an "Article XV: Military Service" which neither subscribes to the changes called for nor reads like the old section, but is a reordered and less expansive passage of the old section:

> While recognizing Human Government as of Divine Ordination and affirming our unswerving loyalty to the Government of the United States, nevertheless we are constrained to define our position with reference to the taking of human life.
>
> Whereas, We as followers of the Lord Jesus Christ, the Prince of Peace, believe in implicit obedience to the Divine commands and precepts which instruct us to "Follow peace with all men" (Heb. 12:14), "Thou shalt not kill" (Ex. 20:13), "Resist not evil" (Matt. 5:39), "Love your enemies" (Matt. 5:44), etc. and
>
> Whereas, These and other Scriptures have always been accepted and interpreted by our churches as prohibiting Christians from shedding blood or taking human life;
>
> Whereas, We as a body of Christians, while purposing to fulfill all obligations of loyal citizenship, are nevertheless constrained to declare we can not conscientiously participate in war and armed resistance which involves the actual destruction of human life, since this is contrary to our view of the clear teachings of the inspired Word of God, which is the sole basis of our faith.
>
> Therefore, be it
>
> Resolved, That the General Council hereby declares its unswerving loyalty to our government and to its Chief Executive, and that we hereby restate our fixed purpose to assist in every way morally possible, consistent with our faith.[3]

The major difference between this and the resolution passed ten years previously is that the concluding statement became a loyalty

---

2. "Final Report of Revision Committee on Essential Resolutions," 29. This is found after the proposed constitution and bylaws in a section of resolutions which "do not logically belong either in a constitution or a by-law. They may be revised and published in a revised and combined copy of the minutes but should not be part of the Constitution and By-laws," "Final Report of Revision Committee on Essential Resolutions," 26.

3. General Council constitution and bylaws, 1927, 28–29.

proclamation instead of a pacifist declaration. What was omitted, perhaps more for purposes of brevity than anything else, were the following
sentiments: "We plainly declare the Holy Inspired Scriptures to be the all
sufficient rule of faith and practice" and "the Scriptures deal plainly with
the obligations and relations of humanity, setting forth the principles of
'peace on earth, good will toward men' (Luke 2:14). However, the Council had not altered its stand on the Scriptures as that stand was articulated
elsewhere.

Little is recorded regarding the intentions of the Council, except that
just before the constitution and bylaws were finally adopted, the Council
moved and carried a resolution to reaffirm its expression of "Loyalty to
the Government."[4] Loyalty had become the primary concern.

No additional mention is made in the records as to how or why Article XV was voted to be included in the bylaws when it had not been in
the earlier proposal, or why certain sections were deleted from the original resolutions. Nevertheless, the section as adopted in 1927 remained
essentially unchanged for the next twenty-five years.

The Decline of Pacifism

The interlude between the two world wars was marked by an uneasy
peace. *The Pentecostal Evangel* continued to produce articles with apocalyptic and eschatological focus similar to those written in the period
prior to World War I. In 1925, the question was raised, "How long will
peace last?" Observing the election of Field-Marshal van Hindenburg,
Germany's war hero, to be President of the German Republic, the *Evangel*
replied, not long. Quoting Sir John Foster Fraser, "Will the combination
of the greater democratic nations, acting on the principle that to be ready
for war is the best guarantee for peace, be successful in preventing war? I
do not believe so." The only solution, the editors wrote, to averting or at
least delaying world war again is prayer. "The world is preparing for war;
the saints are preparing for revival." Three days of prayer had been held
in April and similar days were being called for by church leaders for July
2–4.[5]

The idea of lasting harmony and concord among nations was in-
comprehensible to Pentecostal believers for whom the world was fast

4. General Council minutes, 1927, 73.
5. "How Long Will Peace Last?" 4.

approaching Armageddon. It was the reality of human history as well as their other-worldly perspective which caused them to be skeptical of peace efforts. The inevitability of war would be a fact of life until the coming of the Prince of Peace. Since 1496 B.C., it was noted, the world had enjoyed fewer than 250 years without war. And with Russia, Germany, Italy, and Japan all rearming, it was obvious that tyranny was again coming to the fore. What hope there was rested in the realization that ultimate, universal war was not possible before the rapture of the Church.[6] The theme is reminiscent of that of World War I pacifists and non-pacifists alike who had rejected human peace-making efforts on the basis of their futility.

This other-worldly attitude toward mounting world tensions is strongly evident throughout this period. The rise to power of Mussolini, Stalin, and Hitler were monitored closely in light of biblical prophecy. Though the writers in *The Pentecostal Evangel* did not necessarily "gloat" over world events, their optimism was not concealed. Consider, for example, a response to the imperial rumblings of Mussolini in Italy: "Well, praise the Lord! If the fulfillment of Rev. 13 and 17 is near, the fulfillment of I Thess. 4:13–18 is nearer. Keep looking up! He is at the door!"[7]

Even so, something other than eschatology played a role in causing most Pentecostals to reject pacifism. The variable was the concept that Christians were obligated to obey human government.

Williams championed the loyalist role in the 1930s and 1940s much as his predecessor, Bell, had done earlier. Through his pen as well as in the pulpit, a patriotic note was played as had not been heard before by *Evangel* readers. Unabashedly he proclaimed, "We are Americans."[8] Earthly citizenship was not to be dishonored. "Let us do our best to be good citizens," he preached.[9] Though he had declared that believers are Christians first, then Americans, increasingly he placed emphasis on the dual nature of the Christian's citizenship:

> Some have felt that their allegiance to God forbids their saluting the national flag or respecting the Government of the Nation. We feel sorry for those who sincerely feel thus. They are suffering from being wrongly taught. While "our citizenship is in

6. Panton, "Universal War," 2, 3.
7. "The Mussolini Empire," 3.
8. Williams, "Our Duty as Christian Citizens," 1.
9. Williams, "Christian Citizenship."

heaven" and "we seek a country" those are blessings of hope to be realized when the present age is past and we enter "the everlasting kingdom," our eternal home. But we are also citizens of our native land and subject to its laws. Let us recognize our relationship both to "the everlasting kingdom" which we fondly hope to enter, and to the present civil order of which we are also a part.[10]

Note the change in the concept of the heavenly kingdom. It is identified by Williams wholly in futuristic terms.

The transfer of allegiance to temporal power had two foundations. One was the numerous scriptural injunctions on the subject such as the ruler is not to be cursed; the people are to be subject to the higher powers; rulers are not a terror to good works, but to the evil; and so on. The question of whether this applied to such despotic rulers as the dictators of Germany and Russia was never addressed in this context.

But Williams was quick to point out that the second basis for the Christian's loyal duty was the liberty with which America was blessed. Faith in religion was fundamental in America and had characterized American life. "The provision for separation of State and Church was meant to keep some one religion [from being] considered the only accepted religion, not to remove religion from our national life."[11] The place of the church in the nation was spiritual and moral, not political, though being apolitical did not preclude promotion of loyalty to government. As he would write later,

> Loyalty to God and loyalty to government may go hand in hand in our free United States. It is cause for rejoicing that we can give unswerving loyalty to those who rule over us without having to stifle conscience or deprive the Eternal Sovereign the rights which belong to Him. May this harmony between the makers of our State and the Maker of our destiny continue. *Only in the matter of worship do we own an allegiance more binding than our allegiance to the State.* God must have first claim upon us in this.[12]

Bell and Williams were alike in the matter of refocusing allegiance from a radical commitment to scriptural authority to a more "balanced" obedience. Supreme loyalty was now reserved only for matters of worship.

10. Williams, "Our Duty as Christian Citizens," 1.

11. Williams, "American Nation."

12. Williams, "We Are Grateful for the U.S.A.," 4. Emphasis added.

As long as citizens were granted freedom, particularly religious freedom, the Government was to be granted allegiance in all other matters. As Williams wrote, "We are blessed with unbounded liberty."[13]

Some Pentecostals, however, did not share this reasoning. The most vocal spokesperson was Gee, who wrote a two-part series on "War, the Bible, and the Christian" for *The Pentecostal Evangel* in 1930.[14] Narrow-sighted nationalism and unreserved patriotism were for him the bane of the Christian church, especially as demonstrated in World War I. Decrying the church's inability to mount a united front against militarism, Gee wrote, "Patriotism surged over everything; its virtues were represented as the truest expression of the Christian life, and its sacrifices were upheld as evidencing the very spirit of Calvary."[15] Patriotism should not be allowed to run so wild in believers, he admonished. Gee, however, went further than Williams in arguing for allegiance to the State. Submission to temporal authority was not dependent on political persuasion, he proclaimed; in fact, the Christian had no choice but to be obedient to the leaders. As he saw it, the mandate for such submission was not because of any particular blessings bestowed by the State, but because the Scriptures so dictated. Gee saw no dual allegiance: "The Christian's true citizenship is in heaven. Phil. 3:20, R. V. He obeys the laws of his earthly country in exactly the same way as an alien passing through. His ultimate allegiance is always to his heavenly King."[16] Practically, this meant that God must always come first. The State must be obeyed in all matters, except when the State dictated actions contrary to the laws of God. For Gee, blind patriotism and military service crossed this delicate line.

Because he viewed the Old Testament's regard for warfare as dispensational, it was inapplicable as exemplary material. His doctrine was based on the primacy of the teachings of Jesus. For Gee, the Christian's supreme model was Jesus himself: "No Christian artist has ever represented the Galilean as commanding a machine-gun battalion or piloting a bombing plane."[17] The New Testament church was uniform in following Jesus's example.

13. Williams, "Our Duty as Christian Citizens," 1.

14. Gee, "War, the Bible, and the Christian," 8 November 1930, 6–7; and 15 November 1930, 2–3.

15. Gee, "War, the Bible, and the Christian," 8 November 1930, 6.

16. Gee, "War, the Bible, and the Christian," 15 November 1930, 2.

17. Gee, "War, the Bible, and the Christian," 8 November 1930, 7. Gee was quoting an unidentified "recent worldly periodical."

Gee spoke with respect of chaplains and others who had ministered to the spiritual needs of those fighting in war. He did not even oppose Christians serving in the military, adding that "God meets us in grace during this dispensation."[18] Each Christian was expected to walk in the light he or she had been given, and conscientious objection was a deeply personal matter. But Gee observed that those Pentecostals who had taken a strongly patriotic stand in the last war had mostly gone backward in spiritual power, while "those who put Christ and His Word before all have advanced by divine grace to positions of spiritual leadership."[19] He emphasized, however, that divine blessing did not necessarily represent divine approval. The Christian was called upon to do "prayerful study of the will of God revealed in His Word, and for earnest consecration to do that will at whatever cost, based upon solid conviction."[20]

The editor of *The Pentecostal Evangel* at this time was Frodsham. Though it is difficult to determine how strongly pacifist Frodsham really was, he served on the Executive Presbytery which formulated the Resolution of 1917. In "Our Heavenly Citizenship," written in 1915, he had issued a call for Pentecostals to go beyond nationalism and patriotism and to recognize their heavenly citizenship. He urged his readers to side with the Prince of Peace and not against the Lord and His anointed as the kings of the earth had done. Closing with an apocalyptic description of how God would triumph with his saints, Frodsham couched his pacifism in clearly eschatological terms. For him, the issue was one of being distinct from the world.[21]

Whether this viewpoint remained with him in the 1940s is hard to tell. He served as editor of the *Evangel* through the Second World War during a time when pacifism was vanishing from the teachings of the Assemblies of God. How much he was allowed to express his personal beliefs in editorial policy is uncertain. Occasionally there were brief fillers describing the horrors and the cost of war ("War does not prove which nation is right, but only which nation is strong.—Robert W. Searle"[22]), and pacifist articles by Gee and others appeared in the weekly until

18. Gee, "War, the Bible, and the Christian, 15 November 1930, 2.
19. Gee, "War, the Bible, and the Christian, 15 November 1930, 3.
20. Gee, "War, the Bible, and the Christian," 8 November 1930, 6.
21. Frodsham, "Our Heavenly Citizenship," 3.
22. *The Pentecostal Evangel*, 8 January 1938, 7.

Frodsham's retirement. Significantly, no such views were expressed in print after 1948, the year he resigned.

On one occasion, Frodsham devoted nearly two pages of the *Evangel* to an editorial of his own writing in which he took a decisively pacifist stance. Warning of the looming world crisis, he reminded his readers of the recent ravages of war. "Some of us have not forgotten the horrors of the last war and certainly do not want to see the voices of a number of greedy profiteers and grafters, with visions of bloated bank accounts such as they obtained in the last war, prevailing in inducing our rulers to rush into another great war."[23]

God's will, he declared, is the way of peace. Believers belong to a kingdom "not of this world," the principles of which have been set forth by its King, the Prince of Peace. "The writer has always thought it a peculiar way to show our love to our enemies by pushing bayonets into them."[24] Hope for the world would have to wait for the hereafter, but in the meantime the saints were expected to remain true to the principles of the kingdom.

A careful, scriptural study of the issue of war and military service was printed in 1936 by an author identified only by the initials, R. G. The reasoning used by the author as he wrestled with various standard objections to nonviolence was common to Gee and other Pentecostal pacifists. Among the major themes, the New Covenant (especially the Sermon on the Mount) was sharply contrasted with the Law of the Old Covenant.

His thesis was that Christians "are to resemble God the Father and His Son Jesus Christ, and to explain them to the world."[25] They are therefore to emulate the God of Peace, as portrayed in the New Testament. Echoing Gee's declaration, this source countered that believers are to be governed by biblical obligation, not simple pragmatic reasoning. The question, "What would become of us, if all were to refuse to fight?" is moot for the Christian. "But our question ought to be: 'What is our duty?' Not, 'What will be the consequences of it!' 'Duties are ours; events are God's.'"[26]

---

23. Frodsham, "The Editor's Notebook," 20 February 1932, 4.

24. Frodsham, "The Editor's Notebook," 20 February 1932, 5.

25. R. G., "Our Attitude toward War," 4.

26. R. G., "Our Attitude toward War," 5.

The case of Russian Conscientious Objectors

An intriguing series of correspondence developed when a shift by Russian Pentecostals away from pacifism in 1927 caused a stir in the missions leadership of the General Council. Information about the controversy is contained in correspondence from Paul B. Peterson, general secretary for the Russian and Eastern European Mission (REEM), to Noel Perkin, missions secretary for the General Council.[27] It is enlightening for it focused on the issue of citizenship in a totalitarian state and how Pentecostals were to respond to military draft.

Under government pressure, conscientious objectors were not being tolerated by Russian Pentecostal leaders. Their position, Peterson asserted, was opposite to that of the American Assemblies of God in that a person could not be a member of the Assemblies of God in the U.S.S.R. unless he or she approved of military service by Christians. "This is wrong no matter how many verses of Scripture they may quote to ease their conscience in assuming their position."[28]

The question of military service was a burning issue among the Russian believers. The All-Russian Evangelical Christian Union had been forced to reverse its position and advocate military service for the past several years, and the All-Russian Baptist Union had agreed to the same policy. Now the Pentecostal leaders had also bowed to the government's decree, rather than face prison or worse. Already some Baptists were now in exile because they would not accept the decision of the Baptist Union, and Peterson reported that Russian believers as a whole had always been against military service.

Peterson admitted that the Russian brethren were writing with great care, but the submission by Pentecostal leaders to Russian law saddened REEM officials. "This stand is absolutely unchristian, for certainly no demand by the Soviet government of this nature should be made THE condition for uniting with the Assemblies of God."[29] The response of

27. Peterson was an ordained minister with the Assemblies of God 1927–1943. Peterson, Ministers file. REEM worked in close cooperation with the Assemblies of God missions department during the 1920s and 1930s. Most, if not all of REEM's executive officers held General Council ministerial papers, and in 1939 a proposal was considered and then rejected to merge REEM with the Assemblies of God missions department. See letter from Perkin to Peterson and members of the board of trustees of the REEM, 27 December 1939.

28. Letter from Peterson to Perkin, 21 September 1928.

29. Letter from Peterson to Perkin, 21 September 1928. Emphasis in original.

the Russian Pentecostals was to point out that they were obeying their
government just as American Pentecostals obeyed theirs. It was a difficult
matter for REEM and the Assemblies of God missions department:

> While we wish to be charitable and take into consideration
> the difficulties and persecutions incident to opposing the So-
> viet Russian laws, we do not seem to be able to reconcile their
> attitude with God's word on the point of excommunicating
> members from the assemblies who will not serve in the army
> or urge obedience to the law regarding military service. It seems
> we have to decide which of two evils is greater—to support
> the work in spite of the unbiblical attitude and actions of the
> brethren, or to withdraw our support and consequently have the
> work suffer.[30]

Peterson's response to the Russians was that there should be only
one consideration: what is the Lord's will? "His Word is our only guide
in faith and practice. . . . we must insist upon adherence to the Word
whatever the cost may be."[31]

Eventually Peterson conceded with Voronaeff, a leader in the Russian Assemblies of God, that submission to government and laws was
necessary as long as there were no transgression of the laws and teaching
of Jesus (1 Cor 9:20–23). But to make conscientious objection a matter of excommunication was inexcusable. "We cannot possibly find any
grounds for such action in the Word of God." It was to be a matter of
conscience.[32]

Whether the issue was ever resolved is not known. From the last ex-
tant correspondence on the subject: "If they will not change their attitude
our thought is to gradually decrease our support of the work in U.S.S.R.,
as much as we dislike to do so, because we do not wish to have any part
in strengthening their stand in disfellowshipping believers for the reason
mentioned above."[33] What is pertinent to this study is that Peterson and
Perkin understood pacifism to be a mainstream Pentecostal position and
that there were limitations to the Christian's loyalty to government. Abstaining from military service was a matter integral to faith and therefore
a conviction for which it was better to suffer than to submit.

---

30. Letter from Peterson to Perkin, 13 June 1929.
31. Letter from Peterson to Perkin, 12 July 1929.
32. Letter from Peterson to Perkin, 12 July 1929.
33. Letter from Peterson to Perkin, 4 September 1929.

19

Changing Perspectives in Wartime
(1939–53)

BY 1939 THE WORLD sat on the edge of a kind of impending doom unlike any it had ever faced. Totalitarian machines in Germany, Italy, Russia, and Japan were threatening to sweep the world. Such a crisis placed the church worldwide amid unprecedented dilemma.

Emphasis on Loyalty

In that year the General Council in session sent a telegram to the President of the United States, applauding his efforts for peace, "not the least of which is the maintenance of American neutrality."[1] It would be the last time the Council would urge such a posture; it would also be the last time the Council could affirm simultaneously a non-militarist and a loyalist stance.

In 1938, the year before, the writer of the Sunday school lesson in *The Pentecostal Evangel* had considered the text of Romans 13. Displaying submissiveness, the distinctive characteristic of the Christian, Jesus Christ held himself subject to temporal authority. "He did this when He and all men knew that those powers had been sold out to Satan." Evidently, the moral nature of a government was no precondition for obedience to that government. Only when the state commanded action contrary to what God commanded was it to be disobeyed, and then not arrogantly.[2] An

1. General Council minutes, 1939, 57–58.
2. "Our Attitude to the Government," 6.

accompanying cartoon quoted the verse, "Render unto Caesar the things which are Caesar's—and unto God the things that are God's." Caesar's share was depicted as payment of taxes; God's share was prayer.

Soon the government was going to demand more than just taxes. A world war would call for much greater loyalty, and the Assemblies of God was readier to give it than it had been in the first great conflict. The *Evangel* took its responsibility seriously to stand behind the war effort. A case in point was the 28 June 1941 issue where the cover article interpreted divine intervention as coming on the side of the cause of the Allies.[3] A photograph depicted a boy placing an American flag on the front of a house. On each side just beneath the masthead, a drawing of the Statue of Liberty was accompanied by the verses, "Stand fast . . . in the liberty wherewith Christ has made us free," and "Where the Spirit of the Lord is, there is liberty." On page three, in the middle of an article on prophecy, a banner read, "God bless America." This was followed by "If My people . . . shall humble themselves and pray . . . then will I hear . . . and will forgive."

Other General Council periodicals were also supporting the war effort. An advertisement for *The Christ's Ambassadors Herald* announced that the January issue of the youth publication was "dedicated to the defenders of America—on the fighting front, as well as on the spiritual front."[4]

A speaker at the 1941 General Council addressed the issue of loyalty to government and God. Before posing the question of spiritual loyalty, Elsworth Krogstad promoted the cause of national allegiance. Again, Jesus was the model loyalist. If Jesus was *"absolutely* loyal to the powers then governing,"[5] how much more could Americans be loyal who live in a nation founded on religious principles.

The message had quite a different flavor than anything expressed in the Assemblies of God theretofore. Krogstad spoke of the thrill "Old Glory" brought him on his return to the States and said that anyone disagreeing with the American form of government was welcome to leave. As citizens of this country and a heavenly country as well, American Christians owed their allegiance to the Government not only because of the great freedoms afforded them, but because of the godly heritage of this land. Then he quoted the poem, "The Landing of the Pilgrims," by

3. Argue, "Until I Have Showed," 1.

4. "Defenders of America," 14.

5. Emphasis added.

Felicia Hemans with its line about the land the Pilgrims trod as being "holy ground." Asserting that this was a freedom purchased with great human sacrifice, Krogstad argued that it was precisely because of such a price by the country's forefathers that loyalty was demanded[6]—a complete reversal in attitude from even the non-pacifists of World War II.

At the National Young People's Conference in 1941, Wesley R. Steelberg, who would become general superintendent a decade later, urged the denomination's youth "to be very grateful for the freedom we have." He declared that the purpose of the gathering, held on 4 July, was to express dual loyalty to God and country.[7]

A Righteous Crusade

More was at stake here than just a new-found patriotism. In both world wars, Pentecostals evaluated the involved nations' efforts from a moral perspective. The verdict had been less than clear during the first war, but the sides were better defined in the second. Themes of retribution and repentance once again dominated the war commentaries in the *Evangel*. God was in the process of meting out judgment and not even the United States was exempt. The massive conflict was seen as God's way of dealing with the nation for "her multiplied iniquities." In other words, God was using America's enemies, Japan and Germany, as whips "to punish us for our sins."[8]

At the end of the war, Riggs stated that the most significant sin America had committed was in not fulfilling her special calling to provide an army of missionaries to spread the gospel worldwide. "The Christians have been forced to give one-tenth of their income in taxes and war bonds and their sons to the armed forces of our nation because they had not voluntarily obeyed His commands to give and to go in the holy cause of world missions."[9]

Other sins such as crime and divorce were grievous in America, but she had been given opportunity to repent. Germany's sin, however, led to crushing fall and ruin. This once God-fearing people, the cradle of the Reformation, had sunk into the awful hell of Nazism. "Those murders,

6. Krogstad, "Loyalty to Government," 1.

7. Steelberg, "The Stars and Stripes," 1.

8. Davis, "Nation-wide Prayer," 1.

9. Riggs, "V-E Day," 1.

those blasphemies, those defiances of the God of the Jews and His chosen people, those unspeakable crimes of torture and sadism, and those horrible rapes of nations, have mounted to high Heaven and have brought down the fierce wrath of the Almighty."[10]

Significantly, the *Evangel* continually condemned Germany, while nothing was written regarding Japan. Although Japan was an equally formidable foe, it did not share Germany's religious heritage. Germany had become a spiritual as well as a national enemy.

Opposition was expressed toward Germany on two primary counts: the intense hatred the Nazis evidenced toward the Jews as well as their anti-Christian attitude. In the *Evangel's* most open attack, it declared in 1944 that Germany could not possibly win. "If Hitlerism wins, then the Jew must die, and the Jew cannot die." Citing the intense anti-Semitism of the Nazis, the article presented scriptural documentation to prove the unique historical role of the Jew and the inevitable judgment or the enemies of the Jew. Hitlerism had also set itself up against God. The article quoted from a Nazi booklet that explained that God and Jesus were unacceptable to the Germans."[11]

If blasphemy were not enough, the church itself was being attacked in Germany, even threatened with annihilation. Hitler and Germany were seen as enemies of the church, the Jew, other oppressed peoples, and God Himself. The world was overshadowed by two opposing symbols, the Cross and the Swastika,[12] and this called for a holy war against Hitler's demonic schemes.[13] *The Pentecostal Evangel* sounded the battle cry, "As He died to make men holy, let us die to make men free, / While God is marching on."[14]

Such a portrayal of America's enemy did not, however, include the prophetic overtones that had accompanied other world events. Occasionally, last days signs were identified,[15] but Pentecostal writers did not

10. Riggs, "V-E Day," 1.

11. Cited by Kagan, "Hitlerism Must Lose," 1, 7.

12. "Nazi Storm Trooper," 6.

13. "Heavenly Songs," 8–9. This excerpt is from a review of a book, of which the English version was distributed by GPH, written by Gustav Herbert Schmidt of his experiences at the hands of the Gestapo as a persecuted Pentecostal preacher.

14. Howe, "The Battle Hymn," 3. This spiritual national anthem was printed in its entirety.

15. For example, mention was made that there had never been a war in which traitors played so prominent a role, very significant in the light of Bible prophecy: "in

perceive Nazism to be so prominent in God's prophetic picture. In a favored interpretation of Ezekiel 38 and 39, Germany would be subjugated to a yet stronger northern power, believed to be Russia.[16] While Hitler demonstrated an anti-Christ spirit, his victory was not prophetically inevitable. Pentecostals in World War I had expressed futility in fighting a war already dictated by prophecy, but no such script had been written in the Bible for this war.

America could therefore choose to fight such a perpetrator of evil, her road to victory lying in national repentance and prayer. "As our nation repents and returns to God and the Lord Jesus Christ, great victories may be brought to pass on land, and sea, and in the air."[17] Thousands of "Revival and Victory" prayer cards were distributed through *The Pentecostal Evangel* and GPH. Signers of the card pledged "to spend ten minutes or more daily . . . praying for repentance, revival, and return to God, throughout our land; and for victory for our forces on land and sea and in the air."[18] Monday was designated as the nationwide cottage prayer meeting night.

A front-page drawing headlined "God be with us," depicted Uncle Sam on his knees interceding for the "liberation of enslaved Europe."[19] The *Evangel* called on its readers to pray for revival, mass evangelization, and a speedy end to the war that the gospel might be preached. It declared, "We are praying in the will of God when we make petition for the world's rulers, and that a just peace may be established."[20] A just peace meant the defeat of Hitler and his tyranny.

The battle cry was against human principalities and powers, not people, however. Nothing but compassion was expressed for the common people of the enemy nations, who themselves were more often than not considered victims. To the Pentecostal reader, the spiritual worth of an individual superseded all political barriers. Just prior to America's entrance into the war, a story appeared in the *Evangel* depicting the conversion of seven Red Army soldiers about to face a firing squad in Finland in 1918. Written by a Finnish soldier, it demonstrated great warmth and

---

the last days men shall be traitors." 2 Tim 3:4. "Traitors," 13.

16. Kagan, "Hitlerism Must Lose," 7.

17. Davis, "Nation-wide Prayer," 1.

18. "Victory Prayer Card," 12.

19. Shoemaker, "God Be with Us," 1.

20. "Victory," 1.

compassion for these doomed men, whose conversion to Christ caused the soldier and his friends to forget their hatred and, instead, to make a decision as well for Christ.[21] Similar concern was expressed for the young Nazis of Germany: "We must go to the Continent of Europe and win these young people for Christ."[22] Such concern was more than rhetoric. Marie Juergensen, a veteran missionary to Japan, worked extensively among the Japanese at a relocation center in Idaho.[23] These people were not considered enemies, but helpless innocent victims caught in a war not of their own making.

The Spiritual Battle for Servicemen

Battle lines were being drawn in another sphere as well—the spiritual lives of the American servicemen. In fact, the Council's evangelistic efforts were to have a profound impact on military personnel and on the fellowship itself.

Richey again led the fight. He challenged the 1941 General Council to reach out wholeheartedly to the "cream of the nation" now stationed in the various camps[24] which, he considered, were "the greatest opportunity for home missionary work that ever has been."[25] As others had been doing, Richey called for national repentance, stating that the nation had drifted from God. "America has departed from the Source of all her blessings." His was a cautious patriotism, however. Do you love the Stars and Stripes, he asked his listeners? Acknowledging their national loyalty, he averred that only spiritual faithfulness could keep the nation free. No matter how glorious the nation was, it deserved only secondary allegiance. "This is about the only nation where one flag can go above the national flag, and that one flag is the Christian flag. Thank God it is thus. Let us keep it that way."[26]

Richey was one of many evangelists carrying on the work among the camps. Harry Jaeger ministered extensively across the nation; a Brother

21. "Red Soldiers Were Transformed," 4.

22. "Nazi Storm Trooper," 7.

23. Juergensen, "Japanese Relocation Center," 10.

24. "The Diary of a Delegate," 10.

25. Richey, "Our Army Camps," 12. This article was taken from a sermon earlier preached at Central Assembly of God in Springfield, Missouri.

26. Richey, "Our Army Camps," 2.

Gidman worked among sailors; and a Mrs. Seahold ministered in Civilian Conservation Camps. Father-daughter team, Watson and Zelma Argue, labored similarly in Canada.[27]

Much of the denominational initiative came as a result of action at the 1941 General Council in Minneapolis. The theme of the Council was "Our Place in the Present World Crisis," and a declaration was made that it was "the responsibility of the Assemblies of God to maintain spiritual watchcare over our boys in the Armed Service and to evangelize the unsaved."[28] The Council acted to support this ministry through the erection of tabernacles near military camps. Many of the evangelistic efforts were being accomplished through tent meetings, but more permanent facilities were needed.[29]

With the action of the 1941 Minneapolis General Council, the servicemen's work became a formal program of the Assemblies of God. The ministry was placed in the Home Missions department, though little was developed organizationally until later.

The suggestion was made at the Minneapolis conference that a paper suitable for circulation in the camps be produced by GPH. Myer Pearlman, assistant editor of *The Pentecostal Evangel* and instructor at Central Bible Institute, began work almost immediately on this project. Born of Jewish parentage and raised in England, Pearlman had served as a private in the United States Army during World War I and had since come to be a highly respected Assemblies of God biblical scholar.

The new publication, *Reveille*, proved to be a tremendous success and became one of the most celebrated religious publications of the war. For the first edition, 170,000 copies were printed, including a special edition depicting the British flag for use in Canada. Published quarterly and undated, fifteen wartime issues of *Reveille* were printed and distributed through a mailing list which reached 100,000 names. Thousands more were distributed through chaplains of many denominations. It was the only non-governmental religious publication given free postage to any theater in the world. The cost of the entire program—$450,000—was underwritten by the Assemblies of God constituency.[30]

27. "1,000 Testaments," 13; "Helping the Service Man," 1; and "The Diary of a Delegate," 10.

28. General Council minutes, 1941, 63.

29. General Council minutes, 1941, 64.

30. General Council minutes, 1945, 81.

Reveille's format changed many times, but the simple evangelistic message remained basically the same. Each issue also had an upbeat perspective and was designed with military and patriotic colors and symbols. As a publication for military personnel, it reflected the feelings of the time and served as a motivational influence in the lives of the soldiers. Its purpose, as stated in the dedication of its first issue, was "to awaken your interest in values of life. We feel that faithfulness to these ideals will make you better soldiers as well as better citizens."[31]

References to Hitler and the Axis were frequent.[32] Though the paper exhibited little outright animosity toward the nation's enemies, occasional prejudicial statements were expressed in foxhole lingo: "Troops land on Kiska to give Nips a fitting send-off. Evidently the little brown men were no where to be found."[33]

The Assemblies of God first began participating in the military chaplaincy program in 1941, with Clarance P. Smales being the first to receive a commission. Chaplain Smales was prominently featured at the following General Council and his message later printed in the *Evangel.* Addressing the Council, he said that a good Christian made a good soldier, and that a soldier must have a useful religion, one which was loyal to God and his country. "When our souls come in vital contact with Christ there springs up within our heart more loyalty than ever before for the cause of God and for our country. None of us want to be traitors. Let us then serve Christ with all our might, with all the strength that God gives unto us."[34] It is difficult to determine if religion for Smales simply served a utilitarian purpose for the military cause.

Because of limited organization, J. R. Flower served as a one-man chaplain's commission. He approved applications, sending them on to be processed through the NAE in Washington, D.C., shortly after that organization began operation.

As word spread that the War Department was looking for more chaplains, many Assemblies of God ministers "envisioned an opportunity to serve their country and at the same time to continue in their calling as ministers of the gospel."[35] Most of them were not aware of the

31. *Reveille,* 1:1.

32. *Reveille,* 1:8.

33. *Reveille,* 1:9. "Nips" was a derisive term used of the Japanese.

34. Smales, "Marks of a Good Soldier," 1.

35. General Council minutes, 1943, 34. This statement follows immediately a paragraph mentioning the help the general secretary was affording the Conscientious Objectors.

standards set for the chaplaincy. Qualifications included being a male between the ages of 23 and 34, being ordained with three year's ministry experience, and being a graduate of both a four-year college and a three-year theological seminary.[36] The War Department temporarily lowered the educational requirements during World War II; otherwise, almost no Assemblies of God ministers would have been able to apply.[37] By 1943, eight ministers had been granted commissions.[38] In all, 34 ministers served during World War II; two were awarded the Purple Heart and three the Bronze Star.[39]

In January 1944, a servicemen's department was formally established, and Harry Jaeger was appointed director.[40] *Reveille* continued to be the department's most visible product, but in addition, one and a half million letters were written to servicemen during the war and the department appointed evangelists and provided Victory Service Centers for ministry among the soldiers.[41]

Following the war, the work of the Servicemen's Department rapidly decreased and was placed under the Christ Ambassadors [youth] Department. Then in 1951, the General Council designated the Chaplaincy Commission of the NAE as the official agency to represent the Council in the processing of ministers for commission in the Armed Forces.[42] An Assemblies of God pastor, Douglas G. Scott, became chair of the NAE Commission on Chaplains.[43] During this period, there were sixteen Council ministers serving as chaplains.[44]

This renewed interest in work among servicemen came at the height of the Korean War. Scott challenged the *Evangel* readership with the idea

---

36. Honeywell, *Chaplains of the U. S. Army*, 214.

37. However, these educational requirements for the chaplaincy did much in later years to persuade the General Council for the need to provide post-baccalaureate courses.

38. General Council minutes, 1943, 34.

39. General Council minutes, 1945, 83.

40. The department, established under order of the Executive Presbytery, was later authorized by the General Council. General Council minutes, 1945, 80. Pearlman, who had served as editor of *Reveille* and as coordinator for all servicemen's activities, died in 1943. He was temporarily replaced by Fred Vogler, home missions secretary.

41. Jaeger, "Servicemen's Department."

42. General Council minutes, 1951, 34.

43. Photography caption, *The Pentecostal Evangel*, 2 November 1952, 20.

44. "Chaplain School," 20.

that "the day has arrived when we, as a church, must consider the Chaplaincy to be a definite branch of the church."[45]

Military Involvement and Conscientious Objection

A significant shift had come within the fellowship since World War I. Military involvement by Assemblies of God people in the second great war was not alone due to the justification of this particular conflict. The very attitude toward participation in war in general had changed. The fellowship was proud of its fighting men, partly because this involvement showed the strength of the denomination and demonstrated its respectability as a church body to other religious organizations. Wrote one church historian a decade after the war, "The blood of the noble youth from the ranks of the Assemblies of God flowed with that of all others . . . and they wrote a like glorious page in the history of our land with those of the other great churches of America."[46] As many as fifty thousand men from the Assemblies of God were in the service in 1944,[47] but during the course of the war, the Service Men's Division of the General Council compiled a directory of more than 76,000 names, over a thousand of whom were killed in action.[48]

Conscientious objection, almost entirely lacking in mainline denominations during World War I, grew in those churches during the Second World War. In contrast, it decreased in Pentecostal circles.[49] However, there were still many men in the Assemblies of God opposed to war.

By virtue of office, the person in the General Council most responsible for dealing with pacifists and noncombatants was J. Roswell Flower, now general secretary-treasurer. In 1943, he reported that his office was faced with increased responsibility because of all kinds of war-related requests, including correspondence with local draft boards and even the office of the President of the United States when necessitated by improper classification of ministers and laymen. The general secretary also covered the problems of conscientious objectors who had been consigned to the

45. Scott, "The Chaplaincy," 20.
46. Harrison, "A History," 156.
47. "50,000 men," 12.
48. General Council minutes, 1945, 81.
49. Selective Service System, *Conscientious Objection*, 324.

Civilian Public Services Camps and men who had sought noncombatant status.[50] During the next two years problems related to conscientious objectors decreased, but there were still "a number of our young men who refused all military service on the grounds of conscience."[51]

Three classifications of conscientious objectors were listed. The first category, those actually called Conscientious Objectors, were the men assigned by the National Service Board of Religious Objectors (NSBRO) to Civilian Public Service camps. A total of 11,950 objectors of all types served in the camps during World War II.[52] At least 130 of these were listed as Pentecostals,[53] as many as 35 being from the Assemblies of God.[54] In the second category, 20,000 to 30,000 objectors had refused training in combat units but had been willing to serve in the army in noncombatant work. No figures are available for how many of these were from the Assemblies of God. The third category, numbering about 1,000, were men sent to federal prisons for refusing to do anything or to register or report for induction. Flower knew of none of the constituency who were members of this last group.[55]

The three "peace" churches—the Society of Friends, the Church of the Brethren, and the Mennonites—were bearing the responsibility for conscientious objectors working in the camps and for their families. Since half of these men were from other traditions, the three churches had appealed to the other denominations to aid those members coming from their own ranks.

In 1943 and 1944 Flower made general appeals for funds to assist Assemblies of God conscientious objectors and their families.[56] Flower also asked for names and addresses of men in the Armed Services who had obtained a 1-A-O rating (noncombatant status) since such information was desired for a special ministry to this group.[57] Quite a few sympathizers responded to Flower's appeals, bringing in over $4,500 for

50. "Report of the Executive Presbytery," General Council minutes, 1943, 34.

51. "Report of the Executive Presbytery," General Council minutes, 1944, 44.

52. Schlissel, *Conscience in America*, 162–63.

53. Selective Service System, *Conscientious Objection*, 318–20.

54. *Conscientious Objection* specifies twenty-one, but Menzies, *Anointed to Serve*, 328, notes thirty-five, citing "Quarterly Letter," 24 March 1951.

55. Flower, "Present World Conflict," 2.

56. Flower, "Plight of the Conscientious Objector," 2–3; and Flower, "Concerning the Conscientious Objector," 7.

57. "Wanted," 7.

the fund by the end of 1944. At the 1945 General Council, the total financial obligation to the National Service Board for Religious Objectors had
amounted to more than $16,000.[58]

Required to work hard without pay, conscientious objectors served
in various occupations, including forestry and soil conservation, and as
attendants at insane asylums. Some offered themselves for experimental
work in medical clinics. Flower spoke in praise of these "unsung heroes,
unwilling to fight and yet willing to suffer and die if need be that others
may live."[59]

Not all leaders in the Council agreed with the idea of supporting
conscientious objectors. Robert Brown of Glad Tidings in New York City
wrote to Flower regarding a young man in his church who had refused a
noncombatant role. In fact, he had been the only young man in Glad Tidings not willing to serve. Brown stated that he could not be responsible
for those not wanting to participate in supporting their country because
this was contrary to what he preached. He had no teaching, he wrote, "ad-
vising any one to be a an extreme conscention scrupler [sic]." He taught
that all should have some part in the service of their nation.[60]

Nothing like the intense discussions of twenty-five years earlier took
place in the pages of *The Pentecostal Evangel* during World War II. With
so many Assemblies of God young men joining the Armed Forces, the
question of pacifism was almost irrelevant. Nonetheless, the issue was
raised primarily by three leading spokesmen within Pentecostalism—
Gee, Williams and Flower. Frodsham, editor of the paper, also made a
contribution.

How much responsibility Frodsham did have in setting editorial
policy is impossible to determine. Nothing is penned by him directly in

---

58. No updated figure was given as to the total number of Assemblies of God men
claiming Conscientious Objector status, though the report states that the final cost was
lower for various reasons: "Some of the men sent to C.P.S. camps during the first two
years of the war were discharged on account of physical disability; others were trans-
ferred to mental hospitals, and the forest fire fighting corps; others became guinea
pigs for the medical division of the government, thus reducing the charges during the
last two years of the war below the amount marked up against them during the first
two years." General Council minutes, 1945, 45. While receiving no pay for their work,
conscientious objectors were charged for their room and board at the rate of $30 per
month. The National Service Board of Religious Objectors figured the cost of aiding
the families of these men to be at $50 per month. Flower, "Plight of the Conscientious
Objector," 2–3.

59. Flower, "Concerning the Conscientious Objector," 7.

60. Letter from Brown to J. R. Flower, 12 August 1942.

the pages of the *Evangel* in this period, but correspondence written in 1941 after America entered the war reveals some ambivalence on his part.

In one letter, Frodsham took a firm stand against participation in war. He was writing in reply to a letter addressed to Williams, Pearlman, and him on the question of wartime service. Beginning by establishing his hermeneutic, he wrote that the world was divided into three classes: Jews, Gentiles and the Church of God. The Epistles were written to the Church, but the Gospels also applied to the followers of Jesus. The by-laws of the kingdom to which believers belong were set forth by the King in Matt 5–7. Sounding his long-held theme, Frodsham proclaimed that Christians were citizens of heaven. "We are His witnesses, His ambassadors, and as we walk this earth we are to recognize ourselves as only pilgrims and strangers." He declared that the Christian also fought in a conflict, but it was a war fought in spiritual realms.

Attempting to present a balanced viewpoint, Frodsham cited some practical words from Scripture regarding how a Christian was to lead his life. The believer was to recognize and pray for those in authority; he was to pay taxes; and he was to seek the peace of the city where he lived.

As to war itself, Frodsham referred to the principles already set forth in the Council's minutes: "while being absolutely loyal to the Government we cannot conscientiously take part in the taking of life." This attitude is like that of the Quakers and is in accord with Scripture.[61]

However, in another letter written only a month earlier, Frodsham had argued that it was important for the "boys" to register noncombatant, definitely not a Quaker position. He did not believe that one who took part in a war of defense would be judged as a murderer: "It is quite a different thing to be full of hatred against someone and deliberately destroy that one in time of peace, and for a man to conscientiously defend his home, his wife and his children in time of war; and I believe the reading of the Scriptures makes this distinction quite clear."[62]

Frodsham's influence was probably also evident in the reprinting of an article written by Gee prior to the war. Taken from *Redemption Tidings*, a British Pentecostal publication, the article was prefaced by an editorial comment: "This article . . . expresses the attitude of our own fellowship

61. Letter from Frodsham to Ward, 30 December 1941.

62. Letter from Frodsham to Wattenburger, 26 November 1941. Wattenburger was a conscientious objector who had written to the *Evangel* expressing misgivings about the publication's treatment of the issue of conscientious objection. Wattenburger, letter to the editor, 24 November 1941.

in the matter of military service." The piece itself was written directly to conscientious objectors concerning the propriety of their position and, more specifically, the correctness of their motivation and attitude.

Not at all as ambiguous as Frodsham, Gee admonished his readers to be thoroughgoing in their positions. Though the whole nation (England) was involved in war, there were occupations less directly connected with the actual war machine. "Have we manifested a tenderness of conscience in other matters besides military service?" Gee challenged, calling for a consistency in Christian living, regardless the cost. He made it clear that the objection had to be unequivocally against the whole business of war, not just one particular conflict.

Gee encouraged objectors to make a special study of the Book of Daniel and its four principle characters who "were ready and willing to serve the very State that had persecuted them once their rights of conscience had been established." He added that it is selfish to enjoy the blessings of citizenship without returning whatever service might be possible without any compromise of Christian principle.[63]

While Gee was a staunch objector, Flower appears to have been more of a sympathizer. It is difficult to distinguish between Flower's official attitude and his personal convictions. From the beginning he had been a superb organizational man, subordinating his personal will to that of the church body. In making his appeal for support of conscientious objectors, he was acting in an official capacity, yet there is nothing to indicate that he was acting contrary to his own conscience. Note how he made his appeal: "It is really a disgrace to us as a church movement to forget and neglect our men who are in these C.P.S. camps, whether we agree with their stand for conscience or not."[64] He was being consistent with his lifelong tenets: (1) that denominational respectability is important; and (2) that freedom of religious conscience is vital. "They [the conscientious objectors] are standing for the right of conscience and therefore should be given consideration and protection in a land which is fighting for freedom of conscience and religious liberty." Forgotten and neglected, these men should at least be objects of pity and compassion.[65]

Unusually broadminded, Flower could always esteem persons who held contrasting opinions to his own. All Christians reject the spirit of

63. Gee, "Conscientious Objection," 4.
64. Flower, "Concerning the Conscientious Objector," 7.
65. Flower, "The Plight of the Conscientious Objector," 2.

war, he wrote; some just respond differently: "The difference between the ordinary follower of Christ and the religious objector is that while both believe the war spirit to be anti-Christian, the one submits himself to governmental control while the other refuses to take part in any phase of the war effort."[66] However, Flower did have a preference as to how conscience was to be acted upon. Following the denominational line, his position was to counsel men to noncombatant service. "The universal advice given to our young men was that instead of taking the extreme conscientious objector position it was better for them to ask for noncombatant service."[67]

This less radical position was shared by Williams. A contemporary of Gee in denominational leadership, he, too, called for thoughtful consideration of matters, but he clearly opposed Gee's views. He was very careful to speak for himself and not for the entire movement, saying that the General Council had already declared itself on the subject.[68] The Assemblies of God had no claim over individual conscience, but it had gone on record as a denomination. Inclusion of the 1917 resolution in the General Council minutes both in 1917 and in 1927 was seen by Williams as a definitive statement by the Council, even though it had never been discussed by that body originally. Williams saw that record as a call for loyalty to the government and preference for a noncombatant stance as opposed to an absolute pacifist stance.[69]

In an earlier article, Williams had described the Christian as a dual citizen of heaven and of an earthly nation. Therefore, loyalty was expected for both kingdoms,[70] and such concern for loyalty mitigated against taking an absolute pacifist position. "Surely he [the conscientious objector] would not wish, in the interest of showing his aversion to war, to become an obstructionist to the successes of his own nation, and thus a helper to the enemy."[71] The question for Williams was how far a Christian ought to assist the government in time of war. Again, differing from Gee, Williams

66. Flower, "The Plight of the Conscientious Objector," 2.

67. Quoted in Selective Service System, *Conscientious Objection*, 372.

68. Williams, "The Conscientious Objector," 4.

69. Williams, "In Case of War," 4.

70. Williams, "Christian Citizens," 1.

71. Williams, "The Conscientious Objector," 5.

argued that no one can be absolutely isolated from wartime activities; therefore, the noncombatant position had to be the most logical.[72]

The Assemblies of God could be classified as a conscientious objector organization only in a broad sense, Williams wrote. It certainly could not be considered as unqualifiedly pacifist, since it had pledged to "assist the Government in time of war in every way morally possible."[73] While he affirmed a statement which said, "I cannot reconcile the way of Christ with the practice of war," he admitted that a full-fledged pacifist position was beyond what he could take, were the nation at war.[74]

Williams did not believe that killing in war was the same as murder. In the Old Testament, the same God who gave the Sixth Commandment also authorized going to war at times.[75] But Williams qualified his position on this point, reaffirming his noncombatant stand: "Christians should ever be loyal and helpful to their Government, but it would be well for them to request noncombatant service in time of war."[76]

The arguments of these four men went right to the heart of the struggle within the General Council. It was an issue of loyalty to the kingdom of heaven versus loyalty to kingdoms of earth and a question as to how that balance was to be determined. Gee established first the principle of allegiance to the kingdom of heaven and interpreted submission to human authority in that light. For Flower and Williams, participation in war was a matter of conscience which had to be respected, but loyalty to governmental authority was an unquestionable obligation which took precedence. Frodsham most clearly reflected the inherent ambiguity in the fellowship; he was a pacifist except in time of war.

All agreed on the importance of loyalty to government; the disagreement came on how crucial to the gospel was the spirit of peace. As denominational leaders during the next two decades, Williams and Flower would see their perspective prevail.

72. Williams, "In Case of War," 4.

73. Williams, "The Conscientious Objector," 4, is quoting from the General Council minutes.

74. Williams, "In Case of War," 4. Williams, "The Conscientious Objector," 4, 5.

75. Williams, "Questions and Answers," 22 November 1941, 16.

76. Williams, "Questions and Answers," 27 July 1940, 5.

Limits to Loyal Expression

Every General Council with one exception from 1939 to 1953 considered or passed resolutions which demonstrated the denomination's growing struggle over what its proper attitude should be toward military involvement.[77] This period had begun with a resolution affirming loyalty and peace; it would end with a change in the biblical rationale in the statement on military service.

Williams's perspective, predicated on loyalty and religious liberty, was reflected in a "Religious Liberty" resolution passed by the 1945 General Council. It petitioned the President of the United States to continue occupation of Italy at the request of the Assemblies of God Chaplains and military personnel in order to ensure religious liberty for Protestants: " . . . for this cause and in this behalf, sacrifices having been made by the pledging of our lives, our fortunes, our sons and our sacred honor."[78] This was indeed a contrast with the 1939 General Council which had petitioned the President to remain neutral. Beaman noted that contrary to earlier Pentecostals who looked for the immediate return of Christ and who saw national existence as quite tentative, the new generation sought the preservation of " . . . a government of, for, and by a free people which shall not perish from the earth."[79]

Despite the obvious patriotic stand the Assemblies of God held, it came out strongly against one militaristic development. For nearly a decade the Council fought Congressional consideration of compulsory or universal military training; this had been proposed during World War II and then resurfaced during the Korean War. Universal military training would mean that all young men, with few exceptions, would be drafted upon reaching their eighteenth birthday. They would be given six months of military training and then would enter the Reserves for eight years.[80]

---

77. The General Councils and their resolutions are 1939, resolution on neutrality, passed; 1941, proposal for a ministry to servicemen, passed; 1943, resolution in opposition to compulsory service, passed; 1945, resolution on religious liberty in Italy, passed; 1947, consideration of reformulation of statement on military service, no action; 1951, resolution approving cooperation with the NAE Chaplaincy Commission, passed; and 1953, change in statement on military service, passed. The exception was the 1949 Council.

78. General Council minutes, 1945, 39.

79. Beaman, "Pentecostal Pacifism," 99.

80. "Universal Military Training," 7.

The Council declared its opposition to such a proposal in its 1943 session. The only discussion was whether such a bill was in fact before Congress, but the Council determined to express itself "if and when such a bill does come before Congress."[81] When Congress did consider it and soundly sent it back to committee to die, the *Evangel* expressed elation. "We should thank the Lord for causing the Universal Military Training Bill to be defeated in Congress. . . . To Him be praise." The defeat was attributed to thousands of letters sent in opposition to the bill, to the many Christians who prayed, and to God who answered.[82]

Opposition by the Assemblies of God came from the fear that, if the measure prevailed, "we will become a militaristic nation and will never go back to being a civilian nation." The measure would force America's youth to abandon Christian principles, of which peace was one of the most basic.

> If the old principles of "love thy neighbor" are to be done away with, what principles will take their place? If peace is not basic, then war will be basic—and yet both General Eisenhower and General MacArthur have declared that war is a failure and that war actually destroys that which it is intended to protect.[83]

Though the Council had never expressed opposition to the draft, it did make itself clear on the issue of universal military involvement and further regimentation of American life. The denomination might have been willing to be loyal, but there were still limitations.

Interest was growing, however, in reexamining the official position of the Assemblies of God on the question of participation in war. Was the statement on military service current with where the fellowship currently stood? In 1947, a committee appointed to attempt a reformulation of the statement reported that it was unable to come up with a proposal that would better represent the attitude of the constituency.[84]

Six years later, the statement was altered without comment when the Council voted to omit reference to the Decalogue (Ex 20:13) as a reason for not participating in bloodshed during the time of war.[85] Beaman noted that the change probably reflected a greater theological precision

---

81. General Council minutes, 1943, 26.

82. "No 'Universal Military Training,'" 2.

83. "Universal Military Training," 7.

84. General Council minutes, 1947, 13.

85. General Council minutes, 1953, 60.

than earlier Pentecostals had evidenced, as well as a growing belief that killing in war was not murder.[86]

Participation in the war by so many Assemblies of God chaplains and soldiers did much to affect the fellowship. Chaplains were the chief resource for the military to provide the kind of "public relations" needed with the churches.[87] Beaman noted, "It would only be a matter of time before they would be giving written expression to the justification of the work of a soldier, from the Bible."[88] Menzies saw in the first Pentecostal chaplains the admission of a change from pacifism to nonpacifism. The shift in attitude between the wars was significant.[89]

The growing emphasis on loyalism erupted into unabashed patriotism. In 1947, the Independence Day weekend issue of *The Pentecostal Evangel* displayed on the front page the Statue of Liberty against a background of the American flag. It was a patriotism which called for America to live up to her destiny of greatness in God. On the same front page was a poem which ended, "Thus may our country, good and great, / Be God's delight—man's best estate."[90]

86. Beaman, "Pentecostal Pacifism," 100.

87. Swomley, *The Military Establishment*, 200–209.

88. Beaman, "Pentecostal Pacifism," 96.

89. Menzies, *Anointed to Serve*, 327.

90. Blackburn, "What Makes a Nation Great?" 1.

20

Settling on a Loyal Priesthood
(1954–80s)

THE FIFTEEN YEARS FOLLOWING the Korean War were filled with tension from the Cold War and the buildup in Vietnam. In the Assemblies of God, the movement was struggling to reconcile its changing behavior with its long-held beliefs. Two of the three classic tenets held by the fellowship—loyalty and evangelism—would survive, even flourish. The third, pacifism, would disappear and be forgotten. Fifty years after its adoption, the 1917 resolution would be erased from the General Council's constitution and bylaws, but not before its principles had first been challenged among the masses. The change in doctrine came first at the behavioral level, then in the realm of popular belief, and finally in official statute.

A Growing Ministry to the Military

Even in peacetime the demand to maintain a large standing military force remained and the Assemblies of God representation continued to keep pace. At the end of the 1950s, more than 28,000 of the denomination's men were on active duty.[1] To help meet the spiritual needs of these servicemen, spiritual retreats, for example, were held periodically in Europe.[2] The Servicemen's division began publication of *At Ease* in

1. General Council minutes, 1959, 29.
2. "Spiritual Retreat," 23.

1961, replacing *Reveille* which "retired" with over fourteen million copies produced during its existence.[3]

The chaplaincy program came of age in the historic San Antonio General Council. In 1959, an Assemblies of God Chaplaincy Commission was established so that instead of working through the cooperative program of the NAE, the Council now had direct means of communication with the federal government. The denomination had gained enough respectability to speak for itself: "the United States Government fully recognizes the Assemblies of God as a major Protestant Denomination with an influential voice in behalf of its military Chaplains."[4]

Slowly chaplains developed a level of visibility within the fellowship. The *Evangel* began publishing news of the chaplains, including their training at the U.S. Army Chaplain School.[5] Philip Nichols was reported as the first Assemblies of God chaplain killed as a result of "enemy" action in Vietnam in 1970.[6] In a denomination in which church membership had not been highly promoted, the desire for more chaplains had become a significant reason for pushing membership since chaplaincy quotas were based on such membership. By 1986, there were 85 Assemblies of God chaplains on active duty.[7]

Increasingly, the emphasis had been to place chaplains in the role of missionaries before the Assemblies of God constituency. They were "not in the service to bless bombs and bullets; they are there to witness and demonstrate to those who serve in our armed forces the love, grace, and saving knowledge of God through Jesus Christ.[8]

The military became labeled as a mission field, variously called the "world's greatest" or the "world's most neglected" mission field.[9] The goal of the servicemen's ministry was described as twofold: (1) to reach every

3. McElyea, "The Military Chaplaincy," 11.

4. General Council minutes, 1959, 30. However, the Council continued to process all its chaplains through the NAE until 1967, when it began processing directly with the offices of the Chief of Chaplains in Washington, D.C. The basic function of the Military Chaplaincy program was formally outlined by the Council in 1977. See General Council minutes, 1977, 99.

5. "Enrolled in Career Course," 25.

6. "Chaplain Nichols," 2.

7. Confirmed 11 July 1986 with secretary to Lemuel D. McElyea, secretary, Chaplaincy Department.

8. McElyea, "The Military Chaplaincy," 12.

9. McPherson, "Missions and the Military," 8–9.

unbelieving serviceman with the gospel; and (2) to encourage every Christian serviceman to live a victorious spiritual life during his tour of active duty.[10]

The military was also described as a missions-sending agency, with frequent references made to the tremendous potential for missions inherent in the fact that young Christian men were being sent all over the world, courtesy of the armed forces. One biblical example of a soldier missionary was Cornelius, the Roman officer and first Gentile to receive the fullness of the gospel and the baptism of the Holy Spirit. Why would God choose such military people as Cornelius and friends? "It was because they were the keys which God needed to unlock closed doors." As soldiers, they could go where no Jewish Christian could.[11] So, too, Assemblies of God servicemen could spread the gospel everywhere they went.[12] The government was "financing the greatest missionary army ever commissioned" through the support of military personnel "committed to spreading the good news of Jesus Christ."[13]

Can a Christian serve in the military? This was an often-asked question which referred to the ability of servicemen to keep their faith, not to the morality of participating in war. Instead of articles on how to be a good conscientious objector, advice was given to youth on how to contact chaplains and other Christians once they had entered the service.[14] Tracts were produced showing how others had lived for God in the armed forces,[15] and testimonies were published. Robert Way, appointed as secretary of the Commission on Chaplains and servicemen's representative in 1964, spoke of his own experience in World War II, saying that military service stabilized his own Christian life.[16]

Promoting the positive role of the Christian life in the armed forces became a main priority for chaplains and others responsible for servicemen's ministries. Warren McPherson, who served as servicemen's representative 1954–64, maintained that Christian military personnel could indeed live for God. Zealous to preserve the spiritual well-being of the

10. Way, "Our Mission to the Military," 7.

11. McPherson. "Keys to Closed Doors," 5.

12. Webb, "Ministering to Servicemen in Europe," 6.

13. Mayo, "Who Are These People," 17.

14. Griepp, "Entering Military Service," 6, 11, 12; and McCormack, "Can a Man Serve God," 24–25.

15. Ward, "The Sergeant Thompson Story," 23.

16. Champion, "Welcome, Ways!" 5.

men he served, "he was a living example to contradict the argument many people have that the military is a sidetrack to sin."[17]

The Morality of War

The difficulty with making a commitment to serve people is in trying to retain a prophetic perspective in the proclamation of the gospel to them. How can a particular occupation be considered questionable without alienating those who are so employed? When denominational officials are indirectly promoting the virtues of military service, queries about the moral ramifications of killing enemies are not readily welcomed.

The articles on conscientious objection during World War II were the last printed by *The Pentecostal Evangel.* In 1949, Cunningham replaced Frodsham as editor, and a new era began for the publication. Nothing was published indicating the views of the editorial staff on the question of pacifism, but a memo from the 1950s sheds some light.

The memorandum written by Richard G. Champion, then on the *Evangel* staff and editor after 1985, was attached to an editorial clipped from *Redemption Tidings*, the British Assemblies of God magazine. Deploring the development of the H-bomb, the editorial was a pacifist plea in the tradition of Gee. Bombs and nationalism were out; evangelism was in. "Assemblies of God are officially a Pacifist movement (though not a movement of pacifists)."[18]

Specifically, what Champion opposed in the British editorial was the idea that "if a superintending Providence allows suffering, then it is better to bear it than to retaliate." Champion's response was to call this "an 'ostrich' editorial if I ever read one," referring to how the ostrich sticks its head in the sand.[19]

One *Evangel* reader, a pastor in New York and a former serviceman, did react to what he perceived as the glorification of war in one issue. The cover of the 30 June 1957 periodical depicted what appeared to be an invasion by paratroopers, something not in keeping, the minister wrote, with the denomination's aims or teachings. "It would seem to put us in the position of condoning and even glorifying war and bloodshed." War may be a necessary evil and the ministry of the Assemblies of God among

17. Braxton, "God Bless You, Warren," 9.
18. Editorial, *Redemption Tidings*, 3.
19. Memo from Champion, attached to copy of the editorial.

the servicemen is commendable, "but let us be careful lest we be charged with aligning ourselves with those who promote war and bloodshed."[20]

The morality of war was discussed during the next decade in only two forums. One was Williams's question-and-answer column; the other was a group of articles and books written specifically for servicemen. No more articles or letters to the editor appeared in any Assemblies of God publication affirming the traditional Pentecostal position or even discussing the subject objectively.

Williams, at least, did acknowledge the varied perspectives on war within the movement. Yes, the Assemblies of God had at one time aligned itself with pacifist groups and, no, that position had not changed.[21] In an earlier column he explained that the General Council had never taken a position of absolute conscientious objection and it had never refused to support the government in any way in time of national emergency. The official position consistent with "our beliefs" was one of nonmilitary service, service exempt from bearing arms.[22] Williams pointed out that the fellowship's young men had almost universally refrained from requesting exemption from combat on the basis of conscience.[23]

The idea of conscience was very important to Williams. He had personally talked with many of these Assemblies of God men who had not claimed the exemption and who had not felt it wrong to take up arms in defense of their country. It was a matter, therefore, which must be left to individual conscience. To another question on the propriety of worship of God on Sunday morning and playing volleyball in the afternoon, Williams's reply was negative on the grounds that this would be contrary to the commandment, "Remember the Sabbath Day to keep it holy." The Christian is not to copy the world.[24] Hollenweger noted the irony of these responses:

> It is true that Williams leaves open the question of whether military service can be reconciled with the Christian conscience. Everyone must decide this according to his own conscience.

20. Douglas, letter to the editor, 28 July 1957, 23.

21. Williams, "Your Questions," 28 May 1967, 15.

22. Williams, "Your Questions," 5 July 1959, 7.

23. Williams, "Your Questions," 28 May 1967, 15.

24. Williams, "Your Questions," 12 February 1961, 11.

But that one should not play volleyball on a Sunday afternoon is quite clear to him; it is a compromise with the world.[25]

Readers also frequently raised questions as to whether the Scriptures taught that God was a "man of war" and that killing was forbidden. Invariably Williams sidestepped the issue of the rightness and wrongness of Christians going to war.[26] In fact, his column made only two things clear about how he stood: (1) the issue of military service was a matter of conscience; (2) the Christian's first allegiance was to God, but this did not hinder one's allegiance to country. Therefore, for example, it was not idolatry to salute the nation's flag.[27] For Williams, loyalty and freedom of conscience were always the chief concerns.

The second forum on the morality of war—material written directly for servicemen—was much less objective than Williams's column, even revealing incredulity at the thought of pacifism among Pentecostals. The literature examined was generally of a persuasive nature regarding the rightness of military service and included an article by McPherson[28] and another by an unidentified author writing on the Sixth Commandment in *At Ease*.[29] Two books or pamphlets, both by navy chaplains, were also of significance. One, by Stanford E. Linzey Jr., was written for draftees;[30] the other was by David W. Plank.[31]

The assumption of all these writers was that conscientious objection was not an option. In 1962, McPherson wrote an article on the three-fold decision facing most young men of the day: whether to enlist for active duty; to sign up with a reserve unit; or to wait for the draft. McPherson explained the advantages and disadvantages of each, but never once considered the option of conscientious objection or even noncombatant service. He did write that the old idea that one cannot live for God in the service was a delusion. "In fact, military authorities report that the

25. Hollenweger, *Pentecostals*, 36.

26. Williams, "Your Questions," 7 February 1960, 11; and Williams, "Your Questions," 20 August 1961, 21.

27. Williams, "Your Questions," 5 July 1959, 7.

28. McPherson, "To Join or Not to Join?" 6–7.

29. "The Sixth Commandment," 7–11.

30. Linzey, *Filling Your Boots*.

31. Plank, *Called to Serve*.

consecrated Christian makes the best serviceman."[32] As Linzey put it, "*'To serve or not to serve'* is *not* the question."[33]

When an attempt was made to deal with the Bible's perspective on soldiers in battle, the passage invariably discussed was the Sixth Commandment, "Thou shalt not kill." These writers were apparently unacquainted with classical Pentecostal pacifists who generally did not use the Decalogue as a basis for their belief. But to the new generation, this was the text most often seized upon by those not wishing to fight. Invariably, they came to the conclusion already reached by many pacifists, that this passage dealt with relationships between individuals, not between Israel and other nations. Linzey noted that it did not necessarily forbid the slaying of animals, capital punishment, or the killing of enemies of war.[34] Thus, Plank wrote, the commandment was referring to killing with premeditated malice or hatred. "The soldier is no different than the civilian farmer who feeds the soldier."[35] The writer of the *At Ease* article even went so far as to justify military killing on the basis of the Sixth Commandment: "Is it possible that an extension of the Sixth Commandment suggests that he who neglects to save life is the same as he who takes it away?"[36] But while the article intended to show that the military killer was not included in the Decalogue, it implied that those committing suicide, dying from lung cancer (apparently from cigarettes) or being the "operator of a speeding car" were all included in the injunction.

Jesus's attitude toward war was considered only casually. As he said about the poor, he also said about wars—that they would always be present.[37] He recognized war as a necessary evil, saying, "If my kingdom were of this world, then would my servants fight" (John 18:36). Jesus was not saying that fighting was wrong, but only that it was the wrong time for such fighting. According to the *At Ease* article, the time would arrive when Jesus would engage in war.[38]

Plank and Linzey considered the option of conscientious objection, but almost as an addendum. Besides acknowledging only the

32. McPherson, "To Join or Not to Join?" 7.

33. Linzey, *Filling Your Boots*, 7. His emphasis.

34. Linzey, *Filling Your Boots*, 8.

35. Plank, *Called to Serve*, 21.

36. "The Sixth Commandment," 10.

37. Linzey, *Filling Your Boots*, 8–9.

38. "The Sixth Commandment," 11.

noncombatant option of objection, Plank did his best to dissuade objectors from their position. If, however, the objector had thoroughly examined all the options, had not changed his mind, and had the correct motivation, then "be assured you have the complete blessing of the church."[39] It was as if the primary purpose of the statement was to reconcile the book with the General Council's constitution and bylaws. Linzey went further in accepting the conscientious objector, but in keeping with Gee's teaching he called for the objector to remain loyal. Everyone was to do his part somewhere in the war effort.[40]

Plank called for objectors to examine Romans 13, which he considered a Christian rationale for war set forth most clearly and comprehensively. From the writings of the Apostle Paul, Plank laid out five principles: (1) government and governing authorities are appointed by God and exist at his pleasure; (2) these authorities have been appointed by God to suppress evil and execute His wrath on wrongdoers; (3) every person, without exception, is commanded to obey his rulers, with Paul implying that this is true as long as those rulers function according to their divine commission; (4) such obedience may require service in the armed forces; (5) service in the military is in an official capacity, acting on behalf of the government. Duty to take life fulfills and affirms God's law of love, rather than contradicting it. "Governments, and those who serve them in a just cause, are the means whereby the higher counsels and purposes of God are brought to pass in the world, righteousness is upheld, and God's cause is brought the victory."[41]

Plank and Linzey both affirmed the role of America in executing God's justice in the world. True freedom, they stressed, was a gift from God, and as stewards of life, American Christians must give an account to God for their defense of freedom.[42] "So long as there are those whose covetousness exceeds their desire for justice; so long as there is one man in the world whose appetites and passions are not subdued by the love of Christ, the struggle between freedom and tyranny will continue."[43] They wrote that America had to rise and defeat atheistic Communism

39. Plank, *Called to Serve*, 21.

40. Linzey, *Filling Your Boots*, 9.

41. Plank, *Called to Serve*, 19.

42. Plank, *Called to Serve*, 15.

43. Plank, *Called to Serve*, 14.

and other equally wrong ideologies,[44] that she must defend herself from aggression and protect her "precious" heritage. "Reverently we sing, 'Long may our land be bright, with freedom's holy light.'"[45] This "holy light," they believed, would shine brightly by America maintaining her military might.

This argument for the defense of freedom carried Plank into the sphere of unconcealed militarism, identifying God's peace with mankind's bombs: "Favored you are if you learn to recognize. . . . freedom is a bomb [that] four aircraft-carrier men load aboard a plane at Christmastime with a scribbled note upon its back, 'Peace on earth, goodwill toward men.'"[46]

While questioning the legitimacy of the noncombatant's position, Plank challenged his readers to consider reenlistment.[47] Moreover, he affirmed all Christians serving in the armed forces had been divinely called to wear a uniform. "God's purpose and mission for you is to bring Him glory in the military, and to witness faithfully to the reality of His presence in your life."[48]

Giving high praise to Plank's book, the *Evangel* called it "outstanding" and a book which should be furnished to every young Christian man eligible for service. Plank was described as worthy of a medal for "spiritual guidance and concern for Pentecostal youth."[49] The review was referring specifically to the book's helpful advice to servicemen on keeping spiritually strong, getting married while in service, and abstaining from sins prevalent in military life. In one paragraph, the validity of Plank's exposition of Romans 13 was raised, but the reviewer wrote that Plank was "careful to include valuable information for those having religious convictions against bearing arms."[50]

---

44. Linzey, *Filling Your Boots*, 3.
45. Plank, *Called to Serve*, 15.
46. Plank, *Called to Serve*, 109.
47. Plank, *Called to Serve*, 100.
48. Plank, *Called to Serve*, 34.
49. Caldwell, "Called to Serve," 10.
50. Caldwell, "Called to Serve," 11.

The Cold War

The problem of war took on new complications with the advent of the nuclear age. Generally, the reaction in the *Evangel* toward nuclear build-up was prophetic interpretation and spiritual application. In 1949, the *Evangel* quoted the concern of General Omar N. Bradley, who said the world had grasped the mystery of the atom while rejecting the Sermon on the Mount. "Ours is a world of nuclear giants and ethical infants."[51]

However, the *Evangel* called more often for evangelism and spiritual salvation than for ethical evaluation of the scriptural injunctions regarding peacemaking. The president of Boston University was quoted as terming the hydrogen bomb an evangelistic instrument causing a rise in the religious "tide."[52] The same column recommended that, in face of the possible disintegration of the world, all might find shelter in Christ.

The front page of the 1954 "Revival Issue" of the *Evangel* was covered with a photograph of the world's first hydrogen bomb explosion. The caption read, "Are you ready for Christ's return?" and this was also the title of the feature story which depicted the terrors of the times as a signal to Christians of the near return of their Redeemer.[53] The prophetic response was dominant in the 1950s. The hydrogen bomb was examined in light of Peter's prediction that "the elements shall melt with fervent heat." And what attitude should Christians take in light of such ominous warnings? They should be keeping themselves pure for Christ's return.[54] Radio Evangelist C. M. Ward continued to call people to salvation as he saw the portent of Scripture in the light of world events.[55]

An editorial in 1957 stated that the nuclear buildup was a sign of the end of the age, but it also urged that "the free world must be armed with atomic weapons so numerous and so deadly that no nation would dare to start World War III." While statesmen must try to avert global war, the article continued, such an event was inevitable. Even so, defensive measures were necessary.[56] The denomination and its official mouthpiece were firm in their convictions on two counts: (1) the threat of nuclear

---

51. Cunningham, "The Passing and the Permanent," 9.

52. Cunningham, "The Passing and the Permanent," 2.

53. "Christ's Return," 1–4.

54. Holloway, "Day of Doom," 3, 9.

55. Ward, "The Struggle for Survival," 3, 29, 30. This article was the transcript of his message preached on the weekly radio broadcast, "Revivaltime."

56. "The Missile Age," 2.

war meant the imminent arrival of Jesus; and (2) the gospel must be preached to the lost. In that, the movement was unchanged in the doctrine preached by its pioneers in World War I. But as to what should be done practically, the constituency was divided. Just as the early leaders had struggled between loyal defense of government action and a pacifist stance in light of the inevitability of the first global war, so now ambiguity of conviction reigned. The national call for the erection of bomb shelters pointed up the division of opinion.

The 1957 General Council passed a resolution to support the establishment of civil defense shelters. "In the event of a nuclear attack upon our country, spiritual leaders and workers will be in great demand to comfort the wounded, dying, distressed."[57] Across the Atlantic, British Pentecostals rejected an appeal for civil defense workers, saying "Our greater need is not a guide to the H-Bomb, but a guide from it."[58] It was this same editorial that drew Champion's "ostrich" reaction, but the American Assemblies were no more definitive in their response. When asked if it was right for Christians to build bomb shelters, Williams responded, "I believe this is a matter each person must decide for himself, but I wonder if bomb shelters will prove as effective as some think should the atmosphere become filled with radioactive materials."[59]

Preparation had to be made, even though preparation might be futile. "The Christian hates war, violence, bloodshed, and death." Still, the Christian had to face the truth that war was inevitable. The only option possible was spiritual salvation.[60] An editorial in the *Evangel* considered the options of building or not building shelters and concluded that the only safe solution was to build a spiritual shelter.[61]

In reaction to the failure to ban nuclear tests in 1962, Cunningham wrote, "In vain do men try to make peace with other nations without first making peace with their Creator."[62] He also argued that then was not the time for fear or fatalism, but for compassionate action, particularly intercession and evangelism.[63]

---

57. General Council minutes, 1957, 56.

58. Editorial, *Redemption Tidings*, 2.

59. Williams, "Your Questions," 25 March 1962, 15.

60. Wilson, "Nuclear Explosions and You," 32.

61. Cunningham, "Fall-out Shelters," 3.

62. Cunningham, "April Deadline," 3.

63. Cunningham, "A Time for Action," 3.

If the fellowship's constituents were divided in their opinion as to the value of bomb shelters, they were at one in the belief that "God has founded this great nation,"[64] and that therefore America deserved the loyalty of its Christian citizens, who were also scripturally commanded to be obedient. What this meant to the General Council was that whenever the biblical principle for a decision was unclear, the government position should be supported.

Generally, this allegiance meant that Christians were to pray for those in authority,[65] were to salute the flag,[66] and were bound to obey "rulership" unless, and only unless, it was in conflict with God's laws.[67] God was usually acknowledged as the supreme authority, but sometimes the practical outworking of this was confusing. An *Evangel* cartoon from 1960 is a case in point. "Loyalty to Both," was the caption. The cartoon, underlined with the "Render unto Caesar" passage, portrayed a family saluting the American and Christian flags set apart at an equal height.[68] Forgotten were the words of Richey, who said the Christian flag should be honored above all others, including the American.

The Assemblies of God had come to accept the rightness of each American military action beginning with World War II. America was God's arm of justice in the world and America's cause was true. The American entrance into Vietnam was no different. In the rice paddy, "God is still with us, and our cause is right," opined a poet. The soldier does his "utmost for God and the right." Americans were exhorted to prayer for their sons in battle, be true to their country, and seek divine guidance.[69]

Early in the conflict, the movement acquired its first war hero, Lieutenant Colonel James Robinson Risner, an Assemblies of God member. The first living recipient of the Air Force Cross, an award for heroism, he was featured on the front page of *Time* magazine for his valor. Then in September 1965, he was shot down and taken prisoner by the North Vietnamese. Support for Risner was quickly identified with America and her cause as a "symbol of our servicemen who are giving their best

64. Skipper, "One Nation Under God," 6.

65. Wadsworth, "Praying for Our Government," 11.

66. Williams, "Your Questions," 22 June 1958, 23.

67. Bishop, "Christ and His Enemies," 22.

68. Ramsey, "Loyalty to Both," 22.

69. "In South Vietnam: 1965," 7.

to preserve our freedoms" in the face of those who would "destroy the Scriptures, close the churches, and silence the voices that would speak for God in our generation."[70]

At all levels the fellowship supported the war. It was not the role of the General Council or *The Pentecostal Evangel* to question the rightness of the war, which indeed they deeply affirmed up to the end of the conflict. "To be vocal in criticism that may not be founded on all the facts only tends to discourage the men we are seeking to help." The role of the church was primarily spiritual and its chief task in the war was to support "the boys," wrote Robert Way, the servicemen's representative for the Assemblies of God, who took a two-month tour in 1967 to convey the denomination's "thanks" to those serving in Vietnam.[71]

Letters praising the war effort were not frequent in the *Evangel*, but they contrasted with the total absence of any other view. "In these days of draft-card burning, rebellion, and confusion, young men hardly know where to turn," wrote one pastor, who went on to tell of his son's pride in the nation he was serving and for which he had laid down his life.[72]

At the 1969 General Council, a message of greeting was read from Chaplain Charles Adams, stationed in Vietnam, who asked the Council to "remember the servicemen in Vietnam." The Council immediately took time out to pray for the men.[73]

As in other wars, the spiritual dimension of the conflict was kept in focus. The fight was not against men but against the principalities and powers that control them. Referring to the restrictions being placed on the military leaders attempting to fight "a limited war against a ruthless enemy," the *Evangel* challenged its readers to an all-out spiritual effort in prayer. God could change the situation in the war and bring "our boys" home, but he was being hindered by the sin of prayerlessness. "When will the Christians of America muster the same courage, the same determination, the same spirit of self-sacrifice that its sons are showing in the fight for a free Southeast Asia?"[74]

On rare occasions, the darker side of the war was also portrayed. The *Evangel* published the poem of one mother as "the unspoken cry

---

70. Way, "Christmas in Vietnam," 5.

71. Way, "Mission of Thanks," 11.

72. Holaday, letter to the editor, 10 November 1968, 28.

73. General Council minutes, 1969, 12.

74. Cunningham, "How Wars Are Won," 4.

of every mother sending her sons into war." Speaking of "these troubled years and the attendant anxieties and fears of her heart, she wept, "For this they were not born!" "I hold fast to faith, become acquainted with sorrow— / And lead my sons to make peace with their God.[75]

The Final Demise of Pacifism

Pacifists were conspicuously absent from the ranks of the General Council after World War II. As has been shown, gone too was any affirmation of the pacifist or noncombatant position. During the Korean War, Flower helped men who needed ministerial deferment or conscientious objector status, but the only cases on file are those whom he could not help because they did not follow proper procedure.[76] Flower's advice to a serviceman on one occasion included telling of another man in the armed forces who "has become reconciled to the fact that he must complete his term of service and now recognizes that God can give a man a ministry for Christ even in the Army."[77]

In 1961 an article on conscientious objection was banned from publication in the *Evangel*, just twenty years after Gee's last article on the subject. The Executive Presbytery turned it down in the "unanimous opinion" that it "would not be desirable to air this issue" in the weekly.[78] A decade later, William Suttles was imprisoned for refusing alternative service as a conscientious objector. He wrote to the editor of the *Evangel*, who responded by trying to persuade him to comply with the government's wishes.[79] Though Suttles would not have found even traditional Pentecostal pacifists supporting his refusal of alternative service, the concept of conscientious objection was long forgotten in the Assemblies of God. The 1917 statement had been deleted from the constitution and bylaws five years earlier.

The constitutional change did not occur by spontaneous action. The process took two years, beginning when the 1965 General Council passed

75. Douglas, "Take Now Thy Son," 3.

76. Letter from Erdmann to J. R. Flower, 21 October 1954; and letter from Flower to Erdmann, 4 February 1955.

77. Letter from J. R. Flower to Scholl, 3 October 1951.

78. Memorandum from Webb to Cunningham, 31 May 1961; and memorandum from Webb to Cunningham, 17 July 1961.

79. Letter from Cunningham to Suttles, 8 September 1972, cited by Beaman, "Pentecostal Pacifism," 104.

a resolution committing the Executive Presbytery to appoint a committee to study the statement on Military Service and report to the next council. The motion was made "in view of the fact that there are widespread questions regarding the adequacy" of the current statement.[80] On the same day the resolution passed, the morning service had focused on the work of Assemblies of God chaplains. Stanford Linzey had been the morning speaker, his subject being "Nicodemus and the Kingdom."[81]

The committee was to report its findings at the next Council, but Beaman asserted that "the decision had been made before ever being voted on by the General Council."[82] The basis for his statement is an article released by Warren McPherson, which Beaman dates by internal evidence as having been written after 1965 and before August 1967. In this item, McPherson, by now serving as public relations secretary for the headquarters, explained the current view of the Assemblies of God position on war. The article also featured a conference taking place in Springfield, Missouri, led by Robert Way, servicemen's representative, and a class being offered on "Preparing Youth for Military Service." McPherson quoted Way as saying, "The church must influence the attitude of its young men toward all of life's processes." Since cooperation with properly established authority was right and scriptural, Way could see no difference in "preparing for a tour of duty in the armed forces than in getting ready for any other phase of life." Commented McPherson, "The Assemblies of God is in a continuing program encouraging its members to recognize military service as an opportunity for worldwide missionary service rather than 'a lost chapter in the prime years of a young man's life.'"[83]

Perhaps Beaman was correct in his observation that the decision had already been made by 1967, but if so, the decision process began long before 1965. The denomination had already departed from its historic position; only the statement itself remained to remind constituents of their pacifist heritage.

In the end the revision did not come without considerable discussion. The original study committee proposed that the bylaws article be retained with the addition of one paragraph: "We hereby express our desire to continue to extend fellowship and sacramental ministries to those who

80. General Council minutes, 1965, 61.

81. "General Council Chronicle, Part III," 16.

82. Beaman, "Pentecostal Pacifism," 102.

83. McPherson, "Military Service Policy."

do not choose non-combatant service."[84] Essentially, the committee had determined to affirm the denomination's work among servicemen while preserving the pacifist and loyalist sentiments.

The Council, however, was less than satisfied with the proposal and, after much discussion, the resolution was referred back to committee. It was also moved that the committee be expanded "by at least three members representative of a cross section of the Fellowship."[85] The original committee had considered the opinions of chaplains, pastors, evangelists, and young men then involved in the draft. Significantly, one of the original committee members was Chaplain Leonard Ahrnsbrak, who had recently returned from a tour of duty in Vietnam. He later greeted the Council and spoke of the chaplains and their ministry to the service personnel.[86]

Aware of the dissatisfaction with the earlier proposal, the committee submitted a greatly altered statement which was quickly adopted. The preceding report had accepted the role of the Christian citizen in promoting peace and the need for national defense. It had affirmed loyalty to God as a higher priority over the binding obligations of earthly citizenship. Finally, it had acknowledged the principle of freedom of conscience in the area of military service. But the article approved by the Council that replaced the original article read simply:

> As a movement we affirm our loyalty to the government of the
> United States in war or peace. We shall continue to insist, as
> we have historically, on the right of each member to choose for
> himself whether to declare his position as a combatant, a non-
> combatant, or a conscientious objector.[87]

The committee's first proposal would have affirmed the Council's three historic doctrines of pacifism, loyalty, and evangelism. As it was, the statement that was adopted dropped any pacifist sentiments. Perhaps the new resolution was historically more accurate, for it preferred individual conscience to pacifism, and this had really been the more popular attitude within the movement since its inception. The Council had never

84. General Council minutes, 1967, 14.

85. General Council minutes, 1967, 15. The original committee was composed of Howard S. Bush, chair; Bartlett Peterson, J. L. Gerhart, William H. Robertson, and Chaplain Leonard L. Ahrnsbrak. New members were O. B. Harrup, Daniel P. Kolenda, and Howard Cummings.

86. General Council minutes, 1967, 23.

87. General Council minutes, 1967, 35.

accepted fully the 1917 resolution on pacifism, but it had long approved the ideal of freedom of conscience. If Williams's perspective was in keeping with the heart of the fellowship, then the three dominant themes are better understood as loyalty, evangelism, and freedom of conscience. The new statement addresses at least the first and last.

Adoption of the new resolution also brought another significant change. No rationale was presented as in the original article. Beaman noted that the new article differed from the original most markedly in that it did not condemn killing in warfare and cited no Scriptures.[88] Dempster also questioned this deletion. "Apparently, the pentecostal believer's conscience on war no longer needed to be formed specifically by biblical teaching but was now to be informed by knowledge of certain political, theological and ethical propositions."[89]

In any case, the fellowship openly accepted the change. The *Evangel* reported that the new article reflected "more accurately the current attitude of the fellowship as a whole." The denomination was no longer willing to be committed as a body to a noncombatant or conscientious objector status.[90]

Two almost incidental items of information from the years that followed capture the then prevailing attitude of the movement on the question of war. In 1977, ten years following the historic change, David Ytterock queried a large Sunday School class on ethical attitudes in his Assemblies of God church. Of the 260 persons surveyed, 73 percent said they would use a gun to protect their family, and 60 percent said they would use a gun to protect a neighbor. But 95 percent said they believed "a Christian generally may fight in the defense of his country."[91] Many more people were willing to defend their country than even their own families with the use of a gun.

A minority element within the General Council continued to cling to the pacifist perspective, even though the position was generally suspect as being unscriptural and disloyal to governmental authority. A resolution was introduced at the 1981 General Council in support of a bill to establish the World Peace Tax Fund. The basis for the resolution was that there were still those in the denomination who were conscientiously opposed

---

88. Beaman, "Pentecostal Pacifism," 104.

89. Dempster, "Peacetime Draft," 2–3.

90. "New Bylaws," 7.

91. Ytterock, "Probing Our Moral Identity," 7.

to war on the basis of Scripture.[92] The resolution was defeated; however, as Beaman commented, the proposal was "far from civil disobedience."[93]

92. Sponsored by Chase and Krueggel. "Resolutions Processed," 35–36.

93. Beaman, "Pentecostal Pacifism," 105.

21

Attitudes toward War: A Pragmatic Ethic

BY THE 1980S, FOUR distinct periods could be found in the attitudes expressed by the Assemblies of God with respect to participating in war. The first period was the pre-organizational era through the end of World War I. Pacifism was a popular position throughout the ranks of Pentecostalism, but the roots of its demise were also present in the strong sentiments for loyalty to the government and evangelism. Never would a more open forum be provided on any subject as during this time.

The second period, from 1920 until 1938, was a time of transition as the movement came of age. No Americans were being called to fight in any conflict, so the issue was abstract. But by the end of this period, pacifism, at least in the American Assemblies, would be shelved.

With the commencement of World War II, the third phase began, lasting until the end of the Korean War. During these brief years the practical adherence to the 1917 resolution fell into widespread disuse. By 1953, conscientious objection was a position unknown in the General Council constituency, and in that year the Council made its first substantial alteration in the 1917 resolution, omitting some spiritual bases for the pacifist position.

Finally, from the 1950s on, the fourth phase was marked by total repudiation of the 1917 resolution, the signal year being 1967 when the resolution was erased from the constitution and bylaws exactly fifty years after its adoption. In that Council, the option of a statement embracing pacifism, loyalty, and evangelism was rejected in favor of a much simpler statement endorsing loyalty and freedom of conscience. Following 1967, the Assemblies of God showed no sign of movement on the position. If anything, the principle of loyalty to the state intensified while freedom of conscience was, at best, considered quaint.

Predominant Views

Four primary attitudes have dominated the thinking and behavior of the Assemblies of God constituency regarding participation in war during its history, at least through the 1980s. These attitudes are pacifism, loyalty, evangelism, and freedom of conscience. As with issues previously considered, official and predominant views have tended toward accommodation and cultural standards, especially since the 1930s. But to assume that accommodation was the primary cause in the demise of the pacifist perspective is to overgeneralize, for the doom of pacifism was inherent in the beginnings of the fellowship and in the tensions of holding potentially conflicting beliefs. In the end, freedom of conscience was preferred to a pacifist stance as the commitments to loyalty and evangelism held fast.

Four predominant perspectives influenced the developments of these attitudes: belief in the imminent return of Christ, a changing concept of citizenship, strict allegiance to Scripture, and the overriding commitment to world evangelization.

The belief in the imminent return of Christ has had varying effect on the movement. During the First World War, it led to an otherworldly pacifism shaped by resignation to fate in the face of impending world doom. But in the Cold War, such belief caused the opposite reaction as the fellowship rejected peace movements as futile on the basis of prophecy. Also, the belief in the unique role of the Jewish nation in God's plan has had particular influence on the fellowship, helping it to accept the use of American might in defending Jews and Israel.

The second concept, citizenship, has had some limited relationship to the denomination's understanding of eschatology. Two positions have found varying favor. One is that Christians have a heavenly citizenship which commands their overriding allegiance. All other commitments, including commitment to earthly authority, are secondary and subservient. This belief has consistently marked the Pentecostal pacifist persuasion and has been most evident in the writings of Gee and Frodsham.

The second position, that Christians are dual citizens of heaven and earthly states, has become the standard on which Pentecostal non-pacifists have built their case. Bell and Williams were prominent leaders who espoused this conviction, and chaplains have done much to popularize the belief in recent decades. As dual citizens, Christians are responsible to both God and country. God, of course, has the higher claim, but the mixed allegiance has produced ample ambiguity. Both the Pentecostal pacifist and non-pacifist positions espouse loyalty to human governments, even as they end up in different places.

As with the concept of citizenship, strict allegiance to Scripture has provided a mixed forum of responses. Such adherence in the pioneering days invariably led to a pacifist persuasion, and Pentecostal pacifists have always been distinguished by their careful exegetical study. Non-pacifists, also, have not been without their biblical expounders, especially on the question of loyalty to government. Comparatively, pacifists have tended to emphasize the New Testament and non-pacifists, the Old. For the most part, however, biblical and theological investigation has been lacking among nonpacifists. The earliest spokespersons, Richey and Bell, were purely pragmatic in their approach and the pro-involvement writers of the sixties attempted to use Scripture only to defend their case. What has been missing in recent years has been an expressed desire to research Scripture before determining proper action.

In the end, however, it was the challenge of world evangelization which most won over the Council to the idea of discarding its pacifist heritage. A pacifist denomination could not hope to achieve acceptance from military authorities and gain access to the soldiers. Furthermore, the ability to minister pastorally to a people is related in some degree to the ability to accept the livelihood of that people. Beaman noted the dichotomy inherent in evangelizing military personnel:

> What does one tell soldiers once they are converted? Are they to leave the military? It would seem from a pragmatic point of view, that the answer to these questions would, to a large extent, determine the success of ministry to servicemen. If one answered that the soldier who is born again should stay in the military, one immediately destroys some of the arguments that would keep other Christians from joining in the first place.[1]

The call to reach the American soldier for Christ has been answered by the Assemblies of God in every war since the Hot Springs Council in 1914. Today the chaplaincy program has become a basic part of the denomination's world missions strategy. The Assemblies of God has shifted

---

1. Beaman, "Pentecostal Pacifism," 71.

to a pastoral emphasis, leaving the prophetic task to the traditional peace churches.

A Pragmatic Ethic

The denomination's approach to ethics in this issue is best described as pragmatic. The Assemblies of God did not develop its attitude toward war out of a dogmatic commitment to any established procedure, nor did it simply react to the mainstream of evangelicalism. If anything, the church has proven itself a leader in the task of ministering to military personnel and such involvement has opened the movement to greater acceptance of and by the mainstream denominations.

More than with the other two issues—women in ministry and inclusion of African Americans—the policy on wartime involvement has been formed out of a pragmatic reaction to what works best. The commitment to loyalty, for example, has often been maintained more out of a concern for acceptability than for biblical principle, and this concern for acceptability has been rooted in a desire for unhindered ministry.

While intense discussion and a regard for scriptural authority have marked the development of the denomination's position, it is unfortunate that the fellowship's pacifist heritage has been so thoroughly lost. It is not only the belief in pacifism which has been discarded, but also a healthy commitment to the Word and to the prophetic—regardless of the temporal practicability of the results.

22

In Search of a Pentecostal Ethic

IN ALL THIS REVIEW, what have we discovered about the nature of the fellowship and what its brand of Pentecostalism has to contribute to ethical analysis? Developments within the Assemblies of God at the time this original research was concluding affirmed this study to be more than a theoretical exercise; they showed a need for providing the Council leadership with an ethical framework rooted in its Pentecostal heritage.

Loss of the Prophetic Voice

The ethical history of the Assemblies of God in its first seventy-five years is a case study in the effects of the institutionalization of a movement wherein the vitality of a pioneer spirit is replaced by a defensive self-image and an acceptance of the status quo. The first-generation pioneers had heaven to gain and nothing on earth to lose. By the late 1980s, the fellowship often seemed to have forgotten heaven in search of an earthly kingdom.

What most marked the socio-ethical responsiveness of the Assemblies of God, especially after World War II, was a desire to be accepted by the evangelical community and society at large. Much heritage was forfeited in the name of acceptability, and, all too often, the fellowship fled from the Pentecostal label.

Five theological emphases have been identified in this study as significant factors in the development of the ethical posture of the Assemblies of God: the imminent return of Christ; the authority of Scripture; the present Age of the Spirit; the priority of world evangelization; and

Pentecostal ecumenism. Of the five, three—the authority of Scripture, the priority of world evangelization, and an abiding commitment to working with other Pentecostal and evangelical bodies—continued to have significant impact in the latter part of the twentieth century.

However, the eschatological intensity of the early Pentecostals was no longer present. The doctrine of the rapture and end-time prophecy were widely preached, but such proclamation had lost the truly prophetic edge it once had. Perhaps the General Council failed to heed the warning of C. S. Lewis as quoted in its own publication, *The Pentecostal Evangel*: "Aim at heaven and you will get earth thrown in; aim at earth and you will get neither." Effectiveness in this world, Lewis cautioned, is predicated on attention to the other.[1]

Perhaps not all the eschatological fervor in the early twentieth century was conducive to developing adequate ethical responsibility, but such expectations contained a core of prophetic insight. The first-generation Pentecostals were not simply left-wing dispensationalists waiting for the rapture and speaking in tongues. They had adopted a worldview much more akin to the nineteenth-century holiness Evangelicals than to the twentieth-century Fundamentalists and social gospel advocates. Only the Pentecostals had maintained some earlier evangelicals' expectations that the Age of the Spirit was now a reality. Unlike the Fundamentalists, Pentecostals believed that there was great promise for this present age through the outpouring of the Spirit. Unlike the modernists, Pentecostals realized that their hope was not to be found in this world.

This prophetic edge in the Assemblies of God was largely lost within a decade of the Council at Hot Springs. The 1927 General Council made a significant decision to preserve the status quo at the expense of its ability to prophesy. The fellowship continued to affirm its commitment to the authority of Scripture. It maintained its goal of world evangelization. And it even continued to preach that "Jesus is coming soon" and that speaking in tongues is for today. But it gradually lost its eschatological vision that these are the "Last Days" and that in the Last Days are to be found the fulfillment of Joel's prophecy: sons and daughters, slave and free, young and old will prophesy. Lost was the message of liberation; in its place was the preaching of preservation.

As a result, the Assemblies of God developed a set of moral principles lacking the distinctiveness of a thoroughgoing Pentecostal social

1. C. S. Lewis, in *Decision*.

ethic. Instead, the denomination resorted to three other ethical responses: dogmatic, pragmatic, and reactionary. The dogmatic response has been demonstrated in the fellowship's approach to women in ministry. Ignoring the Pentecostal distinctive on the Spirit's anointing of women, the Council preferred to interpret all scriptural teachings on women in light of Paul's silence passages.

The Council's shifts in its attitudes toward participation in war illustrate the pragmatic posture. Scripture and Pentecostal heritage were sacrificed on the altar of missional and social expediency.

The reactionary approach is most vividly portrayed in the sorry saga of the denomination's attitude toward African Americans. In race relations, the Assemblies of God simply reacted in terms of cultural trends; it never took an aggressive stand based on its commitment to either the Word or the Spirit.

Thoroughgoing Pentecostals

At the 1983 General Council, discussion was raging on the perennial issue of divorce and remarriage for ministers. C. David Gable—a tall, lanky, easy-going pastor from the farming metropolis of Fresno, California—stood to speak. What he had to say carried a significance far beyond the motion on the floor, though it was not taken seriously at the time.

Gable questioned whether the procedure used by the committee which had presented the report before the Council had been Pentecostal enough. "Pentecostal decision-making considers the biblical text, but also asks, 'What is the Spirit doing in the Church?'" Gable said that what the Spirit was doing might shed new light on current interpretations.[2]

At the Jerusalem Council described in Acts 15, all the Jewish Christians knew the texts about separation from Gentiles. However, when they asked what the Spirit was doing in the churches, they were astonished to find that Gentiles were receiving the Spirit. In reexamining the Scriptures again, they discovered a whole new set of prophecies and principles to consider. The believers remained biblical yet changed hermeneutical lenses according to the direction of the Spirit.

Gable explained to the Council that this was what the early Pentecostals and holiness people did regarding women preachers. They did not just follow the lead of other traditions. They examined the Word in light

2. Gable, written statement.

of what the Spirit was doing. Paul's restriction on women in authority had been enough for others, but those Spirit-led pioneers could not forget Joel's prophecy. And the same Paul who talked about women keeping silent had also said that there is neither male nor female in Christ. The pioneers did not ignore the Word; they simply were determined to discover a consistent application predicated on the work of the Spirit.

This approach is what Gable was asking the Council to consider. He reminded the delegates that the first century apostles and the first-generation Pentecostals "had stayed biblical, but formed policy to allow full expression to what the Spirit was doing in the Church."[3]

At the heart of Gable's rationale was a call for a Pentecostal hermeneutic. Full evaluation of that issue lies beyond the scope of this paper, but the concern is related to the current discussion of ethics.

William G. MacDonald wrote that one of the chief contributions Pentecostal theology has made to the church at large is Pentecostalism's championing of a dynamic experience of God.[4] Such focus on experience does not deny that Pentecostal theology is a theology of the Word. "The written Word has both shown us the way and also stood as the absolute criterion for testing all our professed experiences of God."[5]

Anderson also contended that experience, not doctrine, was the primary interest of the early Pentecostals. These pioneers were bound by a common experience, not a common creed: "The Pentecostals sought to recreate a primitive New Testament community of saints, emphasizing individual religious experience, spontaneity, and the free life of the Spirit. For them the only genuine religion was the 'religion of the heart' in which one felt the immediate presence of God and lived a life under the direct guidance of the Spirit."[6]

Pentecostal experience took the pioneers beyond what they expected doctrinally. Pentecostal reality, wrote Gee, was no mere theory:

> When we "came out" for Pentecost we came out not merely for a theory, or a doctrine; we came out for a burning, living, mighty EXPERIENCE that revolutionized our lives. The Baptism in the Spirit which we sought and received was a REALITY, even though we probably understood little of the doctrines involved

3. Gable, written statement.

4. MacDonald, "A Classical Viewpoint," 62.

5. MacDonald, "A Classical Viewpoint," 64.

6. Anderson, *Vision of the Disinherited*, 156.

at the time. How different, then, from the purely doctrinal and theoretical issues involved in this matter.[7]

Thus, Bell was able to state that the Council refused to become narrow and sectarian. The new organization would fellowship with anyone, regardless of his interpretation, as long as one held to "the true teaching of Christ and the Apostles."[8] At the time—February 1916—this statement still allowed for a wide latitude of interpretation.

Pentecostals rooted themselves in the Word in their desire to be attached to the apostles. They saw a dynamic connection between the action of the Spirit in the New Testament days and the current work of God. Their cry "Back to Pentecost" demonstrated that they had forged a link between the intervening years. "Built by the same hand, upon the same pattern, according to the same covenant, they [Pentecostals] too are the habitation of God through the Spirit. They do not recognize a doctrine or custom authoritative unless it can be traced to that primal source of church instruction, the Lord and His apostles."[9]

One difficulty with traditional hermeneutics is that all too often believers have opted for an epistemology which has either abdicated faith for reason, or sought to validate faith "by a category of special pleading in the interests of propositional theology."[10] In either case, faith is seen as rooted in logic, and this leaves uncomfortably unanswered for Pentecostals the question: What role does the Holy Spirit play in the interpretation of Scripture?

Earlier Pentecostals felt uneasy in both the fundamentalist and the modernist camps. They equated the Fundamentalists with the Pharisees who denied the working of God in their day and age and compared the modernists with the Sadducees who denied the power of God at all. J. Roswell Flower observed that the Pentecostal movement had had to think carefully through the relationship between experience and Scripture. Yet he warned fellow Pentecostals that they "must be alert to the dangers of becoming so literal in our interpretations of the Scripture that, like some of the older denominations, 'we deny the power thereof.'"[11]

---

7. Gee, "Tests for 'Fuller Revelations,'" 6.
8. Quoted in Sheppard, "Word and Spirit: Part I," 4.
9. "Back to Pentecost," 4.
10. Ervin, "A Pentecostal Option," 12.
11. Flower, "Fifty Years of Signs and Wonders," 7.

Gerald Sheppard demonstrated that Pentecostals openly violated the hermeneutical rules of dispensationalists, "reading through both the Old Testament and the Gospels as a literal address to the Christian Church and to the contemporary arena in which pentecostals did their theology."[12] The issue here was not a literal versus non-literal interpretation of Scripture. Rather, Pentecostals were fighting against a rigidity which in effect denied the contemporary work of the Spirit. Thus, the early Pentecostals felt free to invert a dispensationalist hermeneutic which ruled out the possibility of charismatic manifestations in the Church Age. Menzies called this hermeneutic reversal a "Pentecostal baptism" of dispensational eschatology.[13] For such believers, Joel's prophecy was meant for present fulfillment.

Two elements distinguish a Pentecostal hermeneutic. First, Pentecostals affirm that God is indeed active in today's world and that He speaks to modern women and men as He did to people in Bible days. God is as much an active causative agent today as He is pictured in biblical writings. Pentecostals insist on the continuity of God's presence in and among the faithful from the creation to the present. Wrote Mark McLean: "Pentecostals . . . assert that God speaks and acts today, just as He did in biblical times."[14]

Second, Pentecostals affirm that the Holy Spirit plays a vital role in interpretation of Scripture today just as He did in inspiring the original text. Sheppard commented that the issue among early Pentecostals was not expressed chiefly in terms of historical accuracy, but whether or not God spoke through Scripture by His Spirit. Sheppard then referred to Frodsham, who wrote that the scholars and critics were concerned about the characteristics of individual writers of the Bible. "God is not concerned about the characteristics of his prophets—he is concerned about their character." For Frodsham, the question, "Did Isaiah write the whole of the prophecy by his name?" is the wrong question. Proper biblical interpretation depends on men and women, scholarly and non-scholarly, who are "tuned by the Spirit to receive the Spirit's message."[15]

What made the early pioneers truly Pentecostal was more than just the ability to speak a language they had not studied, as essential as that

---

12. Sheppard, "Word and Spirit: Part II," 16.

13. Menzies, *Anointed to Serve*, 27.

14. Mclean, "Toward a Pentecostal Hermeneutic," 23.

15. Quoted in Sheppard, "Word and Spirit: Part II," 17.

may be. What made them Pentecostal was that their entire orientation was governed by the bold notion that they were living in the Age of the Spirit. They were thoroughgoing Pentecostals, not just tongues-talking dispensationalists. For more than half a century leading up to the Azusa Street outpouring, countless numbers of spiritually-hungry people had lived with the growing expectation that the Holy Spirit was about to send forth the latter rain.

Now that it had come, nothing could remain the same. They gave up all they had and scattered throughout the world. They suffered ridicule and outright persecution for their beliefs. They risked all because they had encountered Jesus Christ and he had empowered them with his Holy Spirit.

It was not just a personalized experience, for it affected their entire worldview. Because they had been so empowered with the Spirit, they were now unconcerned with society's dictates. No longer were they Americans or Germans or Chinese who happened to be followers of Jesus Christ. They were citizens of heaven who happened to live in America or Germany or China, and consequently, they could not go to war against their own family. God was calling women to preach and who God ordained, they were to also. Blacks and whites alike were being baptized in the Spirit; therefore, they were to learn to live as brothers and sisters in Christ.

It is not essential to determine if these radicals at the beginning of the twentieth century were entirely consistent in their beliefs and actions. Consistency alone does not validate faith. However, it is essential to consider what, if anything, their faith has to offer as a guide to understanding the believer's approach to modern society. Does being a Pentecostal today mean something more than merely being an evangelical with a talented tongue? Does the Pentecostal worldview have any implications for ethics?

Too often in the past a Pentecostal ethic consisted of little more than stale, truncated holiness legalism. To be a good member of an Assemblies of God church, one simply had to be saved, speak in tongues, and refrain from drinking, smoking, dancing, gambling, and going to the movies. Assemblies of God members could not define the actual work of sanctification as easily as their holiness Pentecostal cousins, but they had come to define its implications in much the same vocabulary. And these implications were extremely narrow. The deacons could bar Harold Carter, a black child, from entering an Assembly of God church in Selma,

Alabama,[16] but the young people had "better not be caught dead" inside the local theater.

A Pentecostal Ethical Framework

Unfortunately, up through the 1970s, there had been little formal development of ethical thought within Pentecostal ranks. Holiness Pentecostals had written volumes on the nature, value, and role of sanctification and its application to personal standards. Implications beyond personal dress and behavior had been largely ignored.

Meanwhile, the Finished Work Pentecostals, such as the Assemblies of God, had tended to reject ethical considerations as lacking importance. Standards of holiness had, in varying degrees, been adopted from the holiness Pentecostals. The mandate of evangelism and a desire for an increasingly educated clergy had superseded interest in other implications of a Pentecostal faith in the modern world. Even a growing commitment to a learned clergy had not included courses in ethical analysis.

In a 1983 study of the charismatic movement, Richard Quebedeaux noted numerous works on the subject of Spirit baptism and social change. Interestingly, none of the literature cited was authored by classical Pentecostals.[17] The existence of such a body of literature did speak, however, of an awakening sociopolitical consciousness in larger Pentecostal-charismatic circles.

However, whether or not an ethical consciousness could develop in classical Pentecostal ranks, an observation Kilian McDonnell made in 1970 is worth noting. He argued that the Pentecostal experience does not automatically change a person's political and social attitudes. "Although the Pentecostal experience does seem to elicit a new openness and generosity toward others," McDonnell observed, "it does not endow people with a new passion for political and social justice." The Pentecostal experience could reinforce already existing awareness, but such experience alone would not supply such an awareness.[18]

16. Harold Carter, sermon.

17. Quebedeaux, *The New Charismatics II*, 96: Pulkingham, *Gathered for Power*; Pulkingham, *They Left Their Nets*; Harper, *A New Way of Living*; Christenson, *A Charismatic Approach*; Fichter, "Catholic Pentecostals," 303–10; Fichter, *The Catholic Cult*; Ford, *Which Way*; Fahey, *Charismatic Social Action*; Suenens and Camara, *Charismatic Renewal and Social Action*; Hollenweger, *Black and White*.

18. McDonnell, "Problems in Evaluation," 51.

Quebedeaux described Spirit baptism as an "independent variable." When a newly baptized Pentecostal believer is socialized or discipled in a group committed to social change, that believer will likely move in that direction. "But if the new pentecostal is socialized in a conservative community of faith, he or she will mostly likely come to share *its* position here."[19] Dempster responded that one of the tasks of a Pentecostal theological ethic is to provide an interpretive framework for the Pentecostal experience because no human experience—not even this one—is self-interpreting.[20]

In attempting to demonstrate the personal and social ethical significance of Spirit baptism through glossolalia, Dempster proposed two foundational characteristics of a Pentecostal ethic:[21] one, a Pentecostal ethic is theocentric; and two, it focuses on the action of God.[22] A Pentecostal ethic, Dempster further asserted, is grounded in community, rooted in worship, filled with aspiration, and marked by responsibility.[23] Building on the thought of Stanley Hauerwas,[24] Dempster declared a Pentecostal ethic to be an ethic of imagination. "What is needed most often to stimulate human action in a divided world is the power of imagination," and this can be found through the work of the Spirit.[25]

One other element can be drawn from Dempster's notion of imagination: a Pentecostal ethic is one of transformation. Transformation is a concept already noted in the teachings of Wesley and in the experience of the early Pentecostals who avowed the radical work done by the Holy Spirit in the life of the believer. "An ethics of imagination not only aims at the reenactment of [the biblical] stories, but also at the embodiment of its stories in the formation of the church as the new society."[26]

19. Quebedeaux, *The New Charismatics II*, 166–67. Emphasis his.

20. Dempster, "Significance of Glossolalia," 2.

21. In attempting to describe a Pentecostal ethic, the desire is not to assert that its characteristics cannot also be found in other Christian ethics. Rather, the purpose here is to affirm what a Pentecostal ethic is, and what it is able to contribute to the larger sphere of moral understanding.

22. Dempster, "Significance of Glossolalia," 11, 12.

23. Dempster, "Significance of Glossolalia," 15, 19, 20, 24.

24. Hauerwas, "The Interpretive Power," 55–82.

25. Dempster, "Significance of Glossolalia," 28.

26. Dempster, "Significance of Glossolalia," 31.

Ethics in the Age of the Spirit

In theological and ethical studies within the Pentecostal-charismatic movement, much effort has been concentrated on the experience of Spirit baptism and the enduement of power. Other scholars have focused on the eschatological emphasis in Pentecostalism, though rarely on the relationship between eschatology and pneumatology. Dempster's study of glossolalia is most helpful, but what is also needed is an understanding of the significance that the concept "Age of the Spirit" has had on the Pentecostal worldview. The idea that the present age is indeed the Age of the Spirit enabled the early Pentecostals to move beyond a purely otherworldly dispensationalist eschatology. In fact, many theological contortions were needed just to reconcile dispensationalism and Pentecostalism.

Of all the elements which helped to shape the Pentecostal worldview, this was something distinctively Pentecostal—the Age of the Spirit. Founded in the prophetic utterances of Joel and demonstrated in the reality of Pentecost, the concept of the Age of the Spirit gave to the Pentecostal pioneers the theological and ethical framework with which to certify their experience and existence. That this is the Age of the Spirit means more than any one characteristic of Pentecostalism, such as speaking in tongues. It is the summation of all that is Pentecostal: not tongues alone, or healing alone, or spiritual gifts alone, or the Second Coming alone, or unity alone, or renewal alone. It is all of these and more. The eschatological hope of the Pentecostals was rooted in their expectation that these were the Last Days and that in the Last Days God would pour out His Spirit on all flesh.

Whatever else may be said of a Pentecostal ethic, it must be eschatological and prophetic in nature. The final hope of the believer lies in the blessed hope, this hope that Christ will return and that the fulfillment of all promise lies in the age to come. Even so, Pentecostal believers are aware that there is also fulfillment in the now since the future age has come exploding into the present age through the power of the promised Comforter.

A Pentecostal ethic is also prophetic. The reality of Pentecost is not just to be found in the presence of the Holy Spirit. It is not just eschatologically established in "the Last Days." The reality of Pentecost is equally the promise that sons, daughters, slaves, and freemen will prophesy. There are marked parallels between Peter's assertion of the fulfillment of Joel's prophecy and Jesus's proclamation that the words of Isaiah were being fulfilled.

> The Spirit of the Lord is on me,
> because he has anointed me to preach good news to the poor.
> He has sent me to proclaim
>> freedom for the prisoners and recovery of sight for the blind,
>> to release the oppressed, to proclaim the year of the Lord's favor.[27]
>
> In the last days, God says,
>> I will pour out my Spirit on all people.
> Your sons and daughters will prophesy,
>> your young men will see visions, your old men will dream dreams.
> Even on my servants, both men and women,
>> I will pour out my Spirit in those days,
>> And they will prophesy . . .[28]

Both prophecies were used as inaugural addresses—one for the earthly ministry of Jesus; the other for the earthly administration of the Spirit. Both prophecies assured the empowering of the Spirit. Both highlighted the gift of prophecy, and both spoke of a new world, a new day, in which the barriers and the bondages of the past would be broken.

Isaiah and Joel, Jesus and Peter—all were speaking of prophecy in a much broader sense than that of simply the foretelling of future events. It was God's word, boldly proclaimed, for the immediate day and age. "Thus saith the Lord," thundered the Old Testament prophets, Jesus, and the apostles. And "Thus saith the Lord" is what rings from the lips of modern Pentecostals, attesting to their belief that this is the age of the Spirit, under new authority, that the old order has passed away and all things are become new.

Three themes are evident in the eschatological and prophetic message of a Pentecostal ethic. All three—liberation, reconciliation, and justice—were made manifest in the event of Pentecost.

The Pentecostal message is first a message of liberation. Implied in the inclusive language of sons and daughters, bond and free is the truth that all are now liberated in Christ Jesus. Joseph Flower referred to Joel's prophecy when he concluded that "the Christian church should

---

27. Jesus citing Isa 61:1–2 in Luke 4:18–19 (NIV).
28. Peter citing Joel 2:28–32 in Acts 2:17–18 (NIV).

be in the vanguard of any movement promoting true scriptural liberty for women."[29] Pentecost provides power for deliverance from spiritual, physical, social, and emotional oppression.

The Pentecostal message is also a message of reconciliation. Now men and women, slave and free, are not only liberated in Jesus, but they are also made one in his Spirit. In the opening statement of Acts 2 concerning the day of Pentecost, the disciples were said to be in unity. A significance of the gift of tongues is that the curse of Babel has been lifted. Reconciliation is the result. Writes Dempster, "The outpouring of the Spirit at Pentecost within the framework of 'the mighty acts of God' signifies an action of God's creative power to establish and to empower the eschatological community of believers to be the beach-head of a new humanity characterized by freedom, justice, Shiloam, and unconditional love."[30]

A distinctive feature of the outpouring at Azusa Street was the lack of gender, class, race, and priestly distinctions. In the Spirit all barriers are brought down and the body of Christ is reconciled in true spiritual ecumenicity.

Last, the Pentecostal message is a message of justice. These same men and women, bond and free, who are now one in the Spirit, are also equal before the throne of the Father. Thus, wrote charismatic leader Michael Harper: "Every one of us should be passionately concerned about justice, public morality, and the plight of the undernourished and underprivileged, and a balanced spirituality should reflect really deep commitment to the cause of man's physical as well as spiritual well-being."[31]

According to Dempster, a Pentecostal ethic must avoid what he called a "trivialization" and an "evangelicalization" of the moral life. Trivilialization reduces ethics to inconsequential, personalized, and externalized behaviors. Evangelicalization refers to the assimilation of Pentecostalism into the evangelical mainstream, with the resultant loss of valuable Pentecostal distinctives.[32] Consequently, he advocated that classical Pentecostals learn to follow the Spirit through their own experience, acting on behalf of the poor, the needy, the lonely, and the oppressed. "For unless glossolalia stimulates the joyful response to the God of lib-

---

29. Flower, "Does God Deny," 22.

30. Dempster, "Significance of Glossolalia," 16.

31. Harper, *Walk in the Spirit*, 71–72.

32. Dempster, "Significance of Glossolalia," 46, 47, 65, 66.

eration, the God of social justice and Shiloam, the God of unconditional love, the God of the new humanity, the tongues of men and of angels will still sound like they did two thousand years ago—like a noisy gong or a clanging cymbal."[33]

The task which awaits Pentecostals is to discover the uniqueness and implications of their experience and faith and to answer the question, What, indeed, do the Spirit and the reality of Pentecost through which he speaks have to say to the ageless problems of prejudice, greed, oppression, sexism, and war?

The Pentecostal movement has always affirmed that the Spirit speaks today through inspiration, vision and what Dempster terms imagination. What the Spirit has to say on a given subject must always be considered along with what the church universal and historical has to say.

The Pentecostal heritage affirms that the power of Pentecost is given by the Spirit first and foremost as a transforming agent in the life of the corporate body of Christ. In that baptism by fire is the anointing to proclaim that the Age of the Spirit is here and now. Pentecost is not only a personal experience; it is an eschatological event.

Through Pentecost, the church is empowered for the task of liberation and reconciliation. Yet the church must ever realize that doing is always predicated on being. Moreover, the church must be infused with an ongoing Pentecost in order to fulfill its mission of doing and being.

The Pentecostal movement must recognize that ethics is not simply a set of rules for personal behavior. Ethics is also not a by-product of a church which has lost sight of its evangelistic mandate. Ethical analysis cannot be considered an option only if the church has "time" in the midst of its mission of "doing" for Christ in the world. "Being" Christ to the world is the heart of its mission. To quote Hauerwas, "What the Christian does cannot be separated from what he is, as what he does bears an intimate connection with his character as formed in sanctification."[34] The modern Pentecostal movement adamantly affirms that the Spirit's power is present to transform lives of individual believers, the life of the corporate body, and, in turn, society at large.

33. Dempster, "Significance of Glossolalia," 32.
34. Hauerwas, *Character and the Christian Life*, 206.

23

. . . And Now

IN THE FIRST DRAFT of this book, my dissertation of 1988, I wrote that my hope was this study would assist at least one group, the Assemblies of God, in building an ethical framework for future decision-making. It was a time of great moral crisis for the fellowship with the implosion of the ministries of some of the best-known preachers in the Council, including one of its denominational leaders. The shock of the crisis had far-reaching consequences.

While completing my doctoral work, I accepted an invitation from Edith Blumhofer to share some of my findings with one of her classes at Evangel College. As my talk on the exclusion of African Americans in the General Council ended, a student pointedly asked me, "What are *you* doing about the problem?"

I had not anticipated such a direct and personal question, though I did appreciate it in an awkward sort of way. One always prefers theoretical reflection when engaged with strangers. I explained that I hoped my research was beneficial enough that others could build on it, could make use of it to find solutions that were sorely needed.

I did finish the paper. While its availability to others was limited to academic hounds,[1] the materials from Joseph Flower's file drawer were passed on, as per his instructions, to the Flower Pentecostal Heritage Center, where they have received extensive attention.

---

1. The dissertation itself was made available through Dissertation Abstracts and then ProQuest. A portion of the material from the dissertation was published: See Kenyon, "Black Ministers," 10–12, 13, 20; and Kenyon, "Bishop Mason," 12.

The heart of the dissertation work was always about how the people of God should get on living out what God had called them to be and do. The concentrations on race relations, women in ministry, and attitudes toward war, while each individually important, pointed to a more central concern in the life of faith called ethics. Ethics, with street clothes on, is living out what we believe to be true. For me in my thirties, that meant setting off for parts of Asia where the gospel had limited exposure, desiring to live out what I believed to be true by fulfilling the two Great Commandments and the Great Commission as a Pentecostal in a place of spiritual and temporal need.

The Memphis Miracle

Shortly after I left for the other side of the world, a significant event occurred among American Pentecostals that came to be known as the "Memphis Miracle." I was far removed from all those Tennessee happenings in October 1994 and only heard of them in bits and pieces long after.

The event was a four-day conference themed "Pentecostal Partners: A Reconciliation Strategy for 21st Century Ministry," designed to "lead the Pentecostal movement in America back to its roots as an interracial expression of the body of Christ." Speakers and leading participants read like a Who's Who of black and white American Pentecostal leaders. In the daytime, reconciliation dialogues among a racially balanced group of two hundred ministers and leaders focused on the past, the present, the ideal, and the future. Celebration services in the evenings were open to the public.[2]

The Assemblies of God was highly represented with general superintendent Thomas Trask giving a response in the second dialogue and Pentecostal scholar Cecil M. Robeck Jr., presenting a paper in the first. All this was in the context of the PFNA disbanding in light of its failure at racial inclusion.

When various consultations led to the forming of the PFNA in 1948, neither Oneness Pentecostals nor black Pentecostals were invited. Although it was understood that for many years the Church of God in Christ resisted overtures to join the PFNA,[3] a more accurate picture of

2. "Pentecostal Partners" (brochure); see also, David Waters, "Pentecostals Gather," B1.

3. Kellner, "Divided Pentecostal," 50.

racial exclusion was described by Robeck in his presentation in the first dialogue in Memphis. The uniquely integrated Pentecostal denomination, the Church of God of Prophecy founded by A. J. Tomlinson, had chosen not to participate in the PFNA, "largely because of their [the PFNA's] exclusivist ecclesiology."[4]

In 1958, a representative of the Church of God in Christ did inquire concerning possible membership with the PFNA. The response was that the Church of God in Christ would need to submit a formal application to be reviewed by PFNA's Board of Administration,[5] far short of a warm invitation. Robeck noted that there is "no record of any prior or subsequent applications, formal or otherwise, having ever been submitted to the PFNA."[6] Even more troubling was an observation attributed to Raymond O. Corvin, a member of PFNA's Board of Administration for a number of years, stating in the late 1970s, "...that the all-white PFNA had, in the past, received applications from Black Pentecostals to affiliate, but had 'by agreement' prevented their joining."[7]

Not until 1992 were the first significant steps taken toward healing the seventy-year-old racial divide within American Pentecostalism. In that year, the PFNA Executive Committee agreed to initiate reconciliation. Under the leadership of B. E. Underwood, chair of the PFNA and general superintendent of the white International Pentecostal Holiness Church, and Church of God in Christ Bishop Ithiel Clemmons, a racially balanced task force was named to plan for the Memphis event.[8]

On the second day of the conference, the old white PFNA was dissolved. Although the discussion was closed to the public, witnesses reported that "whites and blacks freely expressed, accepted and repented of their prejudices" with many whites apologizing "for the years of separation."[9] Clemmons expressed surprise at the genuine feeling of repentance on the part of whites, believing that white Pentecostal leaders were committed to reconciliation.[10]

4. Robeck, "Historical Roots," 70.

5. Robeck, "Historical Roots," 57, quoting Minutes of the Eleventh Annual Convention-PFNA (1958), 5.

6. Robeck, "Historical Roots," 58.

7. Robeck, "Historical Roots," 58, quoting from "News Notes on Black Religion," Spirit: A Journal of Issues Incident to Black Pentecostalism 3:2 (1979), 37.

8. Underwood, "Pentecostals Forming," 15.

9. Waters, "Pentecostals End," B1.

10. Waters, "Pentecostals End," B8.

The following day, the delegates adopted a constitution forming the Pentecostal/Charismatic Churches of North America (PCCNA). Most significantly, the constitution called for a twelve-person executive board to be divided equally between blacks and whites, with Clemmons being elected as the first chairperson.[11]

The first action the new organization took was to adopt a "Racial Reconciliation Manifesto," confessing that "racism is a sin and blight" which must be condemned and calling for its end. Racism must be opposed "prophetically in all its various manifestations within and without the Body of Christ." Signers pledged to "work against all forms of personal and institutional racism."[12]

When referring to the Memphis Miracle, observers point to multiple examples of miraculous manifestations—that this conference even happened, that the PFNA willingly dissolved itself, and that a new biracial organization formed. But reconciliation moved beyond mere restructuring when a more spontaneous and very Pentecostal expression happened. After Clemmons declared that "we cannot wait or delay any longer" to deal with the racial division, Donald J. Evans, a white Assemblies of God pastor from Tampa, Florida, spontaneously knelt in front of Clemmons and washed his feet. At the same time, Charles Blake, another Church of God in Christ bishop, began washing the feet of Trask. In response the entire gathering turned into a prayer meeting of repentance and reconciliation.[13]

Without doubt, eyes, ears and hearts were opened, just as they had been in the early days of Azusa Street. Jack Hayford, pastor of Church on the Way in Los Angeles, said he and many white delegates had been made aware of the extent of pain racism had caused as well as their own complicity. "There's no justification for it having taken so long," said Hayford. "The only explanation is that we have been slow to learn how much the community of faith is shaped by the culture."[14]

Something was astir, for similar reconciliation efforts were simultaneously occurring among American evangelicals between the NAE, in whose history the General Council had played a key role, and the National Black Evangelical Association (NBEA). The NBEA had splintered from the NAE over racial tensions in 1963. Don Argue, past NAE

11. "The Miracle in Memphis," 2.

12. "The Memphis Manifesto," 38.

13. S.S., "Reconciliation Dialogue," 7.

14. Quoted in Waters, "Pentecostals End," B8.

president and an Assemblies of God minister, said the NAE had failed to hear the voice of William Bentley, "the father of the NBEA" who had died the year before this reconciliation.[15] "We [NAE] have been the slow ones here," said Argue. "We do not have to deal with the problems of racism day to day."[16]

In contrast to evangelicals in general, Pentecostals had a transracial heritage advantage to live up to. Trask said, "We believe the Holy Spirit intentionally gave us Azusa Street as a beacon of what we might become."[17]

Reflecting on the actions in Memphis, Underwood said that Pentecostals missed a part of their heritage because of this division.[18] "What a difference it could have made during the civil rights movement if all the children of the Pentecostal revival had stood together as a shining example of what God could do to solve the problems of racism and discrimination."[19]

Seemingly overnight, decades of division were being resolved. However, the danger with believing in miracles is that we come to expect instant transformation without the hard process of sanctification, an expectation which can be damning if we have besetting sin. Racism in the American Pentecostal church has been a besetting sin, a spiritual cancer eating away at our God-given mandate. Being a Finished Work Pentecostal, I understand sanctification to be a process, not some once-and-done moment of perfection. Odd then that many Pentecostals in the years following Memphis came to assume that with the miracle, there was nothing more to say or do about the sin of racism in the Pentecostal camp, that all was settled. Nothing could have been farther from the truth.

The hard road ahead was already evident before the Memphis conference even began. L. H. Ford, the Church of God in Christ's presiding bishop then in his eighties, did not attend, nor respond to three invitations to the Memphis gathering.[20] Referencing Ford's absence, Clemmons said reconciliation cannot occur overnight. "It will take time."[21]

There were several reasons for the difficulty of this journey.

15. Morgan, "Interracial Gathering," 50.

16. Quoted in Morgan, "Interracial Gathering," 51. *Brackets in original.*

17. Trask, "Response," para. 16.

18. Grady, "Pentecostals Reject," 66.

19. Underwood, "Recapturing the Unity," 38.

20. Grady, "Pentecostals Renounce," 58.

21. Waters, "Pentecostals End," B8.

First, white Pentecostals had a lot to learn about what black Pentecostals had been struggling with for so long. In a newspaper report later that year referencing the Memphis event, New Jersey district superintendent Joseph Beretta was quoted as saying, "All of a sudden we realized, we're going overseas and there are inner-city needs, there are people in America we have not touched."[22] That in a district that continued to be a forerunner in the Council for inclusion. Even those ahead of the curve, Beretta was intimating, were unaware of how much more had to be done.

In the first of the four Memphis dialogues, Oliver Haney, dean of C.H. Mason Theological Seminary, responded to Robeck's paper by pointing out the extended spiritual blindness on the part of white Pentecostals. What he heard from Robeck's recitation of Assemblies of God history was that none of the fellowship's attempts to deal with racism were ever guided by Scripture. Rather what guided them were the racial attitudes of the fellowship's constituency. Race, Haney declared, superseded the Word of God. "The history of the Assemblies of God . . . clearly demonstrates that they deliberately chose to be guided by the culture."[23] Trask responded that the American Assemblies of God had "failed to keep the dream and example of an integrated Christian community, composed of all races, as modeled at Azusa Street."[24] Such ingrained habits would not be easily eradicated.

Several years after Memphis, I traveled back to Waco, Texas, from my home in Asia. While there, I met the pastor who followed my old presbyter of racist distinction. I noted that the church had changed from Monte Vista Assembly of God—named after the street on which it was located. The pastor explained that the congregation had become concerned that Hispanics might start attending, mistaking it for a Spanish church because of its Spanish-sounding name. Instead, they chose a transformative-sounding Abundant New Life Assembly of God. Transformative or not, the Memphis miracle had yet to reach Waco.

As Trask commented in his Memphis response, "Over the years, we have learned some unacceptable behavior with regard to race relations. We need to unlearn many things and become sensitive in areas where we have had no sensitivity."[25]

---

22. Parsons, "United in Spirit," C8.
23. Haney, "Response," para. 9.
24. Trask, "Response," para. 5.
25. Trask, "Response," para. 20.

Second, black Pentecostals needed time to be sure the change in their white brothers and sisters was real enough for them to feel safe. Clemmons said, "there are wounds that are so deep and that have festered for so long that when it is time to do surgery, there is fear."[26] There was suspicion among some black Pentecostals of white "ecclesiastical imperialism" or the fear of losing their own autonomy if whites joined them. Explained Clemmons, "Black people tend to feel a sense of fear when whites draw too near, a fear of being swallowed up or controlled."[27] Writing shortly after the Memphis event, Clemmons expressed hope "that this new era will promise true reconciliation and not hegemony."[28]

Trask acknowledged this challenge. "As white Pentecostals, we need the wisdom to understand that although our black brothers and sisters forgive us, there is still the human need to release anxiety, express frustration and openly doubt our sincerity."[29] He added that he and his fellow whites were grateful for how "our brothers and sisters in these communities are forgiving us for our flight and welcoming us with open arms."[30]

Part of that process of speaking peace to the fears of our black sisters and brothers is what Robeck's Memphis presentation and this present book have set out to do: to restore truth to our white Pentecostal self-interpretations of history. Wrote Clemmons, "The A/G spin on the materials and primary documents from the historical period between 1907 and 1914 adds to those fears and deep suspicions."[31] He was speaking to white perceptions of that gentleman's agreement between Mason and the white Church of God in Christ. White Pentecostals have much to learn before they can declare the Memphis miracle completed, including the painful truth that perhaps the gentleman's agreement was in the end one-sided, something imposed on a person with lesser privilege, but a heart full of grace.

Third, white Pentecostals would have to demonstrate their faithfulness to the new commitment of racial reconciliation over the long haul. Decades of exclusion would take both time and action to undo. Said Clemmons, Bishop Ford and others were waiting to see more definitive

26. Grady, "Pentecostals Reject," 67.

27. Waters, "Pentecostals End," B8.

28. Letter from Clemmons to Warner, 1 December 1994.

29. Trask, "We Repent," 68; also, Trask, "Response," para. 22.

30. Trask, "Response," para. 15.

31. Letter from Clemmons to Warner, 1 December 1994.

steps taken before they were willing to join in.[32] Regarding blacks getting over their fears and suspicions, the work rests with whites who have much to demonstrate.

White Pentecostals in the PFNA had replaced the old organization with racially shared leadership, but how deep was their willingness to engage black leadership? Would electing Clemmons as chair of the new group be the extent of their willingness to serve under black leadership? In his response in the last dialog of the Memphis gathering, Bishop Blake stated: "There is a long history of blacks under white leadership, but almost no history of whites under black leadership. . . . If it is to be assumed that this trend will continue at any level, then black leaders will perceive little benefit in associating themselves with an interracial fellowship."[33]

How fitting then the closing illustration in Robeck's presentation. The Apostolic Faith Church of God had its origins directly with Seymour. Over time, the Virginia-based movement splintered into various smaller denominations. When Bishop Oree Keyes was elected to lead one of those offshoots, he had a vision of bringing the splintered groups back together. But the other bishops would have nothing of it. Then in 1980, he called a meeting in which he shared his vision with these other bishops and said he volunteered to resign as bishop of his group to facilitate a merger into a single denomination. The others responded, the groups merged, and elected Keyes as Senior Bishop of the newly formed Apostolic Faith Church of God. Such an example, Robeck said, of someone so committed to unity that he was willing to lay his own future on the line. He then urged the PFNA leadership to do the same, which they proceeded to do in disbanding the organization and electing Clemmons as chair of the new organization.[34]

To make room at the table, sometimes someone must give up their seat. While the church should be big enough to welcome everyone, there is limited space at the top. Marginalized people will feel welcomed to the extent that they see those at the front who remind them they are no longer marginalized. Even more, marginalized people will feel safe to the extent that those who hold power are willing to lay down their positions of power for the sake of unity and inclusivity.

32. Waters, "Pentecostals End," B8.

33. Blake, "Response," para. 5.

34. Robeck, "Historical Roots," 70–72.

Trask spoke of the challenge ahead when he said: "I do not want to mislead anyone with the notion that in one great 'microwave moment' we can close the past and go on to an ideal future." Stating that there would be struggles, setbacks and misunderstandings, he said "we are committed for the long haul."[35]

At that time (1994–95), he affirmed the growing color transformation he was witnessing among his American Assemblies of God. "Our church is taking on the color of America as strong ministries flourish among Hispanics, blacks, Asians and a host of other minorities in our culture." Not noted at that moment was that the Assemblies of God district in New Jersey had just elected one of its pastors, Zollie Smith, to be assistant district superintendent, the first black official in the history of the entire fellowship. Trask cautioned that it would take time to realize true biblical expectations, for God "wants the church to be as inclusive as His own grace."[36]

In response to an appeal at Memphis by Leonard Lovett for the white church to repent of its racism, Trask said, "To the extent that I can represent others before the throne of God and before you, I freely do so."[37] Part of his Pentecostal community had sinned in its exclusion of people based on race and had refused to recognize such behavior as sin. The rest of that community had blamed its corporate inaction on the first group and thus was drawn into the same sin. That was the message of repentance and redemption at Memphis to which Trask was responding.

The question remained why recognition of sin took so long. Was it because we had limited our understanding of sin? In 1994, the work was just beginning.

Has a New Day Truly Dawned?

In 2007, circumstances brought my family permanently back to the US. We settled in the Pacific Northwest just in time for the election cycle in which the first black American was elected President. I once again followed closely the interchange between faith and the American public square, this time with the added benefit of hearing from the grassroots via social media. I noted substantial changes in the General Council,

35. Trask, "We Repent," 68; also, Trask, "Response," para. 19.
36. Trask, "We Repent," 68.
37. Trask, "Response," para. 1.

particularly its rapid diversification as well as the first steps it was taking in breaking the glass ceiling for women.

The story of the twenty-first century General Council is that it is transforming into a majority-minority denomination, increasingly reflecting "the ethnic, linguistic, and social diversity that exists in the global church," and closely mirroring the nation's diversity.[38] Far removed from its whitewashed days, the fellowship's percentage of nonwhite adherents had by 2017 risen to 44 percent. For the past eighteen years, the number of white adherents has remained steady[39] while the number of nonwhites has grown exponentially, much of this through immigration. Even the white stability is dependent on immigration.[40] The total number of black adherents, including immigrant blacks, has grown to 10.3 percent. The number of black ministers has increased from less than 1 percent in 2001 to 2.4 percent in 2017, a three-fold actual numerical growth in only seventeen years.[41] Scott Temple, director of ethnic relations for the fellowship, predicts that as early as 2020 the American Assemblies of God will be majority-minority.[42]

Meanwhile, women ministers, while still a minority, have increased significantly, the uptick beginning in the mid-1990s. In 1996, the percentage of women ministers was at 15.6 percent. By 2017, that percentage had increased to 25 percent. In 2016, 14.7 percent of the ordained ministers were female and, although the tally is complicated, 5.1 percent of lead pastors reported were female.[43] These increases are not at the expense of male ministers whose ranks have also grown, albeit at a much more measured rate.

However, ethnic and gender diversity are slow to filter upward into leadership. The area of slowest gains has been at the district and General

38. Rodgers, "2015 Statistics Released."

39. That the number of whites has held steady or close to it is significant in that most Mainline churches have experienced dramatic decrease and even some evangelicals have shown signs of decline. See Rodgers, "2015 Statistics Released."

40. Rodgers writes, "It should be noted that the number of white adherents in the U.S. includes quickly-growing constituents of immigrants from places such as the former Soviet Union and Romania. Without the new white immigrants, the white constituency in the Assemblies of God would be failing even more quickly." Rodgers, "2015 Statistics Released."

41. "Ministers by Race," 26 April 2018.

42. Banks, "Looks to a multiethnic future."

43. From a compilation of the 2016 and 2017 A/G Statistical Reports, 7 December 2017.

Presbytery levels, where turnover is unhurried. "The only way we can include minorities in a significant way is for white people to surrender power, and that's tough," said David J. Moore, Assemblies of God director of intercultural ministries, in 2000.[44] The same can be said of male leaders.

The leadership did find another way to diversify representation: expand the number of positions at the top. The 2005 General Council added representatives to the Executive Presbytery from non-Hispanic foreign language districts and ethnic fellowships, increasing the diversity significantly. Then the Executive Presbytery presented a resolution at the very next General Council to add Executive Presbytery positions for youth (under age forty) and women. Writes Qualls, "For the first time in the history of the Assemblies of God, a woman would be elected to the highest leadership board in the fellowship."[45] The first woman so chosen by the Council was A. Elizabeth (Beth) Grant. Qualls points out that, while nothing barred the Council from electing a woman to the under-age-forty position, only men were nominated.[46]

Pentecostals teach that change, far from being inevitable, comes when willing vessels are empowered by the Holy Spirit to become agents of change. Joyce Wells Booze, an English professor and copastor with her husband, became just such an agent. She and Adele Flower Dalton (sister of Joseph Flower and also a minister) had a significant hand in writing the paper that Flower produced on women in ministry.[47] Flower, with his status and privilege, became the voice for an anonymous committee of spirit-filled women.

Then in the late 1980s, Booze discovered that a couple of fellow professors at Central Bible College, where she was teaching, were actively discouraging female students from taking ministry classes or entering the ministry. Disturbed that this was happening and believing that the fellowship had always been open to women ministers, she went to the college's administration but got nowhere. Remembering Flower's paper, versions of which had been circulating for a decade by then, she wondered if there was now an official statement she could share with her students. She contacted the general secretary's office asking for a position paper on

44. Sack, "The Pentecostal Church in America."

45. Qualls, "God Forgive Us," 191.

46. Qualls, "God Forgive Us," 193.

47. Rodgers, email to author, 17 September 2018. Rodgers is referencing a conversation with Booze.

316 ETHICS IN THE AGE OF THE SPIRIT

women in ministry and was told there was none. Although Flower was the General Secretary, his paper had never been officially adopted.

Booze asked what it would take to get a position paper produced and was told that input from a good number of ministers would help. Immediately she put out the word to fifty or so women friends who were in the ministry, mostly foreign missionaries, to help her advocate for such a positional paper. Within a couple of weeks, Flower's office called her and asked her if she was behind the more than two hundred requests they had received.

The topic was assigned to the commission that produced such papers, a group which happened to be all male in membership. Booze and Deborah M. Gill, another Assemblies of God scholar and pastor, were included as advisors for this particular subject. Flower's paper served as a reference document[48] and Booze remembers that Flower had a hand in writing what the commission prepared.[49] It passed out of committee to the General Presbytery, but not before one of the male members had resigned in sharp disagreement with the conclusions.[50] The General Presbytery adopted the commission's work as an official position paper, "Role of Women in Ministry,"[51] reflecting the same perspective Joseph Flower had presented in his unpublished paper. Finally, the groundbreaking insights of Flower, Booze, Dalton, and others were official. The year was 1990.

Following Grant's election to the Executive Presbytery in the new century, the General Presbytery again adopted a statement worded similarly to the 1990 paper, declaring once more that it could find no "convincing evidence that the ministry of women is restricted according to some sacred or immutable principle."[52] In other words, based on the same biblical passages that had been used to deny eldership to women over the previous century, nothing was found biblically-speaking to deny ministry leadership to women.

At the 2017 General Council, Melissa J. Alfaro, copastor with her husband of El Tabernaculo in Houston, became the first female elected

48. Booze, interview by author, 6 January 2019, telephone.

49. Rodgers, email to author, 17 September 2018.

50. Booze, interview by author, 6 January 2019, telephone.

51. "The Role of Women in Ministry," 28 October 1990, 12–15.

52. "The Role of Women in Ministry," 2010.

to the Executive Presbytery unrelated to gender.[53] Assuming the under-forty position, Alfaro joined a leadership team that had just expanded to twenty-one with a newly created designated African-American position, to which Samuel M. Huddleston, assistant superintendent of the Northern California-Nevada district, was elected.[54] Alfaro and Huddleston joined the most diverse Executive Presbytery to that date, with two women and seven persons of color.

However, it took a special election the following year to validate once and for all that there were no more barriers to women. James T. Bradford, who had been general secretary since 2009, returned to pastoral ministry. Resigning mid-term when neither General Council nor General Presbytery were in session, he made room for his position to be filled by vote of the Executive Presbytery. Donna L. Barrett, lead pastor of a church in Ohio, was duly elected as the fellowship's general secretary, the first time an executive leadership post had been held by a woman.[55] A century after E. N. Bell declared that women could not be elders, the glass ceiling of eldership had been broken.

Still, we must ask if these changes really do reflect a new Pentecostal ethic. Or does the fellowship continue to act out of old moral habits, conforming to the culture around it, leading with a head of pragmatism, and clinging to prooftexts? The questions posed in chapter 1 are yet to be fully answered: What does Pentecostalism bring to the table? Are we any closer to understanding what it means to live in the Age of the Spirit? Have we yet become thoroughgoing Pentecostals?

Certainly, the fellowship is adapting to its new identity. The grass-roots are diversifying because the worldwide missions movement that was set in motion in 1914 has come home to roost. Questions remain: Is that diversity reflected widely in geographical districts and local congregations? What has provided the impetus for the change at the top? Is it because of fresh prophetic vision on the part of leadership in recent years? Certainly, more study is needed to determine movement at the local and district levels as well as perceptions among laity, clergy, and leadership.

While debates on pacifism ended long ago other than in academic circles, the fellowship continues to wrestle with the implications of its

53. Kennedy, "Going Places."
54. Kennedy, "Eight New Executive Presbyters."
55. Forrester, "Donna Barrett Elected."

overriding moral principle of loyalty to government, which in and of it-self has provided inconsistent guidance. Meanwhile, along with the grow-ing involvement of evangelicalism in the political sphere, the General Council has found its voice on specific issues such as religious freedom, abortion, and Black Lives Matter, the last in response to the influence of Church of God in Christ leadership.[56] Ministers and constituents regu-larly weigh in on a wide range of topics from guns to immigration. Do these positions grow out of Pentecostal prophetic insight marinated in the Word? Or do they come from already established political and cul-tural mindsets, as McDonnell and Quebedeaux suggested was the case with previous generations?

What is it that defines a Pentecostal people's stand on issues? And on what issues does it deem appropriate to take a stand? Do we still blindly follow the voices of evangelicalism and society as we did in accepting seg-regation? Are we acting from a purely "what works" perspective, ignoring our theological moorings as we did with the question of pacifism? Or are we merely hiding behind a few preferred texts, as we did for so long with the question of women in ministry?

A lot has been researched and written by and about Pentecostals in the past three decades. A whole new world of Pentecostal scholarship has blossomed in that time and such scholarship includes much reflection of an ethical nature. I suspect some of my original interpretations have not aged well in the intervening years and happily anticipate others revising my findings even as they explore the wealth of data from the thirty-year gap in my observations as well as older materials that are late in coming to light.[57]

While much progress has been made, much more remains to be done. Of the unfinished task, Lois Olena writes that what remains is to "learn from the past in order to avoid similar mistakes in the present, and continue to set out specific strategies for the future."[58] Learning from

56. See, for example, Wood, "Stands with COGIC."

57. See, for example, the extensive material Olena chronicles on the official discus-sion on race conversations at the highest levels in the Assemblies of God. Her review in "I'm Sorry, My Brother," 132–141, as found in Klaus, *We've Come this Far*, expands on the sources that were available when my dissertation was originally written. Other chapters in Klaus, *We've Come this* Far, add to the conversation, as does Mittelstadt and Sutton, *Forgiveness, Reconciliation & Restoration*; and Qualls, *God Forgive Us for Being Women*.

58. Olena, "I'm Sorry, My Brother," 151. For a model of setting out "specific strategies for the future," Olena recommends Synan, "The Future."

the past includes continuing to unearth the testimonies of . . . socially marginalized Assemblies of God ministers, so that we can better tell the full story of the 'Full Gospel.'"[59] Learning from the past also includes understanding more fully why "for many decades . . . [white Pentecostals] allowed the spirit of Jim Crow into their churches."[60]

Old Jim Crow may at last be dead, but does the spirit of Jim Crow live on? Even if an issue, such as the exclusion of African Americans, appears resolved, it is critical to ascertain what caused the issue in the first place and whether underlying causes have also been addressed. If we choose not to root out the causes, we presume both issue and causes are inconsequential to our mission, a presumption we have shown to be detrimental to our mission.

Such is the question a journalist posed to former general superintendent Trask. The journalist asked Trask as to why diversity was not addressed in his keynote message on spiritual vitality at a prior General Council. Trask said he did not consider using that forum to speak to the "spirit of Memphis," focusing only on the need for evangelism, fasting, prayer and Pentecostal passion. He then is quoted as saying that "if the church has spiritual vitality, these other things will take care of themselves."[61]

First, the journalist recognized that matters of an ethical nature are integral to the church's spiritual vitality. Like him, the child of Hot Springs in me knows that for far too long spiritual and ethical conversations have been segregated to the detriment of the spiritual life of the fellowship. How we treat women, people of color, soldiers, conscientious objectors, and a world of violence are much more rudimentary to our spiritual vitality than we have often preached.

Second, Trask's remark indicates that racism and absence of diversity are due to a lack of spiritual vitality. Such an implication begs the question concerning the spiritual vitality of past generations of Pentecostals. Did vitality die in Los Angeles in 1909 or in Hot Springs in 1914 only to be revived in Memphis in 1994? Azusa Street, it must be remembered, was not the finish line, but merely the beginning of the Spirit's work in birthing a new age in the Church.

59. Rodgers, "Walter Evans."
60. Wood, "Stands with COGIC."
61. Sack, "The Pentecostal Church in America."

This conversation between journalist and general superintendent reminds us of the limits we people of the Spirit impose on the voice of the Spirit. "Quench not the Spirit,"[62] was the cry of earlier generations of Pentecostals. Quenching comes when we fail to understand that the Spirit is speaking outside of our predetermined criteria. Wanda Carter, pastor and church planter, black and female, had presumed that one day racists would die off. She came to see that "funerals won't do it." More than funerals, it would take awareness building and education that racism is sin.[63] As Trask said in Memphis, "The most difficult part of our journey may come in the process the Holy Spirit uses to heal us from past racism."[64]

It is not that we Pentecostals have lacked spiritual vitality as much as we have put limits on what we are willing to hear from the Spirit. Pentecostals affirm that McLean is correct when he claims that Pentecostals believe that God still speaks today.[65] The question we must ever ask ourselves is, What is God saying to us about how we live in this world and how we speak prophetically as Pentecostal people to the present generation? Perhaps for such a time as this have we Pentecostals come of age. Would to God that once again our sons and daughters—of all colors—would prophesy.

---

62. I Thess. 5:19 (KJV).

63. Kennedy, "Still bugged," para. 2.

64. Trask, "Response," para. 17.

65. McLean, "Toward a Pentecostal Hermeneutic," 23.

Bibliography

GENERAL

Books

Primary

Bartleman, Frank. *How Pentecost Came to Los Angeles: As It was in the Beginning.* 2nd ed. Los Angeles: n.p., 1925.

Boyd, Frank M. *Ages and Dispensations.* Springfield, MO: Gospel, 1949.

Finney, Charles G. *Revivals of Religion.* New York: 1868: reprint, Chicago: Moody, 1962.

Goss, Ethel E. *The Winds of God.* New York: Comet, 1958.

Henry, Carl F. H. *The Uneasy Conscience of Modern Fundamentalism.* Grand Rapids: Eerdman, 1947.

Horton, Stanley. *The Promise of His Coming.* Springfield, MO: Gospel, 1967.

Parham, Sarah E. *The Life of Charles F. Parham: Founder of the Apostolic Faith Movement.* Baxter Springs, KS: Apostolic Faith, 1930.

Secondary

Anderson, Robert Mapes. *Vision of the Disinherited; The Making of American Pentecostalism.* New York: Oxford University Press, 1979.

Atter, Gordon F. *The Third Force.* Peterborough, ON: The College Press, 1962.

Brumback, Carl. *Suddenly . . . from Heaven.* Springfield, MO: Gospel, 1961.

Bruner, Frederick Dale. *A Theology of the Holy Spirit.* Grand Rapids: Eerdmans. 1970.

Christenson, Larry. *A Charismatic Approach to Social Action.* Minneapolis: Bethany Fellowship, 1974.

Clanton, Arthur L. *United We Stand.* Hazelwood, MO: The Pentecostal, 1970.

Conn, Charles W. *Like a Mighty Army.* Cleveland, TN: Church of God, 1955.

Dayton, Donald F. *The American Holiness Movement: A Bibliographical Introduction.* Wilmore, KY: Asbury Theological Seminary, 1971.

Fahey, Sheila M. *Charismatic Social Action.* New York: Paulist, 1977.

Fichter, Joseph H. *The Catholic Cult of the Paraclete.* New York: Sheed & Ward, 1975.

Ford, Josephine Massyngberde. *Which Way for Catholic Pentecostals?* New York: Harper & Row, 1976.

Frodsham, Stanley. *With Signs Following: The Story of the Pentecostal Revival in the Twentieth Century.* Rev. ed. Springfield, MO: Gospel, 1946.

Gee, Donald. *The Pentecostal Movement.* Enlarged ed., London: Elim, 1949.

Harper, Michael. *A New Way of Living.* Plainfield, NJ: Logos International, 1973.

———. *Walk in the Spirit.* Plainfield, NJ: Logos International, 1968

Hauerwas, Stanley. *Character and the Christian Life: A Study in Theological Ethics.* San Antonio: Trinity University Press, 1975.

Hollenweger, Walter J. *The Pentecostals.* Translated by R. A. Wilson. Minneapolis: Augsburg, 1972.

———. *Pentecostal between Black and White: Five Case Studies on Pentecost and Politics.* Belfast: Christian Journal, 1974.

Jones, Charles Edwin. *A Guide to the Study of the Pentecostal Movement.* 2 vols. Metuchen, NJ: Scarecrow and American Theological Library Association, 1983.

Kelsey, Morton T. *Tongue-Speaking.* Garden City, NY: Doubleday, 1964.

Kendrick, Klaude. *The Promise Fulfilled.* Springfield, MO: Gospel, 1961.

Marsden, George M. *Fundamentalism and American Culture: The Shaping of Twentieth Century Evangelicalism, 1870–1925.* New York: Oxford University Press, 1980.

Menzies, William W. *Anointed to Serve: The Story of The Assemblies of God.* Springfield, MO: Gospel, 1971.

Moberg, David O. *The Great Reversal: Evangelism and Social Concern.* Rev. ed. Philadelphia: Holman, 1977.

Orr, J. Edwin. *The Fervent Prayer: The Worldwide Impact of the Great Awakening of 1858.* Chicago: Moody, 1974.

———. *The Light of the Nations.* Grand Rapids: Eerdmans, 1965.

Pollock, John. *The Keswick Story.* Chicago: Moody, 1964.

Pulkingham, W. Graham. *Gathered for Power: Charisma, Communalism, Christian Witness.* New York: Morehouse-Barlow, 1972.

———. *They Left Their Nets: A Vision for Community Ministry.* New York: Morehouse-Barlow, 1973.

Quebedeaux, Richard. *The New Charismatics II.* New York: Harper & Row, 1983.

Shelley, Bruce. *Evangelicalism in America.* Grand Rapids: Eerdmans, 1967.

Sherrill, John L. *They Speak with Other Tongues.* New York: McGraw-Hill, 1964.

Smith, H. Shelton, Robert T. Handy, and Lefforts A. Loetscher. *American Christianity: An Historical Interpretation with Representative Documents.* 2 vols. New York: Scribner, 1963.

Smith, Timothy L. *Called unto Holiness.* Kansas City, MO: Nazarene, 1962.

———. *Revivalism and Social Reform.* New York: Abingdon, 1957.

Suenens, Leon Joseph, and Dom Helder Camara. *Charismatic Renewal and Social Action.* Ann Arbor, MI: Servant, 1979.

Synan, Vinson, ed. *Aspects of Pentecostal-Charismatic Origins.* Plainfield, NJ: Logos International, 1975.

———. *The Holiness-Pentecostal Movement in the United States.* Grand Rapids: Eerdmans, 1971.

———. *The Old-Time Power.* Franklin Springs, GA: Advocate, 1973.

Articles

Primary

"Back to Pentecost," *Weekly Evangel*, 1 January 1916, 4.

Bresee, Phineas. "The Gift of Tongues." *Nazarene Messenger* 11 (December 1905) 6.

Bryan, Williams Jennings. "A Defense of the Faith Once Delivered to the Saints." *The Pentecostal Evangel*, 1 August 1925, 2–5.

Cox, A. B. "Hot Times in Maryland." *The Christian Evangel*, 25 July 1914, 1–2.

"The Diary of a Delegate." *The Pentecostal Evangel*, 25 September 1943, 4.

Douglas, S. "The Former and Latter Rain." *The Pentecostal Evangel*, 7 October 1956, 8–9. Reprinted from the *Australian Evangel*.

Duncombe, Charles H. E. "Pulling Them out of the Fire." *The Pentecostal Evangel*, 6 May 1951, 4.

Editorial. *The Pentecostal Evangel*. 24 July 1924, 4.

"The Editor's Notebook." *The Pentecostal Evangel*, 27 September 1930, 4–5.

Flower, J. Roswell. "The Basic Unity of Evangelical Christianity." *The Pentecostal Evangel*, 19 June 1943, 8.

———. "Fifty Years of Signs and Wonders." *The Pentecostal Evangel*. Special Issue, 1952, 4–7. Reprinted from *Christian Life*.

———. "The Mark of the Beast." *The Christian Evangel*, 11 July 1914, 1–2.

———. "The Present Situation." *The Pentecostal Evangel*, 8 April 1956, 12–13, 23–24.

———. "Why We Joined the N.A.E." *The Pentecostal Evangel*, 29 March 1947, 12.

Frodsham, Stanley. "Days of Heaven upon Earth." *The Pentecostal Evangel*, 13 May 1944, 4–5.

———. "Disfellowshiped!" *The Pentecostal Evangel*, 18 August 1928, 7.

Gee, Donald. "Tests for 'Fuller Revelations.'" *The Pentecostal Evangel*, 14 February 1925, 6.

"General Council Chronicle." *The Pentecostal Evangel*, 8 October 1961, 9, 10.

Lewis, C. S. In *Decision*. Quoted in *The Pentecostal Evangel*, 24 May 1964, 16.

McIntire, Carl. Editorial. *Christian Beacon*, 27 April 1944, 8.

"A Movement toward Unity." *The Pentecostal Evangel*, 5 August 1922, 1, 7.

"Ordained Elders, Pastors, Ministers, Evangelists and Missionaries of the Churches of God in Christ with Their Stations for 1914." *Word and Witness*, 20 December 1913, 4.

"Pentecostal Evangel Moves to Online News Service." 5 January 2018. https://news.ag.org/news/pentecostal-evangel-moves-to-online-news-service.

"Pentecostal Groups Meet in Historic Convention." *The Pentecostal Evangel*, 20 November 1949, 13.

"St. Louis Unity Meeting not Called by the General Council." *The Pentecostal Evangel*, 14 October 1922, 1.

"The Twelfth General Council Meeting." *The Pentecostal Evangel*, 8 October 1927, 2–10.

"What State is the Most Pentecostal?" *The Pentecostal Evangel*, 24 October 1925, 7.

Williams, Ernest S. "The Pentecostal Movement under Fire." *The Pentecostal Evangel*, 23 July 1927, 2–3.

Secondary

Dayton, Donald W. "The Holiness and Pentecostal Churches Emerging from Cultural Isolation." *Christian Century* 96 (15–22 August 1979) 789.

Dempster, Murray W. "Soundings in the Moral Significance of Glossolalia." In *Pastoral Problems in the Pentecostal-Charismatic Movement*, edited by Harold D. Hunter, 1–47. Cleveland, TN: Church of God School of Theology, 1983.

———. "Pentecostal Church Mission and Social Ethics: Love, Justice, and Just Peacemaking." In *A Light to the Nations, Explorations in Ecumenism, Missions, and Pentecostalism*, edited by Stanley M. Burgess and Paul W. Lewis, 192–223. Eugene, OR: Wipf and Stock, 2017.

Ervin, Howard. "Hermeneutics: A Pentecostal Option." *Pneuma* 3 (Fall 1981) 11–25.

Fichter, Joseph H. "Liberal and Conservative Catholic Pentecostals." *Social Compass* 21 (1974) 303–10.

Hauerwas, Stanley. "The Church in a Divided World. The Interpretive Power of the Christian Story." *The Journal of Religious Ethics* 8 (Spring 1980) 55–82.

Hersch, Eitan D., and Gabrielle Malina. "Partisan Pastor: The Politics of 130,000 American Religious Leaders." 11 June 2017. http: eitanhersh.com/uploads/7/9/7/5/7975685/hersh_malina_draft_061117.pdf.

Kessler, Charles. *Leaves of Healing*, March/April 1969, 11–19. Quoted in Walter J. Hollenweger, *The Pentecostals*, 118. Translated by R. A. Wilson. Minneapolis: Augsburg, 1972.

MacDonald, William G. "Pentecostal Theology: A Classical Viewpoint." In *Perspectives on the New Pentecostalism*, edited by Russell Spittler, 58–74. Grand Rapids: Baker, 1976.

McDonnell, Kilian. "Catholic Pentecostalism: Problems in Evaluation." *Dialog* 9 (Winter 1970) 35–54.

McLean, Mark D. "Toward a Pentecostal Hermeneutic." In *Toward a Pentecostal/Charismatic Theology*, 1–30. N.p.: Society for Pentecostal Studies, [1984].

Outler, Albert C. "Editor's Introduction to 'A Plain Account of Genuine Christianity.'" In *John Wesley*, edited by Albert Outler, 181–96. New York: Oxford University, 1964.

Sheppard, Gerald T. "Word and Spirit: Scripture in the Pentecostal Tradition, Part I." *Agora*, Spring 1978, 4.

———. "Word and Spirit: Scripture in the Pentecostal Tradition, Part II." *Agora*, Summer 1978, 16–17.

Periodicals

The Pentecostal Evangel. Founded as the *Christian Evangel* June 1913. Called the *Weekly Evangel* 13 March 1915–1 June 1918. Finally, *The Pentecostal Evangel* 18 October 1919 to December 2014.

Word and Witness. Published as early as 1912. A monthly eventually merged with the *Evangel*, October 1915.

The World Challenge. Publication of the Division of Foreign Missions, Assemblies of God. Merged with *The Pentecostal Evangel*. April 1959.

Publication Issues

Leaves of Healing. 22 April 1905.
Leaves of Healing. 13 May 1905.

Advertisements

Bryan, William Jennings. Various books. *The Pentecostal Evangel,* 15 August, 1925, 16.
Torrey, R. A. The Return of the Lord Jesus. *The Pentecostal Evangel,* 20 February 1926, 14.

Theses and Unpublished Documents

Blackwelder, Julia Kirk. "Fundamentalist Reactions to the Civil Rights Movement since 1954." PhD diss., Emory University, 1972.
Flower, J. Roswell. "History of the Assemblies of God." 1949. J. R. Flower file, Flower Pentecostal Heritage Center, Springfield, MO.
Gable, C. David. Statement. 1983 General Council. Copy given to author by Gable.

Minutes and Reports

"A/G Estimated Membership by State, 1985." 26 September 1986, Office of the General Secretary, General Council, Springfield, MO.
"Assemblies of God Church Membership." 26 April 1985, Office of the General Secretary, General Council, Springfield, MO.
"Churches on the Official List for Year Ending December 31, 1984." n.d., Office of the General Secretary, General Council, Springfield, MO.
"Church Report—1955-1958." November 1958, Office of the General Secretary, General Council, Springfield, MO.
Executive Presbytery. Minutes. 23 November 1914, 5 July 1922, 16 April 1970.
General Council. Church Directory, 24 September 1987.
General Council. Constitution and bylaws. 1927.
General Council. Minutes. 1914–1987.
General Council. Reports. 1951.
General Presbytery. Minutes. 1939. 1942, 1946, 1949, 1956, 1957, 1958, 1964, 1965.
"Report of Churches for 1955." n.d., Office of the General Secretary, General Council, Springfield, MO.
"Statement of the General Presbytery of the Assemblies of God regarding Social Concern." 21 August 1968, Office of the General Secretary, General Council, Springfield, MO.

Records

Deceased ministers' file, Office of the General Secretary, General Council, Springfield, MO.

Ministers' file, Office of the General Secretary, General Council, Springfield, MO.

Written Correspondence

Frodsham, Stanley H., to Nelson T. Eveleth, 29 July 1943. Frodsham file, Flower
    Pentecostal Heritage Center, Springfield, MO.

Interviews and Spoken Sermons

Carter, Harold. Sermon preached at the North Texas District Council, Reunion Arena,
    Dallas, TX, 7 June 1983. Heard by author.
Flower, Joseph R. Interview by author, 14 January 1986, Springfield, MO.
Flower, J. Roswell. Interview by William Menzies, 26 June 1967. Tape recording. J. R.
    Flower file, Flower Pentecostal Heritage Center, Springfield, MO.
Reynolds, Frank. Interview by author, 13 September 1985, Springfield, MO.

RACE

Books

Primary

Higgins, Walter J. *Pioneering in Pentecost: My Experience of 46 Years in the Ministry.*
    n.p., 1958.
McPherson, Aimee Semple. *This is That: Personal Experiences. Sermons and Writings.*
    3d ed. Los Angeles: Echo Park Evangelistic Assn., 1923.
Mittelstadt, Martin W., and Geoffrey W. Sutton, eds. *Forgiveness, Reconciliation, &
    Restoration: Multidisciplinary Studies from a Pentecostal Perspective.* Eugene, OR:
    Wipf & Stock, 2010.
Montgomery, James, and Bob Harrison. *When God was Black.* Grand Rapids: Zon-
    dervan, 1971.
Parham, Charles F. *The Everlasting Gospel.* Baxter Springs, KS: Apostolic Faith Bible
    College, 1911.
———. *A Voice Crying in the Wilderness.* 3rd ed. Baxter Springs, KS: Apostolic Faith
    Bible School, n.d., first published in 1902.
Wilkerson, David. *The Cross and the Switchblade.* New York: Random House, 1963.

Secondary

Cobbins, Otho B., ed. *History of Church of Christ (Holiness) U.S.A.: 1895–1965.* New
    York: Vantage, 1966.
Dugas, Paul D., comp. *The Life and Writings of Elder G. T. Haywood.* Portland, OR:
    Apostolic Book, 1968.

Jones, Charles Edwin. *Black Holiness; A Guide to the Study of Black Participation in Wesleyan Perfectionist and Glossolalic Pentecostal Movements*. Metuchen, NJ: Scarecrow and the American Theological Library Association, 1987.

A Historical Account of the Apostolic Faith. Portland, OR: The Apostolic Faith, 1965.

Knight, Herbert V. *Ministry Aflame*. Carlinville, IL: Illinois District Council, 1972.

Articles

Primary

"Advisory Committee Makes Plans for World Conference." *The Pentecostal Evangel*, 19 May 1957, 5.

"A/G Looks to Inner-city Ministry." *The Pentecostal Evangel*, 23 December 1973, 27.

Alexander, John. "Campus Unrest." *The Pentecostal Evangel*, 27 September 1970, 6–9.

"And the World Goes On . . ." *The Pentecostal Evangel*, 19 December 1965, 17.

"Annual Evangelists Seminar Focuses on 'Building Strong Families.'" *The Pentecostal Evangel*, 15 February 1981, 24.

Argue, Zelma. "Do the Work of an Evangelist." *The Pentecostal Evangel*, 21 August 1943, 1.

Atkinson, Heidi. "I Was Sure He Was Going to Kill Me!" *The Pentecostal Evangel*, 20 June 1982, 14.

Bacon, L. Calvin. "Eyewitness at a Funeral." *The Pentecostal Evangel*, 14 July 1968, 20–21.

Bartlett, Bob. "Teen Challenge Workers See Victory Ahead." *The Pentecostal Evangel*, 12 September 1965, 22.

Beaver, Flora M. "The Small Church with the Large Vision." *The Pentecostal Evangel*, 15 July 1962, 12.

Bell, E. N. "Questions and Answers." *Christian Evangel*, 28 December 1918, 5.

Bevis, Katherine. "Aunt Katy's Sunday School." *The Pentecostal Evangel*, 12 February 1961, 13.

Bishop, J. Bashford. "Peter Preaches to the Gentiles." *The Pentecostal Evangel*, 4 February 1968, 14.

"Bishop Mason with the Lord." *The Pentecostal Evangel*, 13 May 1962, 27.

"Black Congress on Evangelism Meets." *The Pentecostal Evangel*, 8 November 1970, 28.

Blake, Charles E. "The Future: A Strategy for Reconciliation—Response to a Paper Presented by Dr. Vinson Synan." http://pctii.org/cyberj/cyberj14/blake.html.

Blake, Junius A. "The Undying Flame of Pentecost." *The Pentecostal Evangel*, 31 January 1971, 8–10.

"Bob Harrison Named Consultant on Inner-city Evangelism." *The Pentecostal Evangel*, 31 December 1972, 28.

Bonnici, Roberta Lashley. "A Lesson in Love." *The Pentecostal Evangel*, 15 April 1973, 8–9.

Borden, Darlene. Letter to the editor. *The Pentecostal Evangel*, 17 May 1970, 24.

Boyd, Frank M. "Romanism; What Is Its Place in the Last Days?" *The Pentecostal Evangel*, 16 August 1924, 8.

Brandt, R. L, "Problems Encountered in Evangelical Work Among the American Indians." *The Pentecostal Evangel*, 14 August 1960, 18.

Braxton, Helen. "Overseas Conference Inspires Teachers." *The Pentecostal Evangel*, 30 January 1966, 27.

Buchwalter, Paul R. "Revival Center to Open in Harlem." *The Pentecostal Evangel*, 14 May 1967, 10–11.

Carlson, G. Raymond. "Salt in the Inner City." *The Pentecostal Evangel*, 29 May 1983, 11.

Carothers, W. F. "Attitude of Pentecostal Whites to the Colored Brethren in the South." *The Weekly Evangel*, 14 August 1915, 2.

Carter, Harold. "The Purpose of the Holy Spirit." *The Pentecostal Evangel*, 31 October 1982, 5–7.

Causey, Clyde. "Bushwick Miracle." *The Pentecostal Evangel*, 24 April 1983, 8–9.

"A Chariot of Fire." *The Pentecostal Evangel*, 20 August 1927, 9.

"Church Leaders Meet to Discuss Ways of Reaching Black Americans for Christ." *The Pentecostal Evangel*, 15 February 1970, 29.

"The Colored Auntie's Prayer." *The Pentecostal Evangel*, 24 January 1925, 13.

Cornelius, Sister. "Our Church History." *The Whole Truth*, October 1976, 4.

Cottriel, Fred. "The Immigrants Are Coming." *The Pentecostal Evangel*, 30 November 1986, 14.

Cox, Faye. "Interracial Witnessing." *The Pentecostal Evangel*, 26 January 1969, 5.

Coxe, Paul. "New 'Gang' Church Grows in Brooklyn." *The Pentecostal Evangel*, 25 September 1960, 4–5.

Crosby, Alma Ware. "Witnessing to Negroes." *The Pentecostal Evangel*, 6 August 1961, 7.

Cunningham, Robert C. Editorial. *The Pentecostal Evangel*, 13 August 1967, 4.

———. "How Can We Reach Black Americans for Christ?" *The Pentecostal Evangel*. 26 April 1970, 6–8, 20.

———. "Iniquity Abounding." *The Pentecostal Evangel*, 14 July 1968, 5.

———. "One Nation Indivisible?" *The Pentecostal Evangel*, 13 August 1967, 4.

———. "Social Concern Articulated." *The Pentecostal Evangel*, 13 October 1968, 5.

———. "Wake Up, America!" *The Pentecostal Evangel*, 14 January 1968, 4.

———. "Watts—a Year Later." *The Pentecostal Evangel*, 17 July 1966, 4.

———. "What Christian Citizens Can Do about Crime." *The Pentecostal Evangel*, 14 December 1975, 31.

Davis, Flo. "Revivaltime Originates from El Bethel Assembly." *The Pentecostal Evangel*, 23 June 1963, 22.

"The Diary of a Delegate." *The Pentecostal Evangel*, 18 September 1943, 9.

"The Diary of a Delegate to the General Council at Memphis, Tennessee." *The Pentecostal Evangel*, 25 September 1937, 2.

Doney, C. W. "The Gospel of the Kingdom." *Word and Witness*, 20 March 1914, 2.

Dowie, John Alexander. "God the Father of all Men." *Leaves of Healing*, 24 September 1904, 801–7.

———. "Let Us Go Up to Zion." *Leaves of Healing*, 9 February 1901, 498–501.

———. "The Syrophoenecian Woman." *Leaves of Healing*, 15 December 1900, 236–38.

———. "Zion College Lectures on Prayer." *Leaves of Healing*, 27 October 1900, 16–19.

Dunn, Ruby. "Caught in the Middle." *The Pentecostal Evangel*, 11 November 1979, 32.

"The Editor's Notebook." *The Pentecostal Evangel*, 18 September 1943, 9.

Edwards, Ernest E. Letter to the editor. *The Pentecostal Evangel*, 23 July 1978, 30.

Enyart, Ruby M. "Special Ministries Are on the Move!" *The Pentecostal Evangel*, 20 March 1983, 12–13.

Eubanks, O. W. "Highway Patrolman Pastors New Black Church in Mississippi." *The Pentecostal Evangel*, 8 February 1976, 8–9.

"Evangelical Position on Current Issues Made Clear at NAE Convention." *The Pentecostal Evangel*, 23 June 1963, 21.

Faison, Thurman L. "What Are We Going to Do about Our Cities?" *The Pentecostal Evangel*, 9 January 1972, 8–9.

"Fifth World Conference of Pentecostal Churches." *The Pentecostal Evangel*, 26 October 1958, 8.

"Foreign News Digest." *The Pentecostal Evangel*, 27 October 1963, 26.

"Format, Speakers Announced for August Council on Spiritual Life." *The Pentecostal Evangel*, 16 January 1972, 27.

"From the Mission Field." *The Latter Rain Evangel* (Chicago), August 1924, 14, 15.

Gannon, T. E. "Unrestricted Compassion." *The Pentecostal Evangel*, 15 September 1974, 20–21.

"General Council Speakers Announced." *The Pentecostal Evangel*, 9 May 1965, 29.

"General Council Speakers Announced." *The Pentecostal Evangel*, 26 March 1967, 28.

Gentzler, Lisa. "Assemblies of God Ministers-to-be." *The Pentecostal Evangel*, 27 May 1984, 8–9.

"A God-Blessed Convocation." *The Pentecostal Evangel*, 7 October 1933, 6.

"Go on Wid Dat Prayer." *The Pentecostal Evangel*, 24 April 1926, 9.

Gordon, A. J. "The Present-Day Outpouring of the Holy Spirit Predicted prior to 1896." *The Pentecostal Evangel*, 28 July 1923, 6.

Hall, Don. "Teen Challenge Marches On!" *The Pentecostal Evangel*, 29 December 1963, 10–11.

Haney, Oliver J. Jr. "The Past: Historical Roots of Racial Unity and Division in American Pentecostalism—Response to a Paper Presented by Dr. Cecil M. Robeck, Jr. http://pctii.org/cyberj/cyberj14/haney.html.

Hannah, Marguerite. "Milestones in My Life and Ministry." *The Pentecostal Evangel*, 13 March 1983, 8.

Hansen, David. Letter to the editor. *The Pentecostal Evangel*, 22 August 1982, 31.

Harrison, Bob. "These Things Shall Be." *The Pentecostal Evangel*, 22 October 1967, 2–3.

Haywood, G. T. "Pentecost at Apostolic Faith Assembly." *Christian Evangel*, 27 February 1915, 1.

"Heard at the Council on Spiritual Life." *The Pentecostal Evangel*, 8 October 1972, 6–9.

Hembree, Ron. "Prayers of the Peanut Man." *The Pentecostal Evangel*, 27 February 1983, 4–5.

Hill, E. V. "The Holy Spirit, Our Helper." *The Pentecostal Evangel*, 7 October 1984, 4–6.

Hill, W. Gordon. "Is Yo' Wheat Good?" *The Pentecostal Evangel*, 25 January 1941, 6.

Hitt, Russell T. "Looking Back." *The Pentecostal Evangel*, 9 February 1958, 19.

"Homefront Highlights." *The Pentecostal Evangel*, 28 June 1964, 20.

Horne, Gerald. "Is This My Last Road?" *The Pentecostal Evangel*, 14 May 1978, 7.

"Hot Springs Assembly; God's Glory Present." *Word and Witness*, 20 August 1914, 1.

"Identity, Leadership, Involvement Seen as Keys to Effective Evangelism." *The Pentecostal Evangel*, 29 June 1969, 27.

"Indiana Assembly Sponsors State Prison 'Gospelaires." *The Pentecostal Evangel*, 19 September 1965, 25.

"Jack Seeks Church Help in Solving Rights Woes." *Springfield* (MO) *LeaderPress*, 18 June 1963, 13.

Johansson, Lois. "A 6-year Prayer Is Answered in the Bronx." *The Pentecostal Evangel*, 30 August 1981, 6–7.

Johnson, LeRoy. "Civil Disobedience." *The Pentecostal Evangel*, 14 July 1968, 7.

Jones, Nancy. "The New Neighbors." *The Pentecostal Evangel*, 25 February 1968, 22–23.

Jones, Spencer. "America's Inner-city Churches." *The Pentecostal Evangel*, 30 September 1984, 22–23.

Klaus, Byron D., ed. *We've Come This Far: Reflections on the Pentecostal Tradition and Racial Reconciliation.* Springfield, MO: Assemblies of God Theological Seminary, 2007.

Knapp, C. "Old Nanny's Faith." *The Pentecostal Evangel*, 13 June 1942, 5.

"KS Youth Gets Scholarship and Is Commencement Speaker." *The Pentecostal Evangel*, 8 July 1979, 15.

Lawrence, B. F. "Apostolic Faith Restored, Article VII.—Houston, Texas and W. J. Seymour." *Weekly Evangel*, 19 February 1916, 4.

———. "Apostolic Faith Restored; Article VIII.—Reminiscences of an Eyewitness." *Weekly Evangel*, 4 March 1916, 4.

"Letter from Bro. Parham." *The Apostolic Faith* (Los Angeles), September 1906, 1.

Lyon, Ruth. "Buried Treasure." *The Pentecostal Evangel*, 20 March 1966, 24–25.

———. "Focus on Home Missions." *The Pentecostal Evangel*, 10 October 1965, 12, 13, 27.

Mason, Charles H. "The Kaiser in the Light of the Scriptures." Sermon preached on 23 June 1918. Recorded by William B. Holt. Printed in "Our COGIC Roots." *The Whole Truth*, September 1978, 3–4.

Michael, Stanley. "Revivaltime Choir and Prison Division Collaborate in Prison Evangelism." *The Pentecostal Evangel*, 6 September 1964, 16–17.

Millsaps, Willie. "Willie Millsaps Remembers C. H. Mason at Hot Springs." *Assemblies of God Heritage* 4 (Summer 1984) 8.

"Mississippi: A Venture in Its Cotton Belt." *The Pentecostal Evangel*, 29 April 1973, 10–11.

"'The Most Unusual Sunday School in America.'" *The Pentecostal Evangel*, 8 September 1985, 16–17.

"Negro Evangelicals Form National Association." *The Pentecostal Evangel*, 23 June 1963, 21.

Nelson, M. C. "Inner-City Church Rises in Minneapolis." *The Pentecostal Evangel*, 25 October 1970, 18–19.

———. "On His Own Feet." *The Pentecostal Evangel*, 20 June 1971, 6–7.

———. "They Call Him 'Scotty.'" *The Pentecostal Evangel*, 6 June 1971, 5.

"New Church in Manhattan Starts Church in the Bronx." *The Pentecostal Evangel*, 12 February 1978, 16–17.

"New Heights at Denver." *The Pentecostal Evangel*, 28 September 1975, 30.

"News of the 26th NAE Convention." *The Pentecostal Evangel*, 21 July 1968, 32.

"1975–76 Black Scholarships Awarded to *A/G* College Students." *The Pentecostal Evangel*, 18 July 1976, 29.

"Not Missions, but Churches of God in Christ." *Word and Witness*, 20 August 1912, 2.

"Nuggets from Black Susan." *The Pentecostal Evangel*, 4 September 1943, 8.

Obituary. Ellsworth S. Thomas. *The Pentecostal Evangel*, 11 July 1936, 7.

Olena, Lois. "I'm Sorry, My Brother." In *We've Come This Far: Reflections on the Pentecostal Tradition and Racial Reconciliation*, edited by Byron D. Klaus, 130–52. Springfield, MO: Assemblies of God Theological Seminary, 2007.

"Olric Wilkins Called to Active Chaplaincy Duty." *The Pentecostal Evangel*, 11 November 1984, 31.

Olson, Melford A. "Remembering the Urban Man." *The Pentecostal Evangel*, 27 September 1972, 16–17.

Olson, Nathaniel. "Slavery Still Exists." *The Pentecostal Evangel*, 12 February 1961, 6.

"Our Colored Brethren." *The Pentecostal Evangel*, 12 January 1946, 12.

"Our Colored Brethren." *The Pentecostal Evangel*, 23 August 1947, 6–7.

Parham, Charles F. "Free Love." *Apostolic Faith* (Baxter Springs, KS), December 1912, 4–5.

"Pentecost Has Come." *The Apostolic Faith* (Los Angeles), September 1906, 1.

"Pentecost with Signs Following." *The Apostolic Faith* (Los Angeles), December 1906, 1.

Pinson, M. M. "Trip to the Southwest." *Word and Witness*, 20 August 1912, 1.

Pipkin, Paul. "Servicemen in Taiwan . . . a Challenge and a Blessing." *The Pentecostal Evangel*, 22 November 1964, 22–23.

"Pray for Youth of New York." *The Pentecostal Evangel*, 6 July 1958, 20–21.

"Predominant Prejudices against Black Community Must Be Corrected." *The Lance* (Evangel College), 19 March 1970, 2.

Radumas, Angela. "A Smile Stopped a Black Panther." *The Pentecostal Evangel*, 17 May 1970, 2–3.

"Reaching Blacks in Atlanta." *The Pentecostal Evangel*, 14 January 1979, 20.

Reed, Charles. "Bible Quiz, Talent Search Winners Named." *The Pentecostal Evangel*, 27 October 1968, 22–23.

Reid, Tommy. "Another Mission Field: Our Servicemen Abroad." *The Pentecostal Evangel*, 1 July 1962, 16–17.

"Representatives of 16 Church Bodies Meet in Montreal, Canada, for 16th Annual Convention of the Pentecostal Fellowship of North America." *The Pentecostal Evangel*, 29 December 1963, 16–17.

Ringness, Curtis W. "Reaching Black Americans." *The Pentecostal Evangel*, 25 April 1971, 23.

Ringness, Curtis W., and Leslie W. Smith. "The Now Generation." *The Pentecostal Evangel*, 17 November 1968, 12–13.

Roe, J. M. News item. *Word and Witness*, 20 February 1913, 3.

Rohrer, Norman B. "Religion in Review." *The Pentecostal Evangel*, 17 January 1971, 25.

———. "Religion in Review." *The Pentecostal Evangel*, 9 January 1972, 31.

Sanders, D. Leroy. "To Serve is Still Enough." *The Pentecostal Evangel*, 26 June 1966, 2–3.

San Filippo, Jack A. "There Is Hope in the Ghetto." *The Pentecostal Evangel*, 29 May 1983, 8–10.

Schofield, A. T. "The Good Black Doctor." *The Pentecostal Evangel*, 16 February 1946, 6–7.

"Scholarships Available for Black Students." *The Pentecostal Evangel*, 31 August 1975, 21.

Scott, Charles W. H. "How Can We Reach Black Americans for Christ?" *The Pentecostal Evangel*, 26 April 1970, 7.

"Second Inner-city Pastors Conference Scheduled." *The Pentecostal Evangel*, 15 November 1981, 28.

"Segregation Today and Tomorrow." *The Pentecostal Evangel*, 19 May 1982, 15.

Simkins, J. Robin. "Man with the Battered Grip." *The Pentecostal Evangel*, 11 June 1949, 6–7.

"Skid Row Mission Supports Missions." *The Pentecostal Evangel*, 22 March 1964, 22.

"Southern Missouri Opens Black Church." *The Pentecostal Evangel*, 27 June 1971, 16–17.

"Speakers and Themes Announced for First National Men's Convention." *The Pentecostal Evangel*, 13 April 1980, 26.

Stafford, Mable. "Brown Sugar." *The Pentecostal Evangel*, 19 December 1965, 16–17.

Strobridge, Maxine. "Evangelical Outreach at Deaf Olympics." *The Pentecostal Evangel*, 3 October 1965, 7.

"Swedish Leader to Preach at World Conference." *The Pentecostal Evangel*, 3 August 1958, 15.

"These Churches Defeat Inner-city Problems." *The Pentecostal Evangel*, 10 October 1976, 18–19.

Thomson, Hazel. "Releasing Prisoners, His Specialty." *The Pentecostal Evangel*, 2 April 1942, 6.

"To Preachers." *Word and Witness*, 20 December 1912, 1.

"To Preachers." *Word and Witness*, 20 December 1913, 4.

Trask, Thomas. "The Problem of Racism in the Contemporary Pentecostal Movement— Response to a Paper Presented by Dr. Leonard Lovett." http://www.pccna.org/documents/1994Trask.pdf.

———. "We Repent!" *Ministries Today*, January/February 1995, 68.

Trimmer, Victor. Letter to the editor. *The Pentecostal Evangel*, 9 June 1968, 27.

Underwood, B. E. "Pentecostals Forming New Alliance as a Strategy for 21st Century." *World Pentecost*, Summer 1994, 15.

———. "Recapturing the Unity of the Holy Spirit," *Ministries Today*, January/February 1995, 38.

"War Clouds." *The Pentecostal Evangel*, 31 July 1926, 7. Reprint from "Prophetic News," 9.

Ward, C. M. "J. Edgar Hoover testifies …" *The Pentecostal Evangel*, 4 October 1970, 10.

———. "Signs of the End Time." *The Pentecostal Evangel*, 15 October 1967, 6.

"The Washingtons Hold Good News Crusade in Africa." *The Pentecostal Evangel*, 21 July 1968, 34.

"Welcome in West Africa." *The Pentecostal Evangel*, 6 June 1965, 8–9.

Wilkerson, David. "Teen Challenge Marches On!" *The Pentecostal Evangel*, 5 January 1964, 24.

———. "Teen Challenge; What God Is Doing at the Teen-age Evangelism Center in New York City." *The Pentecostal Evangel*, 31 December 1961, 10–11.

Williams, Ernest S. "Questions and Answers." *The Pentecostal Evangel*, 20 July 1929, 9.

———. "Questions and Answers." *The Pentecostal Evangel*, 7 August 1937, 7.

———. "What of the Jews?" *The Pentecostal Evangel*, 4 January 1941, 2.

———. "Your Questions." *The Pentecostal Evangel*, 24 February 1957, 23.

———. "Your Questions." *The Pentecostal Evangel*, 2 June 1957, 5.

———. "Your Questions." *The Pentecostal Evangel*, 13 October 1957, 9.

———. "Your Questions." *The Pentecostal Evangel*, 2 October 1960, 11.

————. "Your Questions." *The Pentecostal Evangel*, 26 March 1961, 19.

————. "Your Questions." *The Pentecostal Evangel*, 2 April 1961, 13.

————. "Your Questions." *The Pentecostal Evangel*, 26 December 1965, 25.

————. "Your Questions." *The Pentecostal Evangel*, 13 February 1966, 11.

————. "Your Questions." *The Pentecostal Evangel*, 15 October 1967, 7.

————. "Your Questions." *The Pentecostal Evangel*, 25 February 1968, 12.

————. "Your Questions." *The Pentecostal Evangel*, 22 September 1968, 9.

————. "Your Questions." *The Pentecostal Evangel*, 18 August 1968, 21.

————. "Your Questions." *The Pentecostal Evangel*, 24 August 1969, 23.

————. "Your Questions." *The Pentecostal Evangel*, 4 January 1970, 14.

Williscroft, Paul. "Victory in Retreat." *The Pentecostal Evangel*, 7 July 1963, 20–21.

Winley, Jesse H. "The Unequal Yoke." *The Pentecostal Evangel*, 14 March 1976, 6–8. Reprinted from *Reach*.

"With the Lord." *The Latter Rain Evangel* (Chicago), 24 February 1924, 14.

Wood, George O. "Assemblies of God Stands with COGIC in 'Black Lives Matter' Campaign." Charisma News, 12 December 2014. https://www.charismanews. com/politics/20-news/featured-news/46433-assemblies-of-god-stands-with-cogic-in-black-lives-matter-campaign.

"World Pentecostal Conference." *The Pentecostal Evangel*, 24 August 1952, 8.

Secondary

Banks, Adelle M. "Assemblies of God Turns 100, and Looks to a Multiethnic Future." https://religionnews.com/2014/08/06/assemblies-of-god-100/.

Clark, Michael. "FBI File Reveals Endurance of Church Founder." *The Memphis Commercial Appeal*, 10 November 1983, [page number not identifiable].

Clemmons, lthiel. "Insidious Racism in American Religious Statistics." *The Whole Truth*, February 1983, 3.

Grady, J. Lee. "Pentecostals Reject Their Racist Past." *Charisma*, December 1994, 66–67.

————. "Pentecostals Renounce Racism." *Christianity Today*, 12 December 1994, 58.

Hollenweger, Walter J. "A Forgotten Chapter of Black History; The Black Pentecostals Contribution to the Church Universal." *Concept*, June 1980, 27.

Kellner, Mark A. "Divided Pentecostal Groups to Pursue Unity." *Christianity Today*, 25 April 1994, 50.

Kennedy, John W. "Eight New Executive Presbyters Elected." 10 August 2017. https:// news.ag.org/news/eight-new-executive-presbyters-elected.

————. "Still Bugged by Racism." 18 January 2016. https://news.ag.org/News/Still-Bugged-by-Racism.

Kenyon, Howard N. "Bishop Mason and the Sisterhood Myth," *Assemblies of God Heritage*, Spring 1987, 12.

————. "Black Ministers in the Assemblies of God." *Assemblies of God Heritage*, Spring 1987, 10–12, 13, 20.

Lovett, Leonard. "Black Origins of the Pentecostal Movement." In *Aspects of Pentecostal-Charismatic Origins*, edited by Vinson Synan, 123–141. Plainfield, NJ: Logos International, 1975.

"The Memphis Manifesto." *Ministries Today*, January/February 1995, 38.

"The Miracle in Memphis—Racial Reconciliation." *AD 2000 Timelines*, Fall 1994, 1–2.

Morgan, Timothy C. "Interracial Gathering Set." *Christianity Today*, 25 April 1994, 50–51.

"NAE Takes Civil Rights Stand." *Eternity* 14 (July 1964) 34.

Parsons, Monique. "United in Spirit." *Asbury Park Press*, 20 November 1994, C1–2, 8.

"Pentecostal Groups Confront Longstanding Racial Divide to Build Cooperation between Churches." https://www.huffingtonpost.com/2014/02/19/pentecostal-racial-divide_n_4817324.html.

Rodgers, Darrin. "Assemblies of God 2015 Statistics Released, Growth Spurred by Ethnic Transformation." https://ifphc.wordpress.com/2016/06/24/assemblies-of-god-2015-statistics-released-growth-spurred-by-ethnic-transformation/.

———. "New COGIC leader is Graduate of CBC and AGTS." https://news.ag.org/en/News/New-COGIC-Leader-is-Graduate-of-CBC-and-AGTS.

———. "Walter Evans: Rediscovering a Pioneer Black Assemblies of God Minister in Nebraska." https://ifphc.wordpress.com/2017/05/24/walter-evans-rediscovering-a-pioneer-black-assemblies-of-god-minister-in-nebraska/.

Sack, Kevin. "The Pentecostal Church in America." *The New York Times*, 4 June 2000. https://archive.nytimes.com/www.nytimes.com/library/national/race/060400sack-church-side.html.

S.S. "Reconciliation Dialogue Becomes Memphis Miracle." *Advocate*, January 1995, 6–7.

Synan, Vinson. "The Future: A Strategy for Reconciliation." http://www.pccna.org/documents/1994Synan.pdf.

Tinney, James S. "Doctrinal Differences between Black and White Pentecostals." *Spirit* 1 (1977) 36–45.

Waters, David. "Pentecostals End Racial Separation." *The Commercial Appeal* (Memphis, TN), 19 October 1994, B1, B8.

———. "Pentecostals Gather for Reconciliation." *The Commercial Appeal* (Memphis, TN), 18 October 1994, B1.

Publication Issues

Apostolic Faith (Baxter Springs, KS), March 1927.

The Latter Rain Evangel (Chicago), November 1923.

The Latter Rain Evangel (Portland, OR), November 1912.

New Jersey District Advance, June 1987.

San Antonio Light, 19 July 1907.

United Evangelical Action, 15 (15 May 1956).

Word and Witness, 20 October 1913.

Word and Witness, 17 November 1913.

Word and Witness, 20 September 1914.

Youth Alive, Fall 1984.

Cartoons and Drawings

"Looking Our Way." *The Pentecostal Evangel*, 25 February 1933, 10.

Ramsey, Chris. "Crucifixion—1968." *The Pentecostal Evangel*, 4 February 1968, 14.

———. "No Place for Garbage." *The Pentecostal Evangel*, 5 January 1975, 14.

Photographs

"Black Faces—White Hearts." *The Pentecostal Evangel*, 27 June 1936, 8.
Caption. *The Pentecostal Evangel*, 10 June 1962, 22.
The Lower Light, no. 7, pp. 4, 6.
Mason, Charles H. "More Visitors at Memphis." *The Pentecostal Evangel*, 2 October 1937, 4.
Mason, Lelia. C. H. Mason file, Flower Pentecostal Heritage Center, Springfield, MO.
Neeley, Isaac. Missionary group. *The Pentecostal Evangel*, 13 October 1923, 1.
Neeley, Isaac. Missionary group. 1923 General Council. E. S. Williams photograph album, Flower Pentecostal Heritage Center, Springfield, MO.
The Pentecostal Evangel, special outreach issue, 1960, 8.
The Pentecostal Evangel, 10 January 1960, 26.
The Pentecostal Evangel, 26 March 1961, 14.
The Pentecostal Evangel, 15 March 1964, 13.
The Pentecostal Evangel, 16 January 1966, 16–17.
The Pentecostal Evangel, 15 October 1967, 11, 12.
The Pentecostal Evangel, 11 July 1971, 5.
The Pentecostal Evangel, 31 March 1974, 6.
The Pentecostal Evangel, 12 January 1975, 18.
The Pentecostal Evangel, 4 May 1975, 11.
The Pentecostal Evangel, 11 May 1975, 6.
The Pentecostal Evangel, 21 September 1975, 1.
The Pentecostal Evangel, 21 March 1976, 1.
The Pentecostal Evangel, 20 June 1976, 2.
The Pentecostal Evangel, 12 June 1977, 8–9.
The Pentecostal Evangel, 18 February 1979, 18.
The Pentecostal Evangel, 17 June 1979, 2.
The Pentecostal Evangel, 14 October 1979, 1.
The Pentecostal Evangel, 9 December 1979, 1.
The Pentecostal Evangel, 22 February 1981, 17.
The Pentecostal Evangel, 10 May 1981, 3.

Advertisements

G. W. Carver. Biography. *The Pentecostal Evangel*, 23 October 1948, 16.
The Pentecostal Evangel, 22 June 1975, 32.
Youth Alive publication. *The Pentecostal Evangel*, 29 April 1984, 25.

Theses and Unpublished Documents

Cox, A. B. "America and Her Needs." Sermon preached in Dayton, OH, 7 October 1923, A. B. Cox file, Flower Pentecostal Heritage Center, Springfield, MO.
Nelson, Douglas J. "For Such a Time as This: The Story of William J. Seymour and the Azusa Street Revival." PhD diss., University of Birmingham, England, 1981.
Robeck, Cecil M. Jr. "Historical Roots of Racial Unity and Division in American Pentecostalism." http://www.pctii.org/cyberj/cyberj14/Robeck.pdf.

Weeks, Donald Pierce. "A Thesis on the History of the COGIC/Bishop Charles Harrison Mason, and Those Who Helped Make the History." C. H. Mason file, Flower Pentecostal Heritage Center, Springfield, MO.

Minutes and Reports

"Adherents by Race, 2017." 18 June 2018, Office of the General Secretary. General Council, Springfield, MO.

"A/G Annual Church Ministries Report; Vital Statistics Summary, 1985." 16 April 1986, Office of the General Secretary, General Council, Springfield, MO.

"A/G Hispanics: 1975–76 to 1985." 19 August 1986, Office of the General Secretary. General Council, Springfield, MO.

"Churches on the Official List." 1 May 1977, Office of the General Secretary, General Council, Springfield, MO.

"Comparison of Church Membership." 1 May 1977, Office of the General Secretary, General Council, Springfield, MO.

Conference with Blacks. Minutes. 15–16 December 1969, "Black History Files, 1954–1982, Flower Pentecostal Heritage Center, Springfield, MO.

Feasibility Study Committee. Minutes. 10 February 1970, 11 May 1970, "Black History Files, 1954–1982, Flower Pentecostal Heritage Center, Springfield, MO.

Gannon, Theodore E. "Division of Home Missions." 26. In "Biennial Report; The General Council." 1973. Flower Pentecostal Heritage Center, Springfield, MO.

———. "Division of Home Missions." 26. In "Biennial Report; The General Council." 1977. Flower Pentecostal Heritage Center, Springfield, MO.

"The General Superintendent's Report." 14. In "Biennial Report; The General Council." 1971. Flower Pentecostal Heritage Center, Springfield, MO.

"Ministers by Race." 26 April 2018, Office of the General Secretary, General Council, Springfield, MO.

New Jersey District Council. Yearbook. 1962.

"Number of Ministers by District." 31 December 1986, Office of the General Secretary, General Council, Springfield, MO.

"Segregation versus Integration." Special report to the General Presbytery. In Minutes of General Presbytery. 1957.

Records

Gibson, Bruce. Application for ordination certificate. Bruce Gibson file, Flower Pentecostal Heritage Center, Springfield, MO.

Gibson, Bruce. Deceased ministers' file, Office of the General Secretary, General Council, Springfield, MO.

Howard, James Edward. Deceased ministers' file, Office of the General Secretary, General Council, Springfield, MO.

Neeley, Isaac. Deceased ministers' file, Office of the General Secretary, General Council, Springfield, MO.

Robertson, Cornelia Jones. Ministers' file, Office of the General Secretary, General Council, Springfield, MO.

Thomas, Ellsworth S. Deceased ministers' file, Office of the General Secretary, General Council, Springfield, MO.

Washington, Edward. Ministerial credentials, Office of the General Secretary, General Council, Springfield, MO.

Pamphlets, Brochures, and Tracts

Glad Tidings Tabernacle. "Golden Jubilee." May 1957. Marie Brown file, Flower Pentecostal Heritage Center, Springfield, MO.

Olson, Nathaniel. "Slavery Still Exists." Springfield, MO: Gospel, n.d.

"Pentecostal Partners: A Reconciliation Strategy for 21st Century Ministry."

Written Correspondence

Battle, W. L., to Ralph M. Riggs, 31 October 1955. "Black History Files, 1954–1982, Flower Pentecostal Heritage Center, Springfield, MO.

Bergstrom, R. J., to J. Roswell Flower, 26 February 1952. Bruce Gibson file, Flower Pentecostal Heritage Center, Springfield, MO.

Bhengu, Nicholas B. H., to Ralph M. Riggs, 27 January 1955. "Black History Files, 1954–1982, Flower Pentecostal Heritage Center, Springfield, MO.

———, to Ralph M. Riggs, 6 March 1955. "Blacks ministry to/of" file, Office of the General Secretary, General Council, Springfield, MO.

Bogue, J. A., secretary, Northwest District, to J. R. Flower, 15 November 1937. Bruce Gibson file, Flower Pentecostal Heritage Center, Springfield, MO.

Brown, Robert A., to J. W. Welch, 20 February 1917. Robert Brown file, Flower Pentecostal Heritage Center, Springfield, MO.

Carter, Paul S., to Wayne E. Warner, 29 January 1985. Flower Pentecostal Heritage Center, Springfield, MO.

———, to Wayne E. Warner, 16 February 1985. Flower Pentecostal Heritage Center, Springfield, MO.

Clemmons, Ithiel, to Wayne E. Warner, 1 December 1994. Flower Pentecostal Heritage Center, Springfield, MO.

Feick, August, to the General Council of the Assemblies of God, 6 April 1926. Flower Pentecostal Heritage Center, Springfield, MO.

Flower, J. Roswell, to R. J. Bergstrom, 1 March 1952. Bruce Gibson file, Flower Pentecostal Heritage Center, Springfield, MO.

———, to Harry C. Warwick, 10 October 1951. Warwick file, Flower Pentecostal Heritage Center, Springfield, MO.

———, to Ernest S. Williams, 13 July 1939. William Ellison file, Flower Pentecostal Heritage Center, Springfield, MO.

Frodsham, Stanley, to F. D. Davis, Texas District superintendent, 30 May 1942. Frodsham file, Flower Pentecostal Heritage Center, Springfield, MO.

———, to Gerald B. Winrod, 12 August 1941. Frodsham file, Flower Pentecostal Heritage Center, Springfield, MO.

Garlock, John, to Thomas F. Zimmerman, 18 May 1964. "Black History Files, 1954–1982, Flower Pentecostal Heritage Center, Springfield, MO.

Gerhart, Joseph L., to Thomas F. Zimmerman, 2 November 1960. "Black History Files, 1954–1982, Flower Pentecostal Heritage Center, Springfield, MO.

Howard, J. Edward, to J. R. Evans, 17 October 1926. Howard file, Flower Pentecostal Heritage Center, Springfield, MO.

Jones, Ozra T., to Ralph M. Riggs, 5 November 1955. "Black History Files, 1954–1982, Flower Pentecostal Heritage Center, Springfield, MO.

Lyle, B. S., to Ralph M. Riggs. 15 November 1955. "Black History Files, 1954–1982, Flower Pentecostal Heritage Center, Springfield, MO.

Palmer, Leonard, to Ralph M. Riggs. 5 February 1958. "Black History Files, 1954–1982, Flower Pentecostal Heritage Center, Springfield, MO.

Phillips, Everett L., to Noel Perkin, 16 February 1955. "Black History Files, 1954–1982, Flower Pentecostal Heritage Center, Springfield, MO.

Pierce, Willard C., to Harry C. Warwick, 6 September 1951. Warwick file, Flower Pentecostal Heritage Center, Springfield, MO.

Riggs, Ralph M., to W. L. Battle, 29 August 1955. "Black History Files, 1954–1982, Flower Pentecostal Heritage Center, Springfield, MO.

———, to W. L. Battle, 26 September 1955. "Black History Files, 1954–1982, Flower Pentecostal Heritage Center, Springfield, MO.

———, to Nicholas B. H. Bhengu, 20 December 1954. "Blacks ministry to/of" file, Office of General Secretary, General Council, Springfield, MO.

———, to Nicholas B. H. Bhengu, 23 February 1955. "Black History Files, 1954–1982, Flower Pentecostal Heritage Center, Springfield, MO.

———, to Nicholas B. H. Bhengu, 12 October 1955. "Black History Files, 1954–1982, Flower Pentecostal Heritage Center, Springfield, MO.

———, to Samuel Crouch, 31 October 1955. "Black History Files, 1954–1982, Flower Pentecostal Heritage Center, Springfield, MO.

———, to O[zra]. T. Jones, 31 October 1955. "Black History Files, 1954–1982, Flower Pentecostal Heritage Center, Springfield, MO.

———, to F. J. Lindquist, 12 September 1956. "Black History Files, 1954–1982, Flower Pentecostal Heritage Center, Springfield, MO.

———, to B. S. Lyle. 31 October 1955. "Black History Files, 1954–1982, Flower Pentecostal Heritage Center, Springfield, MO.

———, to C. H. Mason, 6 August 1957. "Black History Files, 1954–1982, Flower Pentecostal Heritage Center, Springfield, MO.

———, to A. B. McEwen, 31 October 1955. "Blacks ministry to/of" file, Office of the General Secretary, General Council, Springfield, MO.

———, to Leonard Palmer, 11 February 1958. "Blacks ministry to/of" file, Office ot the General Secretary, General Council, Springfield, MO.

———, to J. O. Patterson, 31 October 1955. "Black History Files, 1954–1982, Flower Pentecostal Heritage Center, Springfield, MO.

———, to Kenneth Roper, 16 January 1956. "Blacks ministry to/of" file, Office of the General Secretary, General Secretary, Springfield, MO.

———, to D. Lawrence Williams, 8 July 1955. "Blacks ministry to/of file, Office of the General Secretary, General Council, Springfield, MO.

———, to Lawrence Williams, 27 November 1957. "Blacks ministry to/of" file, Office of General Secretary, General Council, Springfield, MO.

Robertson, Cornelia Jones, to Harry C. Warwick, 18 September 1951. Warwick file, Flower Pentecostal Heritage Center, Springfield, MO.

Warwick, Harry C., to J. Roswell Flower, 22 September 1951. Warwick file, Flower Pentecostal Heritage Center, Springfield, MO.

Welch, J. W., to Mrs. Louis Schlemmer, 2.5 October 1923. A. B. Cox file, Flower Pentecostal Heritage Center, Springfield, MO.

Westerdorf, Paul, to Stanley Frodsham, 19 June 1936. Frodsham file, Flower Pentecostal Heritage Center, Springfield, MO.

Zimmerman, Thomas F., to Thurman Faison, 27 March 1970. "Black History Files, 1954–1982, Flower Pentecostal Heritage Center, Springfield, MO.

———, to Joseph L. Gerhart, 4 November 1960. "Black History Files, 1954–1982, Flower Pentecostal Heritage Center, Springfield, MO.

———, to Robert Harrison, 27 March 1970. "Blacks ministry to/of" file, Office of the General Secretary, General Council, Springfield, MO.

Interviews and Spoken Sermons

Aman, Mrs. William. Interview by author, 10 February 1978, Waco, TX.

Boyd, Frank M. Interview by author, 18 March 1978, Springfield, MO, tape recording.

Brandt, Robert L. Interview by author, 15 February 1986, Springfield, MO.

Cadwalder, Mary (Mrs. Hugh). Interview by author, 18 March 1978, Houston, TX, tape recording.

Catley, Lawrence. Interview by Society for Pentecostal Studies, 1974 meeting, tape recording.

Collins, Grace. Interview by author, 20 October 1985, Kelso, WA, telephone.

Davis, Frank and Nancy. Interview by author, 18 January 1986, Springfield, MO.

Davis, Frank. Interview by author, 12 February 1986, Springfield, MO.

Flower, Alice Reynolds. Interview by author, 17 March 1978, Springfield, MO, tape recording.

Gerhart, Joseph L. Interview by author, 25 July 1986, Santa Cruz, CA, telephone.

O'Guinn, Carl. Interview by author, 5 February 1986, telephone.

———. Interview by author, 23 May 1985, telephone.

Harrison, Robert. Interview by author, 3 March 1986, Concord, CA, telephone.

Jackson, Gayle. Interview by author, 1 May 1986, Sikeston, MO, telephone.

Jones, Spencer. Interview by author, 3 March 1986, Chicago, IL, telephone.

Kessler, James. Interview by author, 6 March 1986, Springfield, MO.

Peterson, Bartlett. Interview by author, 5 March 1986, Springfield, MO.

Pirtle, Robert W. Interview by author, 6 January 1986, Springfield, MO.

———. Interview by author, 5 March 1986, Springfield, MO.

Richards, John. Interview by author, 18 March 1978, Springfield, MO, tape recording.

Sigmund, Bruce. Interview by author, 31 December 1987, Grambling, LA.

Williams, Ernest S. Interview by author, 18 March 1978, Springfield, MO, tape recording.

———. Interview by James Tinney, 8 November 1978. Tape recording. E. S. Williams file, Flower Pentecostal Heritage Center, Springfield, MO.

WOMEN

Books

Primary

Ewart, Frank. *The Phenomenon of Pentecost*. Saint Louis: Pentecostal, 1947.

Mcpherson, Aimee Semple. *The Story of My Life*. Edited by Raymond L. Cox. Waco, TX: Word, 1973.

Montgomery, Carrie Judd. *Under His Wings*. Oakland, CA: Triumphs of Faith, 1936.

Sisson, Elizabeth. *Faith Reminiscences and Heart-to-Heart Talks*. Springfield, MO: Gospel, n.d.

——. *Foregleams of Glory*. Chicago: The Evangel, 1912.

Woodworth-Etter, Maria B. *Acts of the Holy Ghost, or Life, and Experience, of Mrs. M. B. Woodworth-Etter*. Dallas: John F. Worley Printing Co., 1912.

——. *Holy Ghost Sermons*. Indianapolis: n.p., 1918.

——. *Marvels and Miracles*. Indianapolis: n.p., 1922.

——. *Signs and Wonders*. Indianapolis: n.p., 1916; reprint, *A Diary of Signs and Wonders: A Classic*. Tulsa, OK: Harrison House, 1980.

Secondary

Bruner, Frederick Dale. *A Theology of the Holy Spirit*. Grand Rapids: Zondervan, 1959.

Case, R. H. *Church of God Polity*. Cleveland, TN: Pathway, 1973.

Howe, E. Margaret. *Women and Church Leadership*. Grand Rapids: Zondervan, 1982.

Mathews, Hubert C. *Hubert: Here, There & Yonder*. n.p., 1976.

Mitchell, Robert Bryant. *Heritage and Horizons*. Des Moines, IA: Open Bible, 1982.

Qualls, Joy E. A. *God Forgive Us for Being Women: Rhetoric, Theology and the Pentecostal Tradition*. Eugene, OR: Wipf & Stock, 2018.

Thompson, A. E. *A. B, Simpson: His Life and Work*. Rev. ed. Harrisburg, PA: Christian Publications, 1960.

Warner, Wayne E. *The Woman Evangelist: The Life and Times of Charismatic Evangelist Maria B, Woodworth-Etter*. Studies in Evangelicalism, no. 8. Edited by Donald W. Dayton and Kenneth E. Rowe. Metuchen, NJ: Scarecrow, 1986.

Weber, Max. *The Sociology of Religion*. Translated by Ephraim Fischoff. Germany: J. C. B. Mohr, 1922; English trans. from 4th ed., rev. Johannes Winckelmann, J. C. B. Mohr, 1956; Boston: Beacon, 1963.

Articles

Primary

Alford, Roxie Hughes. "He Shall Baptize You in the Holy Ghost." *The Pentecostal Evangel,* 12 November 1921, 3, 7.

——. "The Baptism of the Holy Ghost and Fire." *The Latter Rain Evangel* (Chicago), January 1922, 18–20.

"Assemblies of God Endorses First Woman Chaplain." *The Pentecostal Evangel*, 13 February 1977, 29.

Bell, Eudorus N. "Questions and Answers." *Weekly Evangel*, 29 January and 5 February 1916, 8.

——. "Questions and Answers." *Weekly Evangel*, 2 September 1916, 8.

——. "Questions and Answers." *Weekly Evangel*, 10 March 1917, 9.

——. "Questions and Answers." *Weekly Evangel*, 26 May 1917, 9.

——. "Questions and Answers." *Christian Evangel*, 25 January 1919, 5.

——. "Questions and Answers." *Christian Evangel*, 17 May 1919, 5.

——. "Questions and Answers." *Christian Evangel*, 14 June 1919, 5.

——. "Questions and Answers." *The Pentecostal Evangel*, 29 November 1919, 5.

——. "Questions and Answers." *The Pentecostal Evangel*, 6 March 1920, 5.

——. "Questions and Answers." *The Pentecostal Evangel*, 3 January 1921, 10.

——. "Questions and Answers." *The Pentecostal Evangel*, 11 June 1921, 10.

——. "Questions and Answers." *The Pentecostal Evangel*, 6 January 1923, 8.

——. "Some Complaints." *Word and Witness*, 20 January 1914, 2.

——. "Women Elders." *Christian Evangel*, 15 August 1914, 2.

——. "Women Welcome." *Christian Evangel*, 13 February 1915, 2.

Booze, Joyce Wells. "Jesus and Women." *The Pentecostal Evangel*, 15 February 1987, 4–6.

Bosworth, F. F. "The God of All the Earth Working at Dallas." *Word and Witness*, 20 December 1912, 1.

Brock, Raymond T. "When Is a 'Head' a Head?" *The Pentecostal Evangel*, 1 November 1981, 6–7.

Brown, Marie. "Pentecost, the Calvary Road." *The Pentecostal Evangel*, 16 September 1951, 3, 12.

Brownell, Ada. "Review of Jessie Penn-Lewis, *The Magna Carta of Woman*." *The Pentecostal Evangel*, 30 January 1977, 30.

Byars, Ross. "Children Are What They Are because Mothers Are What They Are." *The Pentecostal Evangel*, 9 May 1982, 3.

Caldwell, E. S. "Let Us Honor Our Job-holding Mothers." *The Pentecostal Evangel*, 10 May 1981, 12–13.

"A Closer and Deeper Fellowship for the Pentecostal Assemblies of Indiana and the Central States." *Christian Evangel*, 19 July 1913, 1, 2.

Copeland, Ruth. "I Do not Wish to Be Equal." *The Pentecostal Evangel*, 9 May 1971, 6–7.

Cunningham, Robert C. "Let Georgia Do It." *Advance* 23 (February 1987) 4–6.

Dowie, John Alexander. "Address to the Candidates of Ordination." *Leaves of Healing*, 9 March 1901, 624–26.

——. "Having the Seal of the Living God." *Leaves of Healing*, 23 March 1901, 686–91.

——. "Let Us Go Up to Zion." *Leaves of Healing*, 9 February 1901, 498–501.

Earle, Suzanne F. "Her Children Shall Call Her Blessed." *C.A. Herald*, May 1958, 4.

Editorial box. *Christ Ambassadors of the Potomac District* (Washington, D. C.), January 1933, 2.

"Editor's General Council Notes." *The Pentecostal Evangel*, 10 October 1931, 4, 5, 14.

Frodsham, Stanley. "The Editor's Notebook." *The Pentecostal Evangel*, 10 June 1933, 4.

Geiman, Lorrie. Letter to the editor. *The Pentecostal Evangel*, 26 July 1981, 31.

"General Council Meets in St. Louis." *Word and Witness*, September 1915, 1.

"General Council Session." *Word and Witness*, 20 May 1914, 1.

"The General Overseer Sets Sail for America." *Leaves of Healing*, 12 January 1901, 356.

Gentzler, Lisa. "One Woman's Story of Being Born Again." *The Pentecostal Evangel*, 1 August 1982, 4–5.

Gordon, A. J. "The Ministry of Women." *The Alliance Weekly*, 1 May 1948, 277–78, 286.

Jeffries, A. G. "The Limit of Divine Revelation." *Weekly Evangel*, 18 March 1916, 6, 7.

Hahn, Bette. Letter to the editor. *The Pentecostal Evangel*, 15 November 1981, 31.

Hobson, Chuck. "They Call Her 'Sister Pastor.'" *The Pentecostal Evangel*, 13 May 1984, 19.

Hoover, Elva J. "Review of Lois Gunden Clemens, Woman Liberated (Herald)." *The Pentecostal Evangel*, 17 September 1972, 26.

Impellizzeri, Roseanne. Letter to the editor. *The Pentecostal Evangel*, 26 July 1981, 31.

Keys, Leland A. "Where are the Young Men?" *The Pentecostal Evangel*, 21 June 1959, 6.

Lester, Marvin R. Letter to the editor. *The Pentecostal Evangel*, 16 July 1972, 24.

Letter. *Christian Evangel*. 14 October 1913, 8.

Letter. *Christian Evangel*, 26 October 1913, 8.

Letter to the editor. *The Pentecostal Evangel*, 25 April 1976, 30.

M., W. R. "Questions Answered." *The Pentecostal Evangel*, 8 December 1923, 8.

Malmberg, Therese. Letter to the editor. *The Pentecostal Evangel*, 27 January 1985, 30.

"Marie Brown with Christ." *The Pentecostal Evangel*, 25 July 1971, 7

McAlister, Harvey. "A Word from the Other Side." *The Pentecostal Testimony*, May 1936, 23.

McArt, W. M. "Woman's Place and Work in the Church." *The Pentecostal Evangel*, 10 December 1921, 14, 15.

"Millionaire Healers in Douglas." *Douglas Daily Dispatch*, 25 February 1916.

"Mr. and Mrs. Geo. Montgomery." *War Cry*, (n.d.), 12.

Montgomery, Carie Judd. "Cazadera Camp Meeting." *Triumphs of Faith*, 17 (August 1897) 172.

———. "Letters from Mrs. Montgomery." *Triumphs of Faith*, 29 (May 1909) 115, 116.

———. "Letters from Mrs. Montgomery." *Triumphs of Faith*, 29 (June 1909) 121–26.

———. "Miraculously Healed by the Lord Thirty Years Ago; Baptized in the Holy Spirit One Year Ago." *The Latter Rain Evangel* (Chicago), October 1909, 4–10.

———. "Pentecostal Conference, Sunderland, England." *Triumphs of Faith*. 29 (July 1909) 152–54.

———. "The Promise of the Father." Triumphs of Faith. 28 (July 1908) 145–49.

———. "Wonderful Days." *Triumphs of Faith*. 27 (October 1907) 228–29.

"NAE Women's President Says Extension for ERA Makes Women Look Like Poor Losers." *The Pentecostal Evangel*, 29 October 1978, 24.

Newman, Mrs. James. Letter to the editor, *The Pentecostal Evangel*, 26 July 1981, 31.

Obituary. *The Pentecostal Evangel*, 17 April 1977, 25

Orengo, Gloria J. "Serving God and Country." *The Pentecostal Evangel*, 28 June 1981, 4.

Owen, Timothy. Letter to the editor. *The Pentecostal Evangel*, 26 July 1981, 31.

Perkin, Noel. "An Appeal for Lady Missionaries." *The Pentecostal Evangel*, 12 April 1947, 8.

Peters, Charles S. "Help Wanted—Male." *The Pentecostal Evangel*, 18 March 1939, 2.

Pfrimmer, Mildred. Letter to the editor. *The Pentecostal Evangel*, 16 July 1972, 24.

Rabe, Benetta. Letter to the editor. *The Pentecostal Evangel*, 27 April 1975, 30.

Reddout, David. "Focus on Singles." *The Pentecostal Evangel*, 28 October 1984, 6–7.

Reif, Fannie. Letter. *Christian Evangel*, 7 September 1913, 8.

"Rev. R. A. Brown, 75, A Pastor 40 Years." *The New York Times*, 13 February 1948, 21.

"Rev. R. A. Brown Dies; Co-Pastor of Tabernacle." *New York Herald Tribune*, 13 February 1948, n.p.

Riggs, Ralph M. "The Place of Men in the Work of the Church." *The Pentecostal Evangel*, 5 February 1938, 16.

Rohlinger, Mrs. Howard. Letter to the editor. *The Pentecostal Evangel*, 22 June 1975, 30.

Rusk, Rhonda J. "Will the Man of the House Please Stand Up!" *The Pentecostal Evangel*, 13 February 1983, 4–5.

Schuster, Elizabeth. "Leader in World Missions Giving." *The Pentecostal Evangel*, 5 May 1957, 16.

"Should Women Prophesy?" *Triumphs of Faith*, 6 (December 1886) 270–73.

Sisson, Elizabeth. "The Holy Ghost and Fire." *The Latter Rain Evangel*, May 1909, 9.

Smith, Elmer W. Letter to the editor. *The Pentecostal Evangel*, 26 July 1981, 31.

"Southeastern Salutes Women in Ministry." *The Pentecostal Evangel*, 15 April 1984, 28.

"Speakers Announced for Conference on the Holy Spirit." *The Pentecostal Evangel*, 18 March 1984, 25.

"Survey Reveals A/G Men-Women Ratio." *The Pentecostal Evangel*, 16 March 1980, 13.

Towler, Laurence. Letter to the editor. *The Pentecostal Evangel*, 27 August 1972, 25.

Tozer, A. W. "Love and Obey—No Other Way." *The Pentecostal Evangel*, 18 April 1982, 7–8.

"Turkey's Women Unveiled." *The Latter Rain Evangel* (Chicago), December 1924, 20, 21.

Ward, C. M. "His Handmaidens." *The Pentecostal Evangel*, 14 May 1972, 2.

———. "The New 'Bedroom Evangelism." *The Pentecostal Evangel*, 8 February 1976, 12–13.

———. "Women's Lib—Whither?" *The Pentecostal Evangel*, 15 September 1974, 5.

Williams, Ernest S. "A Personal Tribute." *The Pentecostal Evangel*, 25 July 1971, 7.

———. "Questions and Answers." *The Pentecostal Evangel*, 20 April 1929, 9.

———. "Questions and Answers." *The Pentecostal Evangel*, 21 July 1934, 7.

———. "Questions and Answers." *The Pentecostal Evangel*, 11 March 1939, 4.

———. "Sunday's Lesson." *The Pentecostal Evangel*, 25 May 1952, 8.

———. "Your Questions." *The Pentecostal Evangel*, 19 April 1959, 13.

———. "Your Questions." *The Pentecostal Evangel*, 3 July 1960, 11

———. "Your Questions." *The Pentecostal Evangel*, 21 August 1961, 11.

———. "Your Questions." *The Pentecostal Evangel*, 19 April 1964, 20.

Wilson, Mrs. W. Harold. Letter to the editor. *The Pentecostal Evangel*, 21 January 1979, 30.

"Zelma Argue with Christ." *The Pentecostal Evangel*, 23 March 1980, 7.

Secondary

Barfoot, Charles H., and Gerald T. Sheppard. "Prophetic vs. Priestly Religion: The Changing Role of Women Clergy in Classical Pentecostal Churches." *Review of Religious Research*. 22 (September 1980) 2–17.

Forrester, Mark. "Donna Barrett Elected General Secretary." 23 April 2018. https://news.ag.org/News/Donna-Barrett-Elected-General-Secretary.

Hardesty, Nancy. "Holiness Is Power; The Pentecostal Argument for Women's Ministry." In *Pastoral Problems in the Pentecostal-Charismatic Movement*, edited by Harold D. Hunter, 1–15. Cleveland, TN: Church of God School of Theology, 1983.

Kennedy, John W. "Going Places." 11 December 2017. https://news.ag.org/en/News/Going-Places.

Kleeman, Jan. "Mother Flower: Two Rows Back, Two Seats in on the Left, Sunday after Sunday." *Springfield! Magazine* 5 (May 1984) 48–49.

Kunz, Marilyn. "Women and the Evangelical Movement." In *Women and the Ministries of Christ*, edited by Roberta Hestenes and Lois Curley, 161. Pasadena, CA: Fuller Theological Seminary, 1979.

McGee, Gary B. "Three Notable Women in Pentecostal Ministry." *Assemblies of God Heritage* 6 (Spring 1986) 3–5.

Menzies, William W. "Non-Wesleyan Origins of the Pentecostal Movement." In *Aspects of Pentecostal-Charismatic Origins*, edited by Vinson Synan, 81–98. Plainfield, NJ: Logos International, 1975.

Neeley, Jon R. "Maria B. Woodworth-Etter and The Churches of God." *The Church of God Advocate*. August 1975, 2–7.

Overstreet, Sarah. "Mother Flower Remembers." *The News-Leader* (Springfield, MO), 1 December 1984, 48.

Pakkala, Lorraine J. "Aimee Cortese—Confident in Christ." *The Pentecostal Evangel*, 8 July 1984, 3–4.

Riss, Richard. "The Latter Rain Movement of 1948." *Pneuma*. 4 (Spring 1982) 32–45.

"The Role of Women in Ministry as Described in Holy Scripture: A Position Paper Adopted by the General Presbytery, August 1990." *The Pentecostal Evangel*, 28 October 1990, 12–15.

"Studies Suggest Very Few Women Will Fill Evangelical Pulpits." *Eternity*. June 1978, 8–9.

Zickmund, Barbara Brown. "The Struggle for the Right to Preach." In *Women and Religion in America*. Vol. 1: *The Nineteenth Century*, edited by Rosemary Radford Ruether and Rosemary Skinner Keller, 193. San Francisco: Harper and Row, 1981.

Publication Issues

Christian Evangel, 9 May 1914.
The Pentecostal Evangel, 25 September 1943.
"Quarterly Letter," 28 April 1949.
San Francisco Call and Post, 4 April 1922.

Cartoons and Drawings

Ramsey, Chris. "He Had Better Look Again." *The Pentecostal Evangel*, 25 May 1952, 8.

Advertisements

The Pentecostal Evangel, 8 July 1939, 12.

Theses and Unpublished Documents

Albrecht, Daniel E. "The Life and Ministry of Carrie Judd Montgomery." MA thesis, Western Evangelical Seminary, Portland, OR, 1984.

Boyd, Frank M. "Women's Ministry." Flower Pentecostal Heritage Center, Springfield, MO.

Flower, Joseph R. "Does God Deny Spiritual Manifestations and Ministry Gifts to Women?" 4 January 1983, Office of the General Secretary, General Council, Springfield, MO.

"Historical Data of the International Church of the Foursquare Gospel." Aimee Semple McPherson file, Flower Pentecostal Heritage Center, Springfield, MO.

Williams, Ernest S. "May Women Preach?" Flower Pentecostal Heritage Center, Springfield, MO.

Minutes and Reports

"A/G Female Ministers Report, 1977–1986." 22 January 1987, Office of the General Secretary, General Council, Springfield, MO.

"A/G Ministers by Age and Sex, 1985." 17 July 1986, Office of the General Secretary, General Council, Springfield, MO.

"A/G Statistical Reports, 2016." 7 December 2017, Office of the General Secretary, General Council, Springfield, MO.

"Analysis of Rate Gain in Number of Assemblies of God Ministers—1976–1985." 11 March 1986, Office of the General Secretary, General Council, Springfield, MO.

Bethesda Missionary Temple. "Annual Report for 1945." Myrtle D. Beall file, Flower Pentecostal Heritage Center, Springfield, MO.

Manual of the Christian and Missionary Alliance. New York: Christian and Missionary Alliance, 1924.

"Ministers' Ministry Status, 1985." 10 March 1986, Office of the General Secretary, General Council, Springfield, MO.

New Jersey District Council. Yearbook. 1962, 1965–66, 1970–71, 1975–76, 1976–77.

Ohio District Council. Yearbook.1981.

Pentecostal Church of God. Constitution and Bylaws, Minutes, and Directory. 1981.

"The Role of Women in Ministry." General Presbytery, 2010. https://ag.org/Beliefs/ Topics-Index/The-Role-of-Women-in-Ministry.

Records

Alford, Henry Elkert. Credential record. Alford file, Flower Pentecostal Heritage Center, Springfield, MO.

Alford, Roxie Hughes. Credential record. Alford file, Flower Pentecostal Heritage Center, Springfield, MO.

Alford, Roxie Hughes. Credential renewal form, 1922. Alford file, Flower Pentecostal Heritage Center, Springfield, MO.

Alford, Roxie Hughes. Minister's renewal questionnaire, 1922. Alford file, Flower Pentecostal Heritage Center, Springfield, MO.

Beall, Myrtle D. Application form, 14 June 1937. Ministers' file, Office of the General Secretary, General Council, Springfield, MO.

Brown, Mary C. Credential record. Mary C. Brown file, Flower Pentecostal Heritage Center, Springfield, MO.

Brown, Mary C. Ordination certificate. Mary C. Brown file, Flower Pentecostal Heritage Center, Springfield, MO.

Flower, Alice Reynolds. Ministers' file, Office of the General Secretary, General Council, Springfield, MO.

McPherson, Aimee Semple. Credential record. Ministers' file, Office of the General Secretary, General Council, Springfield, MO.

Montgomery, Carrie Judd. Application form. Ministers' file, Office of the General Secretary, General Council, Springfield, MO.

Montgomery, Carrie Judd. Ordination certificate. Ministers' file, Office of the General Secretary, General Council, Springfield, MO.

Pamphlets, Brochures, and Tracts

Bartleman, Frank. "Flapper Evangelism: Fashion's Fools Headed for Hell." Los Angeles: n.p., n.d.

Glad Tidings Tabernacle. "In Loving Memory; Marie Estelle Brown." Brown file, Flower Pentecostal Heritage Center, Springfield, MO.

Written Correspondence

Beall, M[yrtle] D., to the Executive Presbytery, 24 August 1949. Beall file, Flower Pentecostal Heritage Center, Springfield, MO.

Cortese, Aimee, to author, 1 February 1987.

Flower, J. Roswell, to Myrtle D. Beall, 30 August 1949. Beall file, Flower Pentecostal Heritage Center, Springfield, MO.

———, to Andrew Rahner, Plainfield, NJ, 28 January 1947. Rahner File, Flower Pentecostal Heritage Center. Springfield, MO.

Form letter addressed to "Dear Sister" from the Credential Committee, undated. Flower Pentecostal Heritage Center, Springfield, MO.

Havemann, Lorraine (Steffen), to Curtis W. Ringness, 21 November 1958. Alford file, Flower Pentecostal Heritage Center, Springfield, MO.

McPherson, Aimee Semple, to E. N. Bell, 5 January 1922. Ministers' file, Office of the General Secretary, General Council, Springfield, MO.

Osterberg, A. G., superintendent of the Southern California and Arizona District, to J. R. Evans, 28 August 1930. Alford file, Flower Pentecostal Heritage Center, Springfield, MO.

Rahner, Andrew, to J. Roswell Flower, 18 January 1947. Rahner File, Flower Pentecostal Heritage Center, Springfield, MO.

Rodgers, Darrin, to author, 17 September 2018.

[Welch, J.W.], to Mrs. Elbert Alford, 9 August 1919. Alford file, Flower Pentecostal Heritage Center, Springfield, MO.

Williams, Ernest S., to Myrtle D. Beall, 28 April 1949. Beall file, Flower Pentecostal Heritage Center. Springfield, MO.

Interviews and Spoken Sermons

Booze, Joyce Wells. Interview by author, 6 January 2019, Springfield, MO, telephone.
Cortese, Aimee. Interview by author, 18 March 1987, Brooklyn, NY, telephone.
Floyd, David Lee. Interview by Wayne Warner, 26 February 1981. Tape Recording. David Lee Floyd file, Flower Pentecostal Heritage Center, Springfield, MO.
Paproski, John J. Interview by author, 18 March 1987, Trenton, NJ, telephone.
Shedd, Glenroy. Interview by author, 4 February 1987, Springfield, MO, telephone.

WAR

Books

Primary

Bartleman, Frank. *Two Years Mission Work in Europe Just Before the War 1912–1914.* 2d ed. N.p., n.d.
Booth-Clibborn, Arthur Sydney. *Blood against Blood.* 3rd ed. New York: Charles C. Cook, 1914.
Booth-Clibborn, William. *The Baptism in the Holy Spirit: A Personal Testimony.* 4th ed. Dallas: Voice of Healing, 1962.
Gee, Donald. *Wind and Flame.* Croydon: Health, Ltd., 1967.
Linzey, Stanford E. Jr. *Filling Your Boots.* Springfield, MO: Gospel, n.d.
Parham, Charles F. *The Everlasting Gospel.* N.p., 1911, reprint ed., n.p., n.d.
Plank, David W. *Called to Serve.* Springfield, MO: Gospel, 1967.

Secondary

Abrams, Ray. *Preachers Present Arms.* Rev. and enl. Scottdale, PA: Herald, 1969.
Carter, John. *Donald Gee: Pentecostal Statesman.* Nottingham, England: Assemblies of God, 1971.
———. *Howard Carter: Man of the Spirit.* Nottingham, UK: Assemblies of God, 1971.
Dieter, Melvin. *The Holiness Revival of the Nineteenth Century.* Metuchen, NJ: The Scarecrow, 1980.
French, Paul C. *We Won't Murder.* New York: Hastings House, 1940.
Honeywell, Ray J. *Chaplains of the U. S. Army.* Washington, D.C.: U. S. Government Printing Office, 1958.
Lynd, Staughton. *Nonviolence in America: A Documentary History.* American Heritage Series. Indianapolis: Bobbs Merrill Co., 1966.
Meyer, Ernest L. *"Hey! Yellowbacks!"* New York: Day, 1930.
Peterson, Horace C., and Gilbert C. Fite. *Opponents of War 1917–1918.* Madison: University of Wisconsin Press, 1957.
Schlissel, Lillian. *Conscience in America.* New York: Dutton, 1968.
Selective Service System. *Conscientious Objection.* Special monograph no. 11. Washington, D.C.: Government Printing Office, 1950.
Swomley, John M. Jr. *The Military Establishment.* Boston: Beacon, 1964.

Thomas, Norman M. *Is Conscience a Crime?* New York: Garland, 1972.

Whittaker, Colin C. *Seven Pentecostal Pioneers.* Hants, England: Marshall Morgan & Scott, 1983.

Wilson, P. W. *General Evangeline Booth of the Salvation Army.* New York: Charles Scribners Sons, 1948.

Articles

"A. A. Boddy Goes to the Front." *Weekly Evangel,* 19 June 1915, 1.

"Amongst the Soldier Boys; Rank and File Episodes." *Weekly Evangel,* 18 August 1917, 2–3.

"An Ambassador in the Trenches." *Weekly Evangel,* 24 March 1917, 6–7.

"Are You Off to the Front?" *Weekly Evangel,* 11 September 1915, 1.

"Are You Ready for Christ's Return?" *The Pentecostal Evangel,* 6 June 1954, 1–4.

Argue, Zelma. " . . . Until I Have Showed Thy Strength Unto This Generation." *The Pentecostal Evangel,* 28 June 1941, 1.

"Assembly Ministers Attend Chaplain School." *The Pentecostal Evangel,* 2 November 1952, 20.

Bartleman, Frank. "The European War." *Weekly Evangel,* 10 July 1915, 3.

———. "Not of this World." *Word and Work* (ca. 1916), 296–97.

———. "Present Day Conditions." *Weekly Evangel,* 5 June 1915, 3.

———. "Present Day Conditions." *Word and Witness,* June 1915, 5.

———. "What Will the Harvest Be?" *Weekly Evangel,* 7 August 1915, 1, 2.

Bell, Eudorus N. "The Beast of Berlin." *Christian Evangel,* 15 June 1918, 3.

———. "Destroy This Tract." *Christian Evangel,* 24 August 1918, 4.

———. "Loyalty Bonds." *Christian Evangel,* 1 June 1918, 8.

———. "Preachers Warned." *Weekly Evangel,* 5 January 1918, 4.

———. "Questions and Answers." *Weekly Evangel,* 14 April 1917, 9.

———. "Questions and Answers." *Weekly Evangel,* 25 August 1917, 9.

———. "Questions and Answers." *Weekly Evangel,* 24 November 1917, 8.

———. "Questions and Answers." *Weekly Evangel,* 26 January 1918, 9.

———. "Questions and Answers." *Christian Evangel,* 27 July 1918, 9.

———. "Questions and Answers." *Christian Evangel,* 28 December 1918, 5.

———. "Questions and Answers." *Christian Evangel,* 11 January 1919, 5.

———. "Questions and Answers." *Christian Evangel,* 12 July 1919, 5.

———. "A Tremendous Day is To-Day." *Weekly Evangel,* 23 February 1918, 6–7.

Blackburn, Alexander. "What Makes a Nation Great?" *The Pentecostal Evangel,* 5 July 1947, 1.

Bishop, J. Bashford. "Christ and His Enemies." *The Pentecostal Evangel,* 13 March 1960, 22.

Booth-Clibborn, Arthur Sydney. "The Christian and War." *Weekly Evangel,* 19 May 1917, 4.

———. "The Christian and War: Is It Too Late?" *Weekly Evangel,* 28 April 1917, 5.

———. "What is War?" *Weekly Evangel,* 21 April 1917, 2. Excerpt from *Blood Against Blood.* 3d ed. New York: Charles C. Cook, 1914.

Braxton, Helen. "God Bless You, Warren." *At Ease.* January 1965, 9.

Caldwell, E. S. "Called to Serve." Review of David W. Plank. *Called to Serve. The Pentecostal Evangel.* 25 June 1967, 10, 11.

Champion, Dick. "Welcome, Ways!" *At Ease*. Winter 1965, 5.

"Chaplain Nichols Killed in Action." *At Ease*. December 1970, 2.

"Compulsory Military Service: An English Conscientious Objector's Testimony." *Weekly Evangel*, 28 April 1917, 7.

"Concerning Registration for Military Service." *Weekly Evangel*, 2 June 1917, 8.

"The Conversion of a Nazi Storm Trooper." *The Pentecostal Evangel*, 16 October 1943, 6–7.

"The Crisis." *Weekly Evangel*, 21 April 1917, 7.

Cunningham, Robert C. "April Deadline." *The Pentecostal Evangel*, 8 April 1962, 3.

———. "Fall-out Shelters." *The Pentecostal Evangel*, 14 January 1962, 3.

———. "How Wars Are Won." *The Pentecostal Evangel*, 31 March 1968, 4.

———. "The Passing and the Permanent." *The Pentecostal Evangel*, 30 April 1949, 2, 9.

———. "A Time for Action." *The Pentecostal Evangel*, 20 May 1962, 3.

Davis, George T. B. "Nation-wide Prayer for Revival and Victory." *The Pentecostal Evangel*, 9 May 1942, 1.

"Dedicated to the Defenders of America." *The Pentecostal Evangel*, 27 December 1941, 14.

Dempster, Murray W. "Peacetime Draft Registration and Pentecostal Moral Conscience." *Agora*, Spring 1980, 2–3.

"The Diary of a Delegate." *The Pentecostal Evangel*, 27 September 1941, 10.

Doney, C. W. "Salvation for the Soldier Boys; Man's Extremity is God's Opportunity." *Weekly Evangel*, 23 June 1917, 2.

Douglas, Dolores S. "Take Now Thy Son." *The Pentecostal Evangel*, 26 June 1966, 3.

Douglas, William H. Letter to the editor. *The Pentecostal Evangel*, 28 July 1957, 23.

Dowie, John Alexander. "God and Father of All Men." *Leaves of Healing*, 24 September 1904, 805.

———. "Zion College Lectures on Prayer." *Leaves of Healing*, 8 December 1900, 210–12.

"The Missile Age." *The Pentecostal Evangel*, 5 May 1957, 2.

Editorial. *Redemption Tidings*. 15 November 1957, 2–3.

"Enrolled in Career Course." *The Pentecostal Evangel*, 27 February 1966, 25.

"50,000 men." *The Pentecostal Evangel*, 18 March 1944, 12.

Flower, J. Roswell. "Concerning the Conscientious Objector." *The Pentecostal Evangel*, 4 March 1944, 7.

———. Editorial. *Christian Evangel*, 16 January 1915, 3.

———. Editorial. *Weekly Evangel*, 14 August 1915, 2.

———. "The Plight of the Conscientious Objector in the Present World Conflict." *The Pentecostal Evangel*, 3 July 1943, 2–3.

———. "Our Heavenly Citizenship." *Weekly Evangel*, 11 September 1915, 3.

———. "Our Heavenly Citizenship." *Word and Witness*, October 1915, 3.

Frodsham, Stanley. "The Editor's Notebook." *The Pentecostal Evangel*, 20 February 1932, 4–5.

G., R. "Our Attitude toward War and Military Service." *The Pentecostal Evangel*, 2 May 1936, 4–5.

Gee, Donald. "Conscientious Objection." *The Pentecostal Evangel*, 4 May 1940, 4.

———. "War, the Bible, and the Christian." *The Pentecostal Evangel*, 8 November 1930, 6–7.

———. "War, the Bible, and the Christian." *The Pentecostal Evangel*, 15 November 1930, 2–3.

"General Council Chronicle, Part III." *The Pentecostal Evangel*, 24 October 1965, 16.

Gray, James A. "A Voice from England." *Christian Evangel*, 3 October 1914, 1.

Griepp, Frank R. "To C.A.'s Entering Military Service." *The Pentecostal Evangel*, 13 December 1953, 6, 11, 12.

Hall, L. C. "The Great Crisis Near at Hand." *Word and Witness*, 20 November 1913, 1.

"Heavenly Songs in a Nazi Prison Cell; A Review of Gustav Herbert Schmidt's New Book, 'Songs in the Night.'" *The Pentecostal Evangel*, 12 January 1946, 8–9.

"Helping the Service Man." *The Pentecostal Evangel*, 21 February 1942, 1.

Holaday, Kenneth C. Letter to the editor. *The Pentecostal Evangel*, 10 November 1969, 28.

Holloway, D. P. "The Approaching Day of Doom." *The Pentecostal Evangel*, 15 August 1954, 3, 9.

Howe, Julia Ward. "The Battle Hymn of the Republic." *The Pentecostal Evangel*, 10 January 1942, 3.

"How Long Will Peace Last?" *The Pentecostal Evangel*, 23 May 1925, 4.

"In Jail for Failure to Register." *Weekly Evangel*, 30 June 1917, 8.

"In South Vietnam: 1965." *The Pentecostal Evangel*, 26 September 1965, 7.

"Is Christian Civilization Breaking Down?" *Christian Evangel*, 27 February 1915, 3.

"Is European War Justifiable?" *Christian Evangel*, 12 December 1914, 1, 3.

Juergensen, Marie. "First Fruits at Japanese Relocation Center." *The Pentecostal Evangel*, 4 September 1943, 10.

Kagan, Mark. "Hitlerism Must Lose." *The Pentecostal Evangel*, 25 March 1944, 1, 7.

Krogstad, E. Elsworth. "Loyalty to Government and to God in the Present World Crisis." *The Pentecostal Evangel*, 4 July 1942, 1.

Mayo, Samuel. "Who Are These People in Blues, Whites, and Greens?" *Advance* 22 (June 1986) 17.

McElyea, Lemuel D. "The Military Chaplaincy."*Advance* 21 (July 1985) 11–12.

McCafferty, Burt. "Should Christians Go to War?" *Christian Evangel*, 16 January 1915, 1.

McCormack, Orville. "Can a Man Serve God in the Military?" *The Pentecostal Evangel*, 1 July 1962, 24–25.

McPherson, Warren. "Keys to Closed Doors." *The Pentecostal Evangel*, 5 July 1964, 5.

———. "Missions and the Military." *The Pentecostal Evangel*, 7 July 1963, 8–9.

———. "To Join or not to Join?" *The Pentecostal Evangel*, 1 July 1962, 6–7.

"The Mussolini Empire." *The Pentecostal Evangel*, 12 March 1927, 3. Reprinted from *Advent Testimony*.

"New Bylaws on Military Service Adopted by General Council." *The Pentecostal Evangel*, 8 October 1967. 7.

Newby. E. L. "The Great War and the Speedy Return of Our Lord; Light on the Present Crisis." *Weekly Evangel*. 10 April 1917, 1–2.

———. "Light on the Present Crisis." *Weekly Evangel*, 1 July 1916, 6–7, 9.

"No 'Universal Military Training.'" *The Pentecostal Evangel*, 13 April 1952, 2.

"1,000 Testaments for the Soldiers." *The Pentecostal Evangel*, 21 June 1941, 13.

"Our Attitude to the Government." *The Pentecostal Evangel*, 23 ociober 1937, 6.

Panton, D. M. "Universal War." *The Pentecostal Evangel*, 4 July 1936, 2, 3. Reprinted from *The Dawn*.

"The Pentecostal Movement and the Conscription Law." *Weekly Evangel*, 4 August 1917, 6, 7.

"The Pentecostal Movement and the Conscription Law." *Weekly Evangel*, 5 January 1918, 5.

"Pentecostal Saints Opposed to War." *Weekly Evangel*, 19 June 1915, 1.

"The Peril of Universal Military Training." *The Pentecostal Evangel*, 9 December 1951, 7.

"Revival and Victory Prayer Card." *The Pentecostal Evangel*. 13 June 1942, 12.

Richey, Raymond T. "Amongst the Soldiers." *Weekly Evangel*, 13 October 1917, 15.

———. "Amongst the Soldier Boys." *Weekly Evangel*, 16 February 1918, 1, 7.

———. "Evangelizing at Our Army Camps." *The Pentecostal Evangel*, 10 January 1942, 2–12.

Riggs, Ralph M. "The Spiritual Significance of V-E Day." *The Pentecostal Evangel*, 2 June 1945, 1.

Scott, Douglas G. "The Chaplaincy—a Branch of the Church." *The Pentecostal Evangel*, 2 November 1952, 20.

"Servicemen in Europe Enjoy Spiritual Retreat." *The Pentecostal Evangel*, 20 April 1958, 23.

"The Sinister Education of War." *Weekly Evangel*, 20 January 1917, 3.

Sisler, George T. "War 'Profits.'" *Weekly Evangel*, 29 April 1916, 7.

"The Sixth Commandment." *At Ease*, Summer, n.d., 7–11. Adapted from *Holiness Handbook*. Springfield, MO: Gospel, 1966.

Skipper, Vivian. "One Nation Under God." *The Pentecostal Evangel*, 5 July 1964, 6.

Smales, C[larance] P. "Marks of a Good Soldier." *The Pentecostal Evangel*, 25 September 1943, 1.

Steelberg, Wesley. "The Stars and Stripes of Calvary." *The Pentecostal Evangel*, 4 July 1942, 1.

"Traitors." *The Pentecostal Evangel*, 21 June 1941, 13.

"Victory." *The Pentecostal Evangel*, 24 June 1944, 1.

Wadsworth, Ernest M. "Praying for Our Government." *The Pentecostal Evangel*, 11 March 1956, 11.

"Wanted." *The Pentecostal Evangel*, 4 March 1944, 7.

Ward, C. M. "The Struggle for Survival." *The Pentecostal Evangel*, 7 July 1957, 3, 29, 30.

"War! War!! War!!!" *Christian Evangel*, 15 August 1914, 1.

Way, Robert R. "Christmas in Vietnam." *The Pentecostal Evangel*, 19 December 1965, 5.

———. "Mission of Thanks." *The Pentecostal Evangel*, 14 January 1968, 11.

———. "Our Mission to the Military." *The Pentecostal Evangel*, 26 September 1965, 7.

Webb, Bert. "Ministering to Servicemen in Europe." *The Pentecostal Evangel*, 5 July 1964, 6.

Welch, J. W. "An Explanation." *Weekly Evangel*, 19 May 1917, 8.

"When Seven Red Soldiers Were Transformed." *The Pentecostal Evangel*, 27 July 1940, 4.

Williams, Ernest S. "The Conscientious Objector." *The Pentecostal Evangel*, 15 June 1940, 4–5.

———. ". . . In Case of War . . ." *The Pentecostal Evangel*, 19 March 1938, 4.

———. "Our Duty as Christian Citizens." *The Pentecostal Evangel*, 28 November 1936, 1.

———. "Questions and Answers." *The Pentecostal Evangel*, 27 July 1940, 5.

———. "Questions and Answers." *The Pentecostal Evangel*, 22 November 1941, 16.

———. "We Are Grateful for the U.S.A." *The Pentecostal Evangel*, 23 November 1940, 4.

———. "Your Questions." *The Pentecostal Evangel*, 22 June 1958, 23.
———. "Your Questions." *The Pentecostal Evangel*, 5 July 1959, 7.
———. "Your Questions." *The Pentecostal Evangel*, 7 February 1960, 11.
———. "Your Questions." *The Pentecostal Evangel*, 12 February 1961, 11.
———. "Your Questions." *The Pentecostal Evangel*, 20 August 1961, 21.
———. "Your Questions." *The Pentecostal Evangel*, 25 March 1962, 15.
———. "Your Questions." *The Pentecostal Evangel*, 28 May 1967, 15.
Wilson, R. A. Jr. "Nuclear Explosions and You." *The Pentecostal Evangel*, 7 January 1962, 32.
"Your Publishing House and Ours." *Christian Evangel* 15 June 1918, 1.
Ytterock, Dave. "Probing Our Moral Identity." *Agora*, Fall 1977, 7.

Publication Issues

Christian Evangel, 24 August 1918.
Christian Evangel, 21 September 1918.
The Pentecostal Evangel, 8 January 1938.
"Quarterly Letter," 24 March 1951.
Reveilie, 1:1, a, 9.
Zion Banner, 23 September 1902.

Cartoons and Drawings

Ramsey, Chris. "Loyalty to Both." *The Pentecostal Evangel*, 13 March 1960, 22.
Shoemaker, Vaughn. "God Be with Us." *The Pentecostal Evangel*, 24 June 1944, 1. Reprinted from the *Chicago Daily News*.

Photographs and Captions

Caption. *The Pentecostal Evangel*, 2 November 1952, 20.

Advertisements

Ward. C. M. "The Sergeant Thompson Story." *The Pentecostal Evangel*, 2 March 1958, 23.

Theses and Unpublished Documents

Beaman, Jay. "Pentecostal Pacifism; The Origin, Development, and Rejection of Pacific Belief among Pentecostals." Mdiv thesis, North American Baptist Seminary, 1982. Subsequently revised and published, Hillsboro, KS: Center for Mennonite Brethren, 1989.
Harrison, John Irvine. "A History of the Assemblies of God." ThD diss., Berkley Baptist Divinity School, 1954.

McPherson, Warren. "Military Service Policy Restudied by Assemblies." Flower Pentecostal Heritage Center, Springfield, MO.

Robbins, Roger. "Attitudes toward War and Peace." Written for class taught by John Howard Yoder on "War, Peace, and Revolution." 1982. Robbins file, Flower Pentecostal Heritage Center, Springfield, MO.

Williams, Ernest S. "Blessedness of Christian Citizenship; Phil. 3:20, 21." Sermon preached, 4 July 1926. Williams file, Flower Pentecostal Heritage Center, Springfield, MO.

———. "Christian Faith and the American Nation." Sermon notes, n.d. Williams file, Flower Pentecostal Heritage Center, Springfield, MO.

Minutes and Reports

Chase, Michael H. and Joe A. Krueggel. Proposed resolution. In "Resolutions Processed for Presentation to the 39th General Council," 35–36. 1981.

"Final Report of Revision Committee on Essential Resolutions." In Proposed Constitution and Bylaws of the General Council, 26, 29. 1927.

"The Interpretation of the Constitutional Agreements and Essential Resolutions; recommended by the Executive Presbytery 1925." In General Council combined minutes, 24–25, 38–39. 1914–1925.

Jaeger, Harry. "Report Submitted on the Organization of a Servicemen's Department." 4 January 1944, Chaplain's Department file, General Council, Springfield, MO.

"Report of the Executive Presbytery." In General Council minutes, 34. 1943. "Report of the Executive Presbytery." In General Council minutes, 44. 1945.

Records

Peterson, Paul B. Ministers file, Office of the General Secretary, General Council, Springfield, MO.

Pamphlets, Brochures, and Tracts

Bartleman, Frank. "Christian Citizenship." Los Angeles: n.p., n.d.

———. "War and the Christian." Los Angeles: n.p., n.d.

Ward, C. M. "The Sergeant Thompson Story." Springfield, MO: Gospel, 1958.

Written Correspondence

Brown, Robert A., to J. Roswell Flower, 12 August 1942. Robert Brown file, Flower Pentecostal Heritage Center, Springfield, MO.

Champion, Richard G., memorandum attached to editorial. Redemption Tidings. 15 November 1957, 2–3. From the files of the The Pentecostal Evangel office.

Cunningham, Robert C., to William Suttles, 8 September 1972. Cited by Jay Beaman. "Pentecostal Pacifism; The Origin, Development, and Rejection of Pacific Belief among Pentecostals." MDiv thesis, North American Baptist Seminary, 1982, 104.

Erdmann, James E., to J. Roswell Flower, 21 October 1954. J. R. Flower file, Flower Pentecostal Heritage Center, Springfield, MO.

Flower, J. Roswell, to James E. Erdmann, 4 February 1955. J. R. Flower file, Flower Pentecostal Heritage Center, Springfield, MO.

———, to Corporal Edward Scholl, 3 October 1951, J. R. Flower file, Flower Pentecostal Heritage Center, Springfield, MO.

Frodsham, Stanley, to T. L. Ward, Memphis, TN, 30 December 1941. Frodsham file, Flower Pentecostal Heritage Center, Springfield, MO.

———, to Leslie C. Wattenburger. 26 November 1941. *The Pentecostal Evangel* Files, Flower Pentecostal Heritage Center, Springfield, MO.

Perkin, Noel, to Paul B. Peterson and members of the board of trustees of The REEM, 27 December 1939. REEM file, Flower Pentecostal Heritage Center, Springfield, MO.

Peterson, Paul B., to Noel Perkin, 21 September 1928. REEM file, Flower Pentecostal Heritage Center, Springfield, MO.

———, to Noel Perkin, 13 June 1929. REEM file, Flower Pentecostal Heritage Center, Springfield, MO.

———, to Noel Perkin, 12 July 1929. REEM file, Flower Pentecostal Heritage Center, Springfield, MO.

———, to Noel Perkin, 4 September 1929. REEM file, Flower Pentecostal Heritage Center, Springfield, MO.

Wattenburger, Leslie C., to the editor of The Pentecostal Evangel. 24 November 1941. The *Pentecostal Evangel* Files, Flower Pentecostal Heritage Center, Springfield, MO.

Webb, Bert, to Bob Cunningham, 31 May 1961. *The Pentecostal Evangel* Files, Flower Pentecostal Heritage Center, Springfield, MO.

———, to Bob Cunningham, 17 July 1961. *The Pentecostal Evangel* Files, Flower Pentecostal Heritage Center, Springfield, MO.

Author Index

355

CPSIA information can be obtained
at www.ICGtesting.com
Printed in the USA
LVHW010719181119
637665LV00021B/7554